W.C.
Fields:
A Life On Film

W.C. Fields: A Life On Film

Ronald J. Fields

Filmography Compiled by
Richard W. Bann, Research Associate

St. Martin's Press
New York

The publisher gratefully acknowledges
permission from Alfred A. Knopf, Inc.
to quote excerpts from *Lulu in Hollywood*
© 1974, 1982 by Louise Brooks.

Editor: Toni Lopopolo
Editorial Assistant: Andrew Charron
Managing Editor: Carol E. W. Edwards
Copyeditor: Gregory Weber

Fields, Ronald J., 1949-
    W.C. Fields: a life in film.
    1. Fields, W.C., 1879-1946.   2. Moving-picture
actors and actresses—United States—Biography.
3. Comedians—United States—Biography.   4. Comedy films—
United States—History and criticism.   I. Title.
II. Title: WC Fields.
PN2287.F45F56   1984   791.43′029′0924 [B]   84-2052
ISBN 0-312-85311-4
ISBN 0-312-85312-2 (pbk.)

Design by Harry Chester Associates.

First Edition

10 9 8 7 6 5 4 3 2 1

CONTENTS

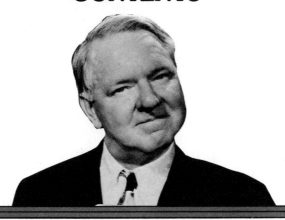

Introduction 7
Key to Reading This Book 9
Prologue 10
First Film—No Title 11
Pool Sharks 12
His Lordship's Dilemma 14
Interlude 18
Broadway After Dark 19
Janice Meredith 20
A Stage Break 23
Sally of the Sawdust 27
That Royle Girl 31
It's the Old Army Game 34
So's Your Old Man 42
The Potters 48
Running Wild 53
Two Flaming Youths 59
Tillie's Punctured Romance 65
Fools for Luck 68
A Time for Change 71
The Golf Specialist 73
Another Interlude 76
Her Majesty Love 79
Million Dollar Legs 82
If I Had a Million 86
The Mack Sennett Shorts
    The Dentist 90
    The Fatal Glass of Beer 95
    The Pharmacist 99
    The Barber Shop 101

Hip Action 107
International House 109
Hollywood on Parade (B-2) 116
Tillie and Gus 119
Alice in Wonderland 125
Six of a Kind 127
You're Telling Me 132
Hollywood on Parade (B-10) 139
The Old Fashioned Way 141
Mrs. Wiggs of the Cabbage Patch .. 148
It's a Gift 152
David Copperfield 162
Mississippi 168
The Man on the Flying Trapeze ... 173
Poppy 181
An Interlude with Radio 187
The Big Broadcast of 1938 190
The Paramount Parting 196
You Can't Cheat an Honest Man ... 198
My Little Chickadee 206
The Bank Dick 217
Never Give a Sucker an Even Break 230
The Laziest Golfer 239
Tales of Manhattan 240
Follow the Boys 243
Song of the Open Road 248
Sensations of 1945 250
Epilogue 252
Acknowledgments 253
Index 254

*With deep love and affection
to my mother, Mrs. W. C. Fields, Jr.,
and to my wife, Pamela Aragona Fields.*

INTRODUCTION

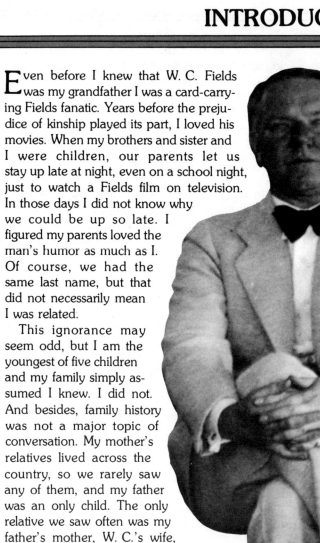

Even before I knew that W. C. Fields was my grandfather I was a card-carrying Fields fanatic. Years before the prejudice of kinship played its part, I loved his movies. When my brothers and sister and I were children, our parents let us stay up late at night, even on a school night, just to watch a Fields film on television. In those days I did not know why we could be up so late. I figured my parents loved the man's humor as much as I. Of course, we had the same last name, but that did not necessarily mean I was related.

This ignorance may seem odd, but I am the youngest of five children and my family simply assumed I knew. I did not. And besides, family history was not a major topic of conversation. My mother's relatives lived across the country, so we rarely saw any of them, and my father was an only child. The only relative we saw often was my father's mother, W. C.'s wife, and she would never talk about her husband. So in my family it was easy for a twelve-year-old not to know his heritage. It was a subject simply not pertinent to my day-to-day living.

I remember clearly the night I found out W. C. Fields was my grandfather. It was late winter in 1962, I was twelve years old. It was a school night but a Fields classic was on, so we were up past our bedtime. The movie was *It's a Gift,* which I had never seen before. From the beginning, the film had us all howling—first the shaving sequence, then breakfast at the Bissonettes', followed by the hilarious drugstore scene. It was the first time in my life I prayed for a commercial break; I needed to catch my breath. Then came the topper, the back porch scene. To this day I believe that bit is one of the funniest routines ever filmed. But that night, the first time I ever saw it, I had to leave the room before it was over. I was in too much pain from laughing so hard. My sister followed me out; she was worried that I was choking. I signaled I was fine and when finally I found my breath again I told her that W. C. Fields was the funniest man who ever lived and that *It's a Gift* had to be the funniest movie ever made. It was obvious to her then that I did not know W. C. Fields was my grandfather. After she told me, she spent the next half hour trying to convince me. Her final argument proved the most persuasive. She noted the remarkable physical resemblance between W. C. and our father. I was related.

My twelve-year-old mind tried to paste this all together. I remember my father rarely talked about his father, and when he did it was usually after a spanking. Then, with logic that eluded me, he used to say, "You're lucky I'm around to discipline you! When I was your age, my father was never home." And then I knew that that father was my favorite comedian. It was difficult for me to picture. Besides the physical similarity and an occasionally quick wit, my father was the complete opposite of W. C. My father was a straitlaced, successful attorney and a very religious man who never smoked and never touched a drop of alcohol in his life. So it was difficult for me to reconcile that lifestyle with his father's legend. But . . .

Learning my heritage changed my life very little. I was twelve and had more important things on my mind. Summer was coming and that meant my last year in Little League. I had to work on my swing so I could break .100 for the first time. Besides there was nothing around our house that yelled, "W. C. Fields is your grandfather!"—no mementos, no pictures, no canes, no hats, no balls. What did change was how I watched his movies. A bit of the fun was taken out now. With familial pride and a tinge of curiosity I laughed less so I could pay closer attention to what he did and said. I wanted to keep an eye out for some family traits.

A year later, my grandmother, W. C.'s wife, died. After her death I helped my father put most of her belongings in storage. With her material was a treasury of W. C. Fields memorabilia—scripts, letters, photos, his vaudeville pool table and cues, cigar boxes—it was a literal ledger of W. C. Fields' life. We hid all of that in the storage room too. I did not think about it much after that. After all, I had more important things on my mind. It was my first year in high school.

Eight years later, my father died and my family had to go through the excruciating process of listing a loved one's assets for the estate, for the government, for taxes, for the lawyers. We took W. C.'s material out of storage and brought it home. It was the same year I quit law school, quit my master's program in English and began my writing career. I had more free time than the other members of my family, so I started cataloguing Fields material. I discovered that my father had started a book on his father, and naturally I felt destined to finish it. It was then, while putting W. C.'s life into that book, that I discovered the depth of W. C.'s genius and gained an understanding of art.

It occurred to me that every great artist takes the particular experiences of his life, remolds them slightly, then puts them on display — and there, through the magic of art, parts of his own life become the general experiences of all mankind, the expressions of one individual understood by the masses. And that is what W. C. Fields did. Fields took his foibles, his loves, his hates, his experiences—shaped them artfully and comically—and made us see them clearly as mankind's idiosyncrasies.

My intention in this book is not only to discuss the facts of Fields' films, enjoy some of his best lines and share the stories of his on-the-set high jinks and backstage intrigues, but also to help you understand the man and his art. I wanted to bring to the reader the etiology of Fields' comedy and genius, to discuss the personal experiences he transformed into his art, to understand how William Claude Dukenfield became W. C. Fields.

W. C.'s movies were a retooling of his life experiences put to a joke, so a book about his films is truly a book about his life as well.

—Ronald J. Fields

KEY TO
READING THIS BOOK

Each film write-up is divided into four main sections. First comes a discussion of the process that begat the particular picture, i.e., Fields' contractual obligations; a look at the conflicts he may have had prior to production with the studio, fellow actors, directors and/or producers; and other pertinent preproduction notes, anecdotes and tidbits. In short, this section will tell of an idea put to screen, the genesis of each film.

Second, you will find the film's plot synopsis. The way I have written this section has been the cause of some debate. My synopses are generally longer than those found in most film books. Some film historians, therefore, have argued that I should cut them down, saying that they do not represent the accepted method of encapsulating. Well, it is my book. . . . They lost the argument.

I am a Fields fan. I love his sense of humor. Most of his films are bad in a purely cinematic sense, but he is superbly funny (of course, my opinion) in almost all of them. Therefore, I felt an extended treatment, especially of his scenes, was called for. For those of you who have already seen a particular film, I wanted to help you remember the joy and fun of the picture. For those of you who have not, I wanted to let you know what you have missed. For both of you I wanted to include in each synopsis as many of W. C.'s great lines and sight gags as possible. Why? Because I am tired of people, particularly at parties, misquoting W. C. His lines are hilarious and should be quoted correctly. For those of you who want to quote them accurately, you will now have them in black and white. Bring this book to your next party.

Each of the synopses is set apart. None will include any ancillary facts, notes or anecdotes pertinent to the Fields historian. These summaries will merely repeat the plot and quote some of the dialogue.

The third section of each write-up will discuss W. C.'s relationship with his co-workers during and after filming: on-the-set anecdotes, fights, filming foibles and the like. It will also include interviews, comments, thoughts and perspectives from those who worked on the particular film under discussion or were otherwise privy to the happenings surrounding the motion picture. Furthermore, this section will include newspaper criticisms from the period, my critique of their reviews and my review of the film.

I began researching this book at home in Los Angeles. There, I spent almost twelve months scouring the twenty-some huge scrapbooks that W. C. Fields had compiled over his years in entertainment. These scrapbooks began in 1896 and traced his public life nearly weekly all the way to 1946, the year he died. They held reviews, good and bad, interviews, in-depth studies, biographical works, letters and even some of his own scribblings, all of which have been used in some manner in this book. From L.A. I continued my research at archives in New York, Washington, London and Paris. Unfortunately, in most cases I found reviews of many of Fields' films cut out of magazines or newspapers or trade publications and pasted to scrapbook pages with no mention of the authors' names or the publications' identities. Thus, in quite a few of my write-ups you will notice that I say, "Most of the critics . . ." or, "All of the critics . . ." or, "A majority of the critics said . . ." without giving you the source or the authors' names. It could not be avoided. But one thing is certain, when I say, "majority" or "most" or "all," it is true, on the basis of the reviews available to me. And in the film analyses where I write, "The majority of critics claimed Fields stole the show," it is a tabulation from those reviews that still exist. It is not the puffery of a Fields relative.

On the other hand, when I opine about W. C.'s work, which I do often, it is purely my honest and humble opinion. Be forewarned, however, in researching this tome Richard Bann and I viewed all of Fields' films available, and, except for a smattering of his pictures, I laughed until I ached every time he took over a scene. I think he was a terribly funny man.

The fourth and last section of each write-up is the filmography. These sections were expertly, diligently and lovingly compiled by my friend Richard W. Bann. Richard gives you the complete (and I mean complete) cast and production credits in these sections. We both decided to arrange the sequence of Fields' movies according to production schedules, not release dates. So, as an example, *Hip Action,* which was released in June of 1933, follows *The Barber Shop,* released in July of the same year, because *The Barber Shop* was made first.

It is also in these sections that Richard and I give you our rating of the particular film under discussion. As I mentioned, Richard and I saw every Fields motion picture obtainable today, and both of us agree that if there is a film in which W. C. appears, even for the briefest seconds, then that film is worth at least one martini, ergo, we use the Martini Rating System. If the film in review is worth only one martini then it is not very good. Two is about average. Three martinis mean the movie is quite good, and four martinis, well, there we have an excellent film, and the only thing we regret is that we did not use the Ten Martini Rating System. Cheers!

PROLOGUE

One day in the mid 1890s William Claude Dukenfield slipped into a Philadelphia vaudeville theatre to catch the Burns Brothers' juggling routine. He was awed by their dexterity and skill. He stayed to see the entire bill but nothing matched the Burns Brothers. On his way home, he could not get that act out of his mind. He sat down under an apple tree, as Isaac Newton had a few years before. He picked up three apples that were lying on the ground, but unlike Newton he did not wonder why they fell, he wondered how he could keep them in the air. He started to toss them, trying to remember just how the Burnses arced three India rubber balls on stage. To his delight and amazement he found he could replicate their juggling. As he noted years later, "I found out I had a fatal facility to juggle."

The boy was fifteen years of age and the oldest of five children. There was Walter, who would team with his brother in vaudeville a few years later. Then came Elsie Mae. Sadly, she would die at a rather young age. Following her was Adel, and in the mid 1890s the youngest, LeRoy, was born.

It was 1895 and Claude, as his family called him, was already a school dropout working for his father, James, a huckster. Early every morning James would pick up his fruit and vegetables along the Delaware River near the Philadelphia docks. His cart loaded, he would tramp the streets of Philadelphia pulling his merchandise and calling out the prices and menu of his stock. Young Claude would follow, using his father's produce to practice his juggling. He quickly added more and more produce to his routine, much to his father's consternation. The boy had uncanny natural coordination, an innate talent accidentally discovered. At night he would gather his friends at their "Clubhouse," an attic over a blacksmith's shop, and put on a show. His friends spread the word of his talent. Soon the young boy was performing for church bazaars and family picnics, taking home spare change from the meager tips, or occasionally grabbing his own gratuities from unattended offering boxes. At one of these bazaars a scout checking on talent for a theatre on Fortescue Pier, an appendage of the Atlantic City boardwalk, saw the boy perform. He was impressed. He wanted him. In that spring of 1896 William Claude Dukenfield signed his first contract to play in a "legitimate" vaudeville theatre. He would be part of the summer fare at an Atlantic City beer hall/theatre.

His sister Adel remembered the night he left. She and their mother, Kate, walked Claude to the train station. Kate had packed some sandwiches for her son and she cried a lot. The boy tried soothing her, promising he would return to Philadelphia soon, but only after he made it big. He could not face his family and friends, to whom he boasted of future successes, unless he made a name for himself. Kate had her doubts and she cried even more; they hugged and then they said their good-byes.

Adel always laughed when asked about the stories of her brother's truculent relationship with his father. She averred that he made up those stories himself. It made for good copy. She remembered "dad" as a tough old man,

reticent and hardworking, but not mean. On the other hand her brother was brash and best described as a juvenile delinquent who teased his father unmercifully because of his thick English accent. She said there was of course friction between the two but her father, James, never threw his son out of the house. Indeed, early interviews with the young entertainer definitely jibed with Adel's remembrances. It was only years later when the famous W. C. Fields was interviewed that he included stories of a harsh childhood under a tyrannical father. It did make good copy.

The beer hall/theatre was the basement of vaudeville. It was a tough initiation to the world of entertainment. In front of the beer hall was a real theatre marquee, very small, but a marquee nonetheless. The young boy billed himself extravagantly—William Claude Dukenfield, Juggler Extraordinaire. It would never fit on that tiny marquee. Besides, the Juggler Extraordinaire clashed with his stage costume, which incidentally doubled as his mufti—outdated baggy pants and shirt, a torn hat and a tattered overcoat. Unceremoniously the theatre manager axed the billing to shreds, and the sixteen-year-old boy was offered as W. C. Fields, Tramp Juggler.

Before the summer stint ended a scout from a vaudeville touring company caught the boy's act. By fall W. C. Fields was playing "two-a-days" from the Mississippi to the Eastern Seaboard. And then more scouts and more touring companies. In 1899 he hitched up with the Irwin Burlesquers, where he fell in love with a chorus girl named Hattie Hughes. He took the beautiful dancer from the chorus and put her in his act.

In 1900, just four short years from Atlantic City, W. C. Fields signed with the most prestigious vaudeville touring company in the world—the Keith Orpheum Circuit. By then his act had changed; to his juggling he had added comedy. And like his juggling the comedy came accidentally too. The young man was a perfectionist, and it seems his natural ire at missing a tossed ball made the audiences howl. He quickly added more mistakes, with various planned and funny displays of anger. It worked. B. F. Keith loved it and that year he made W. C. Fields the headliner on his tour. It was also in 1900 that Fields became a husband. Hattie Hughes and W. C. were married in April in San Francisco.

The newlyweds had the wanderlust. Keith Orpheum played in theatres throughout the world and the young couple wanted to see the world. Fields knew that verbal acts met limited success overseas, so he and Hattie decided to keep the act silent, keep the comedy all physical. There would be no language barrier in the laughs. In 1903 Keith booked them on their first global tour.

A year later W. C. Fields Jr. was born. W. C. made Hattie return to Philadelphia for the birth while he continued touring. The plan was that soon after she left the hospital she would rejoin her husband, bring the boy, and they would turn the act into a trio. Hattie refused, it would be no life for her son. She stayed in Philadelphia while W. C. continued on stage. He pleaded with her to come and share the spotlight with him again, but she was unyielding; she would not raise her boy out of a steamer trunk. She begged him to quit vaudeville and become a husband and a true father, but he was too close to the top, it was not the time to quit. The separation ravaged their love and marriage. Although they never divorced, W. C. was never really a husband or father again. His grief over the estrangement never left him. It became the primary fodder for his comedy for the rest of his life.

For a short time Walter took Hattie's place, but then quit too after a few months. Vaudeville was tough, but W. C. stayed with it, his act a solo once again.

From 1904 until 1915 W. C. Fields traveled the world topping the bill in the best theatres in nearly every country that had a theatre: the Crystal Palace, Berlin; the Folies-Bergère, Paris; the Palace theatres of London and Johannesburg; and just about every Tivoli house on the globe. He played for kings and queens, princes and princesses, and for anyone who could pay the price of admission to a vaudeville show. Now his billing read, "W. C. Fields, The Greatest Eccentric Juggler in the World." And reviewers agreed.

1915 was probably the most important year in W. C.'s career. At thirty-five years of age and after traveling the world for over a decade Fields would finally settle down. Florenz Ziegfeld signed the juggling comedian for his world-famous *Follies*. Fields demanded and received six hundred dollars a week, more than any juggler had ever been paid. So Fields went back to the workbench, cut out almost all juggling from his routine and created an entirely new act. The only thing he kept from his days on tour was his pool routine.

It was a queer time to change. Usually an entertainer alters his performing staple because of audience ennui or the critics' pans, but not Fields. Critics and audiences loved his work. Besides, he was one of the top stars in a world-renowned show, and he had gotten there because of his old routines.

So what made him change his act, indeed his livelihood? He answered that one in a letter he wrote to his sister Adel. He said that since Ziegfeld had made him the highest-paid juggler in the world it proved he was the best juggler in the world, or so he reasoned, and "As a juggler I have nothing more to prove. It's time I try something else."

He wrote skits with dialogue, which were based on the passions of his pastimes—golf and tennis—and of course he still had his pool routine. He poked fun at the games he loved to play and the odd quirks of those who played them. And then in the spring of 1915, from the New Amsterdam stage at 42nd Street near Broadway, New York City, in the *Ziegfeld Follies of 1915,* a theatre audience heard for the first time the raspy, nasal voice of W. C. Fields.

The thirty-five-year-old entertainer was embarking on a new career. No longer was he a funny juggler but a full-fledged comedian who happened to juggle. Now audiences were laughing at what he said, not just what he did.

But 1915 held much more for Fields. It was the year that W. C. would be seen on film for the first time. No irony is lost here that a performer who, after two decades of entertaining, finally finds his voice begins a career in silent films.

FIRST FILM—NO TITLE

Every Fields historian has tagged *Pool Sharks* as W. C.'s first stint in front of the camera, but it was not. To be sure, *Pool Sharks* was Fields' first film distributed theatrically, but many months before that W. C. performed in a motion picture which played to a packed theatre night after night and was reviewed by New York's best critics. The movie was a short piece made by Ed Wynn as part of his routine in the *Ziegfeld Follies of 1915*.

Wynn shot the cast of the Ziegfeld show that year, directing, mapping and staging the performers' movements to perfection. Then he wrote his monologue. For his stage performance he dressed in accepted director's garb and stood in the middle aisle of the theatre. A movie screen would lower over the stage. Wynn's film would

roll and he would direct the performers on film as if they were live. He would bark a command and the actors on screen would respond accordingly, as if they could actually hear him.

For example: W. C., as filmed, would walk onto the screen balancing a few cigar boxes. Suddenly Wynn would yell, "Hey, Fields!" Startled, W. C. would drop the cigar boxes. "You're not on yet! Get off the screen!"

Offended, Fields would gather his props and stalk off. Each night Wynn's timing had to be precise to fit the actors' filmed reactions.

The movie is lost, and the only accounts of what surely must have been an absurd film to see rest in the now tattered yellow columns of those who reviewed the *Ziegfeld Follies of 1915.*

Pool Sharks

—1915—

In 1915, W. C. Fields signed with the important *Ziegfeld Follies,* he became the highest-paid juggler in the world, he talked on stage for the first time in his career and finally Fields' comic genius was joined with the burgeoning motion picture industry. *Pool Sharks* was W. C.'s first legitimate film. It was supposed to be a motion picture version of his famous pool routine, which he had developed in 1903 and had performed nearly every night through vaudeville and now into the *Follies.* It was a grand year for Fields.

Pool Sharks was produced by the English Gaumont Company. They occasionally used New York's Long Island studios to make motion pictures. The English loved W. C.'s brand of comedy. While in vaudeville Fields made at least five extended tours of Great Britain, and twice entertained King Edward VII in command performances. Familiar with W C.'s work, the Gaumont group particularly wanted to capture his pool routine on film. But alas, the movie fell far short of its intent. The pool sequence, actually an insignificant part of the motion picture, relegated W. C.'s amazing juggling feats to trick photography. But there really was little choice. The problem was that Fields performed his pool routine twice a day on the Ziegfeld stage—afternoons and evenings—and his trick pool table, especially designed to enhance his juggling, was too cumbersome to strike in Manhattan, set up in Long Island, strike again and reassemble back on the *Follies* stage for the evening show. Gaumont's only solution was trick photography. Unfortunately, this attempted cinematic simulacrum of Fields' stage routine bears no resemblance to his incredible live pool performances.

The plot of *Pool Sharks* has W. C. and an ugly little fellow, Bud Ross, vying for the attention of a young but homely heroine. The movie begins with Ross showering the young lady with insipid smiles and silly flirtations as the two swing gently on a hammock. Soon Fields joins the lovebirds. He plops himself on the hammock, causing it to spin and—Crash! All three hit the ground. The young woman storms off, leaving the two suitors to fight it out. After a bit of slugging the men search for the woman and find her picnicking with a group of revelers. Ross grabs the empty chair next to the heroine. On her other side sits a young boy. Fields hooks his cane around the kid's chair and yanks it backwards, dumping the boy on the ground. The child runs away crying and Fields usurps his chair. In their competitive struggle to gain the woman's attention, W. C. and his diminutive nemesis accidentally drop a full plate of blueberry pancakes (of course soaked in a thick syrup and topped with butter) on the lady's lap. She stomps off again, leaving her admirers in combat. What a fight! Fields grabs Ross by the hair, pries open one of his eyes and shoves his forefinger into the socket, but in the process W. C. loses his index digit. Vengefully Ross, the flyweight lover, bites off Fields' middle finger, but somehow replaces the forefinger.

The picnickers finally separate the combatants and suggest they play a game of pool. Winner gets the girl. At the pool table they continue their battle, breaking pool sticks over each other's head and throwing punches and pool balls at one another. At the conclusion of the film neither man gets the girl, which is just fine, because the plot has been lost well before The End.

With all the hitting, biting and scrapping, *Pool Sharks* resembles an early Keystone Chaplin movie, lacking, however, Chaplin's grace of movement—a criticism W. C. would have hated. "He's nothing but a goddamn ballet dancer!" Fields had said of Chaplin. It is not a good movie. It is not vintage W. C. It is a very violent film, and Fields' antics seem forced and unattractive, an unfortunate departure from his normally subtle brand of laugh getting. Furthermore, in the entire ten-minute piece Fields juggles four balls for approximately three seconds, a terrible disappointment from a man many considered then to be the greatest juggler in the world.

Nevertheless, the importance of this picture cannot be minimized. It is Fields' first filmed battle with a child. Near the end of the movie W. C. is caught taking great gulps from a bottle of booze, his first recorded affection for "angel's milk." And, after all, this is Fields' introduction to legitimate filmmaking. Today the motion picture affords us a chance to see a slim thirty-five-year-old W. C. Fields performing in front of a camera.

**With a very different-looking
W. C. Fields (left) and Bud Ross.**

POOL SHARKS
One reel
Silent, black and white
Released September 19, 1915, by the Mutual Film Corp.
Produced by the Gaumont Company as *A Casino Star Comedy*
Directed by Edwin Middleton

CAST:
W. C. Fields   The pool shark
Bud Ross   His adversary

Filmed in Flushing, New York.

*At the
pool table
(the studio's table,
not W. C.'s)
with Bud Ross
and Fields.*

*Eyeball
in the corner
socket!
Fields and Ross
in* Pool Sharks.

His Lordship's Dilemma
—1915—

Fields signed for a second motion picture with Gaumont, and it infuriated Ziegfeld. W. C. was probably the first *Follies* star to work in films while performing on the Ziegfeld stage, and the extra load sullied Fields' nighttime performances, taking zip from his juggling and disrupting his timing. Flo tried putting the nix on *His Lordship's Dilemma,* but the Gaumont contract was signed and nothing in the *Follies* agreement proscribed motion picture making. The movie became one more sore spot between the producer and the comedian.

The Ziegfeld-Fields feuds were classic, the natural result of great egos in close contact. Still, they harbored a mutual respect, which mitigated all-out wars to little battles of irritation, and those nettlings enlivened the *Follies* stage. One day when Ziegfeld fired a five-foot stagehand because the employee's shortness offended Flo's sense of beauty in the human form, W. C. hired him. Seizing the opportunity to irritate the impresario, Fields rehearsed the stunted man clandestinely; then, on a night when W. C. knew Ziegfeld was in the audience, he introduced William "Shorty" Blanche to his act.

Not to be outdone, Flo countered shortly thereafter. He secreted Ed Wynn under Fields' pool table and demanded that he mug to the audience throughout W. C.'s turn on stage. Well, Fields was dumbfounded. He could

not understand why the audience howled at all the wrong places, and his timing was cut to shreds. Eventually, W. C. discovered the perfidy. Abruptly, he ended his act, walked in front of the pool table, bowed to the audience and in so doing brought his cue stick back fast and furiously, landing the full meat of the stick on Wynn's forehead. Ed was out for the count.

Ziegfeld disliked comedians, but he knew what the public wanted, and along with his beautiful women the audiences loved the funnymen, and particularly W. C. So, contrary to Flo's personal tastes, he made Fields add more routines to his stage ensemble. Fields reached into his past, dusted off a croquet routine that he wrote in 1908, expunged most of the juggling, added dialogue and transformed the body of the skit from the somewhat esoteric game of croquet to the popular sport of golf. Ziegfeld put it on stage. It received great acclaim. So Gaumont put it on film and called it *His Lordship's Dilemma.* This second movie began immediately upon completion of *Pool Sharks.* It took less than the month of September to film both motion pictures and they were released two weeks apart.

His Lordship's Dilemma has been lost for so long that very few pieces of literature on W. C. even mention the film. Only the still shots and old advertisements recall

Love on the links: Fields' first filmed golf routine.

"Gangway and keep your eye on the ball": His Lordship's Dilemma.

The famous choke shot. Fields with Bud Ross. We do not know the name of the child in the golf bag.

Hmm . . . Where's the men's room? Note the advertised prices!

the motion picture, but nothing in those archives explains the title. The only things we know are that W. C. played a remittance man, and his adversary in *Pool Sharks,* Bud Ross, played his caddy and majordomo. *His Lordship's Dilemma* probably more accurately portrayed Fields' stage golf routine than *Pool Sharks* duplicated the pool routine, because in this film he could use his own stage props. Needless to say, it was easier carrying a golf bag than lugging a pool table to the Long Island Studio.

The response to Fields' golf routine was so enthusiastic in 1915 that he planted variations of the same piece in two silent films in the twenties and made it the subject of his first talking film, *The Golf Specialist,* in 1930. Two years later he put it in the Mack Sennett short called *The Dentist.* And again a golf sequence appears in the 1934 full-length feature called *You're Telling Me,* then pops up four years later in *The Big Broadcast of 1938.* Finally, that same year he put his golf routine to rest in a radio version starring Charlie McCarthy as Fields' caddy.

W. C. always stole from himself. Pool routines show up in four different movies, and nearly all of his stage skits from 1915 to 1928 reappear in the motion pictures he made through the twenties, the thirties and half the forties.

Credited with directing *His Lordship's Dilemma* was William "Silent Bill" Haddock. Upon joining Gaumont in 1915 Haddock had already amassed an impressive list of directing credits at an assortment of long-forgotten production companies, including Kalem, Edison and Kamerphone. It was during his stint with Kamerphone in 1907 that Silent Bill directed the first American talking pictures that utilized synchronized records. And four years later he directed one of the earliest feature motion pictures, *The Clansman.* In so doing he was at the helm of another film breakthrough—it was shot in color. But through no fault of Haddock's, the experiment was abandoned and it remained for D. W. Griffith to screen Haddock's footage, which inspired his version of this property known as *The Birth of a Nation.*

In 1963 producer Sam Sherman interviewed William "Silent Bill" Haddock. At the time Haddock was eighty-six years old and portraying a doctor on a network soap opera. Silent Bill reminisced: "The pioneering days were probably the most satisfying and happiest. A director had no assistant, had to write his own continuity, or shoot off the cuff, look up locations, make up his own prop list and sometimes act in the pictures." When motion pictures were new, pioneers such as Haddock provided the film grammar we take for granted today.

He recalled working with W. C. As Haddock remembered it then, he made *Pool Sharks* with the comedian, although he is credited solely with *His Lordship's Dilemma.* He remembered that once at lunchtime during shooting W. C. and some pals disappeared to enjoy various mood-altering beverages and returned to the set an hour late—driving a stolen garbage wagon.

Unfortunately, *His Lordship's Dilemma* and the garbage truck are lost in the rough somewhere in history and we may never see W. C.'s first filmed golf routine.

W. C. Fields in his earliest recorded bar room scene, with Bud Ross.

HIS LORDSHIP'S DILEMMA ————————
(No rating, unavailable for screening)
One reel
Silent, black and white
Released October 3, 1915, by the Mutual Film Corp.
Produced by the Gaumont Company as *A Casino Star Comedy*
Directed by William Haddock

CAST:
W. C. Fields   Remittance man
Bud Ross   His valet

Filmed in Flushing, New York.

A scene still from the lost film His Lordship's Dilemma, *with Bud Ross.*

Interlude

It was the same year Charlie Chaplin left Mack Sennett to work his magic at Essanay, and Harold Lloyd began his association with Hal Roach. It was 1915 and besides Chaplin and Lloyd no comic contemporaries of Fields' were on film. The Marx Brothers were performing their shtick in the second-rate burlesque houses; Harry Langdon and Buster Keaton still worked the proscenium exclusively; it would be two years before Will Rogers would join Fields on the Ziegfeld stage and still another year before he would make his first movie; and Stan Laurel had not yet met Oliver Hardy.

Even though he was one of the first great comics put on film, Fields did not consider it a significant achievement. After all, in the same year he had already signed with the renowned *Ziegfeld Follies,* and the stage folk then viewed the inchoate film industry more paternalistically than competitively. Furthermore, Flo told his contracted players they could no longer split their time between the *Follies* stage and the silver screen, and anyway the response to Fields' first two films was mediocre. So without much sacrifice W. C. stayed away from motion pictures and settled in with the *Follies.*

Fields played the New Amsterdam stage in New York's Times Square for a stormy seven years, the longest run for any performer in the history of the Ziegfeld show. Despite the critics' uninhibited raves for Fields' work, the comedian constantly fought about comedy with the impresario of female pulchritude. Their views on humor and entertainment were diametrically opposite.

But that mattered little to Fields. He mostly got his way through hook or crook, and besides, the *Follies* years brought great prestige to the juggling comedian as he shared the bill with the top names in comedy: Fanny Brice, Bert Williams, Will Rogers, Ed Wynn, Ray Dooley, Eddie Cantor and others.

But in 1922 Fields left Ziegfeld and joined the *George White Scandals,* a Follies imitation. Flo wanted to keep the independent-minded comedian despite their conflicts because W. C. was a draw. The *Follies* offered Fields over a thousand dollars a week, but George White matched the offer, plus he gave Fields free reign to develop his comic instinct without impediment, and furthermore he would not stop him from filmmaking if the offers came. In the short seven years since 1915, motion pictures began threatening the sacred stage as more and more of the theatre's top names joined the film bandwagon. Now Fields wanted to make pictures, but no offers came his way.

Instead, in the spring of 1923 Philip Goodman, a Broadway producer, asked Fields if he would accept a featured part in a Dorothy Donnelly play. The play was called *Poppy.* Goodman had already signed Madge Kennedy for the title role and wanted W. C. Fields as Poppy's father, Professor Eustace P. McGargle, F.A.S.N. It was Goodman's gamble. Fields was untested in extended narratives. His forte was twenty-minute skits surfeited with juggling stunts. Indeed, Fields himself nearly turned down the part: "I can't remember my lines in a twenty-minute

W. C. Fields greets Philip Goodman, the producer of the Broadway stage play Poppy.

sketch; how the hell can I remember the dialogue in an entire play?'' Goodman pressed harder. He told W. C. he could ad-lib ad infinitum, and if he ever forgot a "must" line, prompters stationed at both ends of the stage would help out. With trepidation Fields left the *Scandals* and signed to play McGargle.

During rehearsals W. C. quit the show a dozen times, frustrated by his inability to remember his dialogue, but each time Goodman coaxed him back. He knew Fields was McGargle.

In September 1923 *Poppy* opened. Fields turned a below-average script into a smash Broadway play. The critics screamed Fields' praises, crowning him the real star of the show. Behind the scenes the cast loved W. C. Every evening the players not on stage stood in the wings to catch what the "old gent" would ad-lib next. In fact it was in this play that Fields invented his famous maxim "Never give a sucker an even break," which became the title of his last starring feature-length film in 1941. "It's the old army game" was also an ad-lib from this play and it too became the title of a Fields film.

W. C. was forty-three years old and *Poppy* was one of the biggest breaks of his career. Because of his performance the movie moguls finally took note of this putty-nosed comedian. Years later this would strike Fields oddly: "The movie people would have nothing to do with me until they heard me speak in a Broadway play, then they all wanted to sign me for the silent movies." The first studio to snare him was Cosmopolitan Pictures, William Randolph Hearst's fiefdom.

But before that . . .

Broadway After Dark

In January of 1924 the following blurb appeared in the movie trade papers: "Warner Brothers Studio will resound with activity in the near future when cameras start to grind in the Harry Rapf production of *Broadway After Dark*. Actual production to begin on January 7, 1924. Rapf recently returned from New York with a couple cans of film under his arm, motion pictures of the Actors Equity Ball in New York where Nora Bayes, Elsie Ferguson, Madge Kennedy, Irene Bordoni, Joseph Santley, Fred and Dorothy Stone, *W. C. Fields,* Irene Castle, Ann Pennington, Vera Gordon, Raymond Hitchcock, Frank Tinney and Paul Whiteman were photographed for a scene in the picture."

Broadway After Dark was ultimately made as a successful vehicle for Adolphe Menjou. A theatrical boardinghouse was the center of the film's events. Carmel Myers, Norma Shearer and Mervyn Le Roy were cast in support, but there is no record of the Fields footage finding its way into the general release prints. So evidently, Fields was recorded on film, but sadly, once again the product was lost.

19

Janice Meredith

— 1925 —

The success of *Poppy* made Fields the talk of New York. It was as if the years he had spent headlining in vaudeville and topping the bill in the *Follies* meant nothing. Now W. C. was hobnobbing with the "crème de la crème": Alexander Woollcott, H. L. Mencken, Ring Lardner, Theodore Dreiser, Heywood Broun and even an occasional visit with Gertrude Stein; and they in turn told New York of Fields' genius.

Meanwhile, in another part of the city, William Randolph Hearst was making a movie at Cosmopolitan Pictures for his protégée, Marion Davies. The film was based on a turn-of-the-century book and play by Paul Leicester Ford named *Janice Meredith*. In this 1920s version Marion Davies played the title role and the American Revolution was featured.

Hearst poured $1.5 million into *Janice Meredith,* an astronomical sum for a movie in those days. (Ms. Davies' twenty costumes alone cost $25,000.) He brought in the great Ziegfeld set designer Joseph Urban to create the scenery, awarding him an enormous salary.

The movie is a romance with the historical facts of the American Revolution foddering the plot. Harrison Ford begins the film as the Meredith family's bonded servant and Janice's secret lover, Charles Fownes. When war erupts with England Charles decides to fight for the American cause, but before marching off he reveals his love for Janice by asking Squire Meredith for his daughter's hand in marriage. The Squire, a member of the Who's Who of early America, refuses to let his daughter marry below her station, and the two young lovers separate in heartbreak.

As a devoted revolutionary soldier, Charles inexorably works his way up the army's ranks and in short order becomes George Washington's right-hand man. The General quickly decides how the young patriot can best serve the cause. Because of Fownes' decidedly English manners, Washington makes him a spy.

Back at the Merediths' estate the Squire spends a great deal of time entertaining the English troops, which lets Mr. Fownes do a considerable amount of spying in his lover's backyard. Their affection grows, eventually leading Janice into a few of Charles' cloak and dagger capers.

Mixed with the love interest are magnificent scenes from our country's revolutionary past: Benjamin Franklin at the imposing Palace of Versailles entreating King Louis XVI to join the colonials against the British; the shot heard round the world at the Battle of Concord and Lexington; lavish parties and period costumes. But the highlight of the historical scenes is George Washington standing like a bowsprit on a canoe leading his ragtag army across the Delaware River.

As the movie comes to a close a new country is born and so is a new Charles Fownes. When the bonded servant, now a revolutionary war hero, returns to the Merediths' home he unveils his true identity. Charles Fownes is not merely the Squire's retainer but none other than Lord Jack Brereton, an English nobleman who years ago changed his name, turned his back on his rank and privilege and headed for the colonies to start a new life. His elevated status and heroic deeds in battle persuade Squire Meredith to agree to Jack and Janice's union. The marriage is performed by Charles Fownes' (né Jack Brereton) former boss, George Washington.

In early March 1924 William Le Baron, the new director general at Cosmopolitan, saw *Poppy* and immediately contacted Fields to play a part in *Janice Meredith*. The footage completed to that point was dull and needed an infusion of gaiety. Le Baron convinced the powers at Cosmopolitan that W. C. was the answer and after some negotiations Fields signed. The comedian worked only one day, April 2, 1924, and received $1,500. Out of the 15-minute film, Fields appeared in only one tight, insignificant three-minute scene. Moreover, he was the only actor in the credits sans an appellation, being described simply as a British sergeant. Furthermore, while all the other actors were dressed in authentic period garb, Fields' white wig was askew, and he refused to doff his stage trademark, a scruffy mustache attached carelessly to his nasal septum. His entire scene could be extricated from the film with no damage to the plot. In short, it appears someone just threw Fields in front of the camaera, said, "Do something funny," he did it, and that was that.

Fields' scene opens with him guarding the captured Charles Fownes, who is tied to a chair in the kitchen of an American mansion the British have overrun. The first shot of W. C. catches him lighting a cigar with a candle. After the cigar is lit he absentmindedly puts the cigar in the candle holder and puffs on the candle. Quickly discovering his mistake, he puts things back in their proper places. He is helping one of the maids sweep the floor when Janice appears. He sees her, takes off his hat and bows gallantly, then replaces his hat accidentally on top of the broom handle. (This is the same gag he used throughout his stage and movie career, generally using a cane instead of a broomstick.) Janice exchanges furtive glances with Fownes, then coyly offers W. C. a drink from a cordial glass. He politely refuses, walks to the cupboard, grabs a tumbler and gives it to Janice. She fills the glass and Fields empties it quickly, then thrusts the cup back for another round. Janice continually flirts with W. C. while keeping his mug filled. He falls for her wiles and both giggle and laugh. Getting a bit tipsy, Fields begins to sway back and forth and Janice gives him a coquettish push. W. C. cutely pushes her back. She giggles again and pushes him a little harder. Not to be outdone in this playfulness, Fields gives her a good shove. Janice, still frisky, but a tad indignant, gives W. C. a final thrust, knocking him against the china closet. He has had enough and they begin their no-push flirting again. Finally Fields drinks himself drunk. Bobbing and weaving, he affectionately hugs his bottle while Janice slips behind him and unties her lover. Soon a cadre of bibulous British soldiers arrive in the kitchen. They discover the spy has escaped and rush out in pursuit. Pulling himself together, Fields follows with a broom in hand ready to fire. He leaves the kitchen but quickly returns. Dropping the broom, he grabs his musket and makes his final exit. End of scene.

It worked nicely. Fields and Davies played off one another well and that made sense. Although Marion Davies claimed *Janice Meredith* was her greatest picture to date, she added, "But I prefer to play comedy. I'd rather make people laugh than cry." It was Hearst who forced her into serious drama, thinking that would make her a legitimate actor and not just a clown. But Miss Davies did her best work in light comedy and one of her finest scenes in this film was the one with W. C.

Janice Meredith opened at the Cosmopolitan Theatre in New York on August 5, 1924, almost two months after its intended premiere, and almost two months before its general release nationwide. The show received good reviews and W. C.'s small skit got grand notices. Within a month of opening, the majority of advertisements for the movie pictured Marion Davies and W. C. Fields, a fine compliment to the comedian who played a mere three minutes in a two-and-a-half-hour production.

There is a fascinating historical note to this film. During the production of *Janice Meredith*, D. W. Griffith was in New York filming *America*, a picture also dealing with the American Revolution. Griffith lacked the huge sums of money Hearst brought to *Janice Meredith*, and he made *America* more as a documentary film than an entertainment piece. Yet, because of the closeness of the themes, Hearst and Griffith agreed that the most elaborate scene in each should not be the same. Hearst chose Washington's crossing of the Delaware as his most impressive re-creation, while Griffith took the midnight ride of Paul Revere. Both films were released about the same time, and although the reviewers of the early twenties praised both, they almost all picked *Janice Meredith* as the superior product. Since then history has judged: Griffith's *America* is called a classic today and *Janice Meredith* a study in ennui.

This opinion of *Janice Meredith* was brought home

at a revival showing of the movie in 1977 at a film convention in Minneapolis. *Janice Meredith* had been considered a lost film until a print was located in England. It was a British release print and they made certain changes to fit their audience. For instance, a pejorative text title which declared, "The redcoats are coming!" was changed to read, "The soldiers are coming!" Anyway, the film buffs in Minneapolis, who had gathered from around the country, were eager to see this newly found "classic." The audience was excited. But as the film rolled on and on, people started to escape the theatre. Except for the scenes with W. C. Fields and Ken Maynard, the film fell flat with this one audience that really wanted to like it. One weary film buff walked out after almost two hours grumbling, "That picture hasn't been lost all these years—it's been hiding."

JANICE MEREDITH

153 minutes
Silent, black and white
Released October 27, 1924, by Metro-Goldwyn-Mayer
Produced by William Randolph Hearst's Cosmopolitan Pictures for MGM
Directed by E. Mason Hopper
Based on the novel by Paul Leicester Ford

Screenplay by Lillie Hayward
Photographed by Ira A. Morgan and George Barnes
Setting by Joseph Urban
Special music score by Deems Taylor
Edited by Walter Futter
Assistant director: E. J. Babille

CAST:

Marion Davies	Janice Meredith
Maclyn Arbuckle	Squire Meredith
Robert Thorne	Patrick Henry
Harrison Ford	Charles Fownes (Lord Brereton)
Hattie De Laro	Mrs. Meredith
Mildred Arden	Tabitha Larkin
Walter Law	General Charles Lee
Holbrook Blinn	Lord Clowes
Lionel Adams	Thomas Jefferson
Joseph Kilgour	George Washington
Nicolai Koesburg	Lafayette
George Siegmann	Colonel Rahl
W. C. Fields	A British sergeant
Olin Howland	Philemon Hennion
Edwin Argus	Louis XVI
George Nash	Sir William Howe
Princess Marie De Bourbon	Marie Antoinette
Helen Lee Worthing	Mrs. Loring
Lee Beggs	Benjamin Franklin
Tyrone Power Sr.	Lord Cornwallis
Mrs. Maclyn Arbuckle	Martha Washington

Wilfred Noy	Dr. Joseph Warren
Ken Maynard	Paul Revere
Spencer Charters	Squire Hennion
May Vokes	Susie
Douglas Stevenson	Charles Mobray
Harlin Knight	Theodore Larkin
Joe Raleigh	Arthur Lee
Wilson Reynolds	Parson McClare
Jerry Paterson	Cato
Isadore Marcell	Innkeeper
Keane Waters	Servant
Edgar Nelson	Tailor
Byron Russell	Captain Parker
Colonel Patterson	Major Pitcarin
George Cline	Trooper Heinrich Bruner
Burton McEvilly	Alexander Hamilton

Filmed at William Randolph Hearst's International Studios in Harlem, New York, with location work in and around New York City, as well as Plattsburg and Lake Placid.

Originally released in Britain as *The Beautiful Rebel*.

A Stage Break

After the day's work at Cosmopolitan, Fields returned to the Longacre Theatre to play Professor Eustace P. McGargle. Then, on June 1, 1924, the star of the show, Madge Kennedy, took a vacation. Victoria White replaced her as Poppy on stage, and W. C. Fields took her spot in the marquee lights. For the first time in nearly twenty-five years in entertainment the forty-four-year-old Fields became a star. That was the way it was in those days. To be called a star an entertainer had to have the lead in a Broadway play. Period! With Madge Kennedy gone, the producer, Philip Goodman, gave Fields the biggest and brightest billing.

On June 2, W. C.'s mother, Kate Dukenfield, came to New York to see her son on his starring night. During intermission that evening Sam Hardy and Will Rogers strode onstage with a bundle of flowers and a stack of telegrams. Nearly every big name in the performing arts wrote letters or sent telegrams praising Fields' ascendancy to stardom, and Sam Hardy and Will Rogers took turns reading the congratulatory notes. Reporters claimed that when Fields finally came out during that intermission the audience gave him a twenty-minute standing ovation. They also reported that this master of extemporization was nearly speechless, mumbling a few thank-you's and walking off seemingly bewildered. Fields had made it to the top once again.

Poppy ran for over a year, then closed in October 1924. Afterwards Fields sifted through countless offers to perform, and by November 14 he made up his mind. Even though they did not like each other they held a mutual admiration; Ziegfeld knew Fields could bring the crowds and Fields knew Ziegfeld could produce. Florenz wanted W. C. again. This time for a musical comedy called *The Comic Supplement* written by J. P. McEvoy, loosely based on the Sunday comic strips, and starring W.C. Fields. Actually, the play was a string of sketches parodying middle-class American life, skits that inevitably portrayed a beleaguered husband writhing under the tyrannical grip of a demanding wife and suffering the wailing and whining of spoiled offspring. The pieces were glued together by song and dance, but the play had no plot to speak of.

Between *Poppy* and *The Comic Supplement* Fields played very different characters. In the former he was a carnival mountebank, a charlatan, a humorous rogue—in the latter a browbeaten middle-class husband. These two plays were the beginning of Fields' motion picture characters. Rarely in W. C.'s film life does he vary from either the lovable faker or the tormented husband. Indeed, many of the lines, scenes and even dialogue in his more famous films can be traced directly to either *Poppy* or *The Comic Supplement. It's the Old Army Game* and *It's a Gift* were nearly complete remakes of *The Comic Supplement,* and some of the bedroom scenes from *The Man on the Flying Trapeze* and *My Little Chickadee,* as well as the one in *It's a Gift,* were once part of *The Comic Supplement.* Fields even performed his golf routine during the play.

As for repeats of *Poppy,* the play was retitled and made into a feature-length silent film, and nearly a dozen years after that Fields made it into a talking feature using the original name, *Poppy.* Then he took the same type of character and put him into two silent films—*Two Flaming Youths* and *Tillie's Punctured Romance*—and two talkies—*The Old Fashioned Way* and *You Can't Cheat an Honest Man.* It is noteworthy that after seeing *Poppy* many of New York's critics commented that if a studio ever made *David Copperfield* into a movie Fields would be the perfect Micawber. Nearly ten years later a studio did make *Copperfield* and Fields played Micawber.

So it is these two plays performed in the mid-twenties that molded the W. C. Fields character we know on film. Fields was perfect for the roles. He knew the characters well—the carnival midway types he met in vaudeville. They were the theatre managers, who with charm and fast talk cheated him out of his salaries. The

McGargle (W. C. Fields) and Poppy (Madge Kennedy) on stage in 1924.

lowly husband henpecked by a shrewish, ostentatious wife and plagued by a sissy son: that role came easily too. It was he, or at least it was how he viewed himself.

Even though estranged from his wife and son, Fields would write a letter and send a check to them every week. Only about three times a year did he get a chance to visit them and these meetings invariably ended in acerbic encounters. Hattie always demanded more money and from the very beginning recruited her son to join her cause. She coached the boy to dislike his father. Fields' hurt was great and was expressed in angry letters to Hattie, but he always sent the checks. Although he thought his son was a mama's boy, a sissy, he worried about him and never failed to ask about him. Years later when the boy became a man, father and son would grow closer to each other, but they would never really embrace. It was painful for the comedian but he used that pain and made it funny. And so it was that the stage and the movie camera provided him the release for the pent-up frustration of being deprived of a family he loved that he believed did not love him back.

The Comic Supplement opened in Washington, D.C., on January 14, 1925. The reviews were mixed. Nearly all of them praised W. C.'s work but complained the production ran too long and lacked continuity. Most of the reviewers, however, agreed that with judicious paring the play would be great for Broadway. It ran two weeks in Washington, then moved to Newark, New Jersey, for a couple more weeks of tryouts. Newark was supposed to be the last stop before the Great White Way. By now Fields had added so much of his own material, particularly through ad-libbing, that he shared writing credits with McEvoy. Ziegfeld, McEvoy and Fields all agreed the piece needed to be cut, but they fought vigorously over where. Ziegfeld settled the matter. After just one month of performances and with somewhat promising reviews he closed the show in New Jersey. Then he took Fields and the best parts of *The Comic Supplement* and put them in the *Ziegfeld Follies of 1925*. The show starred W. C. Fields and Will Rogers. On March 16 that year Walter Winchell wrote, "I can't understand how *The Comic Supplement* got such a deal. Every one of the bits taken from it registered with a wallop and Bill Fields and Ray Dooley ran away with the laughs."

Ziegfeld desperately wanted to sign W. C. to an exclusive contract, because in a writer's loft somewhere in New York City Jerome Kern was completing work on a brand-new play called *Show Boat*. Flo was producing it and the lead role of Cap'n Andy was written for W. C. Fields. But W. C. refused to sign such a binding contract, because he was considering another offer by Philip Goodman. The *Poppy* producer wanted Fields exclusively too, for five years—with Goodman guaranteeing W. C. starring roles in new productions once a year. Furthermore, D. W. Griffith was chasing the new star around New York with a contract to put *Poppy* on film. So negotiations swirled around Fields as he registered hits night after night in the *Ziegfeld Follies of 1925*. Finally he decided. He would keep away from exclusive contracts, work with Griffith on the *Poppy* film and then figure out what to do with Ziegfeld and Goodman after that.

W. C. Fields in the stage play Poppy.

A bedroom scene from
The Comic Supplement *(1925).*

The finale from the back-porch skit in The Comic
Supplement. *This stage routine was reused in two Fields
feature films,* It's the Old Army Game *and* It's a Gift.

Sally Of The Sawdust
— 1925 —

D. W. Griffith was on the move. He was concluding his relationship with United Artists and was ready to join Paramount. But before making movies with his new studio, Griffith produced his own film, *Sally of the Sawdust,* starring Carol Dempster (with whom he was infatuated) and featuring W. C. Fields. Paramount agreed to the independent production, urging Griffith to complete it quickly so he could start working on their projects. They even let Griffith use their Long Island studio, probably to keep an eye on him. It was an experiment for Fields and the director. Although W. C. was a hit on Broadway he had little film fame, and Griffith was unsure of himself in comedy.

The movie was a cinematic reproduction of Fields' smash Broadway hit *Poppy.* Nothing written about the film reveals why Griffith changed the title.

It is a rags-to-riches story of a young girl, Sally, and her lovable, larcenous guardian, Professor Eustace P. McGargle, F.A.S.N. It takes place sometime in the 1880s.

McGargle juggles in a traveling circus while his adopted daughter assists with her fancy dancing and gymnastic tricks. One night one of the trapeze stars in the troupe attempts to rape Sally but McGargle suddenly appears and fights off the attacker. Then and there McGargle decides that the circus life with its lascivious performers is no place for his developing adopted daughter. While packing their belongings he reminisces about how he and Sally first teamed.

Sally's mother was rejected by her wealthy family after she married a circus man. Soon after Sally's birth the marriage went sour, and McGargle, a member of the same circus, looked after the young mother and her baby. One evening Sally's mother fell from the trapeze. On her deathbed she asked McGargle to take care of her infant. She gave him a family heirloom, a locket with her photograph inside, as a reminder of his pledge.

Late one night Sally and her protector sneak away from the circus. After walking great distances, catching rides on freight trains and spending an evening sleeping in a baker's bread oven the two land in Green Meadows, Connecticut. To make a living Sally and the Professor entertain in the private mansions of this wealthy community. One of their first stops is Judge Foster's home, where

Sally (Carol Dempster) and McGargle trespassing on the property of Judge Foster (Erville Alderson). This scene was shot at boxer Gentleman Jim Corbett's estate in Bayside, Long Island. Fields liked the location so much he rented a house in the neighborhood.

Sally and Eustace are the entertainment for a gala function. Sally enchants the crowd with her scintillating dancing, especially attracting young Peyton Lennox, played by Alfred Lunt, who is the son of Judge Foster's good friend. As the McGargles settle down in Green Meadows the Judge notices Peyton's love for the circus girl. He thinks it terrible that his friend's scion would consider falling in love with someone so below his station. To stop further dalliance the Judge orders the arrest of Sally and McGargle, charging them with mendacity.

McGargle escapes, but Sally is caught and dragged into court. The fleeing Professor hears of Sally's fate. He purloins a flivver and after a spectacular chase makes it to the courtroom to prove Sally's acceptable lineage. To support her case he produces the locket. The photograph inside reveals that Sally's mother is none other than Judge Foster's daughter, the same girl he kicked out of the house years ago for philandering with a circus bum. The case is dismissed.

Sally tells her foster father that for all these years she has dreamed of staying in one place and having a home. Peyton obliges and marries Sally. Meanwhile, McGargle has found money and happiness in a lucrative Green Meadows real estate boom. But before he hands Sally over to Peyton he holds her by the shoulders tenderly and says, "Sally, before we depart let me give you one word of fatherly advice. Never give a sucker an even break."

On August 2, 1925, *Sally of the Sawdust* premiered at the Strand Theatre in New York City to generally favorable reviews. Fields' work received the most print, with

Confident of acquittal! W. C. Fields and Carol Dempster in **Sally of the Sawdust**.

the critics predicting an illustrious film future for the funnyman. That was an especially rewarding prediction for Fields, because Griffith gave him the go-ahead to improvise freely on the set, so during shooting W. C. was happy. But Griffith *usually* gave his actors tremendous freedom in front of the camera, knowing that the real film would be made in the editing room.

For *Sally,* Carol Dempster joined Griffith in the editing room, and there she saw how Fields stole the show. She was infuriated and demanded more time on the screen. Griffith loved her and so he threw in an extra $5,000 to shoot a few more scenes with just Carol.

Perhaps because of Dempster's demands or because of Paramount's pressuring the director to hurry, the film was badly edited. In careless cutting between close-ups and medium-range shots sometimes the scenery did not match or actors' positioning and lighting were not in sync. But the biggest error was editing comedy as though it were the usual Griffith melodrama. Normally Griffith would develop characters simultaneously, cutting from one to another until they all met at the end of the film, bringing their different experiences and stories together. But with comedy it is necessary to keep each comic sequence a whole or the joke is lost. Critical to comedy is timing and that comes in neat packages. Griffith cut away from Fields' antics too often, deflating their comic effect.

Another problem with the film rested squarely on Fields' shoulders. Evidently, W. C. simply did not understand the medium. Louise Brooks explains the situation in her delightful book *Lulu in Hollywood.* While Fields was working on *Sally,* Ms. Brooks was at the same studio making *The American Venus* for Famous Players-Lasky. She would often visit Fields' set to watch the filming:

> He paid no attention to camera setups. For each shot, he would rehearse the same business to exasperating perfection while his co-star, Carol Dempster, and the director, D. W. Griffith, sat bored and limp in chairs beside the camera. Long shot, medium shot, two-shot, or closeup, Bill performed as if he were standing whole before an audience that could appreciate every detail of his costume and follow the dainty disposition of his hands and feet. Every time the camera drew closer, it cut off another piece of him and deprived him of some comic effect. . . . As he ignored camera setups, he ignored the cutting room and he could only curse the finished film, seeing his timing ruined by haphazard cuts.

It is precisely for this same reason that Louise Brooks professed "loving the stage Fields more than the film Fields."

Nevertheless *Sally of the Sawdust,* despite its flaws, is worth viewing. Historically, no other Griffith production used exterior shots so extensively. (By the way most of the outdoor shooting was filmed at boxer Gentleman Jim Corbett's estate in Bayside, Long Island.) We also get some nice shots of William "Shorty" Blanche. Remember him? He was the fellow Ziegfeld fired and Fields hired in 1915. Well, he stayed with W. C. all these years. Around the house he was the comedian's factotum, and on the set or on stage Fields used him as his foil. Shorty

McGargle at the top of his form defending Sally in court.

As McGargle, giving us a nice view of Fields' fake mustache.

A tender moment from Sally.

W. C.'s time was free. He was considering Goodman's offer when Ziegfeld asked Fields to return to the *Follies* of 1925. Fields accepted. This, his last round with Ziegfeld, would be short and then followed by contention.

A final note on *Sally:* It is not a fluke that Fields liked the role of Eustace P. McGargle, F.A.S.N., the lovable larcenist. It was well thought out. He knew what worked. In a 1925 interview he was quoted: "No one likes the fellow who is all rogue, but we'll forgive him almost anything if there is warmth of human sympathy underneath his rogueries. The immortal types of comedy are just such men."

SALLY OF THE SAWDUST

104 Minutes (9,500 feet)
Silent, black and white
Released August 2, 1925, by United Artists
Produced by D. W. Griffith, Inc.
Directed by D. W. Griffith
Based on the 1923 stage play *Poppy,* by Dorothy Donnelly
Adapted by Forrest Halsey
Photographed by Harry Fischbeck
Additional photography by Hal Sintzenich
Art direction by Charles M. Kirk
Edited by James Smith
Assistant Director: Frank Walsh

CAST:
Carol Dempster   Title role
W. C. Fields   Professor Eustace P. McGargle, F.A.S.N.
Alfred Lunt   Peyton Lennox
Erville Alderson   Judge Henry L. Foster
Effie Shannon   Mrs. Foster
Charles Hammond   Mr. Lennox Sr.
Roy Applegate   Detective
Florence Fair   Miss Vinton
Marie Shotwell   Society woman
Glenn Anders   Leon the acrobat
Tammany Young   Yokel in the old army game
William "Shorty" Blanche   Stooge

Filmed at Paramount's Astoria Studios in Queens, Long Island. Paramount had no participation in this production, but was anxious to expedite its completion so that D. W. Griffith could begin fulfilling the contract he had signed to produce pictures for them. Additional filming was done on the Long Island estate of James J. Corbett.

Remade as *Poppy* eleven years later, and adapted for radio broadcast on *Lux Radio Theatre* in March of 1938. The premiere release of the Goldwyn Pictures Corporation in 1917 was entitled *Polly of the Circus,* featuring the Griffith actress Mae Marsh, similarly orphaned and raised as a child of the circus.

had a small part in the stage play *Poppy,* appeared in *The Comic Supplement* and now had a small role in *Sally.* Fields would use him again on stage and film. But the most fascinating reason to view the movie is to compare it with the remake, filmed eleven years later, a talking version called *Poppy.* You will discover the effect sound had on Fields' style of performance and what more than a decade did to the man's approach to comedy and the medium.

The filming for *Sally* ended on July 10, 1925, a couple of months later than anticipated. That was a shame, because Ziegfeld and Jerome Kern, worried about rumors that claimed a play which would conflict with *Show Boat* was ready for the boards, rushed their production to stage, leaving Fields behind. So with *Sally* completed and *Show Boat* under a full head of steam,

That Royle Girl

— 1925 —

Surprisingly, Fields and Griffith had a great deal in common. Both loved Old World melodrama, both relished hyperbolic rhetoric and both were great admirers of Dickens. Indeed, for almost twenty years they discussed making a filmed version of *Pickwick Papers*. Sadly, it never came to pass. In short, Fields and Griffith got along famously. Of Fields, Griffith said, "I'm crazy about him. He has a sweet sadness, a gentility, a subtlety. Something about his acting I can't just put into words. He is a great actor and artist. I am going to get him in a picture where he is the whole thing a little later on. I have the greatest admiration for him."

And W. C. on D. W.: "He is the best director I have ever had. He gives actors credit for having some brains. He is one of the finest men I have ever met."

Fields' feelings for Carol Dempster were considerably less sanguine. When asked who his favorite movie

actress was W. C. replied, "Carol Dempster." When asked why he thought so highly of her: "Because I'm working with her right now." Maybe Fields found out what Dempster did in the editing room with *Sally of the Sawdust*.

In any event, soon after completing *Sally of the Sawdust* Griffith, Dempster and Fields would team again. This time the trio would be working for Paramount. Jesse Lasky handed Griffith a script, which was based on a *Cosmopolitan* magazine serial by Edwin Balmer. After reading it the director did not want to make the film. But Lasky cajoled him, saying that only a great director could turn the drab story into a hit. Finally Griffith accepted the job but demanded that his sweetheart, Carol Dempster, take the starring role. Paramount agreed and production began. Incidentally, it began at first without Fields, but in no time D. W. and the Paramount executives realized the picture needed some pizazz and nobody could provide that better than W. C. The part was small, so it would not interfere with Fields' *Follies* work.

That Royle Girl deals with the world of Joan Daisy Royle, Carol Dempster. Daisy is a child of the Chicago slums, but her seedy environment has not corrupted her. In fact in the early going she stares admiringly at a statue of Abraham Lincoln, giving a clear indication of her elevated moral consciousness. Her father, W. C. Fields, is a dipsomaniacal slob who pops up here and there throughout the movie. In order to get out of the house and away from her father, Daisy becomes a modiste model and begins to travel with the swinging crowd of mid-twenties jazz era Chicago. Soon she hooks up with Fred Ketlar, a dance-hall bandleader. Ketlar, played by Harrison Ford, is still married but estranged from his wife, Adele, who has become the playmate of George Baretta, a bootlegger and head of a gangland mob. Meanwhile, Daisy dallies on the fringe of moral turpitude. Ketlar has invited her to his room. At first she is excited. Daisy enters the room full of amour. Ketlar makes his moves and at first she happily goes along, but suddenly she hesitates. She stares at Ketlar's bed, and the mattress slowly transforms into a bust of her hero, Abraham Lincoln. Her excitement turns to shame. She recoils from Ketlar's advances and runs from the room.

Across town Ketlar's wife, Adele, is found murdered. Witnesses claim they saw her estranged husband leaving his wife's apartment about the time of her death. He is arrested and the trial becomes the sensation of Chicago. Calvin Clarke, the straitlaced, crusading deputy district attorney, demands the death penalty. Being a pillar of

W. C. Fields counseling Carol Dempster in D. W. Griffith's That Royle Girl.

integrity and morality he fights off his strange attraction to defense witness Joan Daisy Royle and hammers at her unmercifully in his cross-examination. Ketlar is convicted of murder one and given the death sentence. Daisy knows the bandleader is innocent and she sets out to prove it before the execution. She tries pleading with Calvin Clarke, but he refuses to help her, so she starts alone to find the real murderer. The District Attorney eventually suffers from some doubt and surreptitiously follows Daisy. Furthermore, he is falling in love with her.

Someone tips off Daisy that Baretta, Adele's thug lover, committed the crime. Daisy has to have proof, so she disguises herself in the makeup and clothing from her modeling job and crashes a Baretta party at the Boar's Head Inn. There, she overhears the syndicate boss boast about the murder. Daisy tries to leave but she is discovered and thrown into a basement cell. Suddenly the skies darken and a cyclone hits the building, killing nearly everyone inside except Daisy, who makes a dramatic escape. She finds Calvin Clarke, who had followed her to the Boar's Head Inn, and convinces him of Ketlar's innocence and Baretta's guilt. It is execution day and the two make a mad dash to reach the Governor. They get hold of him a few seconds before the execution and the Governor stays the order.

Ketlar is freed and eternally grateful to his love, Joan Daisy Royle. But Daisy now loves the upright D. A. Calvin Clarke. Ketlar hooks up with a chorus girl and marries her while Calvin and Daisy also tie the knot.

That Royle Girl was released December 7, 1925, and received bad reviews. The critics claimed that W. C. Fields and the cyclone scene saved the picture from total disaster, but that both were added gratuitously. Evidently when the Paramount executives first reviewed the rushes they saw the abysmal state of the film and reportedly threw another $100,000 at Griffith and said, "Now do something!" Thus W. C. and the twister came to the set.

First, about W. C.'s inclusion. It seems it was Fields' role throughout the film to be shoved in here or put there because the picture needed something and nothing else was working. No literature on this film explains exactly how Fields was hired, but credible speculation suggests the following: William Le Baron was now a big shot at Paramount and most likely he and Griffith sat together for the screening of the first disappointing rushes. Griffith must have been acutely embarrassed. It was he who had pushed Paramount to accept as leading lady the particularly mediocre Carol Dempster. (Incidentally, Griffith nearly put himself out of the movie business trying to sell Dempster to the public. The irony is that she made only one more picture, then walked out of her contract with Griffith to wed an investment broker. End of career.) Something was drastically needed to perk up this miserable film. Both Le Baron and Griffith admired Fields' work, so most likely the two quickly agreed that Fields could be the movie's tonic. Fields signed and brought along with him his small pal with the few talents, William "Shorty" Blanche. Shorty was not needed and most likely not even wanted, but Griffith and Le Baron did need W. C., in any package. Fields may have been superfluous to the story, but he evidently was not incidental to its entertainment value. As Mr. Royle he wore loud funny-looking clothes and among other things performed the candle-in-the-mouth cigar-in-the-candlestick routine, which he had introduced a year earlier in *Janice Meredith.*

About the cyclone: Almost all the exterior shots in this film were taken in Chicago with pictures of the Loop and Lakeshore Drive prominent, but the cyclone was filmed on a football field not far from Paramount's Astoria studios. The stagehands created a complete village with a variety of trees, buildings, some telephone poles, a parking lot and cars, all held in place by piano wire. According to the publicity releases, Griffith used twenty-four planes with the propellers on full throttle, then he used fire hoses to shoot water in front of the aircraft, creating the effect of a full-blown tornado. It took five nights to shoot the scene. Although he was not scripted for the scene Fields took a trip to the football field to watch the spectacular storm. When the airplane engines whipped into action their wind caught a heavy peddler's wagon, pushing it slowly onto the set. W. C. jumped into the back of the wagon and pulled its cover over his head. As the wagon larruped in front of the cameras Fields kept lifting the cover and peeking out at the storm. Griffith thought it was so funny he reproduced the scene indoors. He used a wind machine in the studio and brought some Long Island dirt and sand to add realism. They turned on the fan, shot the water and threw the dirt. Every time Fields peeked out from under the blanket he caught the brunt of the onslaught. Griffith got his shot and asked Fields how he was feeling. "I'll be perfectly satisfied if I don't have to go through another cyclone."

Griffith did well with the alleged $100,000 Paramount gave him. The newspapermen praised the two added elements—W. C. and the twister—even though they complained that both were "unnecessary" to what was evidently a terrible picture to begin with. Interestingly, *That Royle Girl* was a carbon copy Griffith film—there is a chase, suspense and a stupendous climax—but even his well-tested formula could not save the bad script.

One last note: The studios used to send press packages to the theatres that exhibited their motion pictures. These kits included ideas for merchandising the particular film scheduled for each week, guaranteeing their brainstorms would bring the crowds. For *That Royle Girl* Paramount suggested the following: "1) Start a Jazz Week in your community. 2) Initiate a Charleston Contest. 3) Have a jazz band in the lobby." Now here is the kicker: "4) Start a contest. Take the best letter of 250 words or less answering, 'Was that Royle girl a victim of heredity or environment or both?' "

THAT ROYLE GIRL _____ (No rating, unavailable for screening)
114 minutes (10,253 feet)
Silent, black and white
Released December 7, 1925, by Paramount
Produced by D. W. Griffith for Famous Players-Lasky Corporation
Presented by Adolph Zukor and Jesse L. Lasky
Directed by D. W. Griffith
Based on the 1925 *Cosmopolitan* magazine serial and novel by Edwin Balmer
Screenplay by Paul Schofield
Photographed by Harry Fischbeck
Additional photography by Hal Sintzenich
Art direction by Charles M. Kirk
Edited by James Smith
Assistant director: Frank Walsh

CAST:
Carol Dempster	Joan Daisy Royle
W. C. Fields	Her father, a drunken confidence man
James Kirkwood	Calvin Clarke, deputy district attorney
Harrison Ford	Fred Ketlar, the king of jazz
Paul Everton	George Baretta, gangster
George Rigas	His henchman
Kathleen Chambers	Adele Ketlar
Florence Auer	Baretta's girlfriend
Ida Waterman	Mrs. Clarke
Alice Laidley	Clarke's fiancee
Dorothea Love	Lola Nelson
Dore Davidson	Elman
Frank Allwortth	Oliver
Bobby Watson	Hofer
William "Shorty" Blanche	Bit

Filmed at the Astoria Studios, in Queens, Long Island, with additional footage shot in Chicago.
   Title also rendered "D. W. Griffith's *That Royle Girl.*"

It's The Old Army Game

— 1926 —

In 1926 they all came after W. C. Fields. First it was Philip Goodman, the producer of *Poppy*. His lawsuit claimed he held an exclusive five-year contract with W. C. Said contract stipulated that the producer would pay the comedian $2,500 a week and 10 percent of gross receipts on any mutual production. The aforementioned lawsuit claimed Fields reneged on the above-mentioned contract.

Following Goodman's court action a fellow named Charles Walton, a casting director for D. W. Griffith,

charged that it was he who had secured stage and film work for W. C. over the past few years, including landing him jobs in the movies *Sally of the Sawdust* and *That Royle Girl*. Walton further argued that because of his work on behalf of Fields, the comedian signed a generous contract with Famous Players-Lasky, Paramount. The plaintiff contended he deserved 10 percent of W. C.'s earnings. The suit claimed Fields made $1.5 million during the few years in question.

The third suit was filed by Florenz Ziegfeld. The

trades asserted that after Fields' last two films Paramount and Hal Roach Studios competed for W. C.'s motion picture services. But both studios wanted exclusive contracts barring Fields from the stage, and so the comedian balked at the offers. At the time he was still playing in the *Follies.* He loved live audiences, and besides by now Ziegfeld had lifted his prohibition against his contracted players sharing their time with the movie industry. The money involved in this split schedule was difficult for Fields to turn his back on. Then William Le Baron fattened Paramount's bid, offering W. C. $4,000 a week for five years, with Fields making three pictures a year. The money and the security were too great for the comedian to refuse and he signed without delay, even though the contract still contained the stage proscription. He quit the Ziegfeld show and now Flo wanted his star back.

Fields' defense held strongly through the three lawsuits, so Paramount and W. C. began their extended association. With the comedian now under his wing, Jesse Lasky predicted, "Fields is going to be the greatest comedy star in the world." The court battles won, Fields began production on *It's the Old Army Game,* his first starring role for Paramount Pictures. It would be a true showcase for W. C.'s visual comedy.

The title came from a phrase Fields made popular in an ad-lib while playing in *Poppy.* Few people understood the origin of the term, which referred to the old shell game, but nevertheless it became a popular phrase around New York, especially among newspaper writers. When one reporter wrote an article about ancient swindles, calling them "the old army game," a United States general wrote a testy letter complaining about the insult to the army and demanding to know the etymology of the term. The writer turned to Fields, who had this answer:

The back-porch scene in It's the Old Army Game, *filmed in Florida. Fields preferred the remake of this routine shot at the Lasky Ranch in California for* It's a Gift *in 1934. Incidentally, that set stood on the Paramount backlot through most of the 1970s.*

The cigar box inferno. Of course the fire department just left.

"My father informed me that immediately following the Civil War the circus drifters and con men working the shell game or three-card monte all used the expression 'It's the old army game. A boy can play as well as a man.' The idea was to inspire confidence in the sucker. I never really got the lowdown from Pa whether he went against the game or was a worker, but he was well up on it."

"The Epic of the American Druggist," *It's the Old Army Game* follows the travails of Elmer Prettywillie, W. C., a no-account Florida drugstore owner. Elmer is trying to get some sleep on his back porch, which is connected to his drugstore. Suddenly a woman drives up to Elmer's business establishment. She is in a great hurry. She gets out of her car and rushes to the door. Clang! Clang! Clang! she rings the bell non-stop. The cacophony brings Elmer out of his deep sleep. Clang! Clang! Clang! He finally recognizes his own bell, throws on his clothes and rushes downstairs. He lets the woman into the drugstore. She most urgently needs a two-cent stamp. Deeply disappointed, but ever the gracious proprietor, Prettywillie makes the transaction and returns to his back porch to catch a few more winks. But the neighborhood is starting a new day and with his noisy family and clamorous trash collectors sleep becomes impossibly frustrating.

Downstairs the woman has mailed her letter but before leaving accidentally trips the fire alarm. This final blow ends Elmer's sleep for good. Firemen with sirens blaring rush to the Prettywillie drugstore. Elmer and the fire company look all over for the fire. No fire! Oh well, as long as they are there they might as well have ice cream sodas. Prettywillie treats. By now it is normal opening time and Elmer's beautiful assistant, Marilyn Sheridan (played by nineteen-year-old Louise Brooks), shows up for work. Just for the chance to stare at Marilyn the firemen decide to go another round on the sodas. On Elmer once again. Soon duty calls and the firemen leave the drugstore, at which time, naturally, a fire starts—in Prettywillie's cigar box.

Prettywillie tries the fire extinguisher. He cannot unhook it from the wall. He aims the hose at the box. Not enough water pressure. Rushing around in panic, he takes a cigar from the burning box and lights it with the fire. It never occurs to Elmer to move the box closer to the water. Finally, the fire simply dies out.

Elmer is overly solicitous to his assistant, trying hard to impress her, but to no avail. She likes him enough, but not in the way he would like her to like him.

At the train station George Parker is in a hurry. He must send a telegram, then return to the train before it leaves. Prettywillie's is the only place in town to send a telegram. At the drugstore he takes one look at Marilyn and forgets his telegram and train. Parker is a confidence man. This is the period of the Florida land rush. New York City is flooded with advertisements of the lush sun-drenched Florida landscape and the New Yorkers are buying property in the Sunshine State sight unseen. Parker wants to reverse the trend. Why not advertise New York land to the Floridians. He wants to rent space in Elmer's drugstore so he can be close to Marilyn. At first Prettywillie fights the idea, but Marilyn, who is impressed with the fast-talking salesman, convinces Elmer to give it a go. Parker offers the druggist a percentage of the take for the space. The deal is made.

Up till now Elmer's business has consisted of selling stamps, giving expensive souvenirs with every purchase, letting people use the telephone and allowing others to take up space playing checkers, but now all that has changed. The land scheme works. Prettywillie's drugstore is packed with Floridians buying New York lots. Elmer is rolling in money. He buys a flivver and one fine day takes his sister, her impudent son and her mother-in-law on a picnic. Mistaking an enormous private Florida millionaire's estate for a park, they begin their outing. First, however, the flivver gets out of control and knocks down a stone wall and a large statue. Oh well, they settle down for lunch. Papers are strewn, food is dropped, cans are thrown, they have turned the exclusive estate into a garbage dump. The little boy wanders away from the outing and finds the millionaire's house. He begins throwing rocks at the statuary on the porch, occasionally missing the target and smashing a window. When Elmer finds his sister's son he reprimands him mildly, then tries the door to the mansion. Discovering the door locked and taking the security measure as an insult to honest taxpaying people, he breaks into the house. He finds some food and brings the manna back to the picnic. Eventually the owner returns and kicks the Prettywillie clan off his property.

Back at the drugstore, a detective discovers Parker's charade but cannot find the swindler. Parker has rushed to New York on "urgent business." When Elmer returns the detective tells him that the land scheme is a hoax and that his nefarious partner has taken it on the lam. Remorsefully, Elmer tries convincing his suckered friends that the deal was a swindle and offers to return their money, but speculation fever is at a frenzy. The customers

Louise Brooks and W. C. Fields in **It's the Old Army Game.**

With Mickey Bennett in "The Epic of the American Druggist," or It's the Old Army Game.

think that Elmer wants their money back because he sold them the land too cheaply. They want more land. Elmer decides to straighten up the mess in New York City. He jumps in his new car and rides.

More trouble in the Big Apple. He arrives driving the wrong way on a one-way street and after some expert dodges he finally destroys his car in an accident. Eventually he finds Parker's office, which is now rubble, and Elmer realizes he has been a party to a crime. He tries turning himself in to the authorities but the cops do not believe his story and kick him out of the station house. After leaving police headquarters he sees a mob of his Florida friends headed his way. He politely and contritely attempts to explain how he had been bamboozled by Parker and that he intends, one way or another, to pay back all their money. The mob will not listen. They are a lynching party now. Elmer realizes their intent and runs to the police station, putting himself in protective custody. The ugly gang stands outside. Soon Parker appears with

Picnic time! Mary Foy and W. C. Fields.

the appropriate deeds for everyone in the crowd. It was not a hoax. After courting Marilyn, Parker had decided to go straight and the entire affair was on the up and up. Prettywillie returns to Florida a wealthy man and Parker gets the girl.

The last card on screen reads, "Moral: A bird in the hand is a hard pill to swallow. In other words, never give a sucker an even break—IT'S THE OLD ARMY GAME."

It's the Old Army Game, Fields' first starring role under his Paramount contract, opened May 24, 1926. The Paramount bigwigs felt Fields would be a great drawing card, but the critics, particularly the New York variety, were lukewarm toward the film. What they praised was Fields' sense of humor and his timing but they said the material he used was old, a little tattered, they had seen it on stage often enough. Furthermore, they said there was no plot, a criticism that haunted W. C. throughout his film career.

Sure the movie used some graying routines. Some of the lines were purloined from *Poppy* and most of the comedic bits came from *The Comic Supplement,* but they were old routines mainly to New Yorkers. This was a nationwide release. There were people west of New York City who never saw *Poppy* or *The Comic Supplement.* As for lacking a plot, who goes to a Fields movie looking for a story? It was his skits, his bits, his characterizations that audiences howled at, not the plots. Eddie Sutherland, who directed W. C. in this film and in several others, observed, "Bill only had one story. It wasn't a story at all really—there was just an ugly old man, an ugly old woman and a brat of a child." Overly simplistic of course, but it was something along those lines and that was all Fields needed to get great laughs.

It's the Old Army Game is a wonderful film and still gets huge laughs at revival screenings today. No need for that distinctive voice with its nasal epithets to attack an audience's risibilities; he could bring the laughs easily with the grace and humor of his movements. *It's the Old Army Game* made W. C. Fields an honest-to-goodness *movie* star.

The incomparable Louise Brooks played the role of Marilyn Sheridan. The year before, at the age of eighteen, she performed in the *Ziegfeld Follies of 1925,* with Fields starring. She and W. C. became very close friends. Almost fifty years later she wrote a sensitive and revealing article about some of her experiences with the comedian entitled, "The Other Face of W. C. Fields," reprinted in her book *Lulu in Hollywood.* Among other things she wrote about their work together on the *Army Game* set.

Ms. Brooks: The picnic scene was "shot on the front lawn of the most lavish estate in Palm Beach, El Marisol, the winter home of a J. P. Morgan partner, Edward Stotesbury. . . . What the producing unit did to the lawn was frightful. During the five days of shooting the litter converted it to a garbage dump, and when the trucks and forty pairs of feet finished their work it looked like the abandoned site of a soldier's reunion. But Mr. and Mrs.

W. C. and Mickey Bennett in the picnic scene.

Amused by his housebreaking skill in this shot from **It's the Old Army Game.**

Stotesbury were thrilled. 'Everybody,' said Mrs. Stotesbury, 'everybody in Palm Beach is driving by to see what is going on here.' "

After the crew wrecked the lawn Mr. and Mrs. Stotesbury invited Fields and the gang in for dinner. Nice people, considering the studio did not pay to reseed their yard.

The great majority of the Florida scenes were filmed in Ocala, Florida, not far from Silver Springs. The people of Ocala wanted to make Silver Springs a rich tourist attraction, so they went out of their way welcoming the company as a means of publicizing their project.

Ms. Brooks: "We were treated to so much southern hospitality that the script got lost and the shooting schedule wandered out of sight. Nobody in Ocala seemed to have heard of prohibition. And if there was a company that needed no help in the consumption of liquor it was ours. Eddie Sutherland [the director, whom Ms. Brooks would marry in July 1926] and Tom Geraghty [the scriptwriter] drank. William Gaxton, Blanche Ring, myself, the crew—everyone drank. Bill Fields drank his private stock apart with his girlfriend Bessie Poole [Fields met Bessie in the *Ziegfeld Follies of 1925*], his manager Bill Grady and his valet, Shorty. We were a week over schedule, Le Baron was wiring, 'All second cameraman's rushes tilted. What are you doing? Sober up and come home!' That's when Eddie decided

that the picnic sequence absolutely must be shot on Mrs. Stotesbury's lawn."

Then she wrote about her role with William Gaxton, who played the male romantic lead: "I knew that our parts as the love interest in a Fields comedy meant nothing but Gaxton had convinced himself that this first job in films would launch him on a successful new career allowing him to escape from years of mediocre vaudeville sketches." It did not work for him. Gaxton was thirty-four years old, playing the part of a much younger man, and it sent him nowhere in films.

Louise Brooks continues that she never did see the film and she thinks it never made money. It did make money but just barely.

How did Fields get along with the thirty-one-year-old director Eddie Sutherland and his assistant Paul Jones?

Ms. Brooks: As far as I know Fields had "no intimate friends and loved only one person . . . Paul Jones, and this is how the three [Paul, W. C. and Eddie] worked together. Fields, Eddie and I first knew Paul when he was the second assistant on *It's the Old Army Game*. He [Paul] would listen to Bill and Eddie argue about the direction of the scene until they ran out of words. Then with some easy comforting remarks he would make them feel just silly enough to laugh at themselves. When it came time to shoot the scene the argument had settled itself, usually in Bill's favor."

Years later, and bitter over his bad treatment in silent films, Fields would blame anyone but himself, and a lot of times Eddie Sutherland came under attack: "I was directed by an ex-chorus boy still in his teens. When I would suggest a gag that had been surefire on the stage for years he would retort, 'But that was on stage, Mr. Fields. The screen is different.' That's bunk. What is funny is funny anywhere." It sounds as if Sutherland stopped Fields from doing his routines. Yet the reporters who visited the set wrote that Fields had unlimited freedom. One writer, however, after commenting on Fields' uncommon liberty on the set did add that at one point W. C. wanted to shoot a kite down with a cap pistol—a positive laugh getter on stage. Sutherland argued strongly against it and finally won his point. Perhaps Fields never forgot that one incident. Furthermore, Sutherland learned the directorial trade as an assistant director to Charlie Chaplin. That was the competition. Fields did not like Chaplin and refused to be guided by anything he did, much less let a Chaplin subordinate tell him what to do.

A side note: Fields himself picked the name Elmer Prettywillie. This was how he got it. He was traveling between *Follies* engagements one night when a suspicious-looking gang in another car passed him on the road and sped ahead. When W. C. rounded the next bend the other car blocked his path. They were highwaymen. Fields quickly decided to pass at a narrow opening between the car and a cliff. He floored it. His car zipped by the bandits and off Fields went flying down the road. He did not stop for a long time and only when he thought it was safe did he pull off to the side to calm down. When he looked up he read the huge sign above the building in front of him: PRETTYWILLIE'S LUMBER COMPANY.

Finally, with *It's the Old Army Game,* Fields' initial starring vehicle, more or less successfully launched, and an exclusive film contract with Paramount in hand, Fields was asked what attracted him to the screen so much that he was willing to repudiate the stage. His response:

An actor's art can be demonstrated far more broadly and more quickly through the medium of the screen. It is not the quantity of money perhaps so much with any other actor as it is the intense desire and satisfaction of demonstrating to the great public that acting impulse *every true actor feels within his breast.* You know, for the people of the stage the impulse of mimicry is an urge, usually demonstrated from earliest childhood, that we cannot deny. The average actor would act whether he starved doing it. Money itself means nothing. It is the reward of pleased multitudes that is pay. That statement may sound flighty but it is true just the same. Ask any actor. And that's the reason I'm leaving the stage. The reason is to become better known by the public in greater numbers. Through the medium of the screen perhaps I can be so successful as to make three million people in the hinterland laugh. If I can make them laugh and through that laughter make this old world seem just a little brighter, then I am satisfied. The question of money doesn't enter into it. Not at all.

Is that so? Hmmm . . .

Looking up Fifth Avenue from 42nd Street. W. C. Fields, getting into the car, departs from Paramount's offices for location shooting elsewhere in midtown Manhattan. The long fur coat is W. C.'s costume for the day's shooting.

IT'S THE OLD ARMY GAME

72 minutes (6,889 feet)
Silent, black and white
Released May 24, 1926, by Paramount
Produced by Edward Sutherland for Famous Players-Lasky Corporation
Presented by Adolph Zukor and Jesse L. Lasky
Directed by Edward Sutherland
Associate producer, Eastern Studio: William Le Baron
Based on the play by Joseph Patrick McEvoy, with certain material derived from four W. C. Fields stage sketches: "The Back Porch," "The Picnic," "The Druggist" and "A Road-Joy Ride," all written by McEvoy and Fields for the *Ziegfeld Follies*
Screenplay by Tom J. Geraghty and J. Clarkson Miller
Titled by Ralph Spence (and W. C. Fields)
Photographed by Alvin Wychoff
Supervising editor: Tom J. Geraghty
Second assistant director: Paul Jones

CAST:
W. C. Fields   Elmer Prettywillie, apothecary and humanitarian
Louise Brooks   Marilyn Sheridan*
Blanche Ring   Tessie Overholt, railroad station agent
William Gaxton   George Parker
Mary Foy   Sarah Pancoast, Elmer's sister
Mickey Bennett   Mickey, his nephew
Elise Cavanna   Morning stamp customer
Josephine Dunn   Society bather
Jack Luden   Society bather
George Currie   Artist
John Merton   Fireman

Filmed at the Astoria Studios, in Queens, Long Island, with location work in midtown Manhattan, and another location jaunt to Florida and the Palm Beach estate of Edward Stotesbury, and also Ocala, Florida.

Remade in part as *The Pharmacist* seven years later, and as *It's a Gift* eight years later.

*Character part has often been listed as Mildred Marshall, but extant prints carry text titles listing Marilyn Sheridan.

So's Your Old Man
— 1926 —

In 1925 Julian Street wrote a short story for *Redbook* magazine entitled "Mr. Bisbee's Princess." It won the O. Henry prize for the greatest American story of the year. In 1926 Paramount changed the title to *So's Your Old Man,* put W. C. Fields in the lead role and produced Fields' second starring movie. It was a comic look at "typical" American family life.

Fields plays a rube, Samuel Bisbee, the local "optometrist, optician, occultist and optimist" for the town of Waukeagus, New Jersey. But in his secret back room he dabbles in his true loves—drinking with his two cronies and inventing. His latest invention, he figures, is going to make him a great deal of money—a shatterproof windshield. His buddies doubt the claim, so Sam takes them outside, fits his new invention to his car and drives the car headlong into a stout oak tree. Back up! Hit it

again! Back up! Hit it again! The car is completely destroyed but the windshield holds together.

At home is Sam's wife, Mrs. Bisbee. She is a relative of "Martha Washington Warren—you know, the Warrens from Virginia." She is a long-suffering woman finally running out of patience with her besotted husband. They have a daughter, Alice, who is "convincing evidence that even poor people can have attractive children." Alice is cooing with Robert Murchison, a boy with a proper heritage from the good side of the tracks "who just reached the ukulele stage of calf love." The youngsters want to marry but Robert's mother, Mrs. A. Brandewyne Murchison, "the bell cow of Waukeagus' social herd," frowns on her son's involvement with "those" people.

Back at the office, Sam has just received an invitation to demonstrate his windshield at an automobile convention.

Back at his home, Mrs. Murchison is trying to convince Mrs. Bisbee to discourage Alice's involvement with Robert. It is just not proper. During the conversation Mrs. Bisbee drops the name of her prestigious relatives and shows Mrs. Murchison her family album proving her fine heritage. Thoroughly impressed, Mrs. Murchison agrees that maybe the marriage is not that unreasonable.

Enter Samuel Bisbee. He is wearing a T-shirt with his suspenders hanging down around his knees. After hearing the conversation he decides to further impress the "bell cow" with his own family scrapbook, a collection of reprobates and criminals, including his cousin Sadie, who was "the best dancer in burlesque until she lost her voice." Pridefully, he extends his hand to shake, looks at it, wipes it on his pants, then puts it out again saying, "I knew your old man when he had just one pair of pants." That does it. Mrs. Murchison, with her nose pointed heavenward, absolutely condemns the union of their families and storms out of the house.

Robert and Alice, who have been waiting outside to hear the outcome, enter, confused. Sam, now offended, retaliates by kicking A. Brandewyne Murchison's son out of his house. Thinking everything is settled, he proudly reads the letter from the automobile convention, but his family, disgusted and crying, walk out of the room, leaving Sam alone with his good news.

Bisbee drives to the convention with his shatterproof windshield attached securely in its place. He parks right in front of the convention hall and enters the building with unabashed confidence. As he meets the automobile magnates he passes out his card: "See the world through a Bisbee window." Then, with absolute pride he announces that his windshield "is harder to break than a blonde's heart." He invites the cadre outside for a demonstration of his breakless glass. Meanwhile, another motorist has pushed Bisbee's car down the road, replacing it with his own. Bunching on the sidewalk the delegates skeptically await the demonstration. With aplomb, Bisbee grabs a brick and heaves it at the window. Crash! The glass shatters. He is puzzled. The car looks like his car, but he could be wrong. The delegates scoff at the folly. Bisbee sees another car parked behind the first. It looks like his also. It must be his. He takes a hammer and clobbers the window. It too shatters. The conventioneers howl. Finally the owners of the cars arrive and chase Bisbee out of town. Sam grabs the first train back to Waukeagus and thinks about the events of the last few days. He has ruined his daughter's happiness and now his invention is a flop. There is nothing left, so Sam decides to take his own life.

He grabs a bottle of iodine and retreats to the train's lounge. He brings the bottle to his lips, but the train shudders and he misses his mouth. Again he tries. No luck. After the third failure he looks out the window and sees a cemetery. He quivers and shakes, then throws the bottle away. As he trundles back to his seat the train lurches forward, thrusting Sam into the beautiful Princess Lescaboura's private car. Because she cut her finger she has a bottle of iodine on the table. Bisbee concludes she wants to end it all just as he was going to do. He has to talk her out of it: "One day you swallow it and the next day you're sorry." He explains his attempted suicide, telling her his tale of woe and then of his ultimate decision to return home and face the dirge. Sam does not know of the Princess's fame, and she keeps it secret by telling him her name is simply Marie.

Bisbee testing his shatterproof windshield at the expense of his car and one oak tree.

W. C. points with pride to photographs of some of the great reprobates of all time, who also happen to be his relatives. The snooty Mrs. Murchison, the "bell cow of the Waukeagus social herd," is not impressed.

With Jerry Sinclair, W. C.'s drinking buddy in So's Your Old Man.

Looks something like a Rockwell illustration, but of course it is a scene from So's Your Old Man. *Bisbee is returning home after a bit of a binge.*

Back in the coach section of the train, two of Waukeagus' gossips sit, astonished to see Sam Bisbee sharing a cabin with a woman. While Sam is talking to Marie he misses the Waukeagus station. The two rumormongers spread the word of Sam's tryst.

After Sam disembarks, the Princess decides to visit Waukeagus and help Bisbee out of the Murchison mess.

When he returns home, he gets a chilling reception from the town's moral wardens. In fact, the only people in town who will talk to him are his drinking pals. The three get drunk in Sam's hidden room. His friends convince Sam that the only way to smooth things over with his wife is to buy her a pet. He buys a pony for her, then heads for home.

By now the Princess has arrived at the station. Of course the Waukeagus elite meet her, headed by Mrs. A. Brandewyne Murchison. At first the townfolk are flattered by the visit, but when the Princess asks for Samuel Bisbee they are flabbergasted. A parade of cars, led by Mrs. Murchison and the Princess, heads for Sam's house. The policemen escorting the entourage keep a lookout for Sam. They find him grazing his wife's pet. Afraid of more trouble, Sam gets down on all fours trying to disguise himself as a pony. The subterfuge does not work. The Princess greets Sam, but he does not recognize her through his whiskey-bleared vision. He stares awhile, then she comes into focus. "Oh, hi, Marie." The informality stuns the stuffed shirts, particularly Mrs. Murchison.

They all go to Sam's house and the old boozer is the toast of the town. Sam hosts a big dinner party for all those folks on the good side of the tracks. Now that Sam has connections the Murchisons agree to the wedding. Robert Murchison's marriage to Alice Bisbee is announced at the party. The Mayor of Waukeagus asks Bisbee to inaugurate the new town country club. He demurs, "I know nothing about golf. I wouldn't even know which end of the caddy to use." The Princess persuades him and the next day he initiates the links with the Princess by his side.

W. C.'s optimism is about to be shattered in this scene shot in midtown Manhattan for So's Your Old Man.

Gregory La Cava directing Fields and Marcia Harris in this scene, which was shot in Queens.

Suddenly, the chairman of the automotive convention pushes his way through the crowd at the first tee. He heads for Sam. Bisbee figures he is in more trouble and the chase begins—Bisbee in the lead with the chairman and the chauffeur a hot second. At the water trap Sam stops short. So does the chauffeur, but the chairman, with contract in hand, cannot stop in time and runs into the drink. The chauffeur tells Sam that they found his car, tested the window, and the chairman is offering a million dollars for the rights. Sam quickly rescues the nearly drowned man and signs the soggy document.

The last scene shows the huge Bisbee mansion, from which the Bisbees and the Murchisons are preparing to go out for the day—except Sam. Before leaving, his daughter turns to her father and says, "I'm the happiest girl in the world."

W. C.: "So's your old man."

Sam stands in the driveway waving good-bye. When the coast is clear his pals come out of the bushes with a jug of cider.

The movie hit the theatres on October 25, 1926. The reviews were mixed. Most said that *So's Your Old Man* was better than *It's the Old Army Game,* but still shy of Fields' potential, concluding that the comedian needed better stories, because Paramount could not depend on just Fields' antics to carry an entire film. Nevertheless, W. C. was building a devoted following, even among the critics. Nary a review pans Fields' comic worth, but they pick on the poor structure of his films, the lack of a strong plot. They loved his comedy but decried the chaos. Not fair criticism. Fields worked best with twenty-minute skits to make a so-called plot. He concluded that so many bits tied together to make a movie which produced belly laughs was a lot better than a tightly structured story which received only occasional chuckles. Time has proved the old vaudevillian correct. Today, a general re-release of *It's The Old Army Game* and *So's Your Old Man* would be reason enough for another full-scale Fields renaissance. The humor is undated, the routines are inventive and the throwaway sight gags are brilliant (casually handing over an axe to aid someone disciplining a child, or extending a lighted cigar while trying to shake hands).

Fields' friend Gregory La Cava produced and directed this movie, the first of a pair on which they would collaborate. The two loved playing golf together and gambling, but most of all they loved drinking and arguing with each other, and boy, did they argue. Although the trade columnists never cited specific causes of conflict they all agreed that the two fought over comedy. It seems what La Cava considered hilarious left Fields flat and vice versa. The scribes claimed the set was a battlefield, with truculent lambasting launched with every new comic scene. Evidently this discord between director and actor caused the picture to run well past its production schedule. In turn this delay may be the reason why Paramount

Candid production shot of a relaxed and laughing W. C. Fields between scenes. Gregory La Cava is looking through the camera on the right. Notice the many reflectors used to film a sunlit golf course on a cloudless day. The stunted man in the middle of the picture walking toward the still photographer is William "Shorty" Blanche.

Samuel Bisbee, the talk of the town, inaugurating Waukeagus' new golf course in So's Your Old Man.

scuttled a previously publicized Fields movie. In April 1926 Paramount announced that W. C. would begin production on *So's Your Old Man* to be immediately followed by the shooting of a picture called *The Wild Man of Borneo*. This is how they were announced:

For Paramount's fifteenth birthday the studio will produce *So's Your Old Man* and *The Wild Man of Borneo*, both starring W. C. Fields. For *The Wild Man of Borneo* Lillian Gish asked for and got the role of the native dancer in a South Seas island picture with W. C. Fields as the shipwrecked yachtsman.

Again, later in April, in the *Motion Picture News*, Paramount bought a full-page color ad announcing:

W. C. Fields in a special comedy production based upon the funniest screen story in years. *The Wild Man of Borneo* by Herman Mankiewicz. The rollicking tale of a dapper boardinghouse Romeo who poses as a Broadway stage star greater than Booth or Irving and who really was the *Wild Man of Borneo* in a cheap Bowery sideshow. Spiced and jazzed up with Fields' own unique side-splitting humor and lavishly produced by the Fields special comedy unit. This will be one of the irresistible offerings of the season. *So's Your Old Man* and *The Wild Man of Borneo;* and following these surefire gold getters

another big W. C. Fields special is coming in Paramount's birthday group of seventy-five all big pictures.

There was no explanation for the thoroughly contradictory plot summaries for supposedly the same picture.

What happened to *The Wild Man of Borneo?* It was made years later but without W. C. In 1941 two of Herman J. Mankiewicz's screenplays were produced, *Citizen Kane* and *The Wild Man of Borneo.* Sometime between 1926 and 1941, MGM had acquired the property rights for *The Wild Man of Borneo.* When they finally made the film they cast Frank Morgan in the role intended for Fields. (Interestingly, it was the second time Morgan took over a part meant for Fields. The other was the wizard in *The Wizard of Oz.* That story is for later.)

Back to 1926. It was at this time that Paramount's out-West facilities were producing and releasing the feature comedies of Harold Lloyd, who had parted company with Hal Roach. Lloyd's grosses were surpassing comedies made by anyone anywhere, Chaplin included. W. C. held promise, but measured against the returns of Lloyd's pictures, he was an also-ran. And with *It's the Old Army Game* and *So's Your Old Man* getting only so-so reviews, William Le Baron and the men in Paramount's gilded East Coast offices worked overtime to find the right script so their comedian could live up to expectations. They had not given up on Fields. Not yet anyway.

SO'S YOUR OLD MAN

67 minutes (6,347 feet)
Silent, black and white
Released October 25, 1926, by Paramount
Produced by Gregory La Cava for Famous Players-Lasky Corporation
Presented by Adolph Zukor and Jesse L. Lasky
Directed by Gregory La Cava
Screenplay by J. Clarkson Miller
Adapted by Howard Emmett Rogers and Tom J. Geraghty
Based on Julian Leonard Street's "Mr. Bisbee's Princess," a *Redbook* magazine short story and winner of The O. Henry Memorial Prize for the best short story of 1925.
Production editing: Ralph Block
Film and title editor: Julian Johnson
Title designs by John Held Jr.
Photographed by George Webber
Associate producer, Eastern Studio: William Le Baron

CAST:
W. C. Fields   Samuel Bisbee, Esq., inventor
Alice Joyce   Princess Lescaboura
Charles "Buddy" Rogers   Robert Murchison
Catherine Reichert   Alice Bisbee
Marcia Harris   Mrs. Bisbee
Julia Ralph   Mrs. A. Brandewyne Murchison
Frank Montgomery   Jeff, Bisbee's fellow scientist
Jerry Sinclair   Al, Bisbee's fellow scientist
Charles Beyer   Prince Lescaboura
William "Shorty" Blanche   Caddy

Filmed at the Astoria Studios, in Queens, Long Island.
    Remade as *You're Telling Me* eight years later.

The Potters

— 1927 —

Satirizing American middle-class family life was a popular theme of 1920s comedies. It began on stage, and one of the first to exploit the theme was J. P. McEvoy in his 1923 play called *The Potters*. Florenz Ziegfeld produced it and Donald Meek starred as Pa Potter. It played Broadway the same year Fields worked the boards in *Poppy* just down the street. *The Potters* was a big hit on stage; in fact, its success spurred Ziegfeld to use McEvoy again, add Fields and have the two collaborate on another play spoofing American middle-class mores. As mentioned, that became *The Comic Supplement*, scenes from which were the delights of the *Follies of 1925*. Paramount was searching for a good solid vehicle to propel Fields' career. *The Potters* was a blockbuster on

stage, easily adapted to film, and could be just the part Fields needed. They acquired the rights and got W. C. to play Meek's original role as Pa Potter, a henpecked husband and disrespected father.

Pa Potter fancies himself a financial wizard but all his schemes end in failure. His wife, son, daughter and prospective son-in-law torment him about this, but Pa Potter never loses faith in his business acumen. Ma Potter has stashed away their last bit of savings, $4,000, so that Pa cannot bring the family to bankruptcy. Pa finds the loot and gives it all to a pair of swindlers for three oil wells, and as a sign of their honesty the crooks throw in a fourth well.

Pa proudly returns home but keeps his deal hush-hush so he can surprise his family when the money comes rolling in. He dreams about how he will spend the prospective treasure—Rolls-Royces, princely mansions, easy living. Suddenly he is shocked from his reverie when he hears the oil lease deal was a scam.

He now has to tell his family. All hell breaks loose. Pa is berated and scolded and then ignored. But a few days later at the pit of his depression and disillusionment he finds out that the supposedly dry wells have turned into gushers. The men who sold him the wells return. They want their deeds back, proffering the $4,000. Wise to their tricks, Pa holds out, eventually bargaining for an enormous sum. With his new great wealth he buys a fur coat, a radio, and fills his pockets with luxury gifts for his family. Pa passes out the gifts and playfully keeps his secret deal quiet. The Potters are bewildered. Finally, Pa turns on the new radio so they all can hear the news of the great oil discovery. Pa Potter finally has respect and money.

W. C. Fields as Pa Potter.

Trying to shave in The Potters. He tried again seven years later in It's a Gift. Note that they painted over the mirror so it would not reflect the camera.

With Mary Alden.

The film was made at the height of the Teapot Dome investigations. In the last scene, when Fields turned on the radio so his family could find out how he got all his money, he picked a station at random. This is what the production crew heard: "The question of whether or not the government oil reserves were deliberately bartered away to private interests is the chief item of concern in the news today and will probably be settled by the jury hearing the case." The coincidence caught the crew and actors off guard. They all burst out laughing, of course, forcing a retake.

The Potters was released on January 31, 1927, but unfortunately, at this writing, the film is lost. All judgments on the film, therefore, must necessarily be based on the comments of the 1927 reviewers. Most of them gave the movie a mediocre mark. They wrote that *The Potters* was less funny than *So's Your Old Man,* but not bad. They complained that it was a little slow in the beginning, yet when it did get to the meat of the plot the laughs came fast and easily. Those reviewers who saw the original stage play with Donald Meek said that much of the spontaneous humor and tender sentiment were, in the words of one critic, "lost in the transition from stage to movie," but, he continued, "it was still a good piece with a rare artist, and the combination is hard to put down."

Up until now Fields had portrayed sympathetic

With Jack Egan.

With Skeets Gallagher and Mary Alden.

characters—a lovable failure or sentimental rogue—but in *The Potters* apparently he played the most sympathetic character to date. He was not the swindler but the object of swindles. He was a buffoon but a good man nevertheless. His family showed him no tenderness whatsoever, even going out of their way to berate him. The only thing that did save him was pure dumb luck. Perhaps the character was too pure, too naive, too touching, for W. C.'s style of humor.

Comments on this film said that Fields' performance was "restrained, subtle and natural," devoid of Fields' pet routines that he had added to his other movies whether or not they fitted. Reviewers further wrote that as Pa Potter, Fields' acting skills were strongly called upon—he jumped from utter dejection to great elation, from frustration and fury to delightful optimism.

It seemed *The Potters* followed a disciplined story line and that may be the reason some critics said that it was not as funny as *So's Your Old Man*. If that be the case, then the reviewers contradicted themselves. If Fields got a strong story, a good plot, which the critics had been demanding, but curtailed his pet bits, then he lost laughs. If he liberally sprinkled the story with his favorite routines, he got the laughs but lost the plot. The critics of the 1920s put him in a no-win situation.

It seems *The Potters* would be a fascinating picture to view, particulary since it is a precursor of such top titles in the Fields canon as *It's a Gift* and *The Bank Dick*. While a strict blueprint for neither, *The Potters* does

Learning a little about oil fields.

A card game from The Potters. *Besides golf and pool, card games frequently popped up in Fields' films. Fields frequently won.*

foreshadow many of the same peccadillos of life dealt with so admirably by Harold Bissonette and Egbert Sousé, which only underscores the loss.

A laugh note: Many of the reviewers took great delight in describing one scene from *The Potters*. Here it is: At one point Pa Potter hails a cab, but the cab keeps going, so Fields takes chase. After blocks and blocks of running he catches the cab, but by now he only has to travel a few more feet. He gets into the cab, the vehicle rolls a couple of feet and Pa gets out. When he pays for the cab the driver makes him pay for the distance from where Pa started the chase.

Paramount had to work harder for W. C. The response to *The Potters* both at the box office and in the newspapers was tepid. They had not lost faith in Fields but . . .

How many aces? A pensive moment for Pa Potter.

THE POTTERS _____ (No rating, unavailable for screening)
71 minutes (6,680 feet)
Silent, black and white
Released January 31, 1927, by Paramount
Produced by Famous Players-Lasky Corporation
Presented by Adolph Zukor and Jesse L. Lasky
Directed by Fred Newmeyer
Based on the 1923 stage play *The Potters: An American Comedy*
Written by Joseph Patrick McEvoy
Adaptation by Sam Mintz and Ray Harris
Screenplay by J. Clarkson Miller
Photographed by Paul Vogel
Assistant director: Ray Lissner
Associate producer, Eastern Studio: William Le Baron

CAST:
W. C. Fields   Pa Potter, office stenographer
Mary Alden   Ma Potter
Ivy Harris   Minnie, daughter
Jack Egan   Bill, son
Richard "Skeets" Gallagher   Red Miller
Joseph Smiley   H. B. Rankin, entrepreneur
Bradley Barker   Eagle

Filmed at the Astoria Studios in Queens, Long Island.
In 1930 Warner Bros. did a series of six Vitaphone two-reel comedies known as *The Potters,* all based on the original J. P. McEvoy property.

Running Wild

—1927—

"I dedicate this picture to the browbeaten Benedicts of the world." (W. C. Fields, from the press book for *Running Wild*.)

So they did it again. They stuck W. C. in a battlefield called "domestic middle American life." Gregory La Cava wrote, produced and directed this second collaboration with W. C. Fields.

Elmer Finch, W. C., heads a mean household. "His first mistake was his second wife," a termagant of the highest order. Her son from her first marriage is an indolent, pernicious, fat early adolescent named Junior, who constantly taunts his stepfather. And naturally, of course, the family dog works to make life miserable for Elmer. The mutt happily attacks Mr. Finch whenever Junior gives the command, while Mrs. Finch watches with satisfaction: "Even the dog knows a boob when he sees one." Then she turns to the magnificent portrait of her first spouse, which hangs over the living-room mantelpiece, and says dotingly, "My first husband was such a noble man."

As for Elmer, well, he is kind of a worthless sort, who suffers from near terminal cowardice. At home he spinelessly accepts the harangues of his wife, the impudence of his son and the malevolence of his dog. It is not much different at work. He is the joke of the toy manufacturing firm where he has toiled for over twenty years without raise or promotion.

Elmer's daughter from his first marriage, Mary, loves her father, but she too is the long-suffering type who patiently yields to Mrs. Finch's tirades. Mary's stepmother detests her and saddles the young woman with all the household chores while letting Junior stuff his mouth and wallow in his fat. Mary is dating Dave Harvey on the sly. His father is Elmer's boss, and Old Man Harvey does everything in his power to discourage his son's romantic interest in the "she's-below-our-dignity" Finch girl.

Elmer's town is preparing for a big bash—the Lions Club dance. Dave wants Mary to go with him, but she cannot—unless she can get a new dress. She has not had one in over ten years, and it looks like she will not get one now, because whenever Elmer gets paid he hands his check to Mrs. Finch, who in turn doles out the money as she sees fit. This morning Elmer asks his wife for some money for the dress. The nerve of him! Mrs. Finch lambasts her husband for his terrible selfishness. Her barrage does not stop until Elmer meekly sneaks out of the house and heads for work.

For many years Elmer's employers have been trying to land Mr. Johnson's enormous annual account. Each year at contract time Johnson flirts with Finch's firm but always signs with the competitor. It is contract time again and Mr. Johnson is scheduled for a big meeting with Mr. Harvey today. Elmer desperately wants to buy his daughter's dress. An idea! If he can land the Johnson account he will get a big commission. He will not have to tell his wife about the money, so he can get the dress and still have cash left over. All he has to do is intercept the account before the big meeting and muster up enough courage to try his own brand of salesmanship. Johnson walks in. Elmer blocks his path to Harvey's office and nervously begins his pitch. He paces back and forth. He puts a cigar in his mouth and lights it. He continues his sales line. When he gets ready to give his closing points he puts his cigar down on a table. Unfortunately, the same table holds a string of firecrackers. The package

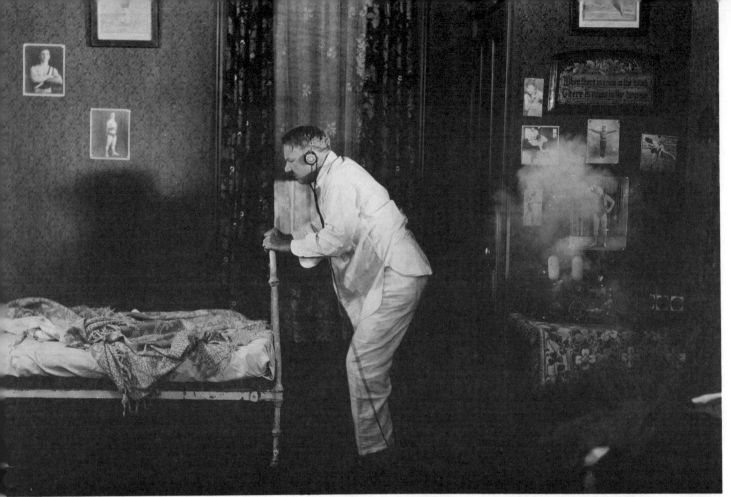

Morning exercises in Running Wild

"Even a dog knows a boob when he sees one." Marie
Shotwell, Rex the Dog and a flinching Elmer Finch.

ignites, sending sparks and blasts throughout the room,
scaring the devil out of Mr. Johnson. Elmer tries to explain: "The fire chief wanted to know if the fireworks
were fireproof." Johnson, incensed, storms out of the
office.

Meanwhile in Mr. Harvey's inner room one of Harvey's bill collectors is telling the boss of his horrible experience trying to collect on Amos Barker's delinquent
account. The man's clothes are torn, his face bloodied
and his eyes blackened. Evidently many of Harvey's
other bill collectors got the same treatment from bully
Barker. While Mr. Harvey tries to figure out what to do
about Barker, Dave Harvey bursts into the office and
defiantly tells his father he wants to wed Mary. Rage! Mr.
Harvey flatly refuses to consider such a proposal. Indeed,
his son will never marry into the worthless Finch clan.
Dave tries a new tack. Give Elmer a chance. Let him try
and collect the Amos Barker debt, and if he is successful
then Dave can marry Mary. Mr. Harvey likes the idea of
getting his useless clerk beaten up and gleefully agrees.

Elmer arrives at Barker's reception room. He hears
yelps, yelling and the sound of furniture breaking coming
from the inner office. Suddenly a couple of men hurtle
through the door followed by the enormous Mr. Barker,
who is dusting his hands off and warning them never to
return. Meekly Elmer exits. He heads back to the office
dejectedly trying to figure out what will happen when he
announces his failure. He sees a horseshoe in the street.
Hoping for luck, he spits on it and throws it over his
shoulder. Crash! It shatters a florist's display window. The

florist runs out and the chase is on. Finch flies. He finds a stage door. He quickly dashes inside. He is on stage. Arvo the hypnotist already has seven volunteers from the audience and he needs an eighth to demonstrate the power of post-hypnotic suggestion. Elmer naturally fits the bill.

Under Arvo's spell, a big slugger of a man becomes a lamb and Finch a lion. Arvo gives Elmer boxing gloves, which Elmer uses to knock out everyone on stage, including Arvo, who then of course cannot take Elmer out of the trance. Elmer is a lion: "I'm a lion." On the way out of the theatre Elmer levels the florist and then heads for Barker's office, all the time yelling, "I'm a lion!" He beats up Barker, admonishing him, "You're a crook and a cheat and a lot of other things I can't remember." Then he easily collects the debt.

Finch rushes from the inner office: "I'm a lion!" He runs into Johnson, who is in town not only on business but also to attend the Lions Club dance. "I'm a Lion!"

Johnson beams when he hears Elmer's yell: "You should have said that in the first place." He gives Elmer the secret Lions' handshake and high sign, then hands over his contract for Elmer's firm.

Elmer runs to his office. "I'm a lion!" Still sporting his boxing gloves he bullies his way into the inner office where Mr. Harvey is conducting a board meeting. Mr. Harvey starts to excoriate Elmer for his intrusion but Finch cuts him short: "Listen, cripple brain, keep your mouth shut and give your ears some exercise." He then gives a stentorian speech on business practices, hands over Barker's payment and Johnson's contract, then hurries out and heads for home: "I'm a lion!"

Mrs. Finch is holding a tea party for some snobby women. Right before Elmer comes crashing in one of the women remarks, "Too bad your husband's not a Lion. He'll miss the ball tonight." Elmer roars in: "I'm a lion!" He kicks the women out of his house, grabs the portrait of the first husband from over the mantelpiece, throws it on the ground and tramples all over it. Then he gives his dog a good kick, grabs his stepson and beats the daylights out of him. "I'm a lion!" He drags Junior upstairs to the bedroom and punches him. Junior falls back, bounces on the bed and returns upright. Elmer hits again. Bounce! Punch! Bounce! Punch! Tiring of that, Elmer takes off his belt and drags Junior into the closet and gives him a thorough whipping. Finished with his stepson, he runs downstairs and gives a present to his daughter, then turns to his wife: "From now on if me or my daughter want a new dress we'll get it."

Suddenly, the cops rush in with Arvo the hypnotist following. After a tremendous fight between Finch and the mob the cops subdue Elmer sufficiently so Arvo can release him from his lion's trance. Elmer remembers nothing of the previous few hours and at first returns to his cowardly self. But he notices that his wife, his son and the dog are treating him with respect and a certain admiration. In walks Mr. Harvey holding a check for $15,000, Elmer's commission on the Johnson deal. With the check Harvey adds a promotion which includes a raise. Elmer plays along well enough to keep his family in line and the promotion alive. His wife likes the new assertive Elmer, the dog cowers from him and Junior walks softly, but best of all Mary can marry Dave.

Elmer at the same desk, the same job and the same pay for the past twenty years.

From a lamb to "I'm a lion!" W. C. with Arvo the hypnotist (Edward Roseman).

Elmer Finch dictates to his family while treading on the photograph of his wife's first husband. Rex the Dog, Mary Brian and Marie Shotwell look on. This is a posed shot from *Running Wild*, but the man walking off the set at right is not posing.

Collecting bad man Barker's delinquent account: *"I'm a lion!"*

Running Wild hit the theatres in late summer 1927 to mostly poor reviews. In one vital respect it was like no other film Fields made. His characterization of Elmer Finch was singular and narrow. In the beginning of the film. W. C. played Elmer so obsequiously that one could not help feel embarrassment for the character, not sympathy. Then when he became the lion, out the window went any of Fields' famous subtlety and precise humor. He was obvious, excessively violent, pushy and coarse. Sure, Elmer was in a trance and certainly not totally responsible for his actions. Indeed, there were cheers when he beat up bad man Amos Barker and applause when he told Old Man Harvey where to get off. And when he attacked the portrait of Mrs. Finch's first husband we loved it. But then he beat up his stepson unmercifully with punches and kicks going far beyond justifiable revenge. A good strong long spanking would have sufficed, but this bordered on torture. And when he turned to the dog he kicked the canine so hard and the mutt cowered so convincingly that it was jolting.

In *Running Wild* Fields lost that special empathy audiences felt for him in his other films. In this picture when he played a toady he played it 100 percent and when he played tough he played it completely. It was the living dialectic—meek Elmer versus pugnacious Elmer resulting in normal-human-being Elmer. It fit the bill of Gregory La Cava's work during this period, using psychological transformations to advance the plot. And his work was great. But it did not fit the Fields style. The comedian seemed sadly miscast for this movie. In almost all his other pictures, no matter how harsh the wifely harangue, W. C. maintained an inner dignity that elicited sympathy for him, and it worked. And when he played the assertive fellow in other films he played it falsely enough to convince the audience that deep down inside he was not such a bad fellow, and that worked. Fields' comedy was subtle and multidimensional. In *Running Wild* it is obvious and one-dimensional. Although he reworked this film eight years later as *The Man on the Flying Trapeze,* he never played a character like Elmer Finch again. I think he learned that the character may work but not for him.

Perhaps the film baffled both the star and the director. It was not working and they knew it. Both knew where their talents stood, both knew they were good. A collaboration should have brought a great picture. But it did not. They fought long and hard on the set, yelled, screamed and threw tantrums, but nothing jelled. They admired each other and stayed close pals throughout the years but they never worked together on a picture again. Maybe each blamed the other for the movie's failure.

Fifty-six years after this picture was made, Mary Brian recalled the relationship between the director and his star: "La Cava was a wonderful, warm, demonstrative Italian. He treated Mr. Fields as if he were quite honored to have him from the stage. Fields was yet an unknown quantity as far as the screen went, but La Cava treated him as a big stage star. The two of them spoke on the same level." Yes, and quite often that level was at a high volume.

Taming Junior (Barnett Raskin).

Elmer giving fisheyes to his bratty stepson.

On the other hand, Fields got along famously with Mary Brian. Ms. Brian debuted in films as Wendy in the original *Peter Pan,* and here she was absolutely delightful as Elmer's devoted daughter. Paramount teamed her again with Fields the following year and later they worked together in Hollywood in *The Man on the Flying Trapeze.* But to get her in *Trapeze* Fields used threats and cajolery, demanding from a reluctant studio that she play his daughter for a third time, which shows how much W. C. respected her talents.

Running Wild was made at the Astoria, Long Island, studios, just minutes away from midtown Manhattan, across the Queensboro Bridge. The movie includes several exteriors shot in the studio's environs. They are no little bonus to the film: prized glimpses of a bright-looking, prosperous and safe New York City. There is an especially nice tracking shot of Fields walking briskly to work through a residential section of Queens dotted with inviting little shops and leafy trees. The same area is physically unchanged today and no less active, just older and no longer flourishing with optimism about its future. The Astoria Studios are still there and, in fact, are coming to life again with the shooting of some current movies. But about a reel's throw away is a nitrate film repository. Many of the films resting there are deteriorating and others were intentionally destroyed. The Astoria complex is coming to life with the cemetery of its history across the street.

RUNNING WILD _____
68 minutes (6,061 feet)
Silent, black and white
Released August 20, 1927, by Paramount
Produced by Gregory La Cava for Paramount Famous-Lasky Corp.
Presented by Adolph Zukor and Jesse L. Lasky
Directed by Gregory La Cava
Adaptation and screenplay by Roy Briant
Based on a story by Gregory La Cava
Photographed by Paul Vogel
Editor-in-chief: Ralph Block
Titles by Roy Briant
Associate producer, Eastern Studio: William Le Baron

CAST:
W. C. Fields   Elmer Finch
Mary Brian   Mary Finch
Claude Buchanan   Dave Harvey, the boyfriend
Marie Shotwell   Mrs. Finch
Barnett Raskin   Junior
Frederick Burton   Mr. D. W. Harvey
J. Moy Bennett   Mr. Henry Johnson
Frank Evans   Amos Barker
Edward Roseman   Arvo, the hypnotist
Tom Madden   Truckdriver
Rex the Dog   Himself
John Merton   Cop

Filmed at the Astoria Studios, Queens, Long Island, after which Paramount closed its Long Island facility and consolidated all production activity in Hollywood.

Remade as *The Man on the Flying Trapeze* eight years later, with Mary Brian re-creating her role as Fields' daughter.

The cast and crew of Running Wild. *Mary Brian seated in the center, with W. C. on her left and director Gregory La Cava on her right.*

Two Flaming Youths

—1927—

In the very late spring of 1927 Paramount made its first attempt to close the Astoria, Long Island, studio. They wanted to consolidate all their production on the West Coast. If they had stuck to their guns *Running Wild* would have been the last film ever shot at the studio. They did not, and a few years later they reopened the lot to accommodate the Marx Brothers' first two talkies and other projects. But then in 1927 most of Paramount's contract players based in New York, including W. C. Fields, started the hegira to the promised land—Hollywood. Many of them felt they would not see New York again. Fields packed his belongings into his Lincoln touring car and in late June drove to California with his girlfriend Bessie Poole. Shorty Blanche still worked for Fields, and he took the rest of W. C.'s belongings, including the dog (Yes, W. C. had a dog called Patsy or Rin Tin Can), and boarded a train for the West. At Ziegfeld's New Amsterdam Theatre, where the lobby housed photographs of the *Follies'* top stars who had performed over

the past decade or so, someone had put black crepe paper around W. C.'s picture with a sign underneath, "Gone to Hollywood."

The forty-seven-year-old Fields was sad to leave New York. He loved the city, but his contract committed him solely to motion pictures, and that now meant Los Angeles. He had to go. He set up house in an exquisite mansion near the top of the Hollywood Hills, from where "on a clear day I can see Catalina Island."

The critics had not liked the last few Fields films. Oh, they praised W. C.—"He is great"; "He is a comic genius"—but they attacked the scripts and the weak stories and the jumbled plots. The box-office draw was not bad, but the studio needed more. They reviewed Fields' career and found that his greatest successes came with *Poppy* and *Sally of the Sawdust,* so they took him out of the house and brought him back to the fairgrounds. Now, however, a little unsure of Fields' drawing power, they decided he needed another comic with him.

Chester Conklin, W. C. Fields and Mary Brian in a scene from Two Flaming Youths.

They assigned Chester Conklin and started production right away on *Two Flaming Youths*. Fields portrays a character named Gabby in this *silent* film.

As Gabby Gilfoil, Fields heads a ragtag bankrupt little carnival. His beautiful young daughter travels with him from place to place, but secretly she longs to settle down. Just as Gilfoil's circus wagon, an elaborate pickup truck with an enormous camper on back, enters Arkosa, Kansas, three tires blow. The wagon limps to the nearest garage, where the young attendant tells Gilfoil it will be a few days before he can get the parts. They are stranded. The young man is attracted to Mary.

Ben Holden is Arkosa's Sheriff. He is courting Madge Malarkey, a punctilious woman who needs $1,500 to get her old hotel back into operation. She kind of likes the Sheriff, but she would like any man with a money roll.

Gilfoil sets up the carnival in Arkosa, trying to attract some greenbacks to pay his debts. He walks through town drumming up business. During one of his strolls he meets Ms. Malarkey. Gilfoil is delighted. Her highfalutin manners and her upper-crust carriage convince Gabby that the woman is rolling in dough. On the other hand Gilfoil's courtly demeanor and braggadocio convince her he has the dollars she needs. They feed off each other's pretense. They court, with both hoping the other will be a financial savior. One day the Sheriff sees Gilfoil with his girl. Jealousy blinds him and he convinces himself Gilfoil

Chester Conklin and W. C. Fields posing for stills between scenes. With the look on W. C.'s face, he could be thinking, Why did they team me with him?

is the dreaded criminal Slippery Sawtelle. The reward for Slippery is $1,500, a fact not at all ignored by Holden and Malarkey. Unfortunately, the Sheriff has not heard the news that the real Slippery has been captured in the next town by a rival sheriff.

Holden hunts for Gilfoil and Gilfoil eludes Holden. Gabby finally lures Holden into his battling kangaroo cage. With the sheriff locked inside the barking begins: "See the town Sheriff fight the battling kangaroo." Ticket sales were never better. In fact, with the money he is getting from this one event Gabby can pay off his past debts.

Soon after the event Holden is told of the real Slippery Sawtelle's capture. He rushes back to Madge knowing that his time spent trying to capture Gilfoil may have helped the fickle woman find someone else who could meet her financial needs. Holden and Gilfoil arrive at Madge's door at the same time. Too late for both of them, Ms. Malarkey has married the wealthy Simeon Trott. In their mutual commiseration Gilfoil and Holden become friends and hatch a scheme. They work out a shell game, "the old army game," to take Trott's money. The Sheriff runs the scam, takes the wealthy Trott and splits the profits with Gilfoil. At the end Malarkey has her money, Gilfoil is out of debt and the Sheriff wins a bundle for himself. Lost in the story was Mary Gilfoil. She ends up with the service station attendant to live happily ever after in Arkosa.

Two Flaming Youths premiered on December 17, 1927. The critics complained again, but this time putting most of the blame on John Waters, the director. Besides booing his simple direction they squawked about the outlandish story and the poor editing. Most reviewers wrote about one scene in particular. The characters walk indoors from a torrential rain but their hair is not wet and their clothes are dry. They did give Waters credit for letting Fields alone on the set, not feeding him gags, letting him use his own adroit business and allowing him to add a hefty amount of "superb juggling, which saved the picture from a complete flop." The critics, it seemed, loved Fields again but not his film. Three thousand miles had not changed W. C.'s luck in motion pictures.

This was Fields' Hollywood debut and it literally nearly killed him. The last sequence filmed was the chase. The Sheriff, thinking Gabby was Slippery Sawtelle, ran after him. Gabby grabbed a bike, the Sheriff got his own, and off they went. Now the script called for Fields to look over his shoulder at the fast-approaching Chester Conklin. When he looked a truck was supposed to back out from behind a building. The scene called for Fields to hit the truck, fall to the ground and roll under the axle while the truck continued in reverse. When the truck cleared him Fields was supposed to get up and run away, using the vehicle as a shield to blind the Sheriff, thus getting a free escape. It was October 3, 1927. They shot the scene at Sky Ranch in the San Fernando Valley, now known as the Paramount Ranch. When Fields fell from the bike he fractured his third cervical vertebra. He could not move,

A close-up of the Gilfoil style of barking from the lost film Two Flaming Youths.

Fields, as Gabby Gilfoil, with his traveling sideshow: "Come one . . . Come all!"

Posed on the set of Two Flaming Youths. From left, Charles Mack and George Moran, Wallace Beery and Raymond Hatton, W. C. Fields and Chester Conklin. Out of the six, only Beery and Fields would become big names in Hollywood. Conklin was a star in the teens, but through the twenties and thirties his popularity diminished. Hatton achieved some moderate success. Moran and Mack, although big in vaudeville as the Two Black Crows, bombed in the few movies they made for Paramount. Incidentally, Fields would later use George Moran in The Fatal Glass of Beer and My Little Chickadee (both times as an Indian) and in The Bank Dick (as Loudmouth McNasty, alias the Wildcat).

THE HUMAN WATCH CHARM
34 INCHES HIGH

Publicity still for Two Flaming Youths, *originally to have been entitled* The Sideshow. *The giant, John Aasen, stands eight foot nine, while the midget, William Platt, stretches to four foot even.*

he could not roll under the axle. The truck kept coming with its huge tire rolling toward the comedian. The crew yelled and screamed, but the driver could not hear them. The truck kept coming. No one moved. Then suddenly Johnny Sinclair, a stuntman, ran for W. C., grabbed his legs and dragged him clear of the tire. A few seconds later Fields would have been crushed. Sinclair saved W. C.'s life.

The crew carried Fields to a car. He sat in the back seat supporting his head in his hands while a man on each side supported an arm, and off they went to the hospital. Since it was the last scene filmed, the accident did not hold up the release of the picture but it put W. C. out of commission for a while.

Fields offered Sinclair money for his heroics but all the stuntman wanted was a job. So W. C. hired him and for every movie he made until the mid '30s Sinclair worked for Fields as a gag writer, stuntman and at least once in front of the camera, where he received billing as "Secretary of Labor" for his role in *Million Dollar Legs*. Eventually Paramount put Sinclair on their payroll as a writer, ending his association with W. C.

While Fields recuperated in the Hollywood Hospital Will Rogers sent the following card: "If we could only call back the old times. I knew you when no truck living could catch you. Are you sure Ziegfeld wasn't driving the truck? Want to see you soon."

The papers wrote almost nothing about the accident but W. C. knew why: "The doctor said I suffered from something in Latin, thus it received little publicity."

Fields also knew the critics hurt his popularity with the Paramount executives. He was worried about his contract. He wrote to the Paramount honchos from the hospital: "I only did it to lighten your burden. I had not been

able to give you a good story up to now so I just had to do something. Sincere good wishes, W. C. Fields."

Two Flaming Youths did poorly in the papers and at the box office, but since the film is lost it is difficult to determine exactly why. It had some fine ingredients besides W. C. For instance, Jack Conway and Herman Mankiewicz wrote the titles. This was only a few years before Conway started to make a big name for himself in motion pictures as a top director, and as for Mankiewicz, he already had his star burning, which would not diminish for years to come. Furthermore, the piece was filled with popular vaudeville acts. This was the film debut for Clark and McCullough and Moran and Mack, topflight names from the stage. Wallace Beery had a part playing with Raymond Hatton in a skit, and Weber and Fields (that was Lew Fields) romped in front of the camera. The title was supposed to be *The Side Show* and with the number of vaudeville acts in the credits it sounds like the original title described the picture well. Last but not least, the film featured Chester Conklin, a fine comic actor, and the winsome Mary Brian. Nevertheless, *Two Flaming Youths* got the complete thumbs down from the critics and the public.

Fields recovered quickly from his broken vertebra and by mid-December he was well enough to start another picture.

TWO FLAMING YOUTHS ⸻ (No rating, unavailable for screening)

55 minutes (5,319 feet)
Silent, black and white
Released December 17, 1927, by Paramount
Produced by John Waters for Paramount
Presented by Adolph Zukor and Jesse L. Lasky
Directed by John Waters

Screenplay by Percy Heath and Donald Davis
Based on an original story by Percy Heath
Titles by Jack Conway and Herman J. Mankiewicz
Photographed by H. Kinley Martin
Fields-Conklin unit supervised by Louis D. Lighton

CAST:
W. C. Fields   J. G. "Gabby" Gilfoil
Chester Conklin   Sheriff Ben Holden
Mary Brian   Mary Gilfoil
Jack Luden   Tony Holden
George Irving   Simeon Trott
Cissy Fitzgerald   Madge Malarkey
Jimmie Quinn   Slippery Sawtelle
(Bobby) Clark and (Paul) McCullough   Themselves
(George) Moran and (Charles) Mack   Themselves
(Wallace) Beery and (Raymond) Hatton   Themselves
The Duncan Sisters   Themselves
(Clarence) Kolb and (Max) Dill   Themselves
(Joe) Weber and (Lew) Fields   Themselves
Savoy and (Jay) Brennan   Themselves

(Phil) Baker and Silvers   Themselves
Benny and McNulty   Themselves
(Jack) Pearl and Bard   Themselves
John Aasen   The giant
Anna Magruder   The fat lady
William Platt   The dwarf
Chester Moorten   The human pin cushion
Lee W. Parker   The tattooed man
John Serresheff   The strong man
Jack Delaney   Himself, a boxing kangaroo

Filmed at Paramount in Hollywood.
  Working titles: *The Side Show* and *The Man on the Flying Trapeze*. Story elements reworked into *The Old Fashioned Way* (1934) and *You Can't Cheat an Honest Man* (1939).

Tribal chiefs pow-wow between scenes of Two Flaming Youths. *A pretty solemn occasion as W. C. Fields is made a member of the Iroquois Indian tribe by Chief Mad Wolf and the equally noble Chief Big Tree, who actually played Indians in several 1930s westerns. As for Fields, he subsequently renounced his affiliation, ending his Indian career as Chief Redskin Nose.*

Tillie's Punctured Romance
—1928 —

In 1914 Marie Dressler, Charlie Chaplin, Mabel Normand and Mack Sennett teamed up to make a historic box-office smash called *Tillie's Punctured Romance*. It was based on the stage play *Tillie's Nightmare*. Mack Sennett wrote and directed the piece, but most importantly it was his first feature-length production. The movie fell a bit short of its potential, but it had speed, slapstick and a great Sennett cast, which made it a big money winner for Sennett's studio. (Incidentally, a young boy named Milton Berle had a small part in that motion picture.)

In 1927 the Christie Brothers wanted to film a remake of *Tillie's Punctured Romance*. Al and Charlie Christie had modest success in the early 1920s with their two-reel comedies, packed with bathing beauties and punch-and-fall comics. But by the late '20s their shorts were sluggish and out of date and they took a distant third to Hal Roach's and Mack Sennett's short comedies. The Christies' studio survived primarily because they occasionally produced a decent feature-length comedy which did well at the box office.

Through some arrangement with Paramount the Christies used W. C. Fields and Chester Conklin, and then got Eddie Sutherland to direct. They hired Monte Brice to rewrite the screenplay. It seems he did a terrible job. The critics said he wrote a movie that bore little resemblance to the original except for the title and a few of the characters (including General Pilsner, played by

Mack Swain, who played the same part in the Sennett version). Then they hired Louise Fazenda, a talented comedienne who specialized in rural types, to take the nominal lead. That created another problem. The Christies had to decide who was the star. Either they could not choose or they were hedging their bets, because their original advertising accessories alternately listed Fields, Conklin and Fazenda atop the bill.

Fields took over Chaplin's role as ringmaster, with Fazenda grabbing Dressler's part as Tillie. (This is another lost film; therefore, once again the following is based solely on the reviews from the period.)

There is intrigue under the big top. The ringmaster, an unsympathetic conniver, wants to take over the circus, but to do so he must kill Horatio Q. Frisbee, the owner of the Frisbee Colossal Circus. The ringmaster decides to feed Frisbee to the lions. The plan backfires. The ringmaster himself is actually caught in the beasts' cage, from which he narrowly escapes. Soon afterwards news of the war in Europe and America's involvement hits the circus, and Frisbee and the ringmaster patch up their differences and decide to enlist. They are too old, so they make up their minds to bring their circus to Europe to entertain the boys on the battlefields. Somewhere on the front lines

His smile always disguised anxiety or treason, as in this scene from Tillie's Punctured Romance. *Tom Kennedy is at far right.*

W. C. and Louise Fazenda. (For many years she was the wife of Warner Brothers producer Hal Wallis.)

they get lost and end up on the German side. At one point their lions escape and run through the German trenches, scattering the troops into retreat, which helps the Allies win the war. And Tillie? All that is known is she was a farm girl who ran away from home to join the circus. What happened to her after that is never made clear.

Ballyhooed as the "new 1928 version of *Tillie's Punctured Romance*," the film was a disaster, according to the critics—terribly produced, terribly directed, terribly written and terribly acted. Undoubtedly the picture did not help Fields' already moribund Hollywood career. One columnist claimed that Fields and Conklin were actually slated to make another film called *Quick Lunch*, in which the two were to play waiters, but someone scrubbed the idea so the comedians could work on this film. Obviously, a bad decision.

By now Louise Brooks was in the second year of her marriage to her director from *It's the Old Army Game*, Eddie Sutherland, a marriage already headed for the rocks. In her book *Lulu in Hollywood* she recalls the making of this film:

> When Eddie Sutherland directed his second Fields comedy, *Tillie's Punctured Romance* . . . Le Baron had already gone to F.B.O. and Fields was finishing his contract at the Hollywood studio. I was married to Eddie during the preparation and production of *Tillie*, which was the worst mess of film making that I ever observed. Even Fields, who ordinarily did not enter the picture until shooting began, came to our house one afternoon to look into the story as it was told to him by Eddie and the writer Monte Brice. I remember Bill sitting quietly listening and drinking martinis from Eddie's two-quart cocktail shaker; I remember him teasing me by dropping my fragile Venetian wine glasses and catching them just before they hit the floor; but I can't remember one word he said about the idiotic plot contrived for the remake of the film . . . it was filled with groans, previewed with moans, shown in a few theatres and then buried in the vaults. Poor old *Tillie* had not a single mourner.

Paul Jones, whom Fields had met during the filming of *It's the Old Army Game*, was the first assistant in this picture. By now Jones and Fields had become close friends. Ms. Brooks gives some insight into Fields' character during this period: "They [W. C. and Paul Jones] had a bond. Women. Paul, too, adored beautiful women who did not adore him." About Paul Jones: "He was in love with a pretty extra girl, Doris Hill, and persuaded Eddie to give her a part in *Tillie*. During production she met Monte Brice and married him."

Also during production Fields broke up with Bessie Poole. On W. C., Ms. Brooks: "He was not a cruel man nor a brave man." Apparently, one day Jones and Fields took a trip to San Francisco, leaving Bessie behind. Fields had a plan. The second he hit the Bay city he would call his lawyer authorizing him to write a check for a large

Chester Conklin, Louise Fazenda and W. C. Fields.

sum, give it to Bessie and then put her on a train headed for New York. He never did follow through with his plan, but soon after he ended his relationship with her anyway.

Fields had a bad time on the set as well. After suffering a broken back in his last picture, he was almost eaten by lions and blown up in this one. The scene in which he was chased by the lions was arranged so that W. C. would run by the lions' cage, and only after he got a substantial lead would the production crew release the lions. Fields was to run into one door and the lions into another right next to it, where raw meat was put as a lure. Unbeknownst to Fields, Sutherland wanted greater action and instructed the crew to let the lions out as soon as W. C. passed the cage. They did. Just as the comedian ran past the bars the lions were on his tail. As he approached his exit with just a slight lead over the beasts, he heard a stagehand shout from behind the door, "Who was the . . . who nailed up this exit." Too late to stop, Fields crashed into the door. Fortunately the lions' exit opened and they went for the raw meat, but as each cat passed it bumped W. C.

Late in the filming, when the circus troupe was lost in Europe and ended up in the enemy's camp and the lions got loose scattering everyone, Fields was supposed to run through a minefield. Fields said that the mines were placed expertly but blown up prematurely. Afterwards he claimed they spent hours picking scrap metal and rusty nails from his hip. Perhaps Fields got the hint that Hollywood did not want him around anymore.

After a short run with miserable reviews *Tillie's Punctured Romance* was taken out of circulation by Paramount, the distributor. Fields had one more movie left on his Paramount contract.

TILLIE'S PUNCTURED ROMANCE

(No rating, unavailable for screening)
57 minutes (5,733 feet)
Silent, black and white
Released March 3, 1928, by Paramount Famous Lasky Corp.
Produced by the Christie Film Company
Presented by Al Christie
Directed by Edward Sutherland
Screenplay by Monte Brice and Keene Thompson
Based on the play *Tillie's Nightmare,* book and lyrics by Edgar Smith
Photographed by William Wheeler and Charles Boyle
Edited by Arthur Huffsmith
First assistant director: Paul Jones

Cast:
W. C. Fields   The ringmaster
Louise Fazenda   Tillie, a runaway girl
Chester Conklin   Horatio Q. Frisbee, circus owner
Mack Swain   General Pilsner, Tillie's father
Doris Hill   Trapezist, the heroine
Grant Withers   Wireless operator, the hero
Tom Kennedy   Property man, the villain
Jean "Babe" London   The strong woman
Billy Platt   The midget
Kalla Pasha   The axe thrower
Mickey Bennett   The bad boy
Mike Refetto   The lion tamer
Baron Von Dobeneck   German officer

Filmed at Paramount in Hollywood.

Nominal remake of *Tillie's Punctured Romance,* fourteen years earlier, directed by Mack Sennett, starring Charlie Chaplin in the equivalent of W. C. Fields' role, and released by Keystone as the first American feature-length comedy. Mack Swain repeated his original role.

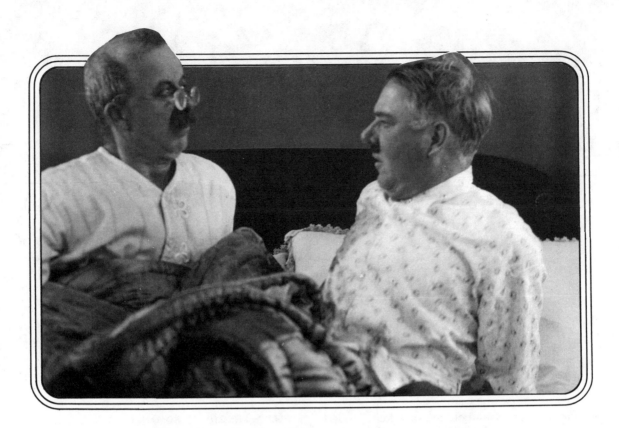

Fools For Luck
—1928—

So far Fields' films had been taking a beating from the critics, yet each movie seemed to have nurtured a growing Fields fan club among those same critics. Heywood Broun, Alexander Woollcott and Ed Sullivan all attested to W. C.'s brilliance but regretted Paramount's inability to get him a good script. Most of the critics claimed that *The Potters* was the closest Fields came to a good story, although, ironically, they had little good to say about the film.

The studio listened. With the failure of the last two circus stories they brought Fields out of the sawdust and back into the living room. Then they handed him a script, a close cousin to *The Potters*, and they kept Chester Conklin again as insurance. This time Conklin was the dupe buying the bogus oil wells and Fields was the swindler.

Richard Whitehead, W. C. Fields, is a slippery sort of businessman. One day he approaches the richest man in Huntersville, Sam Hunter, played by Chester Conklin.

Whitehead sells his oil wells to Hunter, but soon after the sale Hunter finds out the wells are dry. Whitehead refuses to return the money, because he did not know at the time of the sale that the wells were empty. All sorts of fights break out over the deal and, incidentally, interrupt Hunter's daughter's love affair. Right before the big showdown, the wells start pumping the crude, and all live happily thereafter.

Fools for Luck contains a replay of Fields' stage pool routine. When W. C. first moved from New York to Hollywood, Paramount agreed to pay for the pool table's shipping charge. They figured they could use the table. The Christie Brothers used it first in *Tillie's Punctured Romance,* but cut the scene in the editing room. Now Paramount probably wanted their money back on their shipping investment and plopped a pool routine into this, Fields' last film under the current contract.

Here again, the movie should have worked. Charles Reisner was no slouch director; he had been an associate director with Chaplin, and Reisner's films scored a number of hits in the twenties. His most recent picture had been Buster Keaton's very successful *Steamboat Bill Jr.* The screenwriter for *Fools for Luck*, J. Walter Ruben, made a name for himself as a writer, director and producer at MGM and RKO. And of course Fields and Conklin were good, albeit perhaps not together. It seems the film had the right ingredients, but evidently they did not mix well. The critics blasted *Fools for Luck* as soporific, with tired routines and a lethargic plot, dull fare, and with no print known to exist, we cannot judge otherwise. It received miserable reviews, but worse, it was a financial failure.

The picture was released in the summer of 1928. The Fields-Conklin trilogy was now completed. Soon after the trio's release all prints were dispersed, lost, forgotten and unlamented. None is available for fresh re-appraisal today.

Fields' contract with Paramount Pictures was in its option year, but the brass decided not to renew it. The bulbous-nosed comedian with the silly mustache was finished in Hollywood . . . for now.

In 1928 Earl Carroll was released from the federal penitentiary in Atlanta, Georgia. His famous *Vanities* had not played on Broadway for almost two years, since his incarceration for book juggling. But now he was free and ready to produce the *Vanities* bigger and better than ever. He went straight to Hollywood with his checkbook open. He wanted to bring Broadway's former stars back to the boards and New York.

As Richard Whitehead in Fools for Luck. *Whitehead was an appropriate moniker for the Fields character. As a boy, W. C.'s nickname was Whitey, acquired because of his shiny, almost white, blond hair.*

With Sally Blane, the lovely sister of Loretta Young, in Fools for Luck.

With Chester Conklin.

FOOLS FOR LUCK _____
(No rating, unavailable for screening)
60 minutes (5,758 feet)
Silent, black and white
Released May 7, 1928, by Paramount
Produced by Paramount Famous Lasky Corp.
Directed by Charles F. Reisner
Screenplay by Sam Mintz and J. Walter Ruben
Based on a story by Harry Fried
Titles by George Marion
Photographed by William Marshall
Edited by George Nichols, Jr.

CAST:
W. C. Fields   Richard Whitehead
Chester Conklin   Samuel Hunter
Sally Blane   Louise Hunter
Jack Luden   Ray Caldwell
Mary Alden   Mrs. Hunter
Arthur Housman   Charles Grogan
Robert Dudley   Jim Simpson
Martha Mattox   Mrs. Simpson
Eugene Pallette   Bit

Filmed at Paramount in Hollywood.

At the pool table, once again, in Fools for Luck.

Two actors soon to learn that their unique voices would be a great help on their way to fame and fortune: W. C. Fields and Eugene Pallette in a scene from Fools for Luck, W. C.'s last silent effort.

Publicity shot of a comedy team soon to separate. For Chester Conklin the future held decades of bit roles, trading on his former celebrity with Mack Sennett.

A Time For Change

When he reached Hollywood, Earl Carroll had a huge new Broadway *Vanities* show on his mind. One of the first to sign was Louise Brooks, but Carroll's big target was W. C. Fields. By now, Paramount had told W. C. they no longer wanted him, his contract would not be renewed. Fields took it surprisingly well. He never doubted himself. He blamed his failure on the studio. They never listened to him. Had they followed his advice the movies would have been hits. They did not. Some of the films bombed. He was not a failure, the studio was. He was still a star in his own eyes.

Earl Carroll went to W. C.'s house. The comedian offered the producer a chair and a drink and negotiations began. Fields wanted $6,000 a week, plus star billing. Carroll readily agreed to the star billing, but hesitated on the salary. W. C. would consider lowering his price only if his name was written bigger than anything else on the marquee. Earl needed clarification. Bigger than *Earl Carroll*. Bigger than *Vanities*. Bigger than *any* other name on the marquee. Carroll wanted Fields badly. He thought for a while, then agreed and offered $5,200 a week instead of the $6,000. Fields signed. At $5,200 a week W. C. had the biggest long-term contract on Broadway. Furthermore, this was the first and last time *Earl Carroll's Vanities* took second billing. Fields packed his bags, left his California mansion and headed to New York, a not altogether unhappy failure in Hollywood.

The *Vanities* rehearsals did not begin until late June 1928. W. C. had time to kill in New York. He started renewing his old acquaintances from his vaudeville years, including palling around with Moran and Mack. The vaudevillains were booked on a three-week tour of one-night stands through the South and Midwest. During this period, when ethnic humor was at its zenith, Moran and Mack were famous for their "Two Black Crows" routine, a racist takeoff of black jargon and conversation. They asked Fields to join them on the bill. He thought it might be fun to tour vaudeville style again, and he had the time, so he agreed under the following condition: He got star billing. Moran and Mack happily gave it to him, and in early June they hit the road. Two weeks later in Wichita the newspapers reversed the billing and Fields immediately left the show in a huff. Oh, it may have been the billing controversy, but some speculated that Fields wanted out anyway and he just needed an excuse. Apparently the novelty of one-night stands and the nostalgia for the old days quickly waned. He had forgotten the terrible grind of it all. Ironically, soon afterwards, Paramount, with a vacancy to fill on their roster of comedians, signed the Two Black Crows to appear in features. (W. C.'s sentiments might echo the title of their first production, called *Why Bring That Up?*)

By the way, Moran and Mack's career on screen was short and disastrous; but Fields never lost his affection for Moran, using George a few years later in *The Fatal Glass of Beer* and again almost ten years after that in *My Little Chickadee* and *The Bank Dick*.

Back in New York, W. C. started rehearsing the *Vanities;* and on August 6, 1928, the show opened at the Nixon Theatre: "W. C. Fields in the *Earl Carroll Vanities of 1928-29.*" Fields was credited as co-author of the show with Paul Gerard Smith. Basically, what that meant was that Fields wrote only his scenes, but he had a lot of them. His first skit, called "Stolen Bonds," was a satire on the Yukon melodramas, a popular screen theme at the time. He later made it a talking short piece for Mack Sennett called *The Fatal Glass of Beer*. In another skit he spoofed David Belasco. Following that was the "Caledonian Express," parts of which he used in the talking films *Never Give a Sucker an Even Break* and *The Old Fashioned Way*. In "All Aboard" he starred with Dorothy Knapp. They were sailing on the S.S. *Paris* sharing the honeymoon suite. In "School Days" he donned shorts, suspenders, and sucked a lollipop while playing a third-grader in this off-color sketch.

His first scene in the second act he must have loved. It was called "The Cinema." He played a Hollywood producer. It was a well-aimed shot at the boys at Paramount. In "The Mormon's Prayer," "seven palpitating wives and six lustful brides" squirmed on Fields' bed. Fields, as Brigham Young, was down on his knees in prayer asking for strength. In his last scene he played Dr.

Pain in a skit entitled "An Episode at the Dentist," later made into a two-reel short by Mack Sennett.

With W. C. Fields, Beatrice Lillie, Ray Dooley, Joe Frisco and Busby Berkeley, who staged the musical numbers, the *Vanities of 1928-29* was a big hit on Broadway. What a show that must have been! In October they took it on the road. Fields was such a smash that Earl Carroll made him add a few more skits, including Fields' famous old golf routine. For the extra work Fields got a raise to $6,000 a week.

After a few months off in the spring of 1929, the *Vanities* started up again. This time sharing the boards with W. C. was Ben Blue. The *Vanities* finally closed in March 1930. Coincidentally, both Fields and Blue then joined the bill at the Palace Theater for RKO Vaudeville. It seems Mr. Blue had a tendency to abduct other comics' material and play it as his own. Fields performed his golf routine and the "Stolen Bonds" sketch. Ben evidently picked up other parts of W. C.'s *Vanities* routines and performed them at the Palace without permission from W. C. One night Fields left his dressing room to see Blue's act. Soon afterward, on March 24, 1930, the following article appeared in a New York newspaper: "Ben Blue is a comedian in vaudeville. Ben was attacked by thugs last week near the Palace stage door. He was beaten badly. A well known rival comic hired the ruffians. The rival, it appears, did it because Ben is supposed to have thefted his best routines and jokes."

After his two-week stint at the Palace, Fields was again out of work. Every few weeks the New York papers reported that W. C. had rejected this offer or was considering that offer or would accept another offer from such and such studio or so and so producer; but nothing ever happened. Probably W. C.'s agent sent out these blurbs hoping some studio would call to compete for the comedian. Nothing happened. Then in March another one of those notices appeared in the papers. But this time it was for real. Once again it was William Le Baron who breathed life into W. C. Fields' film career. Le Baron had been appointed vice-president in charge of production for RKO Radio Pictures. It was beginning to look as though wherever Le Baron went Fields worked—Cosmopolitan, Paramount, RKO. Le Baron admired Fields, and despite whatever protests were registered from exhibitors, executives or exhausted directors, W. C. was hired. Le Baron believed Fields was one of the most "fascinating characters in the world." So he convinced RKO short-subject producer Louis Brock to use W. C. in one of six shorts in a *Broadway Headliners* series to be made at the Ideal Studios in New Jersey. RKO hailed them as the most expensive short-subject programs ever undertaken by a studio in the East. The studio lied. No matter. What did matter was that Le Baron convinced Brock and Brock wanted Fields.

After getting kicked out of film in Hollywood and after two years back on the Broadway stage, W. C. was going to try movies again. It would be different this time. The film would be "100 percent sound." Fields could talk, tell jokes and ad-lib, but most importantly, Brock would allow Fields to use his own material and to play it just the way he wanted.

The Golf Specialist

— 1930 —

In April 1930 W. C. crossed the Hudson River and started work with Louis Brock at Ideal Studios. Fields' golf routine was well known in New York. He first introduced the comic bit in the *Ziegfeld Follies of 1915,* and later the same year he performed it in the short film *His Lordship's Dilemma.* He kept it in the *Follies* for seven years, then he stored it away for four years. In 1926 he teed it up for his Paramount production of *So's Your Old Man.* Two years later it became a hit on stage again with the *Earl Carroll Vanities of 1928-29.* It never seemed to get moldy, its popularity never attenuated, and Louis Brock wanted it in a sound film. Brock got Monte Brice, who had written *Tillie's Punctured Romance,* as the nominal director, but in fact W. C. directed himself.

The 1928 stage version of the golf routine, as performed for the Earl Carroll Vanities. *Playing Fields' caddy is William "Shorty" Blanche. Two years later it was filmed as* The Golf Specialist.

The first scene begins in the lobby of a posh hotel and country club. The burly middle-aged house dick has just defended his coquettish wife against a would-be suitor by turning him into a pretzel and literally rolling him out of the hotel. The house dick warns of equal retribution to anyone else flirting with his wife and then storms off. His wife, pouting over the loss of attention, plops down on an overstuffed chair. Deep Sea McGurk limps into the lobby. The sight of the fellow pricks her flirting nature and she casually drops her handkerchief in his path. He stops. Looks. Then kicks it back to her as he heads for the desk. He asks for Effingham Bellweather. Apparently Bellweather rented McGurk's boat, then skipped out on the bill. Mr. Bellweather has not come in yet. Deep Sea dictates a message filled with spicy vitriol, then departs. Soon Effingham Bellweather, W. C. Fields, appears. He asks the clerk, "Any messages, telegrams, telephones, televisions?" The clerk hands him MrGurk's message, then looks on gleefully. Effingham reads to himself, then tears it up in little pieces while mumbling, "Silly little girl."

Behind Bellweather a little blond girl tugs on his trousers. "Will you give me a dollar?" she whines while holding up her piggy bank.

Effingham turns. "How old are you, little girl?"

"I'm five years old. Now will you give me a dollar?"

"I'll give you a dollar if you'll sing me a song."

"Give me the dollar first."

"You're not five years old." Fields pushes her aside. The girl remarks defiantly, "That's all right, I have fifty dollars in my bank anyway."

"You have fifty dollars in that bank?"

"Ah-huh."

Bellweather grabs for the bank, but the girl struggles and screams in defense. He stops at her shrill shriek and pats her lovingly on the head, then turns for a final assault. Screams. He stops again. Suddenly a friend of Bellweather's walks up to the desk and, surprised to see Effingham in Florida, asks his business. Effingham: "I'm negotiating for a bank."

The house detective's wife has pushed the little girl to one side, separating the girl and Bellweather. The wife has a fox wrap around her neck. The excess fox hangs down to her fundament, which just so happens is about the level of the little girl's head. Bellweather starts patting the bottom of the fox thinking it is the little girl's blond locks. The little girl, seeing this, says, "You can lift me up by my hair." Effingham, not looking, lifts the fox. The girl says, "Again!" He lifts the tail of the fox a few more times exposing the woman's shapely bottom.

Bellweather still thinks he is lifting the little girl by the hair and comments, "She wants me to do it again so the whole lobby can see it." The house detective walks up, the fox is in the air and the woman is leaning over the counter—a full view. Effingham realizes what he has been doing, smiles at the detective shyly and snakes away across the lobby. The house dick asks his wife if Bellweather has been bothering her. Unaware of the ascending and descending fox, she says no—confrontation avoided.

Later the woman returns to Bellweather to flirt. While they stand in the lobby talking, the little girl puts a stuffed dog next to Bellweather's leg, then, with a watering can, sprinkles water near the cuff of his pants. He feels the water, looks down, sees the dog, puts it together and kicks the dog through the air.

The woman has invited herself to play golf with Effingham Bellweather and they head for the links. On the tee with the girl and Bellweather is a short, dumb, silly-looking caddy, and the golf routine begins. Fields never does hit the ball, what with all the interruptions to his concentration. There is a caddy with squeaky shoes that Fields silences with his oil can. There is paper litter that blows onto the tee that the golfer must fight off. Then the caddy decides to eat his lunch, consisting of a gooey pie wrapped in layer upon layer of paper. The sound of the unveiling is so intrusive that Fields grabs the lunch, sees it's a pie and with derision intones, "Imagine bringing a pie to a golf course. A pint yes! A pie never!" That said, he tries to throw the pie away but some of it sticks to his finger, followed by the long bit of trying to free it. The interruptions continue, including two different female pedestrians casually sauntering across the tee.

Meanwhile, a sheriff has entered the lobby of the hotel on the hunt for Bellweather. He holds a most-wanted poster sporting Effingham's picture. It shows the fugitive dressed in a Klondike outfit. Below the photo is a long list of heinous crimes including "Posing as the Prince of Wales" and "Teaching the facts of life to an Indian." Told that the criminal is on the links, the sheriff and the house dick head for the tee. There they find Bellweather. The culprit's back is to them, so the flatfeet tiptoe up. The lead cop holds the handcuffs and the gun. They reach the golfer just as he starts his backswing. The club strikes the gun, forcing it upward, and it discharges. An enormous bird tumbles from the sky, landing on Bellweather's head, knocking him to the ground. He rises, grabs the bird, heaves it at the caddy and resumes his instruction to the house dick's wife. He still has not seen the two sneaking up on him. He teaches the woman: "In golf it is necessary to keep the wrists together." He indicates the closeness of his wrists. The lawmen slowly slink to their prey.

"Keep the wrists together."

The gildersleeves slap on the handcuffs and lead the criminal off the tee. Confusedly, Bellweather continues to mumble, "Keep the wrists together."

The film was released in August 1930 and was well received. Today, however, some critics complain that the cheap production, particularly of the golf sequence, lacks the dynamism that moving pictures can bring to a stage routine. By keeping the cameras stationary (often a necessity in the cumbersome procedures of recording early sound pictures), these reviewers grouse, the film is nothing more than a Broadway sketch put on the screen. But it is for that very reason the movie is priceless. By comparing Fields' *Follies* script with this filmed golf piece it is easy to see the latter is a duplicate. So with a thinly disguised soundstage passing for a tee and with the camera sitting still like a theatre audience, what we see today is a film of W. C. Fields on stage. That makes it unique and historically illuminating, and instead of being a drawback it's a plus. We see the same routine acted and directed in the same way that the *Ziegfeld Follies* reviewers saw and applauded.

Furthermore, it is easy to discern Ziegfeld's influence on the sketch. When Fields first tried the routine in the *Follies,* Flo was miffed. He wanted the comedian to use some of his *Follies* beauties. W. C. refused. So one night Flo instructed one of his girls to tether a Russian wolfhound and walk the dog across the set through the middle of the scene. She did. Fields glared angrily at her. At first he was speechlessly mad. By the time she got to the end of the stage Fields yelled indignantly, "Nice looking camel you've got there." It brought down the house. Ziegfeld was furious that Fields poked fun at one of his girls, but he had to admit it worked, and W. C. kept it in his act. Later he decided to add a second girl. This one, dressed in riding breeches, walked across the stage and stopped at the tee. She snapped her fingers and said, "Oh, I forgot something."

W. C.: "She probably forgot her horse."

Then on second thought she decided she would not need whatever she had forgotten and continued her stroll. On the way off she stepped on Fields' golf club, breaking the shaft near the bottom. Fields rushed over,

A frame enlargement from **The Golf Specialist.**

Another frame enlargement from the film. It is not known why Shorty Blanche was unable to perform his stage role in this film. Perhaps he was ill.

picked up the shortened shaft and handed it to his caddy: "Here, use this on short holes." These additions made on the *Follies* stage are now preserved on film in the same stage format, a definite bonus for a Fields historian.

There is even icing on this historical cake. In the scene where the sheriff produces a "wanted" poster there is a photograph of Bellweather dressed in Klondike garb. The still was taken from a Fields *Vanities* sketch called "Stolen Bonds." Later the skit would become a Mack Sennett short called *The Fatal Glass of Beer.*

On the negative side, it is extremely difficult to catch some of Fields' classic asides and ad-libs. Since the surviving film negative is so many generations removed from the original, today's "dupe" prints of the subject are often marred by pops, hisses and hash on the sound track. For instance, at one point, when the caddy has brought Fields' patience to an end it sounds like he is mumbling incoherently. But in fact he is mixing his metaphors: "I'd like to wring your neck. I'd like to wash it first then give it a good wring—a ring you could hear for miles and miles." That is followed by another difficult-to-understand crack about the caddy: "I wouldn't get a caddy again for all the tea in China—tea, rice, chop suey or whatever it is they have so much of over there." Then at another point he forgets the "carrying coals to Newcastle" cliché and improvises with "It's like carrying something or another, somewhere or another, as the case may be." But even with the poor quality of the sound track, *The Golf Specialist* is a funny movie, with W. C., sporting his clip-on mustache, performing his most reliable and resilient stage routine.

It was 1930 and W. C. Fields' voice was heard for the first time in a movie theatre—raspy, nasal and slightly whiskey-harsh. It is one of the most imitated voices in the world and certainly one of the most recognizable. That voice was the result of heredity. His mother was an easy mark for bad colds that clogged the sinuses and turned the voice raspy, and her son followed suit. His purposeful

pacing, the muttering asides, the long-drawn-out vowels, and even his noise, he either copied or inherited from his mother. The son obviously thought his mother was funny and used her style on stage and screen, which broke one of the basic commandments of a performer: Never mumble! But by ignoring that rule he became one of the most natural actors on film. Slow and subtle, no matter how crazy the script, how fantastic or absurd, his style made it human, made it believable. Surrounded by the most outlandish situations, he was so natural, we still could see us in him.

W. C. Fields was slim, dapper and fifty years old when a movie audience heard his style of speech for the first time in RKO's one-shot *Golf Specialist,* but it would be a while before he became a talking movie star.

An irony worth noting: One motion picture studio was then making a specialty of filming top Broadway stars performing their stage acts as one-reel short subjects. Eddie Cantor, Burns and Allen, Fred Allen, Harry Richman, Jack Benny—they all made these shorts. This same studio even gambled that the hottest act on Broadway could sustain a feature-length comedy, and they signed the Marx Brothers to pull it off. Of course that studio was Paramount Pictures. At this time their raid of Broadway headliners netted just about everyone except W. C. Fields.

THE GOLF SPECIALIST

Two reels
Sound, black and white
Released August 22, 1930, by RKO
Produced by Louis Brock as part of a *Broadway Headliners* series for RKO
Presented by Radio Pictures
Directed by Monte Brice

CAST:
W. C. Fields   Effingham Bellweather

Filmed at Ideal Sound Studios in Hudson Heights, New Jersey.

Another Interlude

It took only one day to film *The Golf Specialist.* Then, from April to July, Fields did not work, he just had fun. He spent his days playing tennis in Riverside Park on the Upper West Side of Manhattan. He spent his nights going to Broadway plays, then to dinner at Leone's Italian restaurant, where he would stay until early morning holding court at his table. In July he signed a contract with Ziegfeld. W. C. was going to star in another play. It was a reproduction. The original play was written by Jerome Kern in 1925. It was written just for W. C. Fields, but he could not perform in it then because he was filming *Sally of the Sawdust.* Ziegfeld had to get the production out quickly in 1925. He waited as long as he could for Fields

but then had to go ahead without him, hiring Charles Winninger to take Fields' place as Cap'n Andy. The name of the play was *Show Boat.* (Winninger again essayed the role of Captain Andy in the second and definitive film version done in 1936.) Now, in 1930, five years after its Broadway premiere, Fields would finally fill the role that was written with him in mind. W. C. was excited. He was quoted in a newspaper interview then: "Jerome Kern was in a hurry [in 1925] . . . someone else wanted to do *Show Boat,* so Ziegfeld went ahead without me. I regret it now. The pictures weren't so hot as they say, and Captain Andy is a great character. The Huckleberry Finns and Tom Sawyers, they were the kids we liked. And when we

A photo of Ballyhoo on stage. Note the name on top of the poster, "Whitey Duke." Two of Fields' youthful nicknames, "Whitey," because of his blond hair, and "Duke" from Dukenfield. Also note the photo blowup of W. C. Yep! Ballyhoo was W. C.'s.

grew up we had more or less openly acknowledged sympathy with the Falstaffs and Sancho Panzas and with the Captain Andys of the world."

Fields loved the role and a few years later in 1935 he made *Mississippi,* undeniably a relative of *Show Boat,* in which he played the part of Commodore Orlando Jackson, the skipper of a floating cabaret.

Show Boat was scheduled for only a two-week run and not in New York City but right near the Mississippi River in St. Louis, Missouri, at the Municipal Opera House in Forest Park. It was an outdoor theatre that held thousands of people and W. C. liked the size of the crowd. It opened on August 11, 1930, but halfway through the second act it started to pour and they could not finish the play. But for the rest of the run they had clear weather.

Fields added his own material to the play. He brought along William "Shorty" Blanche to do a part and threw in a lot of juggling. The reviewers loved the show. Incidentally, Ziegfeld paid Fields $6,000 a week to play the part of Cap'n Andy Hawkes.

After *Show Boat* Fields went back to New York for more tennis and more pasta. About this same time a fellow by the name of C. C. Pyle was making headlines. Pyle always operated on the fringe of the law. He spent a lot of hours in court. Pyle was a promoter and dabbler in any fast-buck operation. He sponsored a "Bunion Derby," a cross-country foot race, hoping to make a lot of money. It turned out to be a financial disaster. He also promoted marathon dances, tried his hand in the film business and even had a drugstore in Los Angeles. He acquired the store to make enough money to start his own professional football league. He wooed the famous Red "The Galloping Ghost" Grange to push his new league, but the thing went bust. Pyle was a character, and Harry Ruskin and Leighton Brill, under the advisory counsel of Oscar Hammerstein Jr., wrote a play about him. Arthur Hammerstein produced it, Lou Alter wrote the score and Reginald Hammerstein staged the book. The name of the play was *Ballyhoo* and they signed W. C. Fields to play C. C. Pyle. For legal reasons, they

could not use Pyle's name, so they changed it to Q. Q. Quale, but everyone knew the play was about C. C. Pyle. Fields, as Q. Q. Quale, was a fast-talking slick rapscallion who was promoting a "Bunion Derby," the foot race between New York and Los Angeles.

From its inception, the Hammersteins and the writers had Fields in mind to play the lead. They purposely left the plot loose, knowing Fields' inventiveness would help mold the piece. And he ran with it. W. C. cleaned up his old drugstore skit from *The Comic Supplement* and put that in, then he got his baby Austin from his *Follies* routine and drove around the stage in the miniature car. He juggled. He did his cigar-box routine. He played poker with callous cowboys and took them for all their clothes. Then he played the bull fiddle, which gave birth to little violins. He sold stock in his phony peripatetic circus to a dozen different suckers who never see the carnival because "it's on tour." He gambled on a backgammon game and won a horsecart from a fire company. He entered the town of Shamokin, Ohio, riding on a magnificent chariot equipped with a calliope. The Mayor was late, so Quale went ahead anyway, giving his own speech to the crowd, then giving the Mayor's speech and ending it by giving himself the keys to the city. He handled a gun, led an orchestra and stepped cautiously among a throng of creditors. In short, the piece seemed like a playground for all of W. C.'s wild antics.

Ballyhoo opened in New York's Hammerstein Theatre in early December 1930 to very mixed reviews. Heywood Broun could not stop touting Fields in particular and praising the play in general. But most of the other reviewers claimed the plot was so thin and disorganized that they could not call it a play, although, they added, Fields was magnificent.

Much of the material in the show was Fields' old stage stock and much of it was new material, but nearly all of it would show up again in W. C.'s talking films of the thirties and forties. The nights that Fields walked on that *Ballyhoo* stage were probably the happiest moments of his entertainment career. The show was all his—plot be damned.

After only a three-week run and a $140,000 debt Arthur Hammerstein turned off the lights. It is never a good idea to open a Broadway show during the Christmas season. People spend money on presents, not stage plays. Besides, this was the Depression and *Ballyhoo* was an expensive show to see. But beyond all that, Arthur Hammerstein was disgusted with the stagehand union's demands. He claimed they brought the show to its knees. They made the show run in the red by demanding that four men do a one-man job. He said he would never return to the theatre if such unreasonableness prevailed.

For days Hammerstein stewed over the premature closing of the play. He had hoped so much for its success and now it was buried in a theatre closet. His anger kept building. By January 12 he started blaming everyone for the show's death. Here is what he said about W. C.: "The real cause for the unbalanced condition of the book was none other than my friend W. C. Fields, who had been given a legitimate part to play. After rehearsing for six days Mr. Fields was in the same mental condition as when he started and had not learned a line of dialogue. This necessitated my nephew [Reginald Hammerstein] having to reconstruct the original book so that Mr. Fields would be only a specialty artist and not a character." It was probably true, but Fields got great reviews.

Arthur Hammerstein closed the show in early January 1931. In mid-January the cast reopened it with W. C. spearheading the move. When Hammerstein shut down the play Fields offered to work without salary to keep the show open, while the other principals were willing to cut their salaries in half. Hammerstein said no. He repeated his original spiel: As long as the stagehands demanded that four men do a one-man job he was out of show business. He was not going to produce the show under any circumstances. What if the cast took over the production, would he let them use his theatre? Hammerstein agreed, so long as he personally was not involved. Fields began negotiations. The author and composer agreed to forgo their commission for a while. The trades were covering this story scene by scene. In one of them Fields explained how the whole thing worked:

I got to thinking about these boys and girls that have been prancing around rehearsing and banking on this job to see them through the hard winter. And it seemed as if we ought to do everything we could to put this show over for their sakes if not for my own. And we've done it. Of course, the orchestra and the chorus are still on salary, but as far as the principals go, we just share and share alike on what's left after the theatre staff and all the rest of them are paid. The proceeds are brought to my dressing room every night after the show. Anybody can see them that's got a mind to. And if we've given out a certain number of free tickets, so what. . . .

The way things are now, everybody has a right to talk and direct. In some ways that's good and in others it's not so good. If one of the boys in the chorus wears a pair of shoes that isn't just what they ought to be because he says he's got bunions, everyone's on his neck making him do his duty despite the bunions. Everybody's got a lot of bosses in this show. But they all got jobs and jobs is what folks want these days.

Well, that was awfully magnanimous, but you must remember this show was nearly 100 percent W. C. It was his and he was not giving up without a fight. But for the participants to actually take over a play and produce it themselves was a revolutionary idea. No other major company had done that before. New York loved the thought of it. Other stars on Broadway went wild over it. Indeed, every single night some big-name celebrity would make a guest appearance on the *Ballyhoo* stage just to lend support to this unique enterprise of a cast cooperative production. Finally, at the end of February, *Ballyhoo* closed for good.

W. C. had nothing to do now. He would walk Broadway at night and see other shows closing. The Depression hurt the Great White Way badly. The big Broadway names were packing up and heading for Hollywood, hoping to find work there. Fields waited. He would sit in Leone's eating their delicious Italian food and afterwards stay very late, sipping red wine and entertaining his friends at his table. But the lights were dimming in New York City. Broadway was on a stretcher. Fields could wait no longer. In June of 1931 he decided he had to try the movies one more time. He had no offers, he just had to go to California and hope. His only future waited there.

When W. C. announced his decision, Gene Leone threw a bash at his restaurant. He handed out extra platters of spaghetti and free carafes of bootleg red wine for Fields' friends. It was a grand farewell. The next day, after packing his Lincoln touring car, Fields left the city of his past. He said that after crossing the Hudson he turned to see the New York skyline. He said he was sad looking at the buildings of that powerful city. He knew he would never see them again. But mixed with the pain was an exhilaration, a nervousness. At fifty-one years of age he was going to try his hand in films again. They were making sound pictures now, and he hoped the movie people would give him another chance. But he was not sure. He did not know how to begin or who to call or how a Broadway star applied for a job as a movie actor. All he knew was that he had to go. So that is how he left New York City and headed for an uncertain future. He turned to look at the city he loved. He said he knew he would never go back. He started driving again, leaving his past behind and heading for his future in Hollywood.

Her Majesty Love

—1931 —

To most, it seemed as if W. C. fit easily into the relaxed Los Angeles style. Home was a huge luxurious hotel room and he played golf every day and spent many evenings with old friends—Gregory La Cava, Eddie Sutherland, William S. Hart and others. In these early days of his Hollywood career he made all the big parties, usually saying good-night near dawn, leaving everyone with memories of belly laughs. And in these early days in Hollywood the critics did not write about his movies but about his party antics, his juggling of knives and forks and fruit, and they wrote about his jokes and how he kept everybody laughing. But in these early days in Hollywood Fields was not very happy. He was terribly worried. The only executive in the movie business who had faith in the comedian was William Le Baron and he was still in New York. The other motion picture bigwigs knew only that Fields had been to Hollywood once before and bombed; they did not want to talk to him.

In a syndicated series of "as told to" articles by W. C., published in 1934 at the height of the comedian's Paramount popularity, Fields revealed how he got into his first Hollywood "talkie." He claimed that one day he was strolling through his hotel lobby when he ran into Marilyn Miller. They had met when both worked in the *Ziegfeld Follies*. Now in 1931 she was signed with Warner Brothers. She was going to star in a movie soon. Fields and Miller hugged and recalled old times in New York. They talked for a while, then, Fields remembered, she asked him to play her father in her upcoming picture.

"Yes, dear, beautiful girl, and your grandfather as well."

And soon thereafter, as Fields told it, he signed his first Hollywood feature-length talking movie contract.

The movie was called *Her Majesty Love,* a remake of one of the earliest "talkies" made in Germany just two years earlier.

The setting is a cabaret in Berlin. It is a party night. Nearly everyone is popping balloons and running around and all of them are drinking champagne. The men have top hats and tuxedos and the women are dressed in chic clinging dresses. Working the bar is Lia Toerrek, Marilyn Miller. One of the habitués is Fred Von Wellingen, the wealthy son of a ball-bearing tycoon and an officer in the family business, who bets his nightclub pals that he can get Lia to dance with him. His buddies spend their evenings ogling the charming barmaid and more than once have tried to catch her fancy with no luck. They agree to Fred's bet. Von Wellingen tries but fails. Lia teasingly says she will dance with him only if he marries her. Fred has fallen for her charms but does not propose.

The next day we get a look at Fred's working life. He shares his office with his brother. Fred, the playboy, works in his nighttime tux, while his brother wears the proper business suit with the proper gold chain stretched across his proper bulging stomach. The brother disdains Fred's unseemly behavior and flippant manners. But in no time we discover that Fred is the brains of the ball-bearing company and he demands a raise and a new title because of it. His brother fights the idea but after Fred uses a few threats the brother agrees guilefully to bring the matter up at the next board meeting.

The company's board of directors consists of the Von Wellingen clan, a collection of old-stock eccentric stuffed shirts. After a confusing bit of debate they reject Fred's raise and promotion. He storms out promising to quit and join a competitor's firm.

At the cabaret that evening he asks Lia to dance with

A candid shot of W. C. Fields running lines with a production assistant. Same goes for Ben Lyon.

him again and promises he will marry her. She agrees. In the middle of the cabaret they announce their engagement. After the dance she rushes to phone her father. The ringing has awakened Dad, W. C. Fields. At first he does not recognize his daughter's voice. He reaches for his glasses, puts them on, stares at the phone: "Ohhh, it's you. . . . You're engaged? . . . What—in the middle of two A.M.? To who? . . . To whom? . . . Who's him? . . . He . . . him and he are the same? I think you're a little tipsy. Never mind, it's a very good omen for marriage. I was half stewed when I proposed to your mother."

Soon afterwards the wealthy Fred Von Wellingen and Fields, a former vaudeville star and now a barber, meet. They are all headed for the engagement dinner, which coincidentally is also a jubilee celebration for the Von Wellingen ball-bearing business. It is a lavish affair.

Fields is left alone at the buffet line. He flips mashed potatoes on his plate and asks for extra helpings of roast beef. When he starts to leave the buffet a waiter grabs his plate. Misunderstanding the motive Fields quips, "Evidently he's as hungry as I am." He returns to the buffet line and fills a second plate and again a waiter grabs it. He is irritated. The third time he fills his plate and the third encounter with a waiter creates a pushing match. Fred intercedes, telling Fields, "You'll be sitting at the head table, for the present."

W. C.: "Am I going to get a present?"

Fred leads Fields to his seat, and the disaster begins. They put him right next to the number-one Von Wellingen—lemon-faced Harriette Von Wellingen. There is nothing Fields says or does that is right. He talks about his barbershop and old vaudeville. When Harriette tries to find out where the lovers met Fields tells her that they met at the cabaret where Lia works as a barmaid. A disgusting revelation. W. C.: "But it's a very good joint. They get fifty pfennigs for an ordinary glass of beer." Noticing that Harriette does not think well of him, he toasts her to make amends: "Here's to your liver." When a Von Wellingen at the opposite end of the table wants W. C. to pass the éclairs, Fields puts the gooey pastry on the end of a spoon and with careful aim snaps the dessert through the air, landing it perfectly on the plate. When

the man is too dumbfounded to move, Fields takes it as an invitation for another and repeats the flight. All the time he is downing cognacs with gusto. Finally he juggles some of the rolls and then three plates. Lia has to usher him out of the party. When she reprimands him, "What am I going to do with you?" Fields responds, "Take me where there's more cognac." She leads Fields out.

Inside, the Von Wellingens decide they cannot tarnish their family name by joining it with the Toerreks'. It is up to Fred's brother to plead with the playboy offspring to quit the girl. Fred grabs the opportunity. He will renounce the marriage if he gets his raise and promotion. The brother agrees and draws up a contract stating the terms; then they leave to inform Lia.

Lia is expecting Fred. They had planned to attend another family jubilee ceremony and announce their engagement a second time. Fields could not be more thrilled with his daughter's good luck: "I'm so happy for you, to think you're going to get a fine husband and swell family. After you're married and I come to visit I can hear him ask me now, 'Dad, how much do you need?' " Fields has to leave the house to borrow a shirt for the night's festivities. Lia changes from her bedclothes to a nice dress.

Fred's brother waits in a car outside the Toerrek home. Fred knocks on the door. Lia lets him in. They exchange some loving talk and Fred begins to feel awful about his agreement. He cannot tell her the truth. He needs time to think it over. He simply tells her they cannot get married right away or attend the night's party, because he has to go to Copenhagen. Lia is hurt and disappointed but takes it fairly well. Fred leaves and Lia decides to surprise him by showing up at the train station to see him off. Once there, the stationmaster informs her that no Fred Von Wellingen is booked for that train. Ah, now she sees. Infuriated, she stomps over to the Von Wellingen jubilee. She barges in. She gives a tirade on the shabby treatment she has received at the Von Wellingens' hands. She grabs the dinner table, turns it over and rushes out.

Baron Von Shwarzdorf, a monocled old cuckold and Fred's burned-out lascivious friend, admires Lia's spunk and pledges to win her heart. Every day for weeks he sends Lia bouquets of flowers. Thinking they are from Fred, and without reading the card, she throws the flowers out the window. Of course her father, seeing money slip right through his fingers again, tries persuading her to see Fred but to no avail. Eventually the Baron makes a personal call and Lia finds out that he was the one sending the flowers. She is cordial, but she does not want to marry him. The Baron leaves. Fields again sees fiscal security knocking on his door and tries to reason with his daughter: "He's a rich catch. He's rich and he's old. What more do you want? Besides, a rich old man is worth two rich young men and less bother. And you can always look forward to a happy widowhood."

Eventually reason wins out and the marriage is made. Meanwhile Fred, terribly distraught, has been on vacation in Venice. While there, a friend informs him of Lia's marriage. Fred decides to abrogate his agreement and go back to Berlin to win Lia's hand. Too late. He arrives at the marriage bureau just to hear the last words in the marriage ceremony. He leaves without anyone seeing him and heads to the cabaret to drink and remember.

Coincidentally the Baron has decided to take his new bride to the same place for a little dinner before their evening together. The Baron and Lia order. The waiter suggests oysters for the evening: "They're very good for *raising* the appetite" and "These oysters have been in some of the finest beds." At another point the waiter asks the Baron if he would like a little goose. Baron: "I'd like a lot more than a little." Sometime during the dinner Lia and Fred's eyes meet. They are surprised to see each other there. She is immediately drawn to him. He walks to her. They meet in the middle of the empty dance floor and dance to their old theme song. Fred says he will renounce everything to marry her. She says he does not have to. Now that she is a baroness his family will accept her. The Baron sees them dancing and knows he has lost. He agrees to end his seventh marriage, and Fred and Lia live happily ever after.

The movie made it to the theatres in December 1931. The reviews were bad. But once again Fields' role took top honors. That was not too good, as Fields explained: "It was bad luck to stand out in so many films. After *Her Majesty Love* I couldn't get a job for months. The reviewers all raved about me, but what everyone remembers was my last film got terrible notices."

On the set Fields seemed peaceful. No flare-ups were reported between him and the director or other actors, probably because he wanted to keep his nose clean so he could continue working. The only comment made about an exchange between William Dieterle, the transplanted German director, and W. C. was when Dieterle said *Her Majesty Love* was like "Schnapps and beer." To which Fields replied, "For schnapps and beer, I'll take it if you mean scotch and rye."

Her Majesty Love is not a very good film, but Dieterle's direction is snappy; and Fields' fine, although restrained, comedy offset a hackneyed script. Indeed, of all the principals involved with the production only Fields and Dieterle went on to greater successes. Marilyn Miller never caught fire in Hollywood, although nearly every sales technique was tried to push her. Ben Lyon, although a fine actor with good looks and a pleasant speaking voice, never achieved his potential in film. Likewise, Leon Errol never quite achieved the celebrated status in films that he had enjoyed as a stage performer. And Chester Conklin never attained great success in the thirties. (By the way, this picture reunited the team of Fields and Conklin, but their previous films together had had so little impact that this reunion went practically unnoticed.) But fame was still a ways off for Fields, so for now W. C. still had to wait for the studio executives to call for his talents.

HER MAJESTY LOVE

75 minutes
Sound, black and white
Released December 26, 1931 by Warner Bros.-First National
Produced by Warner Brothers
Directed by William Dieterle
Screenplay by Robert Lord and Arthur Caesar
Based on the play by Rudolph Bernauer and Rudolph Oesterreicher
Dialogue by Henry Blanke and Joseph Jackson
Edited by Ralph Dawson
Art direction by Jack Okey
Photographed by Robert Kurrle
Lyrics by Al Dubin
Songs: "Your Baby Minded Now," "Because of You," "Don't Ever Be Blue" and "Though You're Not the First One"

CAST:

Marilyn Miller   Lia Toerrek
Ben Lyon   Fred Von Wellingen
W. C. Fields   Bela Toerrek, Lia's father
Ford Sterling   Otmar Von Wellingen
Leon Errol   Baron Von Schwarzdorf
Chester Conklin   Emil
Harry Stubbs   Hanneman
Maude Eburne   Aunt Harriette Von Wellingen
Harry Holman   Dr. Jeisenfeld
Ruth Hall   Factory secretary
William Irving   The "third" man
Mae Madison   Elli, Fred's sister
Clarence Wilson   Cousin Cornelius
Virginia Sale   Laura Reisenfeld
Gus Arnheim and His Coconut Grove Orchestra   Themselves
Ravero's South American Tango Band   Themselves
Alfred James   Lawyer
Elsa Peterson   Cabaret woman
Lynn Reynolds   Cabaret girl
Geraldine Barton   Teenager
Shirley Chambers   Teenager
Florence Roberts   Grandmother
Frank Darien   Shipping clerk
Donald Novis   Singer
Eileen Carlisle   Bit
Russ Powell   Bit
Scotty Mattraw   Bit
Alice Lyndon   Bit
Henry Lewis Jr.   Bit
Eddie Kane   Well-wisher
Irving Bacon   Valet
Leonard Carey   Headwaiter
Gino Corrado   Hotel clerk
Charles Coleman   Waiter
Oscar Apfel   Registrar
E. Alyn Warren   Director

Filmed at the Warner Bros.-First National Studio in Burbank.

Remake of one of the earliest German-made talkies, *Ihre Majestät die Liebe,* made two years earlier at UFA, with S. Z. "Cuddles" Sakall in the W. C. Fields role.

Million Dollar Legs

—1932—

A nd the long wait. Fields had hoped that *Her Majesty Love* would shoot him back to stardom. It did not. So Fields' agent, Billy Grady, trampled the studios' carpets trying to sell his client. Nothing for nearly six months. Then Herman Mankiewicz, who had written *The Wild Man of Borneo* with W. C. in mind, and who was now a producer in good standing at Paramount, heard of the comedian's fate. Mankiewicz was a kindred spirit of Fields' and he loved the man's work. He had been a drama editor of the New York *Times* and *The New Yorker* in the 1920s, so he knew well Fields' stage popularity. Furthermore Mankiewicz probably felt he could handle W. C.—after all, he produced two pictures with the Marx Brothers. Although Herman did not produce *Million Dollar Legs* (he served as supervisor, while his younger brother Joseph was listed as writing the original story), he definitely was the guiding hand for it. The elder Mankiewicz talked to the Paramount bosses about hiring the unemployed Fields. Well, with reservations—and a cut in salary—the studio gave the comedian another

chance. He would not star, as he did before, but they did agree to give him a substantial role. Fields could care less about the terms. He jumped at the chance, and round two began at Paramount.

Million Dollar Legs is an odd movie, very surreal. Fields plays the President of a backward, bankrupt country called Klopstokia (ah . . . the Wild Man of Klopstokia). In a takeoff of the American presidential campaign slogan "What this country needs is a good five-cent cigar," Fields heralds, "What this country needs is money." In fact the country needs $80 million.

Fields: "We have the zeroes; what we need is the eight." (The satiric parallels to Hoover's presidency in a near bankrupt United States would not pass unnoticed in theatres across the land.)

The president of Klopstokia's cabinet consists of

power grabbers who conspire to unseat the head of state. The only legal means to seize the presidency is to beat the incumbent in arm wrestling. At the conclusion of each cabinet meeting the secretaries of Treasury, Interior, Agriculture, War, Labor, State and Navy challenge the President to a test of strength. Fields keeps winning, but each day the contests become more difficult, particularly against his strongest competitor, the Secretary of the Treasury.

Migg Tweeny, Jack Oakie, an American brush salesman, has just finished selling his wares to Klopstokians and is running to catch his boat back to the States. Tearing through town, he runs right over Angela, the Prez's daughter. They quickly pick up each other and fall in love at first sight. In a swoon, Migg misses his boat. Angela has to get home, but they make a date to see each other again. Migg grabs his brushes, then realizes he does not know the woman's name. Her brother, who is hanging around, tells him her name is Angela. Migg calls out, "Angela!" Every woman within earshot responds. It appears all the women are named Angela. Why not?

When Angela tells the President she has fallen in love, he orders Migg to be arrested and shot. The palace guard catch Migg and put him against the wall right below the President's office window. Ready! Aim! . . . Angela pleads with her father to let her lover go and convinces Dad that Migg could help the country out of its financial distress. From the second floor of the presidential palace Fields yells to his guards to stay the execution. He asks Angela the young man's name.

"I don't know. I just call him sweetheart."

Fields bellows from the window, "Hey, Sweetheart, come up here." Prez hires him as his right-hand man, in charge of bringing the country out of debt, and also orders him to uncover the opposition's plots to take over the presidency.

Migg has no plan at first, so he and Angela take a stroll through the countryside to think. Migg is astonished at the athletic prowess of the citizenry. He sees one man with his girlfriend in his arms jump over a river; he sees another man run nine miles in twenty seconds. Migg's job is simple. He will enter Klopstokia in the 1932 Los Angeles Olympics. Once they win, the country will be besieged with advertising contracts, and the royalties will lift it out of debt. He tells Prez. The Prez likes the idea and makes Sweetheart coach.

Meanwhile, the cabinet sets on a course of sabotage. They cannot have Fields succeed in eliminating the country's debt and thus gain popular support. But how to stop him? They have but one hope, Mata Machree, "The woman no man can resist." She agrees to do what she can to foil the President's plan.

Sweetheart's team is primed, the games are soon, so the gang boards a steamer headed for America. Mata Machree also boards. Meanwhile, Sweetheart's love affair with Angela has reached the singing stage. A Klopstokian custom demands that a suitor learn all the gibberish words to the country's love song, "Boog Oogle Jinx." Sweetheart has it nearly memorized.

Mata gets to work. She seduces every male member of the sports ensemble, destroying their training. Then she makes a date with each one for the same time and the same place a night before the games. The night has come. Each of the athletes has a separate table with candlelight and an extra chair. When Mata saunters in they all rise. Each has been two-timed by the other. A battle: chairs broken, punches thrown, bottles shattered, the entire Klopstokian team fighting among themselves. The next day at the games the team is too damaged and bruised to make the anticipated strong showing.

The last event is weightlifting. Fields represents Klopstokia, and the country is in second place, needing two gold medals to win. The chances to succeed seem impossible. Fields' foremost nemesis, the Secretary of the Treasury, joins the competition as an independent. Fields goes first. He nonchalantly kicks aside the first five hundred pounds. Competition begins at six hundred. He lifts the weight with no difficulty; the same for the Secretary. Seven hundred is a breeze for both. Eight hundred! Fields barely gets the block of weight off the ground. The Secretary asks Mata to give him inspiration. He strains. Mata does a body rippling dance, and that does the trick. The thousand-pound weight is left. Fields gives up. The Secretary looks at Mata for more inspiration, but she has none left: "I have done all I can do . . . in public." The Secretary gives up. A tie, and no one wins. Angela gets an idea. She tells Sweetheart to make her father mad, then he can lift anything. Sweetheart whispers an insult in the Prez's ear, then backs up ready for a fight. Fields just shrugs and nods his head affirmatively. Sweetheart tries again, with the same result. Whatever he says the third time gives the President pause, he thinks, but then agrees again. Giving up, Sweetheart walks over to Angela and inadvertently steps on the President's toe. That does the trick. Angela tells Sweetheart to run. The President hops around in anger and pain, then lifts the thousand-pound block and hurls it at Sweetheart, not only winning the weightlifting gold medal, but the shot put as well. That puts Klopstokia in first place, secures the presidency, insures national solvency and allows Sweetheart and Angela to be wed.

Released in July 1932, *Million Dollar Legs* received top notices in sophisticated urban centers, where it pulled well, but audiences in the heartland were bewildered and the film was not a national success. Again Fields got the best reviews, taking the comedy honors over the star, Jack Oakie. One critic after a rave review for Fields' work added just one complaint: "Someone should tell Mr. Fields that he does not have to wear that silly artificial nose to be funny." So much for informed film criticism in the 1930s.

Million Dollar Legs was clearly intended as a vehicle for Jack Oakie, not W. C. Fields. It was crisply written by Herman Mankiewicz's younger brother, Joseph, who had tailored several properties for Oakie. Oakie's most noted role was in a later political satire, *The Great Dictator,* in which he flat-out stole the film from Charlie Chaplin. But good as he was, Oakie purloined nothing from Fields in *Million Dollar Legs.*

With the absurdist dialogue and the zany political

W. C. Fields as he appeared in Million Dollar Legs, *blowing his own horn possibly to announce his triumphant return to a Paramount picture. This time around he would be heard from.*

setting, the film anticipates the classic style of the Marx Brothers' *Duck Soup,* also scripted with a blitz of outrageous puns, jokes and sight gags by Joseph Mankiewicz. (Coincidentally, Susan Fleming, who plays Angela, would soon leave films for a lifelong marriage to Harpo Marx.) But if Klopstokia suggests ties to the later Freedonia it also indicates a throwback to the old Mack Sennett school. *Million Dollar Legs* is almost as purely a Sennett comedy as ever could be without actually having his name on it. The picture is cast with bizarre-looking actors born and bred on the old Sennett lot: Andy Clyde, Ben Turpin, Vernon Dent, Hank Mann, Eddie Baker, Heinie Conklin, Bobby Dunn, Billy Engle—all Sennett regulars. Several devices are nearly trademarks of Sennett's, such as undercranking the camera to speed up action, using stock footage of an actual event (in this case the 1932 Olympics), then building a picture's premise around it, and of course slapstick, chases and above all parody. The film poked fun at Garbo in her role as Mata Hari, Maurice Chevalier (the Klopstokian love song "Boog Ooogle Jinx" was a nonsense version of the title song from Chevalier's *One Hour with You),* Dietrich, and the government. Parody was the heart of Sennett's comedies.

Furthermore, Eddie Cline, the director, was a disciple of Sennett, having served his apprenticeship as a Keystone Cop. Possibly all these ties with Sennett's legacy are what finally brought Fields together with Sennett himself by the end of the year.

On the set of *Million Dollar Legs* W. C. still maintained a low profile, with the exception of one brief encounter with Eddie Cline. Cline could not understand Fields' modus operandi. The director was accustomed to his actors memorizing their lines and repeating them as written, and he wanted that, particularly in this film. Herman Mankiewicz was so enthused about his brother's story that he instructed Cline to film each and every scene with no deviation of any kind from the written word. But that was never Fields' way. Ad-libbing was his bread and butter, and because of it he turned mediocre scripts into smash comedies. Cline pleaded with W. C., but it did not work. Cline got mad and accused the comedian of "basic incompetence." That did not work either. Fields simply explained, "I ad-lib most of my dialogue and have for years. If I did remember my lines, it would be too bad for me." After a couple of weeks with Fields' freewheeling, Cline had to admit that W. C.'s spontaneity worked and worked well. The two became good friends, with Fields writing warm letters after filming, applauding Cline as "an old peach." In fact later on in their careers Cline was always called in when no other director could handle the comedian.

As for Oakie and Fields, they seemed to get along just fine. Oakie was the star and Fields took the unfamiliar second billing, but W. C. handled the demotion all right. He was just happy to be working and his role was a strong one. The two liked each other. Jack Oakie said of Fields, "If I was king of Hollywood I would make W. C. my court jester. Every morning I would go over to his house for breakfast. Because whenever you go to his house in the morning and tell him you haven't had breakfast yet, he leads you to the bar and says, 'I'm thirsty too.' "

What precisely Fields' relationship with Paramount was at this time is unclear, but intelligent speculation suggests the following: Paramount had tried Fields in the silent years and he failed. The studio was wary of using him again, at least as a star of feature-length pictures. They wanted him tested before signing him to a long-term contract. So most likely they agreed to hire him on a single-movie basis until he proved his worth, instead of either his customary three-picture contract or the industry's normal five- to seven-year term contracts. This theory is supported by W. C.'s Mack Sennett association. Sometime before completing his next two Paramount pictures he made four shorts for Sennett. Now, Sennett had an agreement with Paramount to distribute his films, but no contract has been found between Paramount Pictures and Mack Sennett Studios for the use of Fields. Yet there was a contract between Fields and Sennett with no mention of Paramount. Paramount certainly had the power to stop Sennett from using Fields if they wanted to, but most likely they still felt Fields should be tested, and better Sennett's money than theirs. Moreover, most sources agree that William Le Baron signed Fields to his talking picture contract, and Le Baron had not yet returned to Paramount's roster. Conclusion: W. C. signed his long-term Paramount agreement after mid-year 1933. For the present time, then, Fields simply had to wait for the phone to ring before he knew where he would be employed next.

A final note: *Million Dollar Legs* was the first picture in which Fields did not wear his clip-on mustache. As a young boy playing sleazy vaudeville houses Fields wore a full beard to disguise his youth. Around 1904 he scrubbed the beard but kept the mustache. At first he pasted it on with spirit gum, but it looked real and took too much time to apply. So instead he invented the totally unconvincing clip-on mustache, which he fastened to his nostrils. From certain angles it appeared to be hovering in mid-air under that nose of his. The mustache was outrageous and fully in line with his own outrageous characterizations, but now it was gone. Why he discarded it is not known; perhaps it itched. But for whatever reason, that hirsute ornament, which had been his trademark for over twenty-five years, was thrown away for this picture—discarded forever.

MILLION DOLLAR LEGS

64 minutes
Sound, black and white
Released July 8, 1932, by Paramount
Produced by Paramount
Supervised by Herman J. Mankiewicz (uncredited)
Directed by Edward Cline
Screenplay by Henry Myers and Nick Barrows
Based on a story by Joseph L. Mankiewicz
Photographed by Arthur Todd
Songs: "The Klopstokian Love Song" ("One Hour with You"), "When I Get Hot in Klopstokia"

CAST:

Jack Oakie	Migg Tweeny, American brush salesman
W. C. Fields	President of Klopstokia
Andy Clyde	Major-Domo
Lyda Roberti	Mata Machree
Susan Fleming	Angela
Ben Turpin	Mysterious man
Hugh Herbert	Secretary of the Treasury
George Barbier	Mr. Baldwin
Dickie Moore	Willie, Angela's brother
Billy Gilbert	Secretary of the Interior
Vernon Dent	Secretary of Agriculture
Teddy Hart	Secretary of War
John Sinclair	Secretary of Labor
Sam Adams	Secretary of State
Irving Bacon	Secretary of the Navy
Ben Taggart	Ship's captain
Hank Mann	Customs inspector
Chick Collins	Jumper
Sid Saylor	Starter of the games
Ernie Adams	Contestant
Charlie Hall	Klopstokian athlete
Herman Brix/Bruce Bennett	Klopstokian athletes
Bobby Dunn	Klopstokian athlete
Billy Engle	Klopstokian athlete
Eddie Dunn	Coachman
Al Bridge	Spy in cape
Heinie Conklin	Spy in cape
Herbert Evans	Butler
Lew Kelly	Conductor
Eddie Baker	Train official
Edgar Dearing	Train official
Don Wilson	Stationmaster
Tyler Brooke	Olympics announcer
Hobart Bosworth	Starter

Filmed at Paramount in Hollywood.
Working title: *On Your Mark*. Paramount's 1939 same-named feature, which stars Betty Grable, is not a remake.

They're all in—
IF I HAD A MILLION
a Paramount Picture

If I Had A Million
—1932—

By the summer of 1932 Fields had settled into the Hollywood scene. He rented a magnificent home bordering Toluca Lake, which was the center of a small community of wealthy movie people. Directly across the lake from W. C.'s home was the Lakeside Country Club. Fields loved golf. Almost every day he would row his boat across the pond, dock at the eighth tee, play the full eighteen holes and then row back, thus avoiding a greens fee. He had a lot of free time. His movies did not follow in rapid succession the way his silent movies had. But soon after the end of summer Paramount called again and W. C. joined a rich cast of the studio's stars to make his second talking film for Paramount, *If I Had a Million*. He would be billed eighth on the cast list.

The film is a series of eight short subjects tied by a simple device. John Glidden is a crusty, eccentric multi-millionaire. He believes he is terminally ill and refuses to leave his fortune to his indolent and grasping relatives. Instead, he arbitrarily picks names from a phone book with the intention of giving each lucky person a million dollars. He closes his eyes and picks the first name. John D. Rockefeller! Unacceptable! He tries again. This time it is Henry Peabody.

Peabody, Charlie Ruggles, a timid milquetoast sort, spends his home life under the barrage of a tyrannical wife. His only escape from his stentorian spouse are his frequent nightly trips to the bathroom. The long hours near the porcelain convenience afford him time for needed solitude. But lasting peace is hard to find. Even in sleep he dreams of his battling wife. His work life is no better. He is the long-suffering employee in a china shop working under the despotic scrutiny of a merciless boss. Peabody's nerves are shattered, and that makes him an enemy of anything fragile. Every time he drops a valuable piece of bric-a-brac the cost is subtracted from his already meager salary. Then comes Glidden's million-dollar check. He deals forcefully with his wife, leashes his pet rabbit and marches to the china shop. There he calmly, systematically breaks everything in sight right in front of his outraged boss.

The next recipient of Glidden's million is Violet, a tawdry pavement pounder, heavily rouged and powdered, who works on her back to make ends meet. When she gets the money she happily leaves her shabby working pad and registers at a luxurious Park Avenue penthouse to sleep alone for a change. She climbs between the satin sheets, then suddenly jumps out and throws away her garish stockings, representatives of her former employment. For once she won't need to get dressed again until morning, far away.

Eddie Jackson, George Raft, is the third instant millionaire. Jackson is a notorious check forger on the run—and dead broke. He gets Glidden's check and tries desperately to cash it, but all the banks and newspapers have his mug shot. He is tired and scared. Hours later, and with the million-dollar draft in his hand, he is still without the cash for a night's lodging. At wits' end, he turns the check over to the owner of a ten-cent-a-night rooming house in exchange for keeping his whereabouts secret and letting him sleep quietly. The owner, disgusted with Jackson and his kind, and convinced the check is worthless, lights his cigar using the million as a spill, then reaches for the phone to call the cops.

Emily La Rue, Alison Skipworth, is the fourth lucky recipient of the fortune. She was recently married to Rollo La Rue, W. C. Fields, an ex-vaudevillian juggler. They now own a tea shoppe. When the money arrives revenge is theirs. It seems they both harbor a maniacal hatred for road hogs. Recently they bought a new car, but when driving off the lot a road hog crashed into their shining new auto, completely destroying their investment. With their unexpected bonanza in hand they hire a crew of brave drivers and buy a fleet of cars, then head out to do battle with their highway enemies. The procession spots a road hog. Rollo and Emily give chase. They catch up with the offender and knock the guy clean off the road. They get out of their damaged car and proceed to the next car in line. Putting its driver in the back seat, Rollo takes over the wheel. Another road hog spotted! The chase! Crash! Then to the next car, the two drivers now in the back seat, with Rollo and Emily in command. A road hog! Chase!

Crash! And on it goes in succession until all eight of the new cars are used. Rollo pays the drivers off handsomely and he and Emily live happily ever after.

The fifth recipient of Glidden's magnanimity is John Wallace, Gene Raymond, a condemned convict. His check comes minutes before the authorities lead him to the electric chair. The money cannot save him from justice's swift and brutal decree. They drag Wallace to the chair. Hysterically, he passes from laughing to crying, to laughing, to crying.

Number six is a humble clerk, Phineas V. Lambert, Charles Laughton. Beaten, beleaguered and debased at his job as an insignificant bookkeeper in a large clerical business, he is a lost soul with no future but drudgery. Then the check comes in his morning mail. Without ceremony he puts his pen down on his small desk, gets up, and with steady determination he walks through the labyrinth of desks in the large room until he reaches the plush office of the President. He ignores office decorum and shuffles quietly into the President's boardroom. The President is aghast at the interruption, but Phineas V. Lambert is unperturbed as he blows a magnificent Bronx cheer, or raspberry. Then, with total insouciance, he turns and leaves the office, ending his old life and beginning, undoubtedly, a blissful retirement.

The seventh check goes to a marine named Gallagher, Gary Cooper. He and two of his marine buddies are sharing a room in the brig for popping an officer. They are in the middle of a card game, using fake money, when Glidden arrives with the check. Gallagher looks at the calendar, notes it is April first and treats the draft as an April fool joke. Released from the brig the next day, they all go to Zeb's hot-dog stand. The three are smitten by Zeb's daughter Marie, and each wants to take her to the local carnival, but everyone is broke. Gallagher, remembering Zeb cannot read, pulls out what he thinks is his bogus check for a million dollars and persuades Zeb to give him ten dollars for it. With the loot in hand, Gallagher escorts Marie to the fairgrounds. His pals interrupt their tryst at a midway concession. There a fight breaks out with the barker and the three wind up in the hoosegow again. The next day, while staring through the bars, Gallagher and his two chums see Zeb getting out of a luxurious, expensive car. Gallagher wonders about the check.

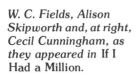

W. C. Fields, Alison Skipworth and, at right, Cecil Cunningham, as they appeared in If I Had a Million.

Rollo and Emily La Rue (W. C. and Alison Skipworth) in this incredibly retouched publicity still for **If I Had A Million.**

Mrs. Mary Walker, May Robson, receives the final check. She is an inmate at a nursing home run by an overbearing and patronizing director. Although the director's intentions seem to be pure, she in fact makes life miserable for the elderly ladies with her well-meant rules and regulations. When Mrs. Walker receives her check she buys the home and turns it into a pleasant, fun-loving place for forgotten grandmothers.

Glidden has taken a real liking to Mrs. Walker and vice versa. Now that his charity has obliterated his obduracy, Glidden's illness disappears and he finds room for love. The last scene catches Glidden talking on the phone in puppy-love whispers, thanking Mrs. Walker for the pies she had baked him.

(Incidentally, John Glidden was played admirably by Richard Bennett, a prominent stage actor and father of Joan and Constance Bennett.)

Released December 4, 1934, *If I Had a Million* received a blasé reception from both critics and audiences. The uniqueness of the structure garnered some praise as revolutionary, but mostly the critics thought it a novelty more than a dramatic change in the art of filmmaking. The structure was unquestionably unique. Each segment was totally self-contained, with a different director handling a different short piece, but therein was the problem: a jarring, variable impact on the audiences.

Anyone who saw the film had his own favorite segments. One tended to praise the piece or pieces he liked the most and in so doing ignored the overall film. Critics and crowds remembered the movie primarily for certain parts and rarely for the whole. Exhibitors found that the "pre-code" prostitute sequence offended prevailing moral tastes, and although its silent eloquence made it quite a sophisticated piece it was frequently excised from

prints. And the mawkish Gene Raymond segment with the electric chair was promptly edited from the original British release after a reviewer aptly described it as "box office anathema."

Paramount was not very impressed with the final quite uneven results. Even though the movie was filled with big names, it played in many outlying areas on the lower half of double bills. But the years have made this movie more acceptable, and it is coming to be considered a classic. Certainly, with the talents it boasts, *If I Had a Million* attracts increasing attention, and if the film was misbegotten it does remain a fascinating venture.

Of all the sequences, the road-hog routine with Fields and Skipworth seems to be the most famous. It is funny and entertaining to a point, but decidedly overrated. Fields in a grandiose Victorian style refers to Skipworth throughout the film in loving hyperbole—"my little phlox, my flower" or "my little chickadee" (a phrase long remembered)—but it is not his funniest piece by a long shot.

Fields' sequence was again written by Joseph Mankiewicz, and although his brother Herman had no official connection with the picture, it was too important to have escaped his consideration and counsel. Herman and Joe played a little "John Glidden" themselves in W. C.'s career when they brought the comedian to *Million Dollar Legs.* And in this picture they undoubtedly had a hand in hiring Fields again. Perhaps they were repaying W. C. for his kindnesses nearly ten years earlier when Fields played in *Poppy* on Broadway. Frequently the comedian entertained Herman in his *Poppy* dressing room, serving drinks out of his wardrobe trunk, which doubled as a bar of Prohibition era booze. One time during a visit Mankiewicz asked W. C. if he would let his teenage brother Joe conduct an interview for the kid's high school newspaper. Fields agreed and Joe published it in his Brooklyn school. After it appeared in print the younger brother received one congratulatory note of approval. It was from W. C. Fields.

Before his work with W. C., Joseph Mankiewicz had

written for another *Follies* star gone to Hollywood, Leon Errol. One picture, *Only Saps Work* (1930), finds Errol chirping the funny bird endearments which Mank would parrot for Fields in *If I Had a Million*. After filming *If I Had a Million* Fields sought out Mankiewicz to buy the jokes Mank had written for him, especially the bird epithets and in particular "my little chickadee." W. C. was told Paramount now owned this material; but according to Mankiewicz, W. C. responded, "I know that, because my lawyer says I don't have to buy it from you, but I'd feel better if I did, because then I'd know it was mine." Joe attributed this to Fields' "incredible punctiliousness about material that is one of the great attributes of the old-time vaudevillian." Jokes were not stolen among honorable performers, and one paid for what one used. W. C. was happy to pay for this material and happy to use it—often. The cost was fifty dollars cash.

Unfortunately, this was Fields' second and last direct association with either of the Mankiewicz brothers. Joseph went on to win four Oscars, two for screenplays and two for directing. Years later Herman would receive his Academy Award for *Citizen Kane*.

For one reason or another Paramount always wanted to hook Fields with someone else, possibly because of the success of Laurel and Hardy, possibly because they did not have the confidence in Fields' lethargic comic style to let him alone. After the failure of mating Chester Conklin with Fields, they tried Alison Skipworth. They probably figured that Fields' bombastic speaking style would counter well with the matronly, tough, down-to-earth Skipworth style. Evidently they hoped for a similar kind of chemistry found in MGM's successful pairing of Wallace Beery and Marie Dressler as "Min and Bill." In *If I Had a Million* the Fields-Skipworth union worked sufficiently well to make the studio want to try it again. But W. C. never did like the idea of teaming with anyone.

IF I HAD A MILLION

88 minutes (2,736 feet)
Sound, black and white
Released December 2, 1932, by Paramount
Produced by Louis D. Lighton for Paramount-Publix Corp.
Production supervised by Ernst Lubitsch
Directors: Stephen S. Roberts, James Cruze, Norman McLeod, Norman Taurog,* H. Bruce Humberstone, Ernst Lubitsch, William A. Seiter and (uncredited) Lothar Mendes
Screenplay by Claude Binyon, Whitney Bolton, Malcolm Stuart Boylan, John Bright, Sidney Buchman, Lester Cole, Isabel Dawn, Boyce De Gaw, Walter DeLeon, Oliver H. P. Garrett, Harvey Gates, Grover Jones, Ernst Lubitsch, Lawton Mackall, Joseph L. Mankiewicz,† William Slavens McNutt, Seton I. Miller, Robert Sparks and Tiffany Thayer
Based on the novel *Windfall* by Robert D. Andrews
Sound recording by Frank Grenbach and Phil S. Wisdom
Episode titles: "The Three Marines," "The China Shop," "The Auto," or "Rollo and the Road Hogs," "The Condemned Man," "The Clerk," "The Forger," "The Streetwalker" and "Old Ladies' Home."

CAST:
Gary Cooper   Steven Gallagher, marine
George Raft   Eddie Jackson, forger
Wynne Gibson   Violet Smith, prostitute
Charles Laughton   Phineas V. Lambert, clerk
Jack Oakie   Mulligan, marine
Charlie Ruggles   Henry Peabody, china store clerk
Alison Skipworth   Emily (Katerina) La Rue, ex-vaudevillian
W. C. Fields   Rollo La Rue, retired juggler
Frances Dee   Mary Wallace
Mary Boland   Mrs. Peabody
Roscoe Karns   O'Brien, marine
May Robson   Mrs. Mary Walker, retired baker
Gene Raymond   John Wallace, condemned murderer
Lucien Littlefield   Zeb, Marie's father
Richard Bennett   John Glidden, wealthy tycoon
Grant Mitchell   Prison priest
Joyce Compton   Marie, waitress at diner
Cecil Cunningham   Agnes
Irving Bacon   Charley Smithers, china salesman
Blanche Frederici   Head nurse, old ladies' home
Dewey Robinson   Cook
Gail Patrick   Secretary at Idylwood Club
Fred Kelsey   Doctor
Willard Robertson   Fred
Kent Taylor   Bank teller
Jack Pennick   Sailor
Berton Churchill   Warden
Edwin Stanley   Mr. Galloway, bank manager
Gertrude Norman   Idylwood resident
Ernest Truex   Mr. Brown
Emma Tansey   Idylwood resident
William V. Mong   Harry, the fence
James Burtis   Jailer
Margaret Seddon   Mrs. Small
Wallis Clark   Mr. Monroe, bank executive

Tom Kennedy   Officer
Tom Kennedy   Joe, carnival tough (two parts)
Frank Hagney   Mike, carnival tough
Charles McMurphy   Mike, bank guard
Henry C. Bradley   Bank guard
Lew Kelly   Prison attendant
Samuel S. Hinds   Attorney
Reginald Barlow   Glidden employee
Clarence Muse   Prisoner
Walter C. Percival   Carnival attendant
Russ Powell   Bartender
Morgan Wallace   Mike, mobster
Hooper Atchley   Hotel desk clerk
Margaret Mann   Idylwood resident
Fred Kelsey   Officer on death row
Robert Emmett Homans   Detective
Eddie Baker   Desk clerk
Joy Winthrop   Idylwood resident
Larry Steers   Glidden's associate
John St. Polis   Glidden's associate
Frederick Santley   Glidden's associate
Herbert Moulton   Glidden's associate
Marc Lawrence   Hood
James Bush   Teller
Tom Ricketts   Elderly man
Bess Flowers   Customer
Fred Holmes   China store clerk
Syd Saylor   Driver
Rolfe Sedan   Auto salesman
Lester Dorr   Pedestrian
Lydia Knott   Idylwood resident
Clair Bracy   Idylwood resident
Bangy Bilby   Idylwood resident

Filmed at Paramount in Hollywood.
*Norman Taurog directed "Rollo and the Road Hogs."
†Joseph L. Mankiewicz wrote "Rollo and the Road Hogs."

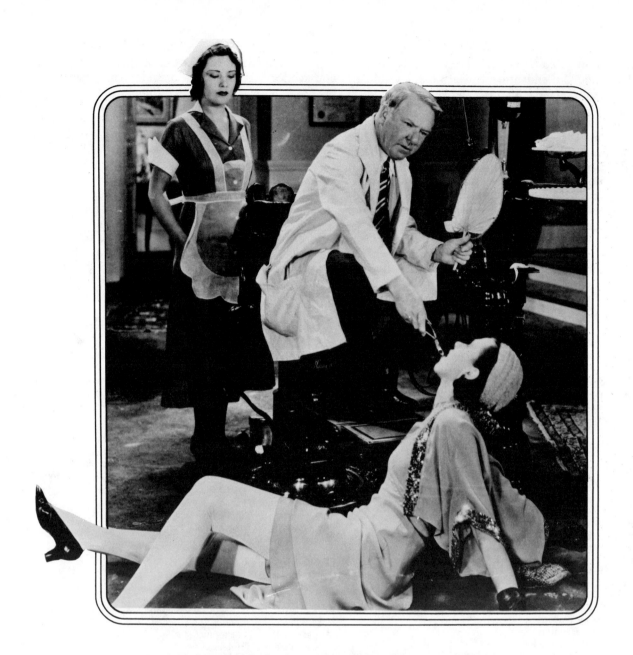

THE MACK SENNETT SHORTS
The Dentist
—1932—

Fields finished work on *If I Had a Million* sometime in late October or early November, then slipped over to the Sennett Studios to start production on four short-subject films. As was mentioned, Fields at the time had no long-term contract with Paramount, just single-picture deals, which meant he was free to work anywhere he could.

It is not odd that Sennett and Fields should team; they had talked of collaborating almost nine years earlier.

In 1923 Fields and Sennett, golfing buddies then, talked of making a movie. Salary and subject had already been decided and W. C. reluctantly agreed to quit the stage and devote his time exclusively under a Sennett contract. Soon afterwards Mack headed back to the West Coast and Fields waited in New York to hear from him. But no word ever came. Now in 1932 Sennett finally called.

Fields made his four short films in quick succession. Sennett paid him $5,000 a week. That was a lot of money for the tight-fisted producer to pay in salary. At the same studio Bing Crosby was cranking out two-reelers for a reported $500 a week. Mack wanted W. C.

Fields' first short, and his finest work for Sennett, called *The Dentist,* was released in mid-December shortly after the premiere of *If I Had a Million.* The film reproduced Fields' 1928 *Earl Carroll Vanities* stage routine entitled "An Episode at the Dentist."

It is morning at the dentist's home. Home and office are in the same building. We find the dentist at breakfast. He is a totally absentminded crotchety man. His daughter has just announced she plans to marry the iceman, Arthur. Fields will put a stop to that: "We're going to order a Frigidaire." No need for Arthur to come to the house anymore.

A phone call from his friend Charley Frobisher reminds the tooth doctor that he has a golf game this morning. He will have time for eighteen holes before his first patient arrives. His daughter tells him where his golf clubs are, and off to the links he goes.

We catch him next in the middle of the game. He has just found his ball and is lining up his shot to the green, ignoring a foursome not yet finished with their putts. The dentist waits for no man. He hits his ball straight and hard.

On the green an elderly man comments on the wonderful salubriousness of golf when—Bam! Fields' ball "cracks him on the sconce," knocking the old man flat. Unconcerned with the unconscious golfer, Fields hunts for his ball, finding it eventually in a sprinkler connection. He will need to check the rule book on this one. He reads: "A ball lying in a sprinkler connection may be dropped without penalty no nearer the hole." He turns his back to the green and readies his drop. He twists his head to check the distance and sees the unconscious man's friends dragging the old duffer off the green. But Fields' eagle eye catches an impediment to his "drop": "Get those teeth out of there too. They're right in my line." The teeth are fetched and Fields drops his ball. The ball lands, then rolls true to the hole. "Down in two!" Frobisher argues. Fields points to the rule book. He must drop the ball no nearer the hole, but it says nothing about the ball rolling after the drop. Frobisher still remonstrates. Fields turns him off: "Don't quibble! Don't quibble!"

The next hole is a "snappy little number." The tee is on the mainland; the hole is on an island in a pond. Fields' first shot lands on the green, then rolls into the water. "Drat!" Those quacking ducks distracted him. His second shot sails clear over the island. It is the caddy's fault this time.

"Don't stand over there. Stand over here."

The caddy obeys, situating himself behind the dentist. His third shot lands in the drink again. That caddy!

"Don't stand behind me when I'm shooting. Stand over there."

"But you told me to stand here, sir."

"Never mind where I told you to stand. You stand where I tell you!" He returns to his next attempt at the

"I'm down in two! Read the card! Don't quibble! Don't quibble!" says W. C. to his dumbfounded pal Bud Jamison in this scene from Fields' initial Mack Sennett short, The Dentist.

drive while he mumbles to Frobisher, "He's so dumb, he probably doesn't even know what time it is."

Frobisher: "Say, what time is it?"

W. C.: "I don't know."

Caddy: "It's ten-fifteen."

W. C.: "Shut up!"

Fields' last shot to the hole again takes a bath. That is the last straw. He steps back and heaves his club into the pond.

A posed still from The Dentist *that does not quite equate with the finished film sequence in which W. C. drops his ball and it rolls into the cup, which gets him "down in two!"*

A scene with Zedna Farley (she could not keep herself from spontaneously laughing throughout the short) and patient Elise Cavanna, a Fields favorite. He first worked with Elise on stage and in the film It's the Old Army Game.

Frobisher: "Oh, wait. You can't do that."

W. C.: "What do you mean I can't do that!" He grabs his golf bag and hurls that into the water. "I can do anything I want!" He takes the caddy and throws him into the water. Then he storms off mumbling, "You can take this golf course and st—" The sound is cut.

Back at the office another golfing buddy is waiting. He wants to set a starting time for tomorrow, but W. C.'s going duck hunting. The dentist loves hunting. The man exits. W. C. dons his outdoors hat, picks up his rifle and dreams about the hunt.

The dentist's first patient is a shapely, attractive woman, played by Dorothy Granger. She sits in the chair, then asks, "You won't hurt my leg, will you?" W. C. is confused. The patient raises her long skirt slightly and explains: "My doctor says I have a very bad leg."

W. C. looks, then concludes: "Your doctor's off his nut. I don't believe in doctors anyway. There is a doctor lives right down the street here. He treated a man for yellow jaundice for nine years. Then found out he was a Jap."

To further explicate her doctor's opinion the woman stands up, puts her back to Fields and tells how this little dog came up from behind and bit her at the ankle. Bending at the waist, keeping her knees locked, she points to the spot where a little dachshund bit her. By doing so she inadvertently highlights her comely fundament, disposing W. C. to suggest, "You're rather fortunate it wasn't a Newfoundland dog that bit you."

She sits back down. Every time Fields comes near her mouth, even with the mirror, the frightened patient screams. Another patient waiting in the outer room hears the screams, hears a jackhammer nearby, puts two and two together and leaves. Soon the woman departs too, without the dentist ever checking her teeth. The dentist does not care; he quickly returns to his hunting reverie.

Another patient enters. The nurse informs the dentist, but the dentist does not want to see another toothache. His mind is on duck hunting. He orders his nurse, "Tell her I'm out!" But the patient, obviously impatient, has already walked into the inner office. Fields sees her and puts down his rifle slowly, and with the sweetest of smiles says, "We've been waiting for you." He leads her to the chair. Then behind her back he excoriates his nurse for not telling "one of these old buzzards" he was out. The patient leans back trying to listen, which infuriates the dentist. He retaliates by stomping on the chair's elevator stick. The patient jerks upward. Still behind her, he repeats the punishment several more times. Then he walks slowly around to the front of her, applying his most hypocritical smile, and lets her down gently. Thoroughly indignant, the patient rises and haughtily begins her exit. Fields stops her: "Just come in for the ride?" For some reason that mollifies her and she returns to the chair. All is ready and he gets to work on the enamel malefactor.

While he is plying the patient's mouth, his daughter descends the stairs and heads for the door. If Arthur cannot come to see her, she will go to see him. The dentist quits his patient and blocks his daughter's path. He spins her around, chases her back upstairs and locks her in her room. He returns to his patient.

Upstairs his daughter takes the grounding petulantly. She jumps up and down in anger, loosening the plaster from the ceiling below.

Meanwhile the dentist and his patient are in a titanic struggle. He is yanking at the tooth. She is reeling in pain. She wraps her legs around his waist. He pulls harder. The patient leaves the chair. The dentist, pulling on the molar, starts walking around the room as the patient holds on like a chimpanzee wrapped around its trainer. The dentist, exhausted but still undaunted, sits the patient back down on the chair. He needs a rest.

As he prepares for another joust with the tooth a huge piece of plaster, set loose by his daughter's tantrum, lands squarely on the crown of his head. He throws down his tools and runs upstairs. He unlocks the door, stalks his daughter and pinches her on the arm in punishment. He returns downstairs, but the patient has escaped. He asks his nurse, "Is that female wrestler gone?"

The last patient is a small man with a long thick beard. His hirsute face hides his mouth. The dentist asks his nurse for a stethoscope. He puts it to his ears. With this he will find the man's mouth.

W. C.: "Now say 'ahh.' "

"Ahhh!"

"Again!"

"Ahhh!"

"Once again. I almost had it."

He finds the mouth, parts the hair and exposes the bushy orifice to the camera. "And a very pretty thing too." Fields grabs the drill and dives in. After some painful drilling, the patient leans over the basin and spits out most of his teeth. Fields wants more. On the way in, however, he brushes the man's beard, which rattles a covey of birds. Excited, the dentist grabs his rifle and hunting hat, but the birds have fled. Undeterred, he pokes the man's beard with the barrel of his rifle looking for more fowl. His nurse interrupts the search to tell her

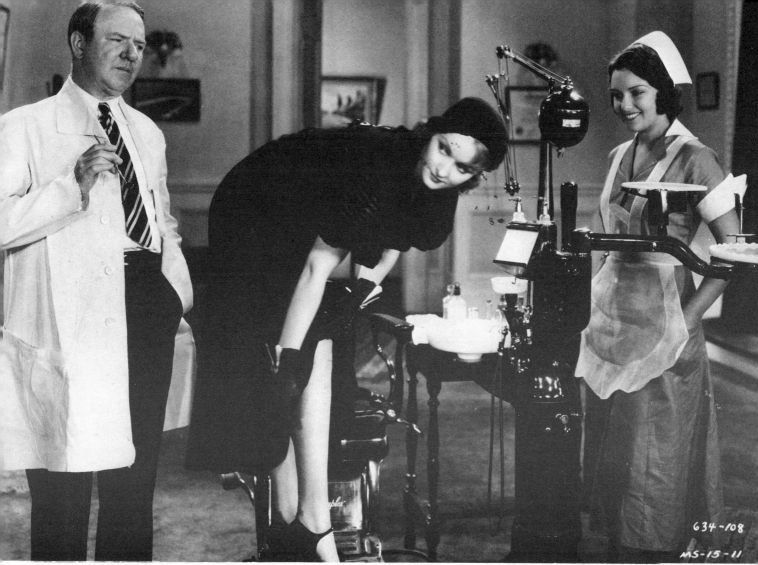

The good dentist with Zedna Farley (nurse) and Dorothy Granger. Ms. Granger would soon begin an eighteen-year career as leading lady with Fields' friend Leon Errol in his long-running series for RKO. So she is rather fortunate it wasn't a Newfoundland dog that bit her.

boss that Arthur has a ladder against the house trying to free the dentist's daughter. Fields throws the gun on the patient's lap and rushes outside. Not only are his daughter and Arthur there, but also the man whom Fields beaned on the golf course and the man's son. The old man points an accusatory finger at Fields. The son brings retribution on Fields with a right cross to the dentist's jaw. Arthur intercedes: "I'd like to see you do that again." Holding his jaw and with worried anticipation on his face, the dentist asks imploringly, "Is it necessary for him to do it again?"

"No!" Arthur lands a retaliatory blow, knocking the fellow out. In gratitude Fields orders fifty pounds of ice from Arthur. No more need for a Frigidaire.

In the original "Dentist" skit on the *Vanities* stage, Fields ran afoul of the law. On September 3, 1928, two officers from the Humane Society walked onstage and arrested Fields during the performance. The charge: onstage cruelty to a canary. During the scene with the bearded patient Fields would stow a canary in his pocket.

At the proper moment he would slyly put the bird in the man's beard and the canary would fly away, then Fields would grab his rifle. This particular evening the bird flew over the audience, then flew back on stage, striking the backdrop and knocking itself unconscious. Harry Moran and Jacob Jacobs from the Humane Society rushed onstage and arrested W. C. They collected the bird as evidence, but before going to jail they rushed the bird to Bellevue Hospital. The bird was D.O.A. Now it was a murder rap.

In front of the judge next day Fields testified, "No, Your Honor, I wasn't cruel to the canary. I took good care of him . . . ah, her. And what the Humane Society says isn't true. No sir! I wouldn't be mean to any bird, not even a chicken." There was more testimony. An autopsy proved the bird died of suffocation and not from a blow to the head. The court speculated that all the photographers (who just happened to be waiting outside the theatre) igniting their flashpowder caused so much smoke the bird could not breathe. Case dismissed. A few of the forty or so newspapermen covering the case commented that the self-satisfied look on Fields' face suggested the entire thing was a publicity stunt. Who knows?

The diminutive ("Is he standing in a hole?") Russian patient is played by a well-disguised Billy Bletcher. While he enacts this role without uttering a word, his specialty in films and radio was voice work. Just a year later his sepulchral tones would provide the huffing and puffing voice for the big bad wolf in Disney's Three Little Pigs.

Another possible publicity ploy was the work of Mack Sennett. Before the release of the film he spread word that the American Dental Association had held up circulation of the movie because they thought it was an affront to their profession. But in fact there was no delay in releasing the picture.

Nearly twenty years later, however, the film did run into real releasing problems. The TV censors of the fifties and sixties felt the scene with Elise Cavanna was too risqué for their medium. That was the scene in which Fields lugged that "female wrestler" around his office. During the bit Elise's dress did hitch high enough on her thigh to reveal garter snaps, and her legs were wrapped around Fields' midsection, but there was obviously no prurient intent. Nevertheless, TV's equivalent of the old Hays Office forced the scene to be expunged before allowing *The Dentist* to be seen in American homes.

Some more facts about the film: The golf sequence was shot at the Lakeside Country Club in Toluca Lake. It was a short row for W. C. to get to that location. His house abutted the lake and had a fine view of the greens.

The name of Fields' golfing buddy in the film was Charley Frobisher, played by Bud Jamison. W. C. took the name from his youth in Philadelphia. Then, William Claude Dukenfield's best friend was Charles Frobisher.

In the *Vanities* sketch Fields called his character Dr. Payne, but in the movie he did not name his persona. Also in the original sketch, when Fields cannot find the bearded man's mouth he tells the nurse, "Pack me a lunch. I may have to go in after it."

Many audiences missed a running gag W. C. used in the short. Each time before putting his little dentist's mirror in a patient's mouth, he breathed on the mirror to clean it, then wiped the breath fog on his smock.

And finally, in the scene in which Fields goes to his daughter's room to punish her for stomping on the floor, one can just barely catch a framed photograph of W. C. Fields on her dressing bureau.

THE DENTIST
Two reels
Sound, black and white
Released December 9, 1932, by Paramount
Produced by Mack Sennett as *A Mack Sennett Star Comedy*
Directed by Leslie Pearce
Original screenplay by W. C. Fields, adapted from his *Earl Carroll Vanities* sketch entitled "An Episode at the Dentist"
Casting by Walter Klinger

CAST:

W. C. Fields	Himself
Babe Kane	Daughter
Elise Cavanna	Miss Mason
Zedna Farley	Dental assistant
Bud Jamison	Charley Frobisher
Dorothy Granger	Patient, Miss Peppitone
Bobby Dunn	Fields' caddy
Billy Bletcher	Diminutive "Russian" patient
Joe Bordeaux	Caddy
Arnold Gray	Arthur, the iceman
Harry Bowen	Joe, the pal
Emma Tansey	Old lady

Filmed at Mack Sennett Studios in North Hollywood, with location work at the Lakeside Country Club.

The Fatal Glass Of Beer

—1933—

The second Fields-Sennett collaboration was *The Fatal Glass of Beer,* another retooling of a 1928 *Vanities* sketch called "Stolen Bonds." W. C. spent ten days adapting it for the screen.

Fields plays the part of Mr. Snavely, a Yukon gold miner. He is preparing to leave his mining cabin and go "over the rim" to his home, where Mrs. Snavely waits. Before leaving, a friendly mountie stops by the cabin. Although the policeman is covered from head to toe with snow, Snavely asks, "Is it still snowing outside?"

Mountie: "To tell you the truth, I didn't look."

The mountie wants Mr. Snavely to sing the ballad of his son Chester's trip to the city and subsequent degradation and imprisonment. Mr. Snavely reaches into his trunk and pulls out a fan, then his dulcimer: "You won't mind if I play with my mittens on, will you?"

He begins his strumming and singing. The song is an unmelodious, unrhythmical dirge of his son's association with college students, who introduced the bumpkin to the curse of drink. They coerced the young lad to down a mug of beer—the fatal glass of beer. After chugging the drink he stumbled out of the bar with the delirium tremens. On the street he met a Salvation Army girl and "cruelly broke her tambourine." In retaliation she "put a mark on his brow with a kick she learned before she had been saved." Chester, well on the road to debauchery,

"How!" . . . *"And how!"* W. C. with George Moran (center) and an unidentified Indian in **The Fatal Glass of Beer.**

then embezzled money from the bank in which he worked and was thrown into the hoosegow. The moral of the song: "To avoid the wicked curse of drink."

The mountie, touched to tears by the ditty, thanks Mr. Snavely and goes off into the night. Fields packs his things and starts to leave the cabin. In the doorway, he stops and comments on the terrible climatic conditions: "It ain't a fit night out for man or beast." Just then a fistful of snow hits him flush in the face. Unperturbed, he closes the door and jumps on his sled, which is pulled by his trusty dog team. "Mush! Mush!" he commands, then spits out a mouthful of snow: "Tastes more like cornflakes." His dog sled includes a dachshund whose feet cannot touch the ground.

Fields returns to his shack "over the rim," where two Indian chiefs are warming themselves at his hearth. After exchanging greetings with "How, Chief," and to the other Indian, "And how," he directs them to the door in pig Latin, translated to "Scram." (That was it for the Indians. They were not used in the film again.) Mrs. Snavely comes out of the kitchen to greet her husband.

He shows her a golden nugget (long "u" on nugget), assuring her it is worth about a hundred dollars, which makes their thirty years in the north country well worth the travail.

At dinner, which consists of a bowl of soup and a three-foot-long piece of dunking bread which Mr. Snavely shares—two feet for him, one foot for his wife—Mrs. Snavely tells him that the creditors knocked on the door again. "They say if you don't pay up they are going to take your dog team."

"They won't take my lead dog, Balto."

"Why?"

" 'Cause I et him."

"You et him?"

"He was mighty good with mustard."

Suddenly, Chester bursts into the room. The ex-con has returned home to "Ma and Pa." The first thing Chester wants to do is go to his old bed, where he "can sleep like a little baby again." Pa suggests he should "lie down and take a little nap first." Chester heads for bed and Pa heads outside to do the chores. "And it ain't a fit night out for man or beast," he announces, theatrically. A fistful of snow hits him flush in the face. Mr. Snavely has to "milk the elk." He searches his herd for his pet elk, Lena, but she is not to be found. He even asks Elmer the elk if he has seen her, but Elmer ignores him. No chance of milking an elk tonight, so he settles for filling the bucket with water from his pump. Ice cubes come pouring out.

Back in the house Mrs. Snavely discreetly asks Chester if he really did steal the money and "them bonds." Yes he did. She tells him she knew it all the time but never told Mr. Snavely, because "it would break the old man's heart if he found out." Mrs. Snavely retires.

Pa enters, and after searching the house dramatically for eavesdroppers, he calls Chester from his room. Young Chester sits at the dinner table.

Pa: "Did you steal them bonds and all that money?"

"Yes I did, Pa," Chester responds, then starts to cry. Tenderly, Pa pats him on the back. "I know you did, Chester, but I'd never tell your ma. It'd break her poor heart if she knew." Pa wants to know where he put the money. "I threw the tainted money away and came back to live with you and Ma for the rest of my life." Coldly and calmly Pa lifts a water pitcher from its bowl and smashes the ceramic vase on Chester's head: "You've come back to sponge on us for the rest of your life." Ma rushes into the room and cracks the bowl over Chester. The boy stands. Pa bats him around a bit and knocks him to the ground. Ma and Pa grab Chester's hands and feet and throw him outside, where "it ain't a fit night out for man or beast." No fistful of snow hits him flush in the face.

The film opened in March to generally poor reviews. From beginning to end Fields' comedy is low key, no slapstick punches or frenzied rushes for laughs. It is a satire of the Yukon dramas of the time, popularized by Robert W. Service's poems about rugged Alaskan life, and as such the movie depends on pure spoofing for laughs instead of the fast-paced bite of the more conventional Sennett films. But besides simply poking fun at the melodramatic northern territory stories themselves, he also took a swipe at the way such films were made, and that is what the critics misunderstood the most. They complained about the obvious phoniness of the process shots, or rear projection scenes, but they were supposed to look contrived. For instance, when he took his dog team "over the rim" through a raging blizzard, he skipped lightheartedly behind his sled knowing the shot looked utterly false. Moreover, when he goaded his dog team with "Mush! Mush!" he spat out some snow and said, "Tastes more like cornflakes." He thus revealed a studio secret: Film snow was cornflakes dipped in white paint. Later in the picture when he searched his herd of elks for his favorite, Lena, he blatantly used a spurious process shot, satirizing the serious films made that way. Even today some critics complain about the substandard production quality of the film, not knowing that most of it was intentional.

Another widely expressed criticism was that W. C. plays hokum. Critics particularly pointed to Fields' running gag. Every time W. C. opened a door or looked through a broken window, a handful of fake snow hit him in the face. But in reviewing the original skit, "Stolen Bonds," S. Jay Kaufman defended Fields: "W. C. is not hokum. The skits are hokum, but W. C. Fields isn't. And if he was, there is nothing wrong with great hokum. It is hokum to have snow thrown at you, but Fields is not hokum in his response. He doesn't spit it out, he doesn't rub his eyes, he does nothing." On film W. C. *did* flinch once. At the end of the movie when he intoned for the last time, "It ain't a fit night out for man or beast," he waited for the fistful of scud to hit him, but none did. After a second or so he covered his face and flinched for the first and only time. Probably the greatest defect in *The Fatal Glass of Beer* is that it is necessary for most people to view the film a number of times to fully appreciate the subtlety of the humor.

The Fatal Glass of Beer caused a breach between Sennett and Fields and the comedian nearly refused to make the last two shorts, *The Pharmacist* and *The Barber Shop*. Sennett and Fields fought hard over comedy and style, particularly on this film. Apparently, Sennett turned sour on it and tried changing it. Fields wrote to Sennett: "Dear friend Mack, You are probably one-hundred percent right, *The Fatal Glass of Beer* stinks. It's lousy. But, I still think it's good . . . I am too good a friend of yours to make what you consider bad pictures. Please let me out of my contract." One part Mack wanted changed was the scene where Fields sings the ballad of his son's demise. W. C. felt it would "kill the picture" if Sennett got his way, showing flashbacks of Chester drinking beer, breaking the woman's tambourine and then being marched off to prison. But Sennett won and it did not hurt the film. Fields' fighting with Sennett over this film got rougher, with W. C. threatening not to continue: "I feel rather reluctant about starting to write a new picture until I have some assurance from you that after it is finished you will not make several changes and calmly send word to me, that if I do not like it in the changed and approved Sennett form, you will give it to someone else." Evidently Sennett had told W. C. that Lloyd Hamilton could take the comedian's place if Fields refused to accept the editing. Fields further railed, "You have been a tremendous success with your formula, but it is new to me and I can't change my way of working at this late stage of the game. When I have the stage all set for a Fields picture and you come in and have everything changed to a Sennett picture you . . . render me helpless. . . . If the pictures I have made are not what you want tear up the contract. . . . I do not believe our business relations are going to be successful. I wish you would agree to terminate the contract and we continue our friendship of yore." Although production had begun in November, general release was delayed until March while Fields and Sennett engaged in the "forty or less friendly fights," as W. C. recalled later.

Fields also sparred a bit with one of the actors. George Chandler, Chester, recalls that *The Fatal Glass of Beer* was a big break for him. And he was excited over one scene in particular, his return home to "Ma and Pa."

It was supposed to be a lengthy close-up on him, a fine break for a budding character actor. But before filming the sequence W. C. looked around the set and saw a bucket behind one of the cameras. He went over, grabbed the bucket and put it next to his seat. The cameras started rolling. Chester walked in the door. The cameras started closing in on Chester, but Fields jumped from his seat, put his foot in the bucket, walked around the table so the camera would catch it all, then kicked the bucket off his foot and greeted Chester warmly. Fields stole the entire scene from Chandler. Chandler said for over forty years he held a grudge against W. C. for the thievery, and for over forty years he refused to see the film. Finally in the early seventies someone coaxed him into watching it. He said that after viewing the picture he lost his grudge. Fields' trick worked so well and fit so nicely he realized W. C. knew exactly what he was doing to spruce up the film.

Fields and Sennett patched up their differences and started work on the next short subject.

THE FATAL GLASS OF BEER
Two reels
Sound, black and white
Released March 3. 1933. by Paramount
Produced by Mack Sennett as *A Mack Sennett Star Comedy*
Directed by Clyde Bruckman

Original screenplay by W. C. Fields, adapted from his *Earl Carroll Vanities* sketch entitled "Stolen Bonds"
Casting by Walter Klinger
Song: "The Fatal Glass of Beer"

CAST:
W. C. Fields   Mr. Snavely
Rosemary Theby   Mrs. Snavely
George Chandler   Chester, the wastrel son
Rychard Cramer   Officer Posthlewhistle of the Mounties
Marvin Lobach   Bartender
Gordon Douglas   College student
Ernie Alexander   College student

Jack Cooper   Officer
Artie Ortego   Indian
George Moran   Indian

Filmed at Mack Sennett Studios in North Hollywood.
Working title: *It Ain't a Fit Night Out for Man or Beast*. Stock footage used from the 1924 Mack Sennett film entitled *Yukon Jake*, which starred Ben Turpin.

The Pharmacist
— 1933 —

Number three for the Sennett-Fields quartet was *The Pharmacist*, released a month after *The Fatal Glass of Beer* in April 1933. Running out of his *Vanities* sketches that would play well on film, Fields reached back to the *Follies of 1925* and introduced to the camera his drugstore sketch originally called "The Druggist." Also from that 1925 routine, Elise Cavanna returned to play his wife. In 1931 Fields used the same sketch in the stage play *Ballyhoo*.

Mr. Dilweg, W. C. Fields, is the proud proprietor of the local drugstore. He has two daughters, an older daughter barely past the prom age, and a bratty pre-adolescent tomboy. His wife is stuffy beyond all reason.

Mr. Dilweg is returning from an errand. He kicks the local kids away from his door and enters the drugstore. Before beginning work he stands over one of his tables where two men are staring at a game of draughts. Fields looks on as one of the contestants slowly reaches for a piece. He checks with the druggist before making his move. Dilweg, with a slight quiver of his head, makes it clear the move will fail. The man retreats, then slowly reaches for another piece. Again, Dilweg coyly shakes his head no. The man retreats. On his third try at a checker Dilweg gives the confident look of a champion. The man

makes his move. With suddenness his adversary jumps all the pieces on the board, ending the game. W. C. shrugs and walks away.

Soon Mrs. Dilweg calls her husband to lunch. He runs upstairs to the family quarters. There he pours gin and vermouth over ice into a cocktail shaker, grabs his daughter's pogo stick, attaches the shaker to the toy, and hands it to his daughter to jump on. She happily bounces up and down on the stick while Dilweg waits. She wants to keep jumping, but the mix is ready, so her father grabs the stick from her. He detaches the shaker and pours his drink while his daughter wails, "You don't love me anymore." Fields raises the stick in anger. Mrs. Dilweg intercedes, "Don't strike that child." W. C., controlling himself: "Well, she's not going to tell me I don't love her."

The phone starts ringing just as the older daughter enters the room. She runs to answer it. It is her boyfriend Cuthbert. Every other word she says on the phone is Cuthbert, "Hello, Cuthbert. . . . No, Cuthbert. . . . I don't know, Cuthbert. . . ." The conversation gives Mr. Dilweg indigestion. He tells his wife, "That Cuthbert is a vichyssoise."

"How do you know that? You've never met him."

"I don't have to meet him. When I was a boy I could beat up all the Cuthberts on my block."

"You have an Uncle Cuthbert."

"I had an Uncle Cuthbert. They hung him. Have respect for the dead."

Because his younger daughter is acting up, Mr. Dilweg dismisses her from the table, but she is still hungry. She starts nibbling on the pet parrot's food—then she eats the parrot. She starts coughing out feathers. Aghast, Fields rushes over and pulls out more feathers. The drugstore doorbell rings. Mr. Dilweg rushes into another room, takes out another birdcage with a huge cockatoo inside, then he runs downstairs.

Two old women are waiting at the counter. They ask to see the female attendant. Fields rushes back upstairs and tells his wife. Mrs. Dilweg complains that her hair is not done and she needs a new dress but agrees to go down anyway after changing her clothes. Fields slips downstairs to the drugstore again, and starts dusting and tidying things up when the phone rings. The customer on the other end of the line orders cough drops, the ones that show a picture of two men with whiskers. No, he cannot split a box. Yes, he will be happy to send them in the truck. O.K.! It is twenty-two convoluted miles to the customer's house; he will send the cough drops right away.

Mrs. Dilweg comes down and the old women ask to use the powder room. Mrs. Dilweg points the way, then glowers at her husband and returns upstairs.

Enter a burly, sour man of about fifty. He says nothing while slowly perusing the counter. He walks parallel to it slowly. Fields, behind the counter, keeps up with him, cheerfully pointing to certain items to pique the fellow's interest. He lifts up a book: "Have you read *Mother India*?" No interest. He points to another book: "Or *The Sex Life of a Polyp*?" Still searching, Fields asks, "Cake à la mode?" Nothing! Still pushing a sale, he walks up to a small puppet dangling from its strings. He pulls on it slightly, "Amusing luttle beggar." The puppet is a replica of W. C. Fields. No sale! He jingles some bells: "Moscow in winter?" Finally, "How about a stamp?"

"Yeah, gimme a stamp."

Fields lifts the sheet, but the customer wants a black one. There are none, but Mr. Dilweg suggests that he could dye one for him. No black stamps! The customer lambasts the Democratic administration in Washington and its penchant to dictate everything in a person's life even "to tell you what color stamp to buy." Fields offers to write to Washington about it, but the man finds that useless. "Why write to Washington. He's dead." Mr. Dilweg chuckles, then quickly starts to tear a corner stamp from the sheet. Not good enough for the old grump; "I don't want a dirty one. Give me a clean one, the one in the middle." Obsequiously, Dilweg obliges, happily cutting through six stamps to extricate the middle two-cent stamp. He handles the stamp delicately, holding just the edges so as not to smudge it, grabs a paper bag, drops the stamp into it, and twists the top tightly. Should he send it? No! No! The customer will take it with him. "That'll be two cents," Dilweg says.

"Do you have change for a hundred?"

"Ah, no, no but thanks for the compliment."

The old man says he will pay for it the next time he comes in. Dilweg has the Dilweg Drugstore Special, a four-hundred-year-old Ming vase with every purchase. He hands it to the customer, who accepts it grudgingly.

Another man enters the store and leans over the counter to whisper something in Dilwig's ear. Dilweg says nothing, but brings a fan from under the counter and turns it on. The fan blows the man's suit coat open, revealing a badge pinned to the vest. Dilweg returns the fan to below the counter and in high dudgeon intones, "Certainly not. I have never sold alcohol here and would never cater to such depraved tastes."

"One day I'm going to catch you and throw you into jail," the Sheriff threatens. Dilweg responds in a whisper, "Maybe and maybe not." The two women have left the rest room and ask Fields for the special of the day. Dilweg hands them the antique vase. They tell him that they figured the powder in the rest room was free so they helped themselves. That is O.K. Then one of the women adds, "I noticed your soap was on a chain."

"Yes it is. Yes it is. It's unfortunate you didn't bring a pair of pliers." The women agree, then leave.

Dilweg returns upstairs, where his older daughter is still talking to Cuthbert. Dilweg looks at the cockatoo cage and sees the bird gone. With vengeance he stalks his younger daughter, hands formed to grab her neck, but before he reaches her he notices the bird on a piece of furniture. He straightens up and pats his little daughter on her head.

The drugstore bell sounds and Fields lumbers downstairs. A woman has fainted and bystanders have carried her into the shop. Someone asks for some brandy, but the officer who tried to catch Dilweg earlier, is standing by and Dilweg puts his forefinger to his lip and denies he has any. After the woman and the crowd leave, shooting starts up outside. Some crooks take refuge in Dilweg's drugstone, guns ablazing. The shooting tears up the place. One of the crooks tells Dilweg to reach for the ceiling. The crook is near the Dilweg phone booth. A man

in the phone booth opens the door and knocks out the crook with the phone receiver. The man is a hero. Dilweg's family has come down to catch the action. Dilweg is shaking the hero's hand and wants to introduce his daughter to his savior. No need, the Dilweg's oldest daughter already knows him. He is Cuthbert.

The Pharmacist, sometimes named *The Apothecary*, particularly in the English release, got generally high marks from the critics. Fields and Sennett were friends again and filming went smoothly. The same cannot be said of the original 1925 version. Ziegfeld had wanted Fields to lend the piece to Leon Errol, who was starring in a Ziegfeld production on Broadway. Fields agreed, but soon afterward Ziegfeld put W. C. in the *Follies of 1925*. Fields wanted his skit back. Flo said no. W. C. used it anyway. When the critics asked about the redundancy W. C. responded, "I want my child back. That's why I'm using it in the *Follies*. I presume it will not continue in both shows. I suppose Ziggy will get it away from me somehow and leave it in, but it will be kidnapping. The scene is my child." It stayed with W. C.

The Pharmacist brought two of Fields' famous screen personas together. He played the aggressive, wisecracking type in the family quarters, but in the drugstore he was meek and groveling. However, out of reach of camera and microphone, Fields maintained a singular personality. Grady Sutton, who played Cuthbert in this, his first job with the comedian, recalled that during the scene with those dear old ladies who wish to use the rest room W. C. came across as sappy in his willingness to accommodate. That was what the audiences saw. But when the stagewise Fields knew the camera and mike were off him he would mumble some uproarious opprobrium at the little ladies, then quickly change demeanor when the scene turned back to him—all in fun.

THE PHARMACIST_____
Two reels
Sound, black and white
Released April 21, 1933, by Paramount
Produced by Mack Sennett as *A Mack Sennett Star Comedy*
Directed by Arthur Ripley
Original screenplay by W. C. Fields, adapted from his *Ziegfeld Follies* sketch of 1925 entitled "The Druggist"
Casting by Walter Klinger

CAST:
W. C. Fields	Mr. Dilweg, title role
Babe Kane	His daughter
Elise Cavanna	His wife
Grady Sutton	Cuthbert Smith, the boyfriend
Lorena Carr	Older daughter
Si Jenks	Checkers player
Joe Bordeaux	Gunman
Efe Jackson	Extra
Jack Cooper	Extra
Emma Tansey	Old lady

Filmed at Mack Sennett Studios in North Hollywood.
Working title: *The Drug Store*. Partial reworking of material first used on film in *It's the Old Army Game*, seven years earlier.

The Barber Shop
—1933—

Fields' last short subject at the Sennett Studios was called *The Barber Shop.* W. C.'s movie persona changed dramatically in the four shorts. In his first, *The Dentist,* he played a tyrannical and unsympathetic father and professional. In this, his last, he portrayed the beleaguered underdog suffering from bumbling mistakes and a wretched wife. The two in the middle synthesized the extremes.

Cornelius O'Hare (Fields), Felton City's town barber, sits in front of his shop sharpening his razor and testing its cutting edge on his tongue. A friend sits nearby reading a newspaper. Mr. O'Hare greets the afternoon strollers with courtesy, but never fails to add a mumbling insult about them to his uninterested friend.

From the second-story window comes the shrill, demanding voice of Mrs. O'Hare. Lunch is ready. Cornelius quickly shifts from the wisecracking observer to the toadying husband and rushes upstairs, grabbing his son Ronald on the way. Ronald likes to tell riddles. Mrs. O'Hare hates riddles. At the lunch table, Cornelius defends his son: "Mr. Lincoln used to be very fond of telling riddles. And that, as much as anything else, made him the fine President that he was." Mrs. O'Hare scowls and Mr. O'Hare cowers, telling Ronald, "Ah, eat your spinach, eat your spinach."

A comical yet loving tribute as W. C. Fields imitates Kate Dukenfield, his mother, in The Barber Shop.

The doorbell to the barber shop rings and Cornelius rushes to meet an Italian gentleman carrying a bass fiddle. Rumor has it that the barber wants a bass fiddle. No, he is happy with Lena, his own bass fiddle, which he keeps in a corner of his shop. The Italian gentleman is disappointed, but as long as he is in town he should go shopping, and he asks O'Hare if he can keep the new bass fiddle in the barber shop with Lena. Cornelius agrees and puts the instrument behind his.

Hortense, the barber shop's manicurist, returns from lunch. Cornelius and she seem attracted to each other and after exchanging cordialities he asks if she would like to hear some music from Lena. Of course she does. He grabs his bass fiddle and gives a tune of his own composition, consisting of banging Lena's strings with the bow. Hortense loves it. Cornelius sadly admits, "My wife doesn't think it's music."

O'Hare's first customer, a gruff young man who wants a shave, sits in the chair. Cornelius vaguely knows the fellow, but cannot quite place the face. The customer understands, "It's all healed up since the last time I was in here." O'Hare neatly places the barber's bib around the man's neck, then hooks it securely under the chair. The customer winces in pain with each stroke of the dull blade. The barber shop is in a basement room and the windows catch passersby from the waist down. A woman stops at the window and adjusts her garter snap, revealing a fine-looking limb. Cornelius catches the show but loses aim with his blade, attacking the man's nose instead of his whiskers. Only the customer's yelps bring O'Hare back to the shave. After a few more painful strokes he notices a spot on the man's chin.

"Is that a mole?"

Affectionately the customer replies, "Yep, I've had it all my life."

Fields swipes at it: "You don't have it anymore."

An enormously fat man walks in and declares to Cornelius that his wife has threatened to leave him if he does not lose weight. He came to the right place. Cornelius has a steam closet. To get the steam pumping O'Hare must run outside and start a superannuated steam engine named Ethel. He coaxes it, "Get hot, Ethel," and the engine spits to life. He returns to the shop and directs the man to the closet, explaining all the safety features—a blinking red light and a loud siren. He further warns the fat man not to stay inside longer than five minutes. The customer places his bulk on the tiny stool inside. Cornelius double locks the doors and returns to his first customer. Next to the barber chair is a dog begging. The customer asks the reason.

"Oh, it's a very funny thing. The other day a man was in here and I was shaving him. The razor skipped, and I cut his ear off. Ever since then he's been hanging around here for a . . . go away, go away!"

O'Hare finishes the shave and now it is time for the hot towels. He turns on the faucet and puts the towels under the gushing hot water. The towels seem warm enough, so he reaches for one of them and scalds his hand. Too hot to hold. He grabs a pair of fireplace coal tongs and gingerly lifts the towels, then drops them on the man's face. The man squeals in pain. "It's all right. It's all right," Cornelius reassures him as he makes sure they are in place completely covering the face.

A baseball drops into the basement. Cornelius has a

*"Get Hot, Ethel!"
Ethel was played
by the steam
maker (or vice
versa) shown
here with W. C.*

*From left to right,
director Arthur
Ripley, W. C. and
John T. Clair
working on the
set of the Mack
Sennett short* The
Barber Shop.

103

few free minutes while the hot towels do their trick, so he runs upstairs with the ball. He wants to show his son, who hit the ball downstairs, what a fine pitching arm he has. He winds up and lets fly, missing home plate and hitting a police officer. Everyone scrambles. Cornelius runs back to his shop. The steam room's light and siren are crying for help, but O'Hare takes the towels off the infuriated shaving customer first. Timidly, the barber asks for payment. The customer draws back a fist, but Cornelius quickly puts on a pair of glasses, and the man stalks out.

W. C. on the lam in **The Barber Shop.**

Finally Cornelius hears the siren and rushes to unlock the steam cabinet. The locks are too hot to touch so he grabs a towel and loosens the fasteners. The enormous fat man has shrunk to a ninety-pound midget and threatens lawsuits and jail. He leaves.

Trying to relieve the tension, Hortense talks about the big news of the day. There has been a bank robbery in Felton City. The bank robber's picture is in the paper, but he is still at large. Oh boy, Cornelius would love to leave work and find the thief. He would throttle him. He tells her he was once a member of the "bare-handed wolf chokers association." Hortense admires his courage. Then Mrs. O'Hare comes down and Cornelius kowtows. She wants to buy new clothes! Cornelius obliges: "Do you have change for a dollar?" She grabs the bill, turns her nose up at Hortense and storms out.

A woman and her young daughter come in. The little girl, who has just returned from a party and is wearing a pointed party hat, wants a haircut. She sits in the chair as Cornelius removes the hat. There is one underneath. He takes that off. Another. He finally decides to cut her hair with the hats on.

Suddenly, a shifty-looking fellow is standing in the doorway. Hortense immediately recognizes the robber. She points him out to Cornelius. He recognizes him too. The man motions for him to come over. O'Hare walks over. The thief wants a haircut and to have his mustache removed. No matter how hard O'Hare tries to convince him that the barber down the street is far superior, it does not work. Cornelius kicks out the girl and her mother and nervously starts to work. Accidentally, Cornelius covers the man's face with the bib. Seeing the opportunity, he runs out of the store, steals a bike and races away. Through fear he loses his direction out of town and inadvertently returns to his barber shop. The robber has also tried to escape the tonsorial parlor, but the local police are searching the streets too carefully to try to run and he returns. Just as Cornelius pedals past his doorway, Ronald hits a baseball which beans his father and knocks him off the bike and down the stairway. In his tumble he knocks down the bandit and lands on top of him. Scared, he tries cajoling the crook, "I like thieves. Some of my best friends are thieves. Why, just last week we had the president of the bank over for dinner."

Some cops arrive in the barber shop and arrest the bandit. Hortense congratulates her employer on the rescue, as do others from the crowd which has gathered. Cornelius accepts their accolades, but their praises are short-lived, because another officer comes down with Ronald under his arm: "Here's the brave little man who caught the robber. He knocked poor Mr. O'Hare off his bike." The officer asks Cornelius, "Are you hurt?" Embarrassed thoroughly, he responds, "Not physically. No." Everyone leaves except Cornelius. From the corner where stand the bass fiddles, the sound of lumber falling to the ground is heard. O'Hare rushes over. He grabs the Italian fellow's fiddle and moves it aside. There, right at Lena's foot, is a stack of baby violins. "Lena, how could you?" He yells in horror. With disgust, Cornelius grabs the other bass fiddle, stands it up straight and kicks it furiously right below the midriff.

If a motion picture can be dedicated to someone because of a scene or two, then this short was dedicated to Kate Dukenfield, W. C.'s mother. He loved her and owed a lot to her, not the least of which was his nose. A photograph taken of her in the early 1900s shows a woman who looked unfortunately yet remarkably similar to the Fields of the 1930s and '40s, with her nose and girth most prominent. In W. C.'s younger days, when he lived with his family in Philadelphia, the Dukenfield clan would sit outside on their porch during summer evenings watching the night come or reading the newspapers and greeting the neighbors who would pass by, just as Philadelphians do today. Kate would roll back and forth on her rocker, darning socks or knitting something for her five children. Then a friend would walk in front of the house. "Oh good evening, Mrs. Frobisher. How's Mr. Frobisher?"

"He's a little under the weather today, Mrs. Dukenfield."

"Oh! That's a shame. That's a shame." Then mumbling to her family: "Last night he was under the table. Two quarts of rye, no doubt."

"Pardon me, Mrs. Dukenfield?"

"I said that's a shame, Mrs. Frobisher, that's a shame."

Now if you look at the first two scenes in the film, it is there where you will find Fields' arcane dedication to his mother. The first shot shows a banner stretched across the town's main street, FELTON CITY'S LIBRARY FESTIVAL. Kate's maiden name was Felton. And the first shot of

Director Arthur Ripley evidently does not like W. C. Fields' music in the Mack Sennett short **The Barber Shop.**

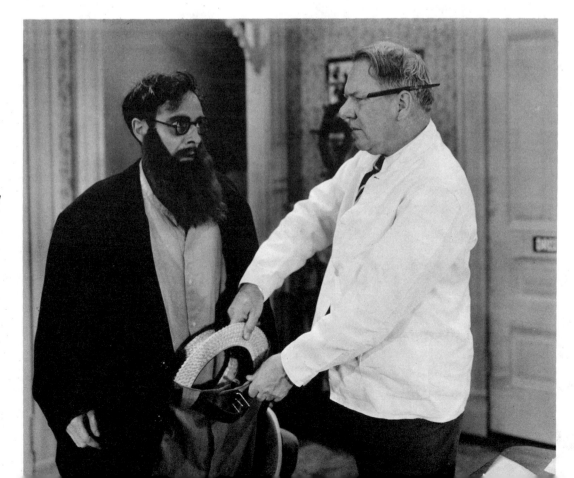

Ethel got too hot! The ci-devant fat man, now a shadow of his former self, and W. C.

Fields catches him sitting on the porch in front of his shop sharpening his razor, greeting the passersby, then mumbling insults about them to his friend, just the way Kate used to do it back in Philadelphia.

The short was released on July 28, 1933, and it received very good reviews. It appears Sennett left Fields alone to create his own magic without interference. And it worked. Of all the four shorts, this one was the most original. Except for two scenes, Lena giving birth to baby violins, and the little girl with the plethora of party hats, both purloined from *Ballyhoo*, it was a completely new piece. He did not take it from any previous stage works, as he did with his other Sennett shorts, nor did he steal it from any of his earlier films.

Also, it seems, W. C. ad-libbed more freely in this short than in the other three. Ronald, Harry Watson, recalled the shooting. As a child actor he never tried extracting meaning from the dialogue. He knew when to say his lines because he remembered the other actor's lines, but if the other actor changed the written dialogue in performance, Harry was lost. With W. C., Watson was lost a lot. The example Harry remembered best was the lunch scene, in which Ronald told his father riddles. One line was "Hey, Pop, what does a mouse and a load of hay have in common?" Fields' written line: "I don't know, Ronald. What does a mouse and a load of hay have in common?" Harry: "Cattle [Cat'll] eat it." But W. C. never gave the written response, so Ronald never knew when to answer. Arthur Ripley, the fine if sometimes erratic director, kept trying to get the scene on track, and Ronald complained that Fields was not saying his lines properly. Fields found the solution. "When I am finished with my line, Harry, I'll kick you under the table. That's your cue." Fields must have loved the idea of kicking a kid. So they shot the scene again. Ronald gave his question and Fields answered, "I don't know Ronald, what does a small rodent and horses' provender have in common?" Kick!

"Cat'll eat it."

The Sennett foursome could hardly be called works of cinematic art. They were very cheaply made, quickly cranked out. Editing was poor, story lines were lost and the acting appeared unrehearsed. But if nothing else it was Fields at his epitome, at home and comfortable. They were really nothing more than vaudeville skits, but for an old stage trouper nothing could come more naturally. Indeed, three of them were simply slightly doctored scenes he played hundreds, if not thousands, of times on stage. In fact, he even utilized some of the same actors. The judgment of most reviewers was correct. They were badly made pictures. But then enters the essence of Fields' purpose: Were they funny? Did they get the laughs? Yes on both accounts. They are funny. Fields' purpose was served, audiences howled and still howl, and belly laughs have a way of dissolving a multitude of sins.

THE BARBER SHOP_____
Two reels
Sound, black and white
Released July 28, 1933, by Paramount
Produced by Mack Sennett as *A Mack Sennett Star Comedy*
Directed by Arthur Ripley
Original screenplay by W. C. Fields, adapted from his *Earl Carroll Vanities* sketch entitled "The Barber Shop"
Casting by Walter Klinger

CAST:
W. C. Fields	Cornelius O'Hare
Elise Cavanna	His wife
Harry Watson	Ronald O'Hare
Dagmar Oakland	Hortense, the manicurist
Fay Holderness	Gloria's mother
John St. Clair	Mr. Flood
Cyril Ring	Bandit
Frank "Fatty" Alexander	Steam room patient
Harry Bowen	Officer
Joe Bordeaux	Extra
George Humbert	Jose, Italian fiddle salesman

Filmed at Mack Sennett Studios in North Hollywood.

Exactly five years after **The Pharmacist** *was released W. C. Fields had the privilege of presenting his friend and producer Mack Sennett with a special Oscar at the 1938 Academy Awards banquet in recognition of Sennett's pioneering techniques in the field of film comedies.*

Hip
Action

— 1933 —

It was 1930. A personable young American golfer won the British Amateur Championship. Later that year the same man won in succession the United States Amateur title, the British Open and the U.S. Open. Bobby Jones, talented, handsome and charismatic, was the first man in history to win the grand slam of golf. So impressive a feat, the sports editors and writers of the period voted Jones the best golfer of all time. His golf made him a national hero; his warmth made him a national idol. He became one of the most popular sports heroes ever, and that is where Hollywood came in. Seizing the national tide of affection, Warner Brothers signed Jones to star in a series of short subjects designed to teach the game of golf—Bobby Jones instructional reels. It was a tough assignment even for this much loved superstar with the magnetic personality—instructing golf on film could be very, very dull. So to avoid boredom, each short featured a major movie star like Loretta Young, James Cagney, or Edward G. Robinson. The stars' light comedic mugging purposefully intertwined with Jones' lesson lent a pleasing air to excellent instruction. Perhaps more important to the series' success, however, was that Jones never lectured the audience, just the stars. The movie idols played inexpert golfing enthusiasts, emphasizing certain flaws in

their game which Jones would correct while the theatre audiences listened in. That made it fun.

The actors wanted to be part of a Jones film, even though they received no compensation for performing. George Marshall, the series' director, recalled that the stars considered it a privilege to be counseled on their game by the popular golfing great. But their unpaid participation may not have been quite as magnanimous as it seemed. Most of the stars in these shorts puttered around the links on weekends, and like Fields they bet substantial sums on the outcome of eighteen holes. Any help from Bobby Jones could translate into financial benefits at the nineteenth hole.

Bobby Jones made, appropriately, eighteen of these delightful and instructive one-reelers. Each was critically acclaimed, but the reviewers' grandest kudos fell to the one-reeler that featured W. C. Fields. With the comedian's stage and movie background full of golfing skits, one would expect Fields to be the first star to work with Jones. He was not. Indeed, Fields' turn did not arrive until the last package of six was filmed.

Jones himself recalled the series fondly, noting that each short contained a story line, but the script was flexible. There was room for improvisation.

In the Fields-Jones collaboration William B. Davidson (later the Sheriff in *My Little Chickadee)* and Warner Oland (of the Charlie Chan and Fu Manchu pictures) tag along with Jones for the first few minutes.

As the threesome stroll down the fairway, the camera catches Fields skulking in the rough. Jones is about to tee off as Fields looks on. The ball explodes off the tee. Amazed, Fields cringes: "Land o' goshen! . . . I don't believe it." W. C. surreptitiously follows Jones to his next lie, a fairway shot to the green. Boom! Another blast by the golfing great straight toward the flag. That is too much for Fields to handle. He shudders. "I still don't believe it." Jones' awesome shot has shamed W. C. into quitting the game for good. He starts to leave, swearing that he will never set foot on a golf course again. Jones sees Fields and hears the muttered pledge and objects warmly. He soothes W. C. and talks him into discussing the problem. Oland, Fields and Jones find a comfortable spot under a large oak tree and sit down. Despondent about the state of his game, Fields talks while unconsciously juggling three golf balls. The juggling impresses Jones: "You do that pretty well."

"I've devoted a lot of time to it."

Jones suggests that with the same kind of practice Fields could improve his golf. The champ asks the comedian to demonstrate his swing. W. C., normally a decent golfer, exaggerates his bad form. And now for the title: it seems Fields swings with egregious hip action. Teacher Bobby Jones takes his cue and in a studio setting demonstrates the proper hip action. Back to the golf course for some more banter, then a return to the studio for more instruction, and so on.

With the gorgeous Bel Air Country Club as a setting and Jones' casual style and the friendly conversation with Fields, this one-reeler was a very pleasant film. Moreover, historically *Hip Action* was important not only for the relaxed candid portrait of Fields, but the clear respect the comedian gave the golfing great. Easily W. C. could have upstaged Bobby Jones, but he did not. He reined in his usually affected speech pattern and added no muttering asides, thereby leaving the focus of the film on Jones' instruction. It was a generous tribute to Jones and a compliment to Fields for so graciously relinquishing the spotlight. You can be certain that this respectful approach was Fields' sole decision. He would not have done as much simply on the command of director George Marshall. But that is a story for later.

Sadly, this film is not available for public showing. What is worse is that neither Warner Brothers nor the Library of Congress admits to owning even simple reference copies of the eighteen one-reelers. Two more or less complete sets of prints are known to exist. One is housed at the Wisconsin Center for Theatre Research in Madison, but they can be seen only through 16-mm private screenings by appointment. The other is the sole complete 35-mm set, locked in an Atlanta, Georgia, bank safe deposit vault held by the Bobby Jones estate.

HIP ACTION
From the Bobby Jones *How to Break 90* series, entry number three
One reel
Sound, black and white
Released June 24, 1933, by the Vitaphone Corporation
Produced by Warner Bros. Pictures and the Vitaphone Corp.
Directed by George E. Marshall
Story by Andrew Bennis
Photographed by Arthur Todd
Edited by Al Clark

CAST:
Bobby Jones   Himself
W. C. Fields   Himself
Warner Oland   Himsef
William B. Davidson   Himself

Filmed at the Bel Air Country Club near Beverly Hills.

International House

— 1933 —

Fields finished the Sennett four in January and soon after that he completed the Bobby Jones short. Now he had to wait again for a studio to call. This time, however, he was a lot more optimistic. His friend and benefactor of earlier years, William Le Baron, had moved out from the East and was now sitting in a big office at Paramount. And W. C. knew Eddie Sutherland, his former director, was searching through cast lists trying to put together a group of actors for a planned Paramount extravaganza called *International House*. Sutherland knew Fields was available and wanted him. Sutherland worked hard to convince the studio to use Fields for the film. He had no trouble getting the nod from Le Baron, but some of the other Paramount executives hesitated. Those people remembered Fields' tepid notices from the silent era and could not forget that the last two feature-length Paramount productions in which Fields performed got a thumbs-down reception from the critics.

Sutherland argued that W. C. got good reviews even though the pictures failed, and that argument seemed to sway the doubters. Maybe, too, they had seen his funny work in the Sennett shorts. They finally agreed and Fields signed for *International House* at the end of April, guaranteeing him four weeks of work for $3,000 a week. Peggy Hopkins Joyce, who had worked with Fields in the 1917 *Ziegfeld Follies,* took top billing, and Fields, as Professor Quail, grabbed the second slot.

Dr. Wong has invited a group of international bidders to the International House Hotel in Wuhu, China, to auction the rights to his newly invented radioscope (television). All the bidders are arriving, including General

Director Eddie Sutherland (sitting down holding the golfing wedge) joins the principals in the cast of International House *for this publicity photo. The car is Fields' baby Austin, which he used in the* Ziegfeld Follies of 1925 *and later in the* Earl Carroll Vanities. *On the hood are Lumsden Hare and Franklin Pangborn; standing atop the car are Burns and Allen; holding the dog is Sari Maritza; staring at her is Bela Lugosi; Stu Erwin is behind the wheel.*

Petronovich, the Russian representative, but the American Electric Company legate, Tommy Nash, is nowhere near Wuhu. He is stuck in Shanghai, where he just missed the last train. He decides to telegraph Wong begging him to hold off on the bidding until he can make it there. Meanwhile, Peggy Hopkins Joyce finds out she too missed the last train to Wuhu. She also has to get there. She wants to marry a millionaire, and whoever wins the rights to Wong's invention will be fabulously wealthy. That is when she will begin her own bidding. Nash finally locates a car and he will drive through the China desert to get to Wuhu. Joyce catches wind of Tommy's transport and persuades him to take her along.

Back at the hotel, the manager, Franklin Pangborn, informs Wong that Nash has sent a telegram asking the scientist to hold up the demonstration. Wong quickly agrees. He is pretty sure the American will be the highest bidder. Wong will entertain no offers until Nash arrives. Now Wong wants to test his invention and asks Pangborn if he would like to see the six-day bicycle race in Madison Square Garden. The scientist is trying to tune in the show but is having difficulty finding the channel. During one of these attempts he focuses in on a plane ready to depart from a dilapidated Mexican airport. Professor Quail sits behind the controls. He is loading up for his return trip to Kansas City with a cargo of beer—cases and barrels of beer. Quail, piloting his own autogyro—part airplane, part helicopter—leans out of his cockpit window to return his last glass of beer to a tray his butler holds. The tray already has about fifteen empties. With the pilot and plane loaded, Quail makes a wobbly takeoff.

Back to Tommy Nash and Peggy Hopkins Joyce. After a breakdown in the desert the two finally arrive at the hotel, where Nash's fiancée, Carol Fortescue, has been waiting patiently. When Carol sees her betrothed appear with the blond bombshell, she is incensed. Peggy heads for the registration desk and there runs into an ex-husband, General Petronovich. He tells her he plans to buy the radioscope. Carol starts thinking about remarrying him.

Meanwhile, Dr. George Burns' nurse, Gracie Allen, of the hotel medical duo, reads an article on the front page of the Wuhu newspaper. Many cities throughout the world report a number of people injured by beer bottles falling from an airplane. Above the item is a photograph of Professor Quail and a diagram of his tortuous flight path.

Outside the doctor's office Carol tells Tommy Nash that all is forgiven: Ms. Joyce explained everything to her. Nash is relieved, but Carol notices a disorder. His hands are cold and his cheeks hot. The eminent Dr. Burns and his nurse walk up and quickly diagnose Nash's condition—measles. Petronovich overhears the report and concocts a scheme to keep Nash away from the demonstration and therefore the bidding. He will report Nash's ill-health to the health inspector, suggesting Nash be quarantined. Off he goes to put his plan into action.

At night there is a huge bash on the roof garden of the International House, where Dr. Wong will demonstrate his new invention and the bidding will get under way. But there will be cocktails and dinner beforehand. During the festivities an empty Mexican beer bottle drops through the open roof and lands on a table. Then another! And a third! With all eyes turned upward, in comes Quail's autogyro, *The Spirit of Brooklyn*. The flying machine makes a soft landing on the International House stage. From the cockpit out pops Quail's head: "Say, is this Kansas City, Kansas, or Kansas City, Missouri?"

Miss Joyce chirps, "Wuhu!" Quail thinks she is flirting and acknowledges her with his "Woo-hoo!" but still wants to know where he is. He turns to Pangborn. The manager, fastidious and sissified, tells him, "Wuhu!"

Quail mumbles, "Woo-hoo to you too." Then he looks down on the huge posy attached to his lapel. He pulls it off and throws it away: "Don't let the posy fool you. Now where am I?" Ms. Joyce tells him he is on the roof garden of the International House.

"Never mind the details. What town is it?"

Pangborn; "This is Wuhu, China."

"Then what am I doing here?"

Pangborn, forever the poseur, now effeminately put out: "Well, how should I know?"

Quail tries again: "Then what is Wuhu doing where Kansas City ought to be?"

Indignantly, Pangborn suggests, "Maybe you're lost."

"Kansas City is lost. I am here." Fields disembarks and heads straight for Joyce's table. After a certain amount of desultory conversation, Ms. Joyce asks Quail if he would like to join her in a glass of wine.

"You go in first. I'll join you if there's enough room."

Then the quarantine is announced. The authorities have gone way beyond Petronovich's suggestion and quarantined not only Nash but the entire hotel. Wong then announces his demo will be postponed until tomorrow at ten A.M. in his room. This will allow everyone to get a bed for the night. The guests rush from the ballroom to

Another cast shot from International House: (from left) Stu Erwin, Peggy Hopkins Joyce, W. C. Fields, Gracie Allen, George Burns, Franklin Pangborn, Edmund Breese and Lumsden Hare.

Quite possibly the last tangle in Wuhu, or a "Chinese noodle swamp."

"Here's a chance for you to have a laugh on every other girl in the world." It is obvious he is getting nowhere, so he turns to Wong: "Sold to the man with the wrinkled stomach."

Then Quail heads downstairs to sign in. There is chaos around Pangborn and the registration desk. Quail disdains the long queue, climbs over the counter and falls into the extended telephone lines on a busy switchboard, disconnecting all the calls. He refers to the mess as a "Chinese noodle swamp." Untangling himself, he signs in. Pangborn is in a tizzy, then precisely when he is on the verge of murder or suicide, Quail knocks over the mail rack, spilling all the letters, messages and keys to the floor. At which point he announces to the infuriated manager, "Young man, if you're not very careful you'll lose my trade." Exit.

Meanwhile, the General tries getting back into the hotel but finds out his quarantine scheme worked too well. He is told to register across the street at the Lotus Garden. Coincidentally his room at the Lotus Garden is directly across from Peggy's suite at the International House.

While the General settles in, W. C. is in quest of a room. The first suite he tries is a woman's bedroom. She screams and he makes a hasty retreat. Forewarned, he peeks through the keyhole of another room, then walks away shaking his head. "What won't they think of next?" Finally he finds a door open and walks in. He starts getting ready for bed. Then Peggy enters. Obviously it is her room. She starts preparing for sleep. By incredible coincidence they miss each other. At one point they both go out onto the balcony for fresh air and neither sees the other. Petronovich on the other hand sees them both and becomes blind with rage. He still lays claim to his ex-wife. He struggles to open his window to shoot Quail. Joyce and the Professor return to bed, still not aware of the other's presence. Finally Quail's snoring awakens Peggy and she screams. Soon afterward Pangborn and a posse are at her door and W. C. escapes by the balcony. Petronovich sees him, shoots and misses.

The Professor walks into Wong's room, where the radioscope demonstration is under way. His clothes are

the registration desk in the lobby, except for Professor Quail, who walks from table to table collecting abandoned wine bottles. Wong and Joyce also remain in the roof garden. Wong thinks Quail is the representative from the American Electric company and is extremely solicitous to him. He asks the Professor where he intends to sleep this evening.

W. C.: "I will sleep on my right side with my mouth open."

Wong tells Quail that he always sleeps on his stomach, to which Quail replies that that would cause a wrinkled stomach. Obviously the scientist is offering his room as a place for the Professor to flop for the evening. But Quail turns to Joyce and asks if there are any other offers. She looks disgusted.

Peggy Hopkins Joyce with the wealthy Professor Quail. This is the only film in which Fields actually ends up with the girl, albeit not for love.

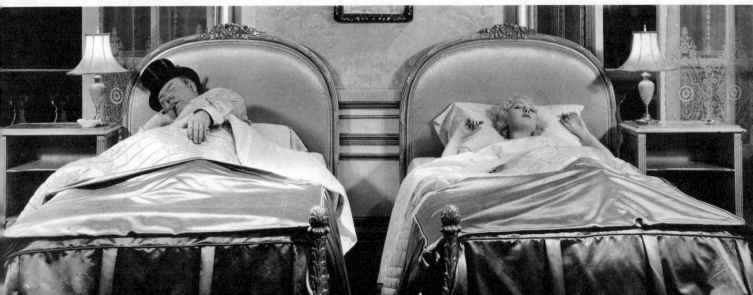

on backwards and he exits to change. Wong is still trying to catch the six-day bike race, but this time tunes in Colonel Stoopnagle and Budd doing a routine about stoopnocracy. Then Wong dials some more and raises Rudy Vallee. The Professor returns to the room while Vallee is still warbling, and Quail wonders aloud, "How long has this dogfight been going on?"

From the television Rudy responds, "Hey, don't interrupt my number. Hold your tongue and sit down."

"Hold your breath and lie down, you howling hyena," Quail demands. But Vallee continues. Out of patience, W. C. stuffs the end of his cane into the moving works of the invention, sending off sparks and automatically changing the channel to a fleet of battleships on maneuvers. Quail, affronted with the show of military might, takes out a gun and fires at the lead ship, sinking it with one shot.

W. C. F. with P. H. J. in Professor Quail's baby Austin. The truncated car actually worked.

Professor Quail's autogyro **The Spirit of Brooklyn.** *Most likely this contraption did not work. Looks like a cold day.*

Next morning Quail wakes up in bed next to Wong. He puts a cigar in his mouth and orders a drink. Peggy calls up and suggests to the Professor that they escape this quarantined place in his autogyro. He agrees. Then Wong finds out Quail is not the American representative. Later that day Wong gives another demo and this time instead of the six-day race he catches Baby Rose Marie singing. By now Nash has escaped from his room and gets together with Wong for another demo, and this time the Chinese scientist tunes in Cab Calloway singing "Reefer Man." Nash loves the invention and presents the highest bid.

Outside, Pangborn, the health inspector, Dr. Burns and Nurse Allen decide that Nash's illness was simply a harmless rash and the quarantine is lifted.

By now Quail has returned to his flying machine and retrieved his baby Austin, a miniature car, and has driven to Hopkins' front door. Peggy gets in and sits down. She is sitting on something, she intones; but Quail knows exactly what it is: "I lost mine in the stock market." Then a meow is heard.

Peggy: "What's that?"

W. C.: "It sounds like a body squeak."

Then after a bit more driving Peggy insists, "I tell you I am sitting on something. Something's under me. What is it?"

She rises slightly and a small cat walks out.

W. C.: "Ah, it's a pussy."

The General, who has already made it back to the hotel and has recently threatened anyone who bought the rights to the radioscope, catches Quail and Joyce. Peggy indignantly gets out of the car to lambast her jealous ex-husband, but when she closes the car door behind her, her skirt gets caught and rips off. When the General notices his ex-wife in nothing but her underwear he sees red. Quail takes off and the chase is on. Finally, the Professor runs into Tommy and Carol. The couple had overheard Petronovich's threat—and are now trying to escape, too. The three drive to the autogyro, where Peggy is waiting. They drive up the plane's ramp, and off they fly to safety. Once again, however, Ms. Joyce is sitting on something.

W. C.: "What again, my little cupcake?"

Oh yes, she is sitting on something. This time when she rises there is a whole litter of cats on the seat. She asks, "I wonder what their parents were?"

W. C.: "Careless, my little nut cake, careless."

A nice candid shot of W. C. and Ms. Joyce. It seems only Stu Erwin knew the still photographer was shooting.

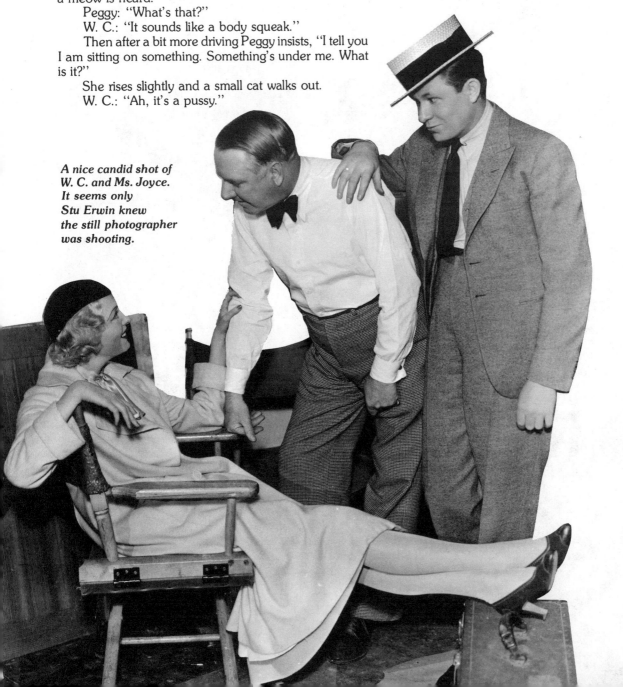

The reviewers loved it, and they particularly praised W. C. To a man they claimed he stole the show, and he did. The picture began with all the earmarks of another elegant and stylized humor piece, made popular in the early thirties. Even Burns and Allen seemed more reserved than normal. Into that came Fields, broad, loud and brash. The contrast was obvious and hilarious, and it drew your attention to the odd man out, in this case W. C. Moreover the character itself was made for thievery. Into an elegant hotel landed an autogyro piloted by a drunk, and containing a miniature car which was used to drive from floor to floor in the hotel. One could not help but steal a show with that setup. Paramount could deny Fields no longer. Critically and at the box office W. C. proved his worth.

The studio offered him a contract for $15,000 a picture, three pictures a year. That was about the same salary W. C. received for his last three Paramount movies, including *International House*. No! If they wanted him they would have to pay. He countered—$100,000 a *picture*, three pictures a year. They compromised—$100,000 a *year*, three pictures a year for three years. Agreed! Then Fields wanted a promise from the Paramount brass. He demanded more freedom on the sets, and certainly more latitude than he was given in the silent days. The studio assented. Of course they could not promise him complete freedom to dictate to directors but certainly more than he had before. His waiting in Hollywood was over. He would now be in a full production swing guaranteed for three years. Whew!

How did Fields get along with director Eddie Sutherland? Eddie Sutherland, you will remember, directed W. C. in a couple of silent films including *It's the Old Army Game*. When Paramount refused to renew Fields' silent film contract because his movies generally were both critical and financial failures, the comedian blamed quite a few people for his walking papers, including Sutherland. As was noted earlier, he accused Sutherland of being a tyro, and an ex-chorus boy who knew nothing of W. C.'s type of humor. He became particularly irate when he recalled that Sutherland had nixed an old stage gag favorite of Fields', shooting a kite from the sky with a pistol. Sutherland claimed it would not play on film. They yelled at each other and they would not talk with each other and finally the director got his way and the bit was axed. Well, it seems the two had mellowed. Fields used essentially the same gag in this film, this time using a gun to sink a battleship on a television screen. Sutherland let him do it. Indeed, the newspaper people wrote accounts about W. C.'s freedom on the set, saying Sutherland never directed him, he just let him run.

The comedian was so pleased he completely reversed his opinion of the director: "He's not only Holly-wood's grandest guy, but one of its best comedy directors."

W. C. cherished this hands-off attitude by a Hollywood studio, and years later claimed it was this newfound liberty that made him a star this time around in Tinsel Town. Fields was now ready to put his *own* work to the Hollywood test.

A shaky side note: There is a now famous clip taken during the filming of this movie. It shows Fields and two other actors playing their parts on the set when suddenly a chandelier starts to swing, then a vase and lamp fall from a table. Earthquake! At the first movement of the earth the cameraman ran out of the soundstage leaving the camera grinding, and it catches a cool, calm Fields gently giving orders for everyone to take it easy, walk slowly and do not panic. And although the clip lasted a short few seconds, it is a unique view of W. C. Fields.

INTERNATIONAL HOUSE
70 minutes
Sound, black and white
Released June 2, 1933, by Paramount
Produced by Paramount
Directed by Edward Sutherland
Screenplay by Francis Martin and Walter DeLeon
Based on a story by Louis E. Heifetz and Neil Brant
Music and lyrics by Ralph Rainger and Leo Robin
Photographed by Ernest Haller
Song: "Reefer Man"

CAST:
Peggy Hopkins Joyce   Herself
W. C. Fields   Professor Quail
Stuart Erwin   Tommy Nash
Sari Maritza   Carol Fortescue
George Burns   Doctor Burns
Gracie Allen   Nurse Allen
Bela Lugosi   General Petronovich
Edmund Breese   Doctor Wong
Lumsden Hare   Sir Mortimer Fortescue
Franklin Pangborn   Hotel manager
Harrison Greene   Herr Von Baden
Henry Sedley   Serge Borsky
James Wong   Inspector Sun
Sterling Holloway   Entertainer: sailor
Rudy Vallee   Himself
Colonel Stoopnagle and Budd   Themselves
Cab Calloway and His Orchestra   Themselves
Baby Rose Marie   Herself
Ernest Wood   Newsreel reporter
Edwin Stanley   Mr. Rollins
Clem Beauchamp/Jerry Drew   Cameraman
Norman Ainslee   Ticket manager
Louis Vincenot   Hotel clerk
Bo-Ling   Chinese girl at cigar counter
Etta Lee   Peggy's maid
Bo-Ching   Bellhop
Lona Andre   Chorus queen
Andre Cheron   Guest

Filmed at Paramount in Hollywood.

Hollywood On Parade B-2
—1933—

Paramount had Fields locked in their stables once again, so now they wanted to promote him. Paramount knew how. All the studios promoted their contract players by circulating publicity stills, but some of the studios went so far as to produce one-reel vignettes of their stars at work and play—a sort of fan magazine on film. Paramount was one of those studios. They made these short-subject movies to push the different stars, directors and producers working on their lot and to advertise their company as a factory where the best dreams in Hollywood were manufactured. They made a series of these promotional films and called them *Hollywood on Parade*. They were well done and entertaining, with

Paramount's best talent frolicking candidly in front of the camera. The stars' appearances in these one-reelers were done gratis, as a means of obliging the studio or generating a little extra publicity for themselves—or perhaps because they were simply fun to do.

Lewis Lewyn, the producer of the *Hollywood on Parade* series, made similar inside-Hollywood short subjects at other studios, but none were as good as these twenty-six entries spanning two seasons. It is a mystery why this series is almost never revived for theatrical or non-theatrical exhibition. Shots of Paramount's backlot are fascinating and it is always exciting to catch the studio's great names gamboling in front of Lewyn's cameras. These cinematic tours treat us to top stars, sometimes in costume, many times in off-the-set togs, stars walking to and from stages, stars at their homes, stars at premieres. Some of the routines were hastily staged, while as many more were spontaneous.

Each short was cut like a newsreel, with several disparate sequences strung together, often with only the flimsiest pretext of continuity. The tone was genial and frivolous, and budgets were nominal and could be written off to promotion even in the unlikely event they did not return their cost.

Particularly impressive were the cast lists. One is hard put to imagine Mary Pickford on film with Mae West, or W.C. Fields with Groucho Marx, or Ruth Etting with

Duke Ellington, and yet all do appear in the same eleven-minute *Hollywood on Parade* short number B-2, although few of them actually had scenes together.

W. C. Fields brightened at least two second-season *Hollywood on Parade* entries. In B-2, his initial appearance, he is one of several luminaries paraded before a convocation of motion picture exhibitors at the Paramount lot. The convocation consists of a great mass of people crowded around a tiny platform. In the middle

This is the kind of nonsensical photo that major studios would circulate to promote their contract players, and Paramount had just signed Fields to a term contract. Naturally, all these young ladies were announced as dancing girls to be seen in W. C.'s forthcoming film. Of course, they were never part of a Fields production.

With their newest star corralled in a three-year contract, Paramount not only wanted to exploit him in their Hollywood on Parade *series but also sent their publicity department out to take still photos of the comedian which they would pass out to the trades for further promotion. Here Fields points to a pair of his prized possessions. This shot was taken in front of his Toluca Lake home.*

of the stage is one skinny microphone from which the different stars will speak. Fields wends his way through the throng. Only the top of his head can be seen until he climbs onto the platform. He heads directly to the microphone and is just about to speak when he spots his stooge Tammany Young on stage playing a game of checkers with a Paramount executive. Following a routine he reprised from *The Pharmacist*, W. C. hovers over the board earnestly, silently studying the strategy. Young slowly brings his hand to a checker. He looks to Fields for approbation. Slyly, subtly Fields grimaces and shakes his head slightly—it would be a calamitous move. Tammany retreats. He tries another piece. Again with slight miming Fields lets his stooge know the move is wrong. Young retreats. Third try. Fields gives Tammany a knowing grin. Young proudly pushes his checker onto another square. Jump! Jump! Jump! His opponent completely clears the board. Fields smiles at his pal apologetically, stares at the board in wonderment and leaves, snaking through the throng again. He never said a word.

The beauty of this superbly mimed sketch lay in its subtlety, a model of precise timing. Fields underplayed each gesture and yet that live audience of film exhibitors responded uproariously to every move, every gag, even the slightest twitch of his head. And as a bonus we have the rare opportunity to catch Fields at his most well practiced skill—working an audience. And he did it without benefit of props, speech, sound effects or even a costume, just hard-earned proficiency.

There were a couple of other interesting scenes in this one-reeler. During a shooting break from *Cleopatra*, Cecil B. De Mille introduced several actors and two slave girls from his current production. They were all in costume. And during his turn at the microphone Cary Grant acknowledged he was a bridegroom of two months, then excused himself to return to the set.

With the fun filming over, Fields had to get back to the hard work of making comedy feature-length movies.

HOLLYWOOD ON PARADE (B-2) _____
One reel
Sound, black and white
Released September 8, 1933, by Paramount
Produced and directed by Louis Lewyn for Paramount

CAST:
George Burns   Himself
Gracie Allen   Herself
Jack Haley   Himself
Irving Pichel   Himself
Bing Crosby   Himself
Mary Brian   Herself
Adolphe Menjou   Himself
Katharine De Mille   Herself
Cary Grant   Himself
Cecil B. De Mille   Himself
Dale Van Sickel   Himself
W. C. Fields   Himself
Jean Rogers   Starlet
Gertrude Michael   Actress in *Cleopatra*
Henry Wilcoxon   Actor in *Cleopatra*
Tammany Young   W. C. Fields' stooge

Filmed at Paramount in Hollywood.

Tillie And Gus
—1933—

With the promoting of W. C. out of the way for a while, Paramount was ready to showcase Fields in a full-fledged comedy vehicle. It was summer and Fields began work on his first sound feature starring role for Paramount. Although the studio lengthened Fields' creative leash they still tethered him by insisting on teaming him with another comic, Alison Skipworth. Their segment in *If I Had a Million* was the high point of that film, and the studio erroneously felt that Fields needed a sidekick to

make his movies work. Anyway, the script was ready and filming began.

Mary and Tom Sheridan should have inherited a lot of money from Mary's father's will, but Phineas Pratt, the family lawyer and executor of the estate, through chicanery and bookkeeping magic, had usurped most of the

For a man who liked children only if they were properly cooked, W. C. seems to be enjoying himself here. The same cannot be said of Baby LeRoy. . . . Hmmm, maybe that is why Fields is enjoying himself.

inheritance and had put the young Sheridans into deep debt to him. Pratt already owns a riverboat, and Tom and Mary have just inherited one. It was the only thing in the will Phineas could not outright steal, but he is after it anyway. He hates the thought of competition with his riverboat franchise, so with larcenous magnanimity he offers to wipe out Tom and Mary's red ink if they will turn over title to the boat. The beneficiaries, however, want to

On the train with Tillie and Gus and card shark Mr. Green, played by Walter C. Percival.

keep it, because it is their only means of support. Pratt figures they will eventually cave in and gives the couple time to think it over.

Tom and Mary smell a rat and need help. Luckily, assistance is on the way in the form of Uncle Gus and Aunt Tillie Winterbottom. They have been summoned to the small town because they were mentioned in the will. The two are missionaries, but unfortunately the course of the Lord's work makes it impossible for them to live with each other anymore. Tillie ostensibly spreads the word to heathens in China, while Gus tries to convert Alaska. But alas, it seems their billing is less than accurate. Tillie *does* work in China, but she was running a saloon and bordello, which she just lost in a crap gamble. And Gus *is* in Alaska, but standing trial for cheating at cards.

When the telegrams reach them they both quickly take off for the river town, hoping to seize some of the inheritance. Accidentally they meet at the ticket line in a train station. After their customary greetings (they pull guns on one another), they settle down on the train, realizing they better act civilly and keep up the missionary sham in order to garner some of the money. They quickly fall into their old tricks. Gus sees some fellows playing poker and asks to join. "Poker? Poker? Let me see, is that the game where one receives five cards and if there's two alike that's pretty good, but if there's three alike that's much better?" The card sharks graciously open their game to this new sucker. Gus sits down. Tillie remains standing and looks over the other men's shoulders while telling stories: "By the way, I saw those two sailors off the ship today." Gus says, "Yeah?" The opponent asks for three new cards to join his pair of jacks. Tillie takes note and continues her talk: "Three more sailors joined them." Full house—jacks and kings.

Finally they arrive at the river town and find the inheritance gone and Pratt nefarious. But they like the Sheridans and decide to help them keep their ferry franchise. They convince Phineas they should race the old inherited riverboat against Pratt's fast new ship, winner take all. The next morning Gus takes over the operation of the steamboat. A sign that reads GENTLEMEN hangs over a door on the boat. Gus takes his captain's hat and puts the GENTLEMEN sign where CAPTAIN should go. He is ready. The boat needs a lot of repairs, including a new paint job. Gus gets to work. On the local radio station a "how to" program is telling him how to mix paint. Gus does it in a completely slapstick way. He keeps pace with the instructions in the beginning but slowly loses control as the radio instructor gives directions faster and faster. Of course the bit ends with Fields throwing whole cans and bottles into his big paint bucket, then finally giving up the entire enterprise.

The evening before the race, and with Tillie's help, Gus designs his own bit of euchring against Phineas Pratt. He dons a diving suit with a steel helmet and jumps into the water behind Pratt's boat. Tillie works the air pump on the pier. Gus ties the boat to the dock. He is ready to surface but cannot because the Captain of the other boat has walked out onto the dock to talk with Tillie. He puts his burning pipe in front of the air vent, filling Gus's steel helmet with smoke. Finally the Captain leaves and Tillie pulls Gus out of the water. Gus opens the window to his helmet and a cloud of smoke pours out. He looks at the camera: "Is there a doctor in the house?"

The next morning the gun starts the race. The Sheridans' boat takes off, but Pratt's struggles to move; eventually it breaks away, taking the dock with it. During the race, near-catastrophe hits the Sheridans' boat. On the main deck Gus had stacked a pile of logs to be used as fuel for the steam engine. To keep Baby King out of the way the Sheridans had put him in a metal bathtub, which they had tied to one of the logs. At one point the logs roll off the deck and into the drink, dragging Baby King with them. At first King is fine, but then he pulls the bathtub plug. Tillie and Gus see the horror and Gus springs into action. He unties the lifeboat and jumps in. The lifeboat starts to sink, but Gus has another explanation: "The river's rising."

He finally saves King and brings him back to the boat. But now there is no fuel. Again Gus to the rescue. He finds old boxes of fireworks and Roman candles and sends them down to Tom in the engine room. Bang!

Boom! The explosions really get the old boat sailing. With rockets screeching from the smokestack, the Sheridans cross the finish line first. After the race, Phineas Pratt, burning in anger, falls off the dock. Gus rushes to save him, extends his cane, and hooks the larcenous lawyer around the neck. Gus dunks him while asking questions about the probating of the will. Near drowning, Pratt admits his perfidy and promises to return the ill-gotten money to Tom and Mary. The kids are so grateful to their aunt and uncle they give them a good part of the dough. That evening we see Tillie and Gus walking to dinner at the Sheridans', singing "Bringing in the Sheaves."

Tillie and Gus hit the theatres in October 1933 to so-so notices. The picture lacked the great belly laughs and sustained humor of the later Fields films, but it did have a definite charm to it. Fields played a compassionate crook, a Robin Hood taking from a thief and giving to the poor, with a little on the side for himself. Missing was the

A fascinating production still taken during a skull session while on location at Malibu Lake for Tillie and Gus. *Around the circle counterclockwise from the left, Clifford Jones, Jacqueline Wells, Alison Skipworth, Clarence Wilson, W. C. Fields (with cigar and wearing glasses), Barton MacLane, Francis Martin and unidentified. Note the boom mike and arc lights hidden in the eucalyptus trees.*

The good guys: the Sheridans (Clifford Jones and Jacqueline Wells) and the Winterbottoms (Skipworth and Fields).

Gus ready to paint the Fairy Queen. A very delicate operation!

bravado of *International House* or his cruelty in *The Dentist* or his pure spinelessness of *The Barber Shop*. In this film he acted with the self-assurance of a con man plying a well-rehearsed art, but doing it with flinches, frowns and a kind soul. It is one of Fields' more gentle movies. Even though he shared the screen with his future nemesis Baby LeRoy, in this, their first job together, W. C. played with the child tenderly, almost with an avuncular concern. A few more pictures down the road with the kid and that will all change.

Part of the problem with *Tillie and Gus* was the direction. This was Francis Martin's first and last time directing a feature-length comedy film. He helped write this movie and collaborated on *International House*. Prior to that he acted in a few short comedies of the silent era and wrote and directed even more shorts, but his direction in this feature-length film needed more snap. Indeed, *Tillie and Gus* seemed much longer than its mere fifty-eight minutes. The comedy was almost too calm and lacked the punch the concept portended.

However, not all the blame should be pinned on Francis Martin. After all, he did have a few headaches on the set. Just before the steamboat race the Sheridans' entry almost sank. The scenes on the river were filmed on a pastoral little secluded lake in the Santa Monica Mountains called Malibu Lake. It has not changed much over the years. Before filming the race, the boat suddenly listed sharply to one side. Martin ordered the actors ashore. Stagehands rushed on with buckets and started bailing out the hold. For four hours they bailed, but the water level never lowered. Finally the director called the

The production crew notices the still photographer, and as the motion picture cameraman points him out W. C. turns and—click! With Baby Leroy and Alison Skipworth filming on Malibu Lake in a climactic scene. Note the hands (only) of Clarence Wilson grabbing the dock. He is treading water but is blocked from view by Alison Skipworth.

fire department. They rushed to the scene with pumps and for five hours those pumps strained, but with no luck. The water level had not altered. At one A.M., and giving up hope, Martin called the man who had built the boat: "She's sinking and sinking fast. She's sprung a leak," he hollered. The builder yawned. "She can't spring a leak." The director was enraged. He saw the boat sinking with his own eyes. The carpenter agreed to come to the site. There, with the pumps still sweating and Martin raving, the builder lazily said again that the old boat just could not spring a leak. The director: "All I know is we've been pumping water out of her hold for nine hours and it comes in as fast as we pump it out."

The builder: "She ain't got a hold."

Martin, flustered: "I don't care what the technical term is, all I know is we've been pumping water out of her interior for nine hours." The builder started laughing. "She ain't got an interior any more than a raft. She's flat on the bottom, sitting on drums. You've got all that heavy stuff on one side and that's what makes it lean over.

You've been bailing Malibu Lake into Malibu Lake for nine hours."

The near sinking of the vessel was not the only delay in the filming. The scene in which Fields queries, "Is there a doctor in the house?" had to be shot at night. Fields followed the script and climbed up on the dock. The camera zoomed in for the close-up. Then suddenly instead of his lines, Fields looked down at his fins and said, "Primo Carnera's bedroom slippers."

"Cut!" The joke was funny, but it did not fit, and with the close-up the joke would be lost on an audience. Fields argued with Francis Martin, claiming everyone knew Carnera had big feet. But after about half an hour of arguing Fields gave in to his director. They set the scene up again. Fields climbed on the dock. The close-up. Fields looked down at his fins and said, "Charley Frobisher's bedroom slippers."

"Cut!" Fields argued that the name Charley Frobisher always got a laugh. Martin again explained it would not work. Some of the stagehands figured Fields had lost his old ad-libbing touch; the genius was gone. It was now after midnight and W. C. agreed to do the scene again. This time it went as written: "Is there a doctor in the house?"

"Cut. Take! Print!" That is what the director wanted. Everyone could go home. Some of the crew noticed Fields seemed particularly pleased. And why not? The old master had not lost his genius. His contract called for eight hundred additional dollars every time he worked past midnight. "Goldentime" it is called today. He knew exactly what he was doing.

Again, the reviews for *Tillie and Gus* were adequate, with most of the critics knocking the direction and complaining that Paramount should not team Fields with Skipworth, "they do not play well together." But, here we go again, the notices gave the overall picture mediocre marks but praised Fields' work.

The critics were not the only ones singing W. C.'s praises. After *Tillie and Gus*, MGM took a serious look at

the comedian. Near the end of November the Culver City studio approached Paramount for the loan of Fields' services. They wanted to match him with Marie Dressler (who coincidentally had just completed *Tugboat Annie)* in a prospective motion picture called *Fercke.* The negotiations were tough. Paramount wanted more than money; they wanted to swap stars of equal stature. They asked for Jimmy Durante, Joan Crawford, Robert Montgomery or Norma Shearer. MGM finally offered Durante. Paramount, after some reflection, decided that the "Schnoz" was not big enough to match Fields and wanted another actor as well. What finally obviated the negotiations was Marie Dressler's death. At the time she was the number-one box office attraction in the country and had been for several years. In her next to last picture, *Dinner at Eight,* she was billed first above no less than Wallace Beery, John Barrymore, Lionel Barrymore and Jean Harlow. Dressler and Fields would have been a great combination to see.

TILLIE AND GUS

58 minutes
Sound, black and white
Released October 13, 1933, by Paramount
Produced by Douglas MacLean for Paramount
Directed by Francis Martin

Screenplay by Walter De Leon and Francis Martin
Adapted from a story by Rupert Hughes
Photographed by Benjamin Reynolds
Art direction by Hans Dreier and Harry Oliver
Song: "Bringing in the Sheaves"

CAST:

W. C. Fields Augustus Q. Winterbottom	Harry Dunkinson Bartender
Alison Skipworth Tillie Winterbottom	Irving Bacon Nosy extra at gambling table
Baby LeRoy/Ronald LeRoy Overacker The "King" Sheridan	Billy Engle Sailor
Jacqueline Wells/Julie Bishop Mary Blake Sheridan	Herbert Evans Butler
Clifford Jones/Phillip Trent Tom Sheridan	Maurice Black Bit
Clarence Wilson Phineas Pratt, executor	Brooks Benedict Mr. Black
George Barbier Captain Fogg	Walter C. Percival Mr. Green
Barton MacLane Commissioner McLennan	Cyril Ring Mr. White
Edgar Kennedy Judge Elmer, "Old Naked-Skull"	Ted Stanhope Telegraph clerk
Robert McKenzie Defense attorney	Ferris Taylor Juror
Master Williams High Card Harrington	Ed Brady Barfly
William Irving Man in tall silk hat	Harry Schultz Kibitzer
Ivan Linow The Swede	Jerry Jerome Customer
Lon Poff Juror	Frank O'Connor Reporter
James Burke Juror	Eddie Baker Race judge
Frank Hagney Jury foreman	
Lew Kelly Sourdough, hotel manager	Filmed at Paramount in Hollywood, with location work at Malibu Lake
John "Blackie" Whiteford Man at bar	in the Santa Monica Mountains.

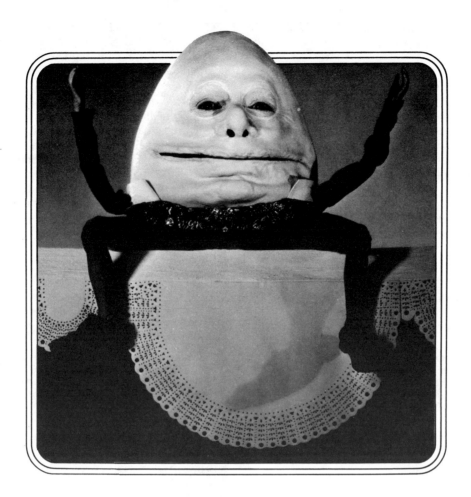

Alice In Wonderland
—1933—

Paramount dropped Fields from top billing in his next two pictures. They were not punishing him or expressing disenchantment with his work, but rather billing was dictated by the types of films and story lines. *Alice in Wonderland* was a Paramount extravaganza packed with the studio's glittering luminaries as well as with some of its minor lights. Except, of course, for Alice, a role originally intended for Ida Lupino, all of the players were listed alphabetically. So Fields' name falls behind Billy Barty's and Gary Cooper's, but above the likes of Cary Grant and Baby LeRoy.

Alice in Wonderland, a film version of Lewis Carroll's classic satire of English royalty, falls far short of being called a classic, too, but nonetheless it was smoothly made, charmingly portrayed and, with the star-studded cast, historically interesting. The film stays true to the book, duplicating Carroll's wild fantasies with amazing cinematic tricks. Accented with animation and splendid

costuming, the book comes to life with all the horror and some of the gaiety of the original work. But this accuracy of the film is its bane. The literal visualization of Carroll's saga excludes the exercise of imagination inherent, and necessary, in the author's work. So after the uniqueness of the art direction, costumes and cinematography wears off, the film becomes a bit tedious.

Furthermore, even though the costuming was magnificent it was slightly distracting. With the actors so elaborately garbed, or in some cases mere voice-overs to animation or puppets, one could not recognize the actors visually—one had to guess an actor by the sound of his voice. Such guessing games took the viewers' attention away from the story. The most recognizable voice, according to the critics, was, of course, W. C.'s. The reviewers said that the audiences immediately recognized Fields' voice and instantly started laughing. They also claimed that W. C. once again walked away with the laughs and the movie. The first was *If I Had a Million.* In this case, the character he played helped him purloin the piece.

Fields played Humpty-Dumpty, unrecognizable except for that hilarious voice, as a gruff, complaining, grouchy sort of oval. He sits on top of a wall; an enormous egg with skinny little legs sticking out. After old Humpty falls and splits to pieces, he continues to grumble and complain and moan and groan. It was a small bit but funny, and it stood out as the only purely humorous sequence in the motion picture, thanks to W. C.'s playing it for all it was worth.

Norman McCleod captained this film. It was a strange choice of directors. McCleod was best known for his fashionable romantic comedies. But he performed adequately in this film, and most of all it appeared he left W. C. undirected, allowing the comedian to use his own unique humor as Humpty-Dumpty. (It still brings smiles to think of W. C. as this big old cranky egg.)

Even though the literal reproduction of *Alice in Wonderland* made the movie more a horror story than a fanciful, whimsical satire, it is worth seeing. The imaginative cinematography, the costuming and the fine appointments of the film make it a pleasure to view. Although, admittedly, it is distracting guessing the actor playing the character, it is also fun.

The film made the Christmas list in 1933. Then Paramount put Fields into another movie in which he would not star but would steal.

ALICE IN WONDERLAND _____

90 minutes
Sound, black and white
Released December 22, 1933, by Paramount
Produced by Louis D. Lighton for Paramount
Directed by Norman McLeod
Based on *Alice's Adventures in Wonderland* (1865) and *Alice through the Looking-Glass* (1871) by Lewis Carroll
Screenplay by Joseph L. Mankiewicz and William Cameron Menzies
Photographed by Henry Sharp and Bert Glennon

Edited by Ellsworth Hoagland
Music by Dimitri Tiomkin
Musical director: Nathaniel Finston
Sound recording by Eugene Merritt
Art direction by Robert Odell
Technical effects by Gordon Jennings and Farciot Edouart
Masks and costumes by Wally Westmore and Newt Jones
Pageantry by Le Roy Prinz

CAST:

Charlotte Henry	Alice
Richard Arlen	Cheshire cat
Roscoe Ates	Fish
William Austin	Gryphon
Billy Barty	White pawn and the baby
Billy Bevan	Two of spades
Colin Campbell	Garden frog
Harvey Clark	Father William
Gary Cooper	White knight
Jack Duffy	Leg of mutton
Harry Ekezian	First executioner
Leon Errol	Uncle Gilbert
Louise Fazenda	White queen
W. C. Fields	Humpty-Dumpty
Alec B. Francis	King of hearts
Skeets Gallagher	White rabbit
Meyer Grace	Third executioner
Cary Grant	Mock turtle
Ethel Griffies	Governess
Lillian Harmer	Cook
Raymond Hatton	Mouse
Sterling Holloway	Frog
Edward Everett Horton	Mad hatter
Roscoe Karns	Tweedledee

Colin Kenny	Clock
Baby LeRoy	Joker
Lucien Littlefield	Father William's son
Mae Marsh	The sheep
Charles McNaughton	Five of spades
Polly Moran	Dodo bird
Jack Oakie	Tweedledum
Patsy O'Byrne	Aunt in the portrait come to life
Edna Mae Oliver	Red queen
George Ovey	Plum pudding
May Robson	Queen of hearts
Charlie Ruggles	The March hare
Jackie Searl	Dormouse
Alison Skipworth	Duchess
Ned Sparks	The caterpillar
Will Stanton	Seven of spades
Ford Sterling	White king
Joe Torrillo	Second executioner
Jacqueline Wells/Julie Bishop	Alice's sister

Filmed at Paramount in Hollywood.
British adaptations of the Lewis Carroll stories were filmed in 1950 and 1972. Walt Disney released his animated version in 1951.

Six Of A Kind

—1934—

Fields does not appear in *Six of a Kind* until the second reel, which helps explain why he did not receive top billing. This was just the beginning of W. C.'s Hollywood "talkie" career. A few more years down the road and Fields will be able to demand and get the top honors for just cameo roles. For this film Charlie Ruggles and Mary Boland lead Fields in the listing with Burns and Allen following.

It was not difficult for Fields to usurp the show from the other actors, because W. C.'s big scene was his old standby, the pool routine, a version of his 1915 original. He cut out most of the juggling and added a hell of a lot of laughs, and it was the hit of the film. This is not meant to imply that George Burns and Gracie Allen had little to offer. Indeed, their comedic bits were top-notch, and Gracie's funning, particularly, nearly matched Fields'; but in the end there was probably nothing that could better W. C.'s old but polished pool routine.

J. Pinkham Whinney, or Pinky as his wife calls him, a middle-aged New Jersey bank teller, is planning a second honeymoon with his spouse, Flora. They are going to make a cross-country road trip to Hollywood. The day has come and Pinky goes to his bank to collect some papers before heading out, and he brings his briefcase. Coincidentally, that same day another teller, Ferguson, has just embezzled $50,000 and put the loot in a briefcase identical to Whinney's. Quickly Ferguson devises a plan. He will exchange briefcases with Pinky, then find out his itinerary, and at a point safely away from town he will again exchange briefcases and make a run for it.

Mrs. Whinney, ever the budget saver, advertised for fellow travelers for the trip west. Pinky at first fought the idea, but as always he acquiesced to Flora. George Edwards and Gracie De Vore answered the ad, and on the day of departure, show up with their enormous Great Dane, Rang Tang Tang. The dog demands the front seat, Flora is afraid to argue, and off the five go to California.

Gracie's persistence forces the Whinneys to go west by another route, altering the itinerary Pinky left at the bank and thus foiling Ferguson's plans. The Whinneys' second honeymoon, filled with the inimitable Burns and Allen madcap mishaps, leads them to Nuggetville, Nevada, where Sheriff "Honest John" Hoxley, W. C., sometimes keeps the peace but most of the time hangs out at the Nuggetville Hotel kibitzing with Mrs. K. Rumford, the proprietor, or shooting pool with his pal Dr. Busby.

Mrs. Rumford, nicknamed "the Duchess," has just received the Whinneys' wired request for two rooms for an evening, apparently the first guests she has entertained in quite some time. She tells the Sheriff that she might make some money for a change, then warns him not to spend it. Then with her ire a bit high she asks disdainfully, "Why do you drink so much?"

" 'Cause I like it." Cannot argue with that.

Mrs. Rumford continues sounding off, listing John's disgusting habits. Finally having heard enough, John interrupts: "According to you everything I like to do is either illegal, immoral or fattening." With that he leaves the registration desk and enters the poolroom. Dr. Busby is waiting for him by the water cooler. The good doctor takes a professional look at his friend and comments about his rather flushed appearance. John tells him why he looks the way he does: Last night "the duchess and I sat up till four playing pinochle. Killed three quarts of rye." Incredulously the doctor asks, "The Duchess drank?"

"No, she doesn't drink." He fills a glass of water and talks about his symptoms: "I feel as though the Russian army'd been walking over my tongue in their stocking feet." He takes the glass of water to his lips, cowers at the thought, pours the water back into a bucket, takes out a flask and downs the contents in a matter of seconds. Now for pool. Fields checks the pool cues and grabs one. It is warped and bowed. The Doctor points it out: "It's crooked."

"I'd like to see something in this joint that isn't crooked." Sheriff John Hoxley lines up his shot.

"Tell me, Sheriff, how did you ever get the name of 'Honest John'?" The Sheriff's answer is simple and short: "The time of which I speak I'm tending bar up at Medicine Hat. A guy used to come in there with a glass eye. I used to wait on him. He used to take this glass eye out and put it in a tumbler of water. He comes in one day and he forgets the glass eye. I found it. The next morning I gave it back to him. Ever since that time I've been known as Honest John." To recite these lines takes Honest John a good five minutes, during which he attempts to shoot the cue ball and break the rack. The routine ends with John trying a massé shot on the cue ball. He raises the stick straight over the ball and comes down hard. The pool cue misses the white ball, and passes all the way through the table. John quickly grabs the ball basket, puts it over the hole, snatches his hat and coat and casually leaves the room with his arm around Dr. Busby: "And ever since that time I've been known as Honest John." (After the five minutes of aiming at the cue ball, he hits it only once—a miscue. The ball passes the racked balls completely, bounces up from the back cushion and fires back, knocking John on the forehead.)

Meanwhile the foursome from the East has arrived at the Nuggetville Hotel. George decides to go shopping and enters the local haberdasher's. John is behind the counter looking at the clothing. George mistakes him for the salesman and asks him about certain items. John tries to interest him in a hat and puts it on to model, then a coat, then a pair of trousers and finally some boots, but George is not interested in any of it. So Honest John gives up and leaves fully clothed.

Back at the hotel, Mrs. Rumford has received a letter from the New Jersey police informing her that Whinney is an embezzler. While Mrs. Rumbord searches for the Sheriff, Ferguson has popped up in Nuggetville to get Whinney's briefcase before the cops get there. But John walks in, and Ferguson hides in a storage room. After interrogating Whinney, Fields leans against the storage room door, accidentally locking Ferguson inside. While he is trying to release the real crook and incarcerate Whinney, a couple of investigators from the East show up with the knowledge that Ferguson is the guilty one, not Whinney. John says he knew it all the time and gladly turns over the criminal. John gets a reward for the capture and Pinky and Flora are given a couple extra weeks of vacation.

Six of a Kind opened in February 1934, two months after *Alice in Wonderland,* and it received kind reviews. This was the fifth talking movie Fields made for Paramount in which he did not star, and yet nearly all the reviewers claimed he stole. *Million Dollar Legs, If I Had a Million, International House, Alice in Wonderland* and now *Six of a Kind* brought the newspapermen to their feet applauding Fields and his ability to walk away with a film. This time the movie itself got fairly good notices and the critics proclaimed a winner for

W. C. with George Burns.

W. C. with James Burke (left), Dick Rush and Alison Skipworth.

A study of the serious business of comedy on the set. Caught off guard are W. C. Fields (with glasses and toothpick), director Leo McCarey (with back to camera), Gracie Allen and Mary Boland. The man sitting in the background sporting the same type of hat worn by W. C. is in fact Fields' double.

After a thorough and exhaustive investigation, Sheriff Honest John Hoxley presents his case to, from left, Gracie Allen, Mary Boland, Charlie Ruggles and George Burns, and then accuses the wrong man.

Paramount. The studio caught on, and immediately after releasing *Six of a Kind* they hired Fields' old friend from the *Comic Supplement*, J. P. McEvoy, to write a sequel using the same six main characters, this time calling it *Three Pair*, production set for May. Undoubtedly Paramount wanted to enhance Fields' part and that is why they hired McEvoy, but the idea never got off the ground, possibly because Fields objected to sharing the limelight again, particularly as only one half of a comedy team which itself had to compete with two other comedy teams. Anyway, most of the notices claimed there was too little Fields in *Six of a Kind* and wondered in print whether or not Paramount had conjured a sinister plot against the comedian. Ed Sullivan put it most bluntly: "They [Paramount] thought they could put Fields to rest by surrounding him with veteran film comedians, but Fields outfoxed them and ran away with the show."

Whether Fields really did outsly the slick executives or not, one thing is clear. He put to rest their propensity to push Alison Skipworth, or, for that matter, any other comedian, on him. It finally became obvious to the studio honchos that W. C. could sustain a film without teaming him with anybody. They quickly dropped the idea of using the comedian in *Three Pair*.

Every critic who wrote about the movie hailed the pool routine as one of the funniest bits on film. Fields first performed the skit in Australia in 1905 and brought it all the way through vaudeville into the 1915 *Ziegfeld Follies.*

Then he performed a poor copy of it on film in the *Pool Sharks*, 1915. He kept it in the *Follies* for seven more years, and then in 1928 it was put on film again. In 1915, his original pool table simply wore out. He had a new one built for the *Follies*, and that was the table he used in this film. It still exists, and it bears the scars of constantly repeated tricks—one in particular. When W. C. tried to line up his shot he would put his left hand on the butt of the stick and would use his right hand for a guiding bridge. When he stroked to shoot, he would pull back his left hand too far and the stick would leave the right hand bridge. He would follow through with his shot as if all was normal, but the stick, now unguided by his right hand, would strike the side of the pool table. Today that side of the table is pockmarked and dented by the point of the cue stick.

Six of a Kind introduced a new Fields foil. Shorty, who for years was Fields' manservant, and whom the comedian used frequently as his stooge on stage and on film, died soon after they moved to Hollywood. Fields still needed a sidekick. At a party someone reintroduced him to Tammany Young. Young had been playing bit parts in movies for the past decade, including an uncredited appearance in the Fields film *Sally of the Sawdust*, in 1925, but up until now his greatest fame had come as a result of his gate crashing propensity. He often bragged that there was no party he could not crash. Most of his antics occurred in New York, but in the early thirties he moved his show to Hollywood. W. C. took stock of this short, dumb-looking party crasher, and realized he had found Shorty's replacement. He hired him as his factotum and then, just as he did with William Blanche, put him on film as his personal foil. He had used him in *Hollywood on Parade* (B-2), but this was Young's true movie debut with his boss. The joke traveled around Hollywood that for the first time Tammany Young was paying for his entertainment.

The recrudescence of Fields' stardom was at hand. His clear expropriation of *Six of a Kind* convinced Paramount that their comedian could stand on his own.

A short note: The great director Leo McCarey helmed this picture. Neither from the tabloids of the period nor in interviews with W. C.'s fellow workers are there any hints of bitterness between Fields and McCarey. Indeed, Grace Bradley Boyd for one recalls that McCarey promoted a happy and creative atmosphere on the set. About his dealings with Fields she says, "Bill Fields, bless him, really didn't need any direction and Leo was happy to let him go."

Soon Fields' insecurity in Hollywood would end, his docility dissolve and his legendary battles with producers, directors and actors would begin anew.

SIX OF A KIND

65 minutes
Sound, black and white
Released February 9, 1934, by Paramount
Produced by Paramount
Directed by Leo McCarey
Screenplay by Walter De Leon and Harry Ruskin
Based on an original story by Keene Thompson and Douglas MacLean

Music by Ralph Rainger
Photographed by Henry Sharp
Art direction by Hans Dreier and Robert Odell
Edited by Le Roy Stone
Sound recording by Eugene Merritt

CAST:
Charlie Ruggles   J. Pinkham Whinney, bank clerk
Mary Boland   Flora Whinney
W. C. Fields   Sheriff "Honest John" Hoxley
George Burns   George Edwards
Gracie Allen   Gracie De Vore
Alison Skipworth   Mrs. K. Rumford, innkeeper (the Duchess)
Grace Bradley   Trixie
Bradley Page   Ferguson
William J. Kelly   A. B. Gillette, bank president
James Burke   Sparks, detective
Dick Rush   Steele
Walter Long   Butch, robber
Leo Willis   Mike, robber
Lew Kelly   Joe, bank guard
Alfred P. James   Tom
Tammany Young   Dr. Busby

Lee Phelps   Airline official
Irving Bacon   Philipsburg House desk clerk
Paul Tead   Accountant at the *Daily Morning Globe*
Harry Bernard   Man in eyeshades
Robert McKenzie   One of the boys
George Pearce   Tourist
Verna Hillie   Safety deposit clerk
Florence Enright   Tourist's wife
William Augustin   Cop
Kathleen Burke   Woman
Neal Burns   Gillette's secretary
Marty Faust   Porter
Phil Dunham   Drunk
Sam Lufkin   Glen Falls hotel clerk

Filmed at Paramount in Hollywood.
Working title: *Republicans and Sinners*.

You're Telling Me

—1934—

With Fields rejecting the idea of sharing the laughs again with five other comedians, the sequel to *Six of a Kind—Three Pair*—never got off the ground. So what to do with McEvoy? Well, someone decided to remake one of Fields' more successful silent films, *So's Your Own Man,* and J. P. McEvoy was assigned to write the dialogue, which meant W. C. had his hand in it. Both versions followed the Julian Street 1925 short story called "Mr. Bisbee's Princess." This was the first time since Fields came to Hollywood that Paramount entrusted him to carry the comedy and the story solo.

With only minor exceptions the movie's plot duplicates *So's Your Old Man.* Therefore in order to avoid redundancy the synopsis in this case will merely point out the differences between the two films. For instance, instead of inventing the shatterproof windshield, Samuel Bisbee—W. C. Fields—has created the puncture-proof tire. And in the scene in which Sam tries placating his infuriated wife by buying her a pony, this time he buys

her an ostrich. Of course, the biggest difference from *So's Your Old Man* is the use of full sound instead of title cards, and with Fields' classic delivery that gives this remake full impact. The pacing in this 1934 version is slower, more refined, more methodical in setting up the jokes, and therefore in perfect harmony with W. C.'s speaking style.

In comparing these two films, one silent, one sound, and so nearly identical, it is easy to see why Fields suffered in his non-speaking films yet made a hit in talkies. The stage star who knew how to build a scene intentionally and slowly to garner the greatest laughs was stymied without a voice. It has been argued that throughout Fields' vaudeville career he never said a word, and therefore he should have fit in perfectly with the silent film medium. But in his mute vaudeville years Fields was more of a juggler than a comedian. It was not until he added dialogue in 1915 that he became more of a comedian than a juggler. That makes all the difference.

The two movies begin slightly differently. This film opens with Sam Bisbee drunk and staggering home late at night. He knows he is in trouble with his wife. He reaches the porch and takes off his shoes in the hope that he can sneak in without waking her. Shoes off, he tries to unlock his door. He cannot focus and his key slips by the lock on each try. He has an invention for just such emergencies. He takes a funnel from his pocket and places the small end over the lock. Then he pushes his key against the wide mouth of the funnel and shoves the key down, right into the lock. He is in the house. He tiptoes down the corridor and turns into the living room, getting tangled in the decorative ropes that separate the hallway from the living room (This is a running gag.) His wife is not asleep but waiting disgustedly for her husband. It is after midnight, but Sam tries to convince her it is the "shank of the evening." He looks at his watch. "It's only half past eight." From here the story follows the original. The Bisbee daughter is out late with the Murchison boy, and Mrs. Bisbee is worried sick. Pauline Bisbee finally comes home and announces her plans to marry Bob Murchison. And so on.

The first scene at Fields' invention shop, the little room behind his "Optician, Optometrist, Oculist, Occultist, Optimist" shop, has more jokes and funnier bits. For instance, W. C. tells his two pals about his newest invention—a burglar-catcher chair: "A thief comes into your house. You get friendly with him; offer him a drink. You lead him to this chair. When he sits down, this steel ball comes up and cracks him on the sconce, thusly." Sam demonstrates by putting his foot on the chair, and as advertised the steel ball flies up from behind the chair, "killing him immediately." The scene continues and Sam swills a few drinks then inadvertently sits in his burglar chair. The steel ball crashes against his skull. He is out. His buddies continue drinking and talking, paying no mind to their unconscious friend. After a while Bisbee wakes with a dull groan; he looks at the ball and shudders. Since he is not dead, it is evident to Sam that his device needs more work.

(Fields liked this scene, particularly because it broke a time-honored rule of comedy: "A good comedy rule is that the audience should not know what is coming. In this film I got a laugh when the audience knew exactly what was going to happen in the burglar chair scene.")

Another split from the original *So's Your Old Man,* is the names given to Bisbee's bibulous buddies. Their original monikers were Jeff and Al, but in this remake Fields named them Doc Beebe and Charlie Bogle. (Charles Bogle later became a pseudonym for Fields' writing credits.) Probably just for good copy, or perchance the story is true, but this was how Fields explained the origins of the two names: "During vaudeville I was stuck in a small town in upstate New York. It was during prohibition and I asked the hotel clerk if he could locate some nose varnish. He tried to get some gin among other things. All was hard to get so I ended up with some 'mountain dew' and it was very good. I never would have gotten the stuff if the hotel clerk hadn't known Dr. Beebe, who knew Charlie

Here comes the Princess Lescaboura, the beautiful Adrienne Ames, escorted by W. C. and director Erle C. Kenton.

Bogle, who knew the guy who knew the guy who made it."

Fields enhanced the suicide scene in this film. He stayed close to his character as an inventor. Instead of trying to drink the iodine straight from the bottle, he pours some of the liquid on his invention, a collapsible spoon. His hand shakes and the fluid spills on his shirt. After a few more tries he spots the cemetery, shivers and decides against killing himself. (Many of the critics said Fields' ability to make suicide comical was a stroke of genius "that even the great Chaplin could not successfully accomplish.") Later in the scene, when Sam mistakenly thinks the Princess Lescaboura is out to take her own life and he sits down to talk her out of it, W. C. shows incredible warmth and sentiment. It is one of the most tender scenes of Fields' career.

Again, instead of a shatterproof windshield, Bisbee demonstrates his puncture-proof tire. But this time when he goes to the boardroom, police officers push his car out of a no-parking zone and leave their car in its place. When the tire executives come down to the street to see Bisbee's demonstration, Sam pulls out a gun and a baseball glove. The bullet should bounce off the tires and Sam should catch the lead with his glove. When he shoots, the tire goes flat. He is baffled. He tries again; another flat. Again; the third flat. One more time; that is all four. The cops return, see the damage and chase the fleeing inventor. Just as in the original, eventually the board chairman finds Sam's car and tests the tires himself. The invention is a success. But by this time Sam's in trouble in his hometown, because of the gossip that claimed he was cavorting with a younger woman on the train (the Princess Lescaboura). To pacify his wife, Sam buys an ostrich. And, just as in the original, the Princess

Mrs. Bisbee (Louise Carter, left) showing Mrs. Murchison (Kathleen Howard) her family album, proving beyond doubt that she does come from good stock, the Warrens of Virginia. Note the decorative ropes attached to the curtains separating the two rooms in the background. Fields used them as a running gag. Every time he walked through the archway, particularly after drinking, he would almost hang himself.

14-87-52

decides to come to Sam's town to help poor old Bisbee out. The same things happen. There is a big party at the Bisbee home, Bob Murchison and Pauline Bisbee announce their marriage, and Sam's invited to inaugurate the new town golf course. The next day on the links Fields performs basically the same golf routine with minor changes. Tammany Young took Shorty's part as the caddy. Also, when the chairman of the board shows up to offer Sam money for this puncture-proof tire the Princess

Mrs. Murchison (Kathleen Howard) responds warmly as Sam Bisbee extends a hearty handclasp in this scene from You're Telling Me.

pipes up and increases the offer. A bidding war is on, with Bisbee eventually receiving one million dollars. The film ends the same way as the original. At the Bisbee mansion, the Murchisons and the Bisbees are heading out for a Sunday drive except for Sam, who stays home to guzzle a jug of redeye with his friends Doc Beebe and Charlie Bogle.

The Bisbees no longer live in Waukeagus, New Jersey, but in Crystal Springs. The exterior shots of Crystal Springs took place in a small town not far from Los Angeles called Sierra Madre. The production company had a lot of trouble in Sierra Madre. One of the Hollywood trade papers explained the difficulty:

The cast of *You're Telling Me* shot some scenes in the town of Sierra Madre, but now Paramount and the cast have declared an embargo on the town. They went there this week [February 3, 1934] to shoot scenes. They rented a frame cottage. When time came to record with camera and sound, the lady of the house next to the studio cottage turned on her radio. Gnashing of teeth prevailed. They approached the lady and she said she had a right to play her own radio in her own sitting room. The assistant director paid her ten dollars to shut it off. More scenes had to be shot the next day, but when Fields and his troop got to Sierra Madre bright and early, a little boy ran indoors, told his mother the movie people were there, and in a jiffy the radio was going again. Then the

136

The burglar-catcher chair. From left, W. C., Robert McKenzie and James B. "Pop" Kenton.

One of those "tranquil" streets in Sierra Madre. W. C. is standing near the boom mike wearing a derby.

Relaxing with a drink as Tammany Young, Fields' majordomo and fellow actor, shows his respect for his benefactor.

You're Telling Me with, from left, Adrienne Ames, Del Henderson, Louise Carter, W. C., Tammany Young, Kathleen Howard and George Irving.

little boy and his brother were out in the yard not ten feet from the scene of action playing hockey with cans and broomsticks, yelling their heads off. An ambassador from the movie outing went to see the woman, but she wanted one hundred dollars to turn off her radio and get the kids inside. At that point the movie people did an automobile trip in a Paul Revere style to the office of the Sierra Madre chamber of commerce and the chief of police. The chief and the chamber secretary hurried up to talk things over with the lady and asked her in the name of civic pride to lay off—which she did for payment of one hundred and fifty dollars. But as the shooting was starting the lady two doors away and her family moved a bunch of card tables into the front yard and this ambitious woman began selling sandwiches and lemonade to all the curious who had been attracted to the scene. In between clinks of glasses and the hum of chatter Fields went through the scenes of his script, but all you have to do now is say Sierra Madre to Bill and he will fall into a swoon.

The direction of the film by Erle C. Kenton, a journeyman director who began with Sennett, was workmanlike and the quality of the film is pleasing. It is a very funny movie with some nice serious touches. Most of all,

it is a complete story and probably has the strongest plot of any of Fields' Paramount films. It proves that W. C. was not only a comedian with a unique style, look and delivery, but also he was a fine actor.

An interesting side note: In the credits, the following is noted, "Music by Arthur Johnston and lyrics by Sam Coslow." However, except for a little background music, there are definitely no lyrics. Before filming got under way a press release announced that Johnston and Coslow wrote a song for Fields. Perhaps he sang it in rehearsals, and the idea of making the movie a musical died then and there.

A non-musical note: Ray Bradbury, the writer of some of Hollywood's most imaginative science fiction, told the *Hollywood Reporter* of the time he met W. C. Fields while *You're Telling Me* was in production. Bradbury was fourteen then and awestruck upon arriving in Hollywood from Illinois. One of his first adventures was to roller skate from Pico and Western to Melrose Avenue and the famous Paramount gate. When he got there he excitedly handed his autograph book to a departing W. C. to inscribe the first entry. Fields obliged without expression and returned the boy's book and pen saying, "There you are, you little son of a bitch."

Fields in a publicity shot with the director of You're Telling Me, *Erle C. Kenton, and Erle's father, appropriately thumbing through a family photo album, James B. "Pop" Kenton.*

YOU'RE TELLING ME

67 minutes
Sound, black and white
Released April 6, 1934, by Paramount
Produced by William Le Baron for Paramount
Directed by Erle C. Kenton
Screenplay by Walter De Leon and Paul M. Jones
Adapted from "Mr. Bisbee's Princess," a 1925 *Redbook* magazine
  short story by Julian Leonard Street
Dialogue by J. P. McEvoy
Music by Arthur Johnston and lyrics by Sam Coslow
Photographed by Alfred Gilks
Art direction by Hans Dreier and Robert Odell
Edited by Otho Lovering
Sound recording by Earl S. Hayman

CAST:
W. C. Fields   Sam Bisbee, optician, optometrist, oculist
Joan Marsh   Pauline Bisbee
Larry "Buster" Crabbe   Bob Murchison
Adrienne Ames   H.R.H. Princess Lescaboura
Louise Carter   Mrs. Bessie Bisbee
Kathleen Howard   Mrs. Murchison
James B. "Pop" Kenton   Doc Beebe
Robert McKenzie   Charlie Bogle
George Irving   Pesident of the tire company
Jerry Stewart   Frobisher
Del Henderson   Mayer Brown
Nora Cecil   Mrs. Price

George MacQuarrie   Crabbe
John M. Sullivan   Gray
Vernon Dent   Fat man in train
Tammany Young   Caddy
Lee Phelps   First cop
Dorothy Vernon Bay   Mrs. Kendall, haughty passerby
Edward Le Saint   Conductor
Elise Cavanna   Mrs. Smith, gossip
Eddie Baker   Motorcycle police escort
James C. Morton   George Smith, gossip
Billy Engle   First lounger
George Ovey   Second lounger
Al Hart   Third lounger
Alfred Del Cambre   Phil Cummings
Frederic Sullivan   Mr. Murchison
William Robyns   Postman
Harold Berquist   Doorman
Frank O'Connor   Second cop
Florence Enright   Mrs. Kelly
Isabelle La Mal   Rosita
Hal Craig   Motor cop
Josephine Whittell   Bit

Filmed at Paramount in Hollywood, with location work not far from Los Angeles in the town of Sierra Madre.

Remake of *So's Your Old Man*, eight years earlier. The one-reel non-theatrical excerpt from this film is entitled *Much Ado About Golf*.

Hollywood On Parade B-10

—1934 —

With a couple of feature-length films under his belt, it was back to "promotion" for Fields and his second appearance in the *Hollywood on Parade* series. His work in B-10 was clearly impromptu, and little more than a pleasant throwaway. W. C., accompanied by Chico Marx, literally walked through the scene.

In what laughingly passes as a story line, a foursome of Earl Carroll's show girls are returning east by train. They are playing strip poker (what else?) and reminiscing about their stay in Hollywood. Ah, they remember with suspicious fondness their encounter with W. C. Fields on

the Paramount lot, and we are shown the event via flashback.

Spotting their prey, the Earl Carroll lovelies hurdle some hedges and intercept W. C. and Chico Marx, who is hardly recognizable out of costume and on his feet. It seems the comic pair had finished shooting for the day and are intent on leaving the studio. They are expensively dressed, smartly groomed and doubtlessly would wind up being the cynosure of high spirits somewhere that evening. The stars sign a few of the girls' autograph books. Then W. C. produces one of his own and asks the girls to sign his ledger . . . and include telephone numbers and addresses. After a few giggles and titters W. C. excuses himself. He has to go golfing. That is the end of his bit. We then cut back to the girls' game, and as the short progresses, so do the flashbacks and so does the strip poker. Sadly, time runs out after eleven minutes and we never find out who won the card game.

HOLLYWOOD ON PARADE (B-10)

One reel
Sound, black and white
Released April 27, 1934, by Paramount
Produced and directed by Louis Lewyn for Paramount

CAST:

Oscar Smith	Stuttering train porter	Gladys Henderson	Bride	W. C. Fields	Himself	Dick Powell	Himself

Oscar Smith — Stuttering train porter
Beryl Wallace — Earl Carroll show girl
Dorothy Daws — Fan dancer
Helen Kelly — Fan dancer

Gladys Henderson — Bride
Wilbur Clayton — Groom
Jack Oakie — Himself
Chico Marx — Himself

W. C. Fields — Himself
Jack LaRue — Himself
Buster Crabbe — Himself
Richard Arlen — Himself
Mitchell Leisen — Himself
Duke Ellington — Himself
Claudette Colbert — Herself
George Raft — Himself
Groucho Marx — Himself
Mary Pickford — Herself

Dick Powell — Himself
Mae West — Herself
Jimmy Durante — Himself
Max Baer Sr. — Himself
George Givot — Himself
Walter Huston — Himself
Ruth Etting — Herself
Clark Gable — Himself
Rhea Langham — Herself
Filmed at Paramount in Hollywood.

And more Paramount publicity. Here is how they captioned this one: "Telephone service deluxe.... When W. C. Fields, Paramount comedian, goes down to the beach to disport himself, so to speak, he manages to keep in touch with the outside world via a mammoth telephone and four dancing chickadees from the Paramount Studio."

The Old Fashioned Way
—1934—

It had worked and it had worked well. The reviewers loved it and so did the public. Paramount had taken a moderately successful silent Fields film called *So's Your Old Man,* reworked it for sound, renamed it *You're Telling Me,* and made it a hit. The Paramount brass probably patted themselves on the back for that one, then hunkered down to find a way to repeat the formula.

Meanwhile, on the other side of the Hollywood Hills in the San Fernando Valley, W. C. Fields was banging out a "new" script called *Playing the Sticks.* Well . . . Fields called it new. When a reporter asked him where he got the idea for his scenario W. C. told him that it came about one night while he was standing in line to see a motion picture. An old man had introduced himself. The fellow said that he had owned a vaudeville theatre many years ago which was terribly in the red. Fields, traveling with a stock company then, had performed in the man's theatre. That one show had saved the manager's business.

"If it hadn't been for your company," the old man said, "I would have had to close." Then the fellow

wanted to know if there was anything he could do for W. C. in return.

"You already have, my good man, you already have." After which, Fields told the reporter, he went home, wrote the story and the next day sold it to Paramount.

Meanwhile, back on the other side of the hills, the trades touted a new script which had been submitted to Paramount by H. M. "Beanie" Walker. It was called *Grease Paint* and designed as W. C.'s next starring vehicle. And there was another script called *The Great McGonigle,* and the trades advertised yet another one entitled *Hearts and Flowers.* Well, final credits on the film read that *The Old Fashioned Way* was based on an original story by Charles Bogle (W. C. Fields) called *Playing the Sticks.* This "original" and "new" business may have been a bit misleading, because barely hidden behind minor plot changes, *Playing the Sticks* was simply a retooling of *Two Flaming Youths.* Instead of playing Gabby Gilfoil, W. C. became the Great McGonigle, leading not a circus but a company of traveling mendicant thespians

. . . and there was a brass band at Bellefontaine—unfortunately not for the Great McGonigle Company. Note the bass drum. It reads, "Knights of Mathias—Bellefontaine, Chapter 418."

who play *The Drunkard* in small-town fin-de-siècle gas-light theatres. But the story itself—Fields and the Sheriff vying for the affections of an obnoxious wealthy widow—was the same, and so were most of the attendant follies. The important differences, however, were that Fields had more freedom this time around, he was allowed to create new scenes, and as this was sound, he could ad-lib to his heart's content.

W. C. was taking a chance. *Two Flaming Youths* by all accounts was a terrible movie. Evidently Fields was sure of himself. Now with sound, and the studio loosening his leash, he felt confident he could turn the former bomb into an explosion of laughs.

When Paramount received Fields' script they must have been elated to see that their star thought as they did—turn another W. C. silent into a talkie. For whatever reasons, Walker's original concept was abandoned in favor of *Playing the Sticks,* which of course was renamed *The Old Fashioned Way.*

The Great McGonigle's group of rambling actors is waiting in the train for their leader, Mark Antony McGonigle, to arrive. Their next performance of *The Drunkard* is scheduled for Bellefontaine. Outside on the train platform the Sheriff, with summons in hand, also awaits the severely indebted impresario. The officer is sure to nab him this time. With a gleeful look on his face he slyly holds the piece of paper behind his back.

Luck would have it that McGonigle approaches from that direction. He sees the summons, walks up quietly and lights it on fire. With the document sufficiently aflame, McGonigle, cigar in hand, casually walks in front of the Sheriff. The Sheriff stops him. Confident of his catch, he happily intones, "I have something for you." He reveals the now flaming document, which McGonigle uses to light his cigar. He graciously thanks the enraged officer and boards the train. Next stop Bellefontaine!

McGonigle addresses his mutinous crew with Micawber optimism, promising that Bellefontaine will bring them fame and fortune, a promise evidently made many times before. When the conductor demands tickets from the troupe McGonigle points him to his dimwitted majordomo, Marmaduke Gump. That trifle out of the way, McGonigle sits down next to his daughter.

Another passenger passing in the aisle accidentally drops his sleeping berth ticket and McGonigle puts his foot on it. When the coast is clear he picks up the berth ticket, but Betty, his daughter, scolds him for the dishonesty and tells him to return it. He agrees easily. He will look for the rightful owner, but he warns his daughter not to expect him back soon because he might play a few rounds of Parchesi before retiring. He heads for the sleeper car, finds the bunk designated on his ticket and hops into bed. With the original ticket owner yelling and screaming, McGonigle causes a hornets' nest of trouble, but in the end he keeps the usurped sleeper.

The next day while freshening up in the lounge Fields gives a fat Turk some sage counsel. The Turk has complained about insomnia. McGonigle: "I have the perfect cure for insomnia—get plenty of sleep." After instigating more havoc in the sleeping car McGonigle returns to his charges in the coach section.

His sleepy, grouchy company moan and complain, but McGonigle hypes them with more promises for their Bellefontaine engagement. He reads a telegram he has just received which claims that the house has been sold out in advance, so wrote their agent, Snead Hearn. When the company hears the name they know the letter is bogus and grumble their derision.

As the train slows to a stop at Bellefontaine, McGonigle optimistically states that he would not be surprised if a brass band were awaiting their arrival. His troupe has heard it all before. But there, in the town of Bellefontaine, *is* a brass band playing its heart out. The entire company is pleased and astounded, the most astounded being McGonigle.

Mark Antony leads his little family of players off the train. He is carrying a cane and wearing a top hat and a billowing coat with an enormous sunflower attached to the lapel. As the band continues playing, McGonigle thanks the citzenry for the warm reception and recounts in redolent verse the trials and tribulations of those such as himself whose sad lot it is to wander the world knowing only fame, adulation and wealth. At the end of his speech McGonigle extends his hand to the head of the welcoming committee, but alas, all the hoopla has been for the high-muck-a-muck of a local brotherhood lodge. The leader, who has been trying to push his way past McGonigle, finally breaks free and performs the ceremonial handshake with the greeting committee. The lodge chieftain is the same fellow McGonigle dislodged from the sleeping berth the night before.

Undaunted, McGonigle and his troupe parade into town waving to the citizenry. Finally he leads his players to Mrs. Wendelschaffer's boardinghouse. Soon after they arrive, the lunch bell sounds, followed immediately by a wild stampede of hungry boarders. With all the other boarders sitting at the table slurping soup, McGonigle takes the opportunity to introduce himself in the most pompous manner. Finished with the spiel he sits down next to Cleopatra Pepperday, an obnoxious, silly but wealthy widow. The wealth and the widowhood attract McGonigle, even though he thinks she looks "all dressed up like a well-kept grave."

Cleo has a baby son named Albert, who greets McGonigle with "Dada," much to McGonigle's horror. In order to win Cleo's bank account, however, he tolerates not only the billing but the little brat's irreverence for the Great McGonigle's talents. Even when Baby Albert, really Baby LeRoy, dumps McGonigle's watch in molasses, the impresario holds his anger. Cleo apologizes, hoping the stunt did not hurt the watch, but McGonigle eases her concern: "How can you possibly hurt a watch by dipping it in molasses? It just makes me love the little nipper all the more."

Albert continues to bother McGonigle, tweaking his nose and such, which surprises Cleo: "I don't know why he's behaving like this. You should see him when he is alone."

"Yes, I'd like to catch him when he's alone."

The Great McGonigle with his daughter, Betty (played by the gorgeous Judith Allen).

Baby LeRoy grabbing a fistful of nose as the owner looks on.

In between scenes on the set of The Old Fashioned Way *with W. C. and Jan Duggan.*

Suddenly one of those newfangled motorcars putt-putts down the street. The luncheon crew rushes outside to see the horseless carriage, except for little Albert and McGonigle. Albert walks to the doorway and, putting his hands on his knees, bends over. McGonigle makes sure the opportunity is as perfect as it seems. He checks the room for any witnesses, sees the coast is clear and kicks Baby Albert square on the seat of his pants. Contentedly, McGonigle walks away leaving Albert sprawled on the floor. The "Great" then turns his attention to wooing the wealthy Cleopatra Pepperday. He finds her in the parlor, sits down next to her and intimates he has room for her talents in his stock company. Flattered and willing to show her wares, she sings a turturous little ditty about collecting seashells at the seashore. Although McGonigle is nauseated, he is also penurious and therefore compliments the screeching soprano on her extraordinary talent. Cleo is flattered and boasts, "I can act as well as I can sing."

McGonigle: "I'm sure of it." He promises her a future on the stage, with his help of course. But in order to secure fame for her he will need considerable financial assistance. Cleo gladly agrees.

Unfortunately, competing for Ms. Pepperday's affec-

tions is Bellefontaine's Sheriff Jones. He sees McGonigle courting his Cleo. He must foil the actor's plans. He finds something shifty in McGonigle's style, so he checks the criminal records and discovers that the impresario is wanted for default of payments throughout the country. He wants to put McGonigle and his crew in the pokey. But Cleo threatens never to see him again if he does. She has been given an important line in McGonigle's production and cannot tolerate the thought of her cicerone thrown in jail before her debut. She settles the issue by clearing McGonigle's debt with her own money.

It is performance night. Cleo paces backstage practicing her line, "Here comes the prince." Onstage McGonigle plays the malevolent Squire Cribbs. He has doctored the original *Drunkard* skit a bit, adding his own lines here and there, such as "It ain't a fit night out for man or beast." The play stinks, but McGonigle continues in the best tradition of stage actors: The show must go on even in the face of adversity—falling curtains, wrong sets and incorrect cues. At intermission Cleo wonders why she has not been called yet. McGonigle calms her, promising that her debut is at hand. The intermission also affords Joe Morrison, playing the part of Wally Livingston, a chance to sing solo "A Little Bit of Heaven Known as

Mother." Wally is from a rich family, but he dropped out of school to pursue a stage career. He hooked up with the Great McGonigle troupe and now has fallen in love with Betty McGonigle. Betty loves him yet she knows he should be back in school. His love is too strong. He cannot leave her. Meanwhile, old man Livingston, angry that his son dropped out of school, and infuriated that he signed up with the no-account McGonigle company, has finally caught up to his son in Bellefontaine. Backstage, father and son fight over Wally's future. Wally wants to marry Betty, the father will not hear of it under the present circumstances. Betty says she will marry Wally only if he returns to school, and finally all agree.

With *The Drunkard* over, the Great McGonigle returns to the stage to perform his wonderful juggling routine. He balances twelve cigar boxes, he juggles four balls, he balances a stick on one foot, then kicks it over to the other foot, and he retrieves apparent "mistakes" with amazing precision. Baby Albert ends the act by tossing a tomato, which hits Fields' nose. The curtain drops. "Drat!"

Backstage, Gump hands McGonigle a telegram. The show has been cancelled. McGonigle keeps the distressing news quiet until he can figure out what to tell his troupe. In his dressing room he overhears Wally and

Judith Allen coddling W. C. in this publicity still. In real life there was talk they were having an affair, which could explain the somewhat embarrassed look on Fields' face.

Making movies is tougher than it looks. Everyone crowds around and stares, no one may laugh or applaud, while the actor performs what he believes to be surefire laugh getters. Here W. C. is pulling a sewing needle from his posterior in this scene from The Old Fashioned Way.

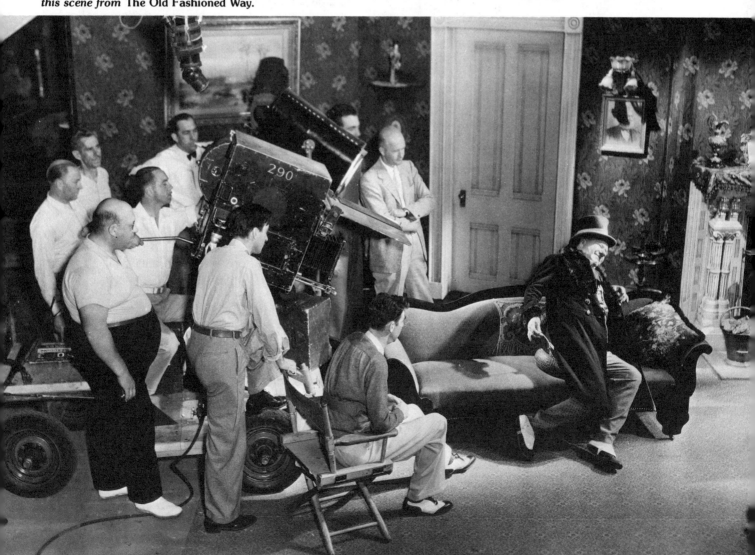

Traveling on a velocipede with that "Trojan infant Baby LeRoy." Again Fields has Baby LeRoy perched on his shoulders (see photo from Tillie and Gus*). This picture was taken in front of a Paramount soundstage.*

Betty talking about marriage. Betty does not know what to do. She cannot leave her father. McGonigle hears this and walks into Betty's dressing room. He tells her he has just received an invitation to head for New York immediately. They want him for the stage, but sadly only him, so he is forced to leave his daughter. Both Wally and Betty feel relieved and they tell him about their plans to marry. He announces that now they will *all* be happy.

The movie ends showing Fields on a soap box barking the glories of an old-fashioned Indian medicine that cures hoarseness. "Even the most stubborn cases of hoarseness." His voice scratches. The harder he talks the less he can be heard. He then takes a swig of his own medicine and his voice booms louder and clearer than ever. It is the Yackwee Indian Medical Discovery and Pine Tar Remedy.

Released in mid-July 1934, *The Old Fashioned Way* received hefty praise from the critics, and it made good money at the box office as well. The film reassured Paramount that Fields could carry a movie solo. Furthermore, it proved that, given a free hand, W. C. could collect praise, money and laughs.

The Old Fashioned Way bore the distinctive mark of a Fields frolic. Except for Joe Morrison singing "A Little Bit of Heaven Known as Mother," one could easily see Fields' hand in every scene. (Incidentally, this was Joe Morrison's screen debut; he was a radio personality of the time, famous as the singer of "The Last Roundup.") Of course the shadow of *Two Flaming Youths* loomed throughout the story line; but with sound and Fields' generous ad-libbing *The Old Fashioned Way* looked brand-new.

For the first time since his silent days, W. C. included a fat bit of juggling in a movie. Several Paramount execs were transplanted New Yorkers who knew all about Fields' notorious tossing talent. They wanted to add it to his talking movies, but up until now he had always demurred. He was in his mid-fifties. He knew the zip and timing of his once perfectly fluid ability was dying. In the old days he even avoided coffee because it might have made his nerves less reliable while tossing a hat or ball. Now he knew his love for alcohol had certainly taken away his sureness in a throw. It was his pride that held him back. Time had robbed him of his gifts, he thought. But this film was tailor-made for a strong spot of juggling and Fields knew it, and so he finally acceded to the studio's longtime cajoleries and juggled in *The Old Fashioned Way*.

The piece was shot by a stationary camera. He was on stage. It was as if the viewer was part of a vaudeville audience watching W. C. Fields, Juggler Extraordinaire, ply his trade. It is difficult to believe that some of his talent was missing in this piece. It is a wonderful look at his amazing juggling ability.

Fields also included in his script parts of *The Drunkard*. It is not surprising how the idea of his stock company performing that play came to him. A year earlier, a group of Los Angeles actors revived the vintage play. The original was intended as a morality play to highlight the evils of the "devil's brew," but by 1934 the hackneyed script, the melodramatic direction and the recent repeal of Prohibition made this serious drama a hilarious satire. Undoubtedly Fields went to see it. He used some of that Los Angeles cast, and *The Old Fashioned Way* premiered on the first-year anniversary of the L.A. revival.

W. C.'s newfound creative freedom probably came from his understanding producer, William Le Baron. This is the first talking film on which the two friends worked— at least officially. Of course they were pals in New York, it was Le Baron who got Fields started at Paramount in the silent days, and he probably had a hand in signing Fields to his most recent long-term Paramount contract; but this was the first Fields talking film in which Le Baron was given screen credit. He in turn let his friend do almost anything he wanted for the picture, including drinking on the set. Up until now Paramount had been quite anxious about Fields' tippling, but Le Baron knew W. C.'s penchant for the brew and let him drink freely as long as it did not interfere with his work. It never did. Anyway, to Fields it was not drinking; he was taking his "treatment." This was how the "treatment" euphemism got started.

It seems that drinking was not the only cause of Paramount's anxiety with Fields. His nose caused some nervousness. Figuring that Fields was probably sensitive about his enormous proboscis, they made sure no one ever teased him about it. During the lunch scene with Baby LeRoy, the little nipper grabbed that enormous Fields trademark and twisted it. The production crew held its breath. They waited for W. C. to rail against the child, but instead the comedian played along. Later someone respectfully asked W. C. if he was sensitive about his large facial appendage.

"To the contrary, I take inordinate pride in my nose. Indeed, I have treatment done on it every day." At which point Tammany Young walked over and gave Fields a drink (pineapple juice and rum, his favorite concoction in the early thirties). He raised his glass: "My daily treatment."

Fields' incessant drinking shocked many reporters. They said W. C.'s dressing room was the best-stocked bar in town. Some of them added, if any other actor was caught drinking on or off the set he would be fired before the ice melted, but not Fields. However, they all agreed that the booze never seemed to affect the comedian.

Evidently something did affect Fields, however. Her name was Judith Allen. The trades were filled with stories of a love affair between the two. Apparently there was one. It was short-lived.

From love to hate. The trades also talked openly about the feud between Baby LeRoy and W. C. Fields. It was of course publicity, and Fields added fodder to the rumors. Paramount claimed they reserved forty square feet of space on a wall so Fields could post his complaints about the child. On one sign Fields wrote, "I am mad at Baby LeRoyoff. Baby LeRoyoff has libeled me. He says I stole his bottle. Baby LeRoyoff is all wet. Baby LeRoyoff is a menace, he steals scenes." The studio kept the feud going in the trade papers, and it was all in fun. On the set it was a bit different. In the scene in which Fields kicked Baby LeRoy in the fundament, the original blow was solid. He knocked the kid in the air. The Paramount people demanded it be cut, fearing a roar of disapproval from the audience. Fields fought for it. They compromised, with Fields promising that if they reshot the scene he would not kick the little chap so hard. When asked why he fought so fiercely to keep the piece in the film, Fields responded, "There's not a man in the world who hasn't had a secret desire to boot a kid."

THE OLD FASHIONED WAY
66 minutes
Sound, black and white
Released July 13, 1934, by Paramount
Produced by William Le Baron for Paramount
Presented by Adolph Zukor
Directed by William Beaudine
Based on an original story entitled "Playing the Sticks," by Charles Bogle (W. C. Fields)
Screenplay by Garnett Weston and Jack Cunningham
Photographed by Benjamin Reynolds
Music by Harry Revel and lyrics by Mack Gordon
Songs: "Rolling in Love," "A Little Bit of Heaven Known as Mother" and "The Sea Shell Song"
Art direction by John Goodman
Sound recording by P. G. Wisdom

CAST:
W. C. Fields   The Great (Mark Antony) McGonigle
Judith Allen   Betty McGonigle
Joe Morrison   Wally Livingston
Jan Duggan   Cleopatra Pepperday
Nora Cecil   Mrs. Wendelschaffer
Baby LeRoy (Overacker)   Albert Pepperday
Jack Mulhall   Dick Bronson
Joe Mills   Charles Lowell
Samuel Ethridge   Bartley Neuville
Emma Ray   Mother Mack
Ruth Marion   Agatha Sprague
Richard Carle   Sheriff from Barnesville
Tammany Young   Marmaduke Gump, company manager and amicus curiae
Lew Kelly   Sheriff Walter Jones
Adrienne Ames   Girl in audience
Clarence Wilson   New Philadelphia Sheriff Prettywillie
Edward Le Saint   Conductor
Billy Bletcher   Man who throws tomato
Otis Harlan   Mr. Wendelschaffer
Robert McKenzie   Checkers player
Dorothy Ray   Bertha
Georgie Billings   Kid in railroad car
Oscar Apfel   Wally's father, Mr. Livingston
Maxine Elliott Hicke   Waitress
Davidson Clark   Passenger who loses ticket
Marvin Lobach   Man sleeping beneath Fields
Oscar Smith   Porter
Sam McDaniels   Porter
Duke York   Stagehand
Sam Flint   Man with the mallet
The Cast of *The Drunkard*:
Larry Grenier   Drover Stevens
Ruth Marion   Mary Wilson
William Blatchford   Landlord of the saloon
Joe Morrison   William Dowton
Jeffrey Williams   Mrs. Arden Rencelaw
W. C. Fields   Squire Cribbes
Samuel Ethridge   Edward Middleton (drunkard)
Judith Allen   Anges Dowton
Donald Brown   The minister
Tom Miller   The villager

Filmed at Paramount in Hollywood.
    Parts cut from the final release print: Del Henderson, Fred Holmes.
    Reworking of *Two Flaming Youths* of seven years earlier. Working titles: *Hearts and Flowers, The Great McGonigle* and *Grease Paint,* which was the title of the original story submitted in January by H. M. "Beanie" Walker. Originally Fields was to have played a tragic clown with a broken heart and was to have been directed by Walker's friend and Our Gang's mentor, Robert F. McGowan. Then Elliott Nugent was assigned the direction in late March, before William Beaudine ultimately took over and received screen credit as director.
    The one-reel non-theatrical excerpt from this film is entitled *The Great McGonigle.*

Mrs. Wiggs Of The Cabbage Patch

—1934—

In the midsummer of 1934, W. C. Fields, Jack Cunningham and Norman McLeod took Richard Arlen's yacht and went sailing for a week to turn an original story by W. C. Fields into a working script. A reviewer noted, "Can you imagine that a story written by these three and under such conditions would bother to have a plot?" When they came back, and after spending some time drying out, production began on the consensus favorite Fields film, *It's a Gift.*

Meanwhile, on another part of the studio grounds Pauline Lord and Zasu Pitts were shooting *Mrs. Wiggs of the Cabbage Patch.* This was the third of four times a studio would make a movie based on Alice Hegan Rice's melodramatic story of the same name. Norman Taurog was directing. Taurog directed Fields in *If I Had a Million* a few years earlier. Evidently, after seeing the rushes for *Mrs. Wiggs,* the director decided that the show definitely needed a comic lift. He immediately thought of Fields, knew he was working on the lot, persuaded the comedian to take a short hiatus from *It's a Gift* and put him to work in *Mrs. Wiggs of the Cabbage Patch.*

It is Thanksgiving at the Wiggs home, a family suffering from abject poverty. Mrs. Wiggs heads the household of five children, Billy, Australia, Asia, Europena and Jimmy, and their dog named Klondike. A few years earlier the ruminative Mr. Wiggs "thunk" himself into a long journey and has not been seen since.

The Wiggs family Thanksgiving dinner is nothing more than leftover stew. But they are thankful even for that much. Mrs. Wiggs has a rich friend, Miss Lucy. She feels sorry for poor Mrs. Wiggs and sends over a real feast for Thanksgiving, turkey and all the trimmings. The stew is put aside and the table is ready for a great meal. Mrs. Wiggs wants to share her good fortune with her equally downtrodden friend Miss Hazy, Zasu Pitts, and invites her to dinner. Suddenly, Bob Redding, Miss Lucy's fiancé, shows up. He and his betrothed are in the middle of a lovers' spat and he desperately wants Mrs. Wiggs' advice.

While pouring out his troubles, Bob notices little Jimmy's terrible cough and arranges a hospital room for Mrs. Wiggs' youngest boy. Without Bob's help Mrs. Wiggs could not afford the professional care. So all in all the Wiggs clan has a very good Thanksgiving.

A few days before the holiday Billy, the oldest son, received a worn-out horse from a traveling salesman, who gave it up for dead. The Wiggses nursed the old mare to health and now after the holidays the horse is strong enough to pull Billy's wagon. Now the boy can make some money selling kindling wood. For one wagonload he gets five tickets to the local theatre. That evening the excited Wiggs family heads for the performance, except for poor Jimmy, who lies in the hospital in serious condition. Suddenly during the show Mrs. Wiggs is paged. She has to go to the hospital. Jimmy is dying. She makes the trip in time to see the young boy pass away.

After a time of mourning, Mrs. Wiggs pulls herself out of depression and to distract her mind decides to help Miss Hazy secure a husband. They go for a mail-order mate. Mr. C. Ellsworth Stubbins, W. C. Fields, answers the advertisement and sends a picture of himself—young and dapper. This is the man for Miss Hazy. But when Mr. Stubbins finally shows up Miss Hazy is shocked to see a gin-drenched broken-down old ham actor. He explains the difference between the young picture and the real thing, giving a tale of woe; and though not overly zealous, Hazy does take a liking to the man. She will marry him. But Stubbins balks. After entering the house and tripping flat on his face, then dispensing with the customary amenities, he explains his fondness for food and will only marry Hazy if she can cook. She cannot, but she does not tell him that. That evening Mrs. Wiggs cooks a scrumptious meal and gives it to Miss Hazy. Hazy serves it to Mr. Stubbins, taking credit for the fine meal. Delighted with the results of this culinary test, Stubbins agrees to marriage.

More trouble brewing. The Wiggses' landlord, Mr. Bagby, has threatened to foreclose on the Wiggs home unless they can pay him twenty-five dollars for the mortgage. Bob and Miss Lucy catch wind of the debt and place advertisements in newspapers throughout the country, hoping to locate Mr. Wiggs and get him back home to help his family out of the jam. No need for the ads, because suddenly Mr. Wiggs returns home just as sorry-looking, thoughtful und beleaguered as when he left. Undaunted by his panhandler looks, Mrs. Wiggs searches her husband's pockets for the twenty-five-dollar dun, and much to everyone's delight finds the exact amount folded neatly in Mr. Wiggs' pants. Furthermore, Bob and Lucy make up. Everyone is happy, and they gaily go to Miss Lucy's and Bob's wedding.

Fields' shadow, Tammany Young, helps his ailing friend through the Paramount lot. Fields severely twisted his ankle while playing tennis and it made production of Mrs. Wiggs of the Cabbage Patch a painful experience.

Reaching the silver screen on October 19, 1934, Mrs. Wiggs of the Cabbage Patch received mostly miserable reviews. Indeed, the best comment complimented the piece for not being worse than it was. But without exception the critics liked Fields' work and most said he saved the film from (as one reviewer wrote) "box office anemia singlehandedly due to his popularity." Even with W. C., however, the film could not be saved from universal pans. It was difficult to blame anyone in particular for its failure. After all, the film worked well in the silent versions, but for a nation made threadbare by the miseries of the great Depression, romanticizing poverty was tactless, if not downright stupid. Fortunately, with Fields' and Zasu's comedy and Taurog's consistently fine direction the movie took a step up from an insult to just an old corny story. Unfortunately, Fields did not appear on screen until the last twenty minutes, too late for him to bring the outdated plot to a comedic level. The film was just barely successful at the box office, and all the credit

Fields interrupted the production of It's a Gift *to film his scenes in* Mrs. Wiggs. *After a week of work with director Norman Taurog, W. C. went back to the* It's a Gift *set. Here he stands with his mentor and longtime friend William Le Baron (center) and* It's a Gift *director Norman McLeod.*

Miss Hazy (Zazu Pitts, left) being introduced by Mrs. Wiggs (Pauline Lord) to her mail-order husband, Mr. Stubbins.

belonged to the now popular Fields and Norman Taurog, according to the trades. This is not to say the rest of the actors were bad but that the story was ill-timed.

Apparently Taurog and Fields got along quite well. There was a story, however, that after filming one particularly troublesome scene and after many retakes the camera ran out of film. Taurog cut production: "Camera reloading!" Fields headed for his dressing room. It took a few minutes to reload the camera, then Taurog yelled, "Company onstage!" All the actors filed back to the set. After a few more minutes the sound machine ran out of film. Taurog yelled, "Cut, sound reloading!" Fields headed back to his dressing room. Again it took a few minutes to reload the sound equipment, and then Taurog yelled, "Company on stage!" Everyone returned except for W. C. Taurog set up the scene, then noticed Fields was absent. "Where's Bill Fields?" From W. C.'s dressing room came the nasal twang: "Fields reloading."

Fields played this film in a great deal of pain. A week prior to production he tore the ligaments and tendons in his ankle. On the set he used crutches until his scene came, then Tammany Young would hand his boss a cane and take the crutches away, and Fields tried to walk as best he could. In fact at one point he apologized to Taurog for forgetting his lines, complaining that "this darn bad leg bothers me so much." Somewhat bewildered, Taurog replied, "That's all right, Bill, but this is the first time I've ever heard of anybody talking with his feet."

It is curious that Fields would take so many of these utility-player roles. Either he was simply grateful to be working or anxious to prove himself, and doing so with the confidence that he could steal any film with any role. So many of these Paramount features are not Fields vehicles. Contemporaries such as Chaplin, Will Rogers, Harold Lloyd and the Marx Brothers would never have served as secondary figures. Then, perhaps, there was an unwritten agreement between W. C. and Paramount or Le Baron that he would do these roles when asked and in kind he would be granted freedom on his own sets. If that is the case, we can be grateful *Mrs. Wiggs* gifted Fields with the freedom to create a masterpiece. After a week with her, W. C. went back to shooting *It's a Gift*.

MRS. WIGGS OF THE CABBAGE PATCH

80 minutes
Sound, black and white
Released October 19, 1934, by Paramount
Produced by Douglas MacLean for Paramount
Presented by Adolph Zukor
Directed by Norman Taurog
Screenplay by William Slavens McNutt and Jane Storm
Based on an original story by Alice Hegan Rice and Anne Crawford Flexner
Photographed by Charles Lang
Art direction by Hans Dreier and Robert Odell
Songs: "Comin' Thro' the Rye," "Glow Little Glow Worm," "Wait Till the Sun Shines, Nellie," "Listen to the Mocking Bird" and "Swanee River"

CAST:
Pauline Lord — Mrs. Elvira Wiggs
W. C. Fields — Mr. C. Ellsworth Stubbins
Zasu Pitts — Miss Tabitha Hazy
Evelyn Venable — Lucy Olcott
Kent Taylor — Bob Redding
Charles Middleton — Bagby
Donald Meek — Mr. Hiram Wiggs
Jimmy Butler — Billy Wiggs
George Breakston — Jimmy Wiggs
Edith Fellows — Australia Wiggs
Virginia Weidler — Europena Wiggs
Carmencita Johnson — Asia Wiggs
George Reed — Julius, servant
Mildred Gover — Priscilla, maid
Arthur Housman — Dick Harris, the drunk
Walter Walker — Dr. Barton
Sam Flint — Mr. Jenkins, railroad agent
Edward Tamblyn — Eddie, usher
Del Henderson — Theatre manager
Lillian Elliott — Mrs. Bagby
James Robinson — Mose
Bentley Hewlett — Box-office man
Al Shaw — First comedian
Sam Lee — Second comedian
George Pearce — Minister
Earl Pingree — Brakeman
Ann Sheridan — Girl
Tyler Brooke — Ticket taker

Filmed at Paramount in Hollywood.

Three other versions of *Mrs. Wiggs of the Cabbage Patch* were made: in 1914 by California Motion Picture Corporation, and in 1919 and 1942 by Paramount.

Its A Gift

—1934—

The critics liked W. C. Fields, audiences loved his fun making, and the former Paramount doubters now felt he could carry his own in a movie—no problem. Receiving what was reported as near carte blanche from the studio, Fields started production on possibly the funniest film of his career, *It's a Gift*. Once again W. C. resurrected some surefire stage material and put it on the screen. And once again the stage material was from the 1925 play called *The Comic Supplement*, co-written by W. C. and J. P. McEvoy. Many of the set pieces in this film first appeared in movie form in the silent *It's the Old Army Game*. Although the plot was similar, this new film was more than a simple remake of Fields' silent movie.

Fields plays Harold Bissonette, who is the father to two disrespectful offspring and the husband to a complaining, pompous termagent, Amelia Bissonette. (She wants her name pronounced Mrs. Bis-o-nay, and Harold has a devil of a time reminding his friends of the correct pronunciation: "Never call me Mr. Bissonette in front of Mrs. Bissonette. It's Bis-o-nay.") His low standing in the household is immediately evident. It is morning and

Harold is shaving in the bathroom. He is standing in front of the mirror. Mildred, his late-adolescent daughter, bursts in, cuts in front of her father, opens the mirror to pull something from the medicine cabinet, closes the mirror, opens it again, pulls out a brush, closes it, starts brushing her hair, and all the while her father is trying to shave. He gives up. Harold grabs a small mirror, ties it to an electric light string and tries it again. The mirror keeps turning in a circle. Finally he faces the mirror toward the ground, brings over a small stool, lies supine looking into the dangling mirror and continues to shave. He does not notice his daughter has left. Amelia enters the bathroom to read a telegram to her husband, but seeing him in the peculiar position demands to know what he is doing. Defensively Harold points to the mirror that his daughter usurped and starts to explain, but Mildred is gone, so he cowers back to the big mirror.

Finishing his toiletries, Harold dresses and heads downstairs for breakfast. Unfortunately, at the top of the stairs he steps on his young son Norman's formerly missing skate and flies down the full flight, landing in the breakfast room flat on his back. He picks himself up and sits at the table, taking a carnation from his lapel and a cigar from his pocket. Unconsciously, he sticks the flower in his mouth and puts the cigar in his water glass. The table conversation centers on Uncle Bean's imminent demise and the resultant inheritance for the Bissonette's.

Norman spills the beans to his family that his father is going to buy a California orange grove with the willed money. Mildred's boyfriend, John Durston, a real estate salesman, has arranged the sale. During the conversation Harold has grabbed for eggs, bacon and some pancakes, but each time either Mildred, Amelia or Norman has gotten there first and finished off the last bit of food. Harold is stuck with just coffee. He wants some sugar. He checks the sugar bowl, but it is empty except for a few granules stuck to the side. He pours his coffee into the sugar bowl, swishes it around, then pours it back into his cup. With Norman's news Mildred runs out of the room crying. She thinks her father is an ogre for disrupting the family with his orange grove scheme and forcing her to leave her love, John Durston. This leads Amelia into her worn-out tale of woe: how she has struggled so gallantly to keep the family together and how Harold has done all he can to tear it apart. During the sermon Harold sneaks away from the table and walks into the kitchen, where Mildred is crying. With bravado, but in a whisper, he tells his daughter, "Listen you all got to realize one thing. That I"—he looks over his shoulder to make sure Amelia cannot hear and says in a lower voice—"am the master of this household."

Harold runs the town's grocery store. He heads for work. The front door of his store consists of two matching window doors. One of them is open. A little girl, Jane Withers, plays hopscotch in front of the store, but Harold shoos her away—bad for business. He fidgets with his key and lock for a while and then discovers that the other door is already open. He enters to find his assistant, Everett (played by Tammany Young), already working.

The first customer is a man in a hurry. He needs ten pounds of cumquats. Harold begins to write down the

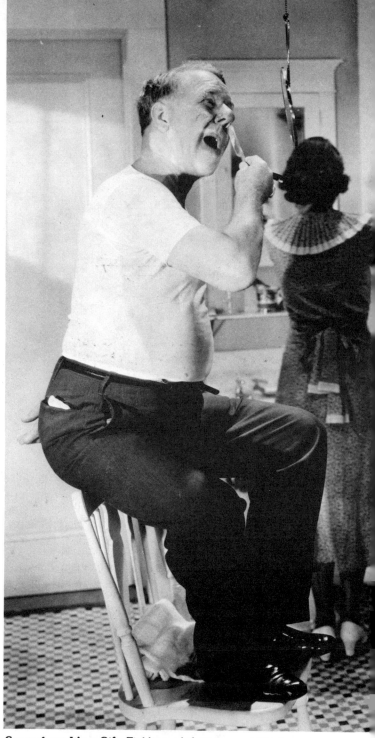

Scene from It's a Gift. *Fields used the same routine in* The Potters, *a silent film. For comparison see a similar photograph under that title.*

order, but suddenly he sees his blind and near-deaf friend heading straight for the closed door with his cane wagging dangerously close to the glass. In a tizzy, Mr. Bissonette yells to Everett, "Open the door for Mr. Muckle! Open the door for Mr. Muckle the blind man!" The dim-witted assistant cannot quite make out the command, so Harold rushes to the door himself. Too late! Mr. Muckle's cane has shattered the glass. Muckle admonishes Bissonette: "You got that door closed again."

Harold Bissonette giving a helping hand to Mr. Muckle (Charles Sellon), "the house detective over at the Grand Hotel." Counting International House, that made two jibes at the MGM film in which "nothing ever happens. . . ."

"It's all right. It's all right," Harold cajoles through Mr. Muckle's hearing horn. He places the blind man on a chair directly across from a pile of light bulbs and some glassware. He pleads with him to stay seated: "Please, Mr. Muckle. Please, dear."

"How about my cumquats?" Harold rushes back to the counter and begins to write the order again. Crash! A light bulb falls. Mr. Muckle swings his cane menacingly over the pile of bulbs. Crash! Another one falls.

"Please sit down, Mr. Muckle! Please, honey!" Crash! Harold leaves the counter and rushes to Muckle. He grabs him. Muckle struggles and there goes the glassware. Bissonette must get the old man out of his store. What does he want?

"Chewing gum!"

Bissonette grabs the gum, wraps it in a huge package and hands it to Mr Muckle: "That'll be five cents please!"

"I'm not going to lug that with me. Send it!" That will be fine. Mr. Muckle leaves, sticking his cane through the other door window this time. Harold helps him to the curb, checks the placid street and lets Mr. Muckle go the rest of the way. The road erupts in heavy traffic, with cars, trucks and trolleys just missing the blind man. Harold winces and shudders with each passing, but Muckle makes it.

"How about my cumquats?"

Harold runs back into the store. The cumquat man demands, "How does he rate all this attention. Who is that man?"

"He's the house detective over at the Grand Hotel."

Now Harold is ready to write down the order for cumquats. One problem: "How do you spell it?"

"C-u-m-q-u-a-t-s!"

Harold writes. "Oh, ah, c-u-m . . ." He looks at the man quizzically.

"Q-u-a-t-s! Quats! *Quats!*"

"Two quats?"

Harold gets the spelling right just as Amelia enters. It seems Uncle Bean has died. Harold excuses himself again from the customer and goes to the back room to discuss the details. Uncle Bean was at a picnic and choked on an orange, got a heart attack and died instantly.

"I didn't know oranges were bad for the heart."

"It was the excitement."

"Oh, yeah . . . the excitement."

From the counter: "How about my ten pounds of cumquats?"

Amelia: "If you don't have any cumquats, why don't you tell him?" The man storms out.

Just as Amelia leaves, John Durston enters. He tells Harold that his real estate company has made a big mistake. The land they sold him is barren, nothing can grow on it, but his company is willing to refund the money. No deal! Harold figures the company wants the deed back because they found out the place was sold too cheaply. He kicks Durston out.

Meanwhile, Mrs. Dunk, the Bissonettes' neighbor, enters and wants to buy some food. "What do you have in the way of steak?"

"I have nothing in the way of steak. I can get right to them."

She orders her meat and asks Everett to babysit her little boy, Baby Ellwood. Harold brings the steak out, weighs it, along with part of his arm, and writes up the bill. Now he has time to dream of his "typical California orange ranch.'' With Bean dead, the $5,000 inheritance will be enough to buy the whole thing. It's a gift. He goes back to his counter and sees Baby Ellwood wading in a pool of molasses. Ellwood had turned on the spigot to the molasses keg. Harold berates his assistant, but Everett has a defense: "I told him I wouldn't do it if I was him.'' Mrs. Dunk returns, screams, grabs her baby and promises never to enter the store again. Bissonette turns to Everett: *"I hate you!"* He closes the store and hangs a sign: CLOSED ON ACCOUNT OF MOLASSES.

He returns home. With the orange grove deal history, Harold suffers through a wailing harangue from his wife—all afternoon, into the night and right up to the wee hours of the morning. It is four-thirty now, both are in bed, but the lecturing has not stopped. The phone rings.

Harold: "Should I answer the telephone, dear?"

"Naturally!"

"Yeah . . . naturally." Harold rises painfully from the bed and gets the phone. "Hello . . . No, no, this is not the maternity hospital." He returns to bed.

Amelia: "Who was it on the phone?"

"It was someone who wanted to know if this was the maternity hospital."

"What did you tell them?"

"I told them no, no it wasn't the maternity hospital."

Amelia props herself on her elbow and looks accusingly at her husband: "Funny thing the maternity hospital should be calling you at this hour."

"They weren't calling me, dear. They wanted to know if this was the maternity hospital."

Falling back to her bed in mock hurt: "Now you change it. Don't make it any worse. How do you expect anyone to get any sleep around here with you hopping in and out of bed all night, tinkering around the house, waiting up for telephone calls. I have to get up in the morning; make breakfast for you and the children. I have no maid, you know, probably never shall have one . . ."

Slowly Harold gathers a blanket and walks stoically out of the room to the back porch. It is on the second floor of a three-level apartment building. He sets up his bed on a porch glider which is connected precariously by chains to an overhead beam. Harold tests the chain and beam's strength. It will work. He lies down. Silence. Crash! The beam cracks at the pillow end of the glider, leaving Harold at a harsh angle. He gets up and brings a chair over to prop up that end of the couch. He tries to sleep again, but the milkman arrives. He has only one delivery, Mrs. Dunk's on the third floor. The milkman climbs the three flights of stairs while his milk bottles rattle and chime against their metal containers. The sound wakes Harold: "A special favor—please stop playing with those sleigh bells."

The man leaves cereal, milk and a coconut, which he places cautiously on the windowsill, then he returns downstairs, milk bottles chiming. Then quiet again. Bissonette tries to sleep. Bam! The coconut falls from the sill and starts a raucous trip down the three flights of stairs, banging into metal trash cans on each landing. Now wide awake, Harold decides he might as well hook the chain back to the cracked beam. He stands on the chair.

A dandy-dressed insurance salesman stops at the bottom of the back porch, sees Harold and asks, "Is this Prill Avenue?"

Without turning around, Harold mumbles, "No it is not."

"Is there a Prill Avenue in the neighborhood?"

"I don't know."

"Do you know a Carl LaFong? Capital 'L,' small 'a,' capital 'F,' small 'o,' small 'n,' small 'g.' Carl LaFong."

Bissonette has attached the glider precariously and

Baby Ellwood Dunk (Baby LeRoy) and Everett (Tammany Young) eating all the profits at Harold's general store in **It's a Gift.**

walks over to the railing. He looks down at the salesman and slowly, contemptuously he drawls, "No, I don't know a Carl LaFong, capital 'L,' small 'a,' capital 'F,' small 'o,' small 'n,' small 'g.' And if I did know Carl LaFong I wouldn't admit it." That said, he returns to his glider, tests its strength and lies down, covering his head with his blankets.

The intruder continues: "He's a railroad man and he leaves very early in the morning."

Mumbling: "He's a chump."

"I hear he's interested in an annuity policy."

"Isn't that wonderful?"

"Yes it is." Seizing on a possible entree, the man bolts upstairs. "The public's buying them like hotcakes." Reaching the second floor, the salesman looks down on Harold Bissonette's covered frame. "Maybe you would be interested in such a policy." From under the blankets Harold mumbles, "No, I would not." Ignoring the last comment, the salesman continues: "What's your age?"

"It's none of your business."

Undeterred, the dapper fellow pulls a guidebook from his pocket, looks down on the covered human frame and surmises, "I'd say you're a man of about fifty."

"You would say that."

The insurance man looks up fifty in his book. "Fifty, fifty, fifty . . . ah, here we are. If you buy a policy now you could retire when you're ninety on a comfortable income."

At this point the door opens to the Bissonette apartment and slowly, sanctimoniously Amelia walks out: "If you and your friend wish to exchange ribald stories, please take him downstairs."

Harold is irate. "My friend! I never want to see him again."

"Then why did you invite him up here?"

"I! Invite him!" He pushes Amelia aside and runs into the house. He returns quickly with a meat cleaver raised to kill and chases the salesman to the steps. The man runs all the way down while Bissonette yells after him, "And I suppose if I live to be two hundred I'll get a velocipede."

Amelia returns to the house, the salesman is gone and Harold lies down again. All is quiet. He falls asleep. Then up on the third floor Baby Ellwood is playing with a bunch of grapes. He is sitting next to a hole in the landing. Coincidentally the hole is directly over Harold's head. Playfully Ellwood drops a grape through the hole, hitting Mr. Bissonette square on the proboscis. The still slumbering grocery store owner turns his head slightly and starts to snore. A second grape sails through the hole. Bull's-eye! A direct hit into Harold's mouth. He gags, coughs and spits the grape back through the hole— a perfect shot at Baby Ellwood's face. Ellwood retaliates by dropping the entire bunch through the hole. It lands on Harold's face. He grabs the grapes, looks and intones, "Shades of Bacchus." He throws them away and returns to sleep. Not satisfied with the grape bombs, Ellwood seizes an ice pick and lets it fly. It lands inches away from Harold's head and sticks in the couch's wooden armrest. Enough! Harold snatches the pick and stalks upstairs. He holds the pick menacingly over Ellwood's head: "Even a

worm will turn." Just then Mrs. Dunk comes out onto the porch, surveys the scene and accuses Harold of trying to give her kid the colic by feeding him grapes. She escorts the poor little nipper back inside.

Harold returns to his floor and tries to get some sleep again, but here comes Mrs. Dunk's teenage daughter out of the third-floor apartment. She is going shopping. She jumps noisily down the three fights of stairs. By the time she gets to the bottom, Mrs. Dunk has also come out and stands at the railing. The daughter stops on the lawn and calls up to her mother. It seems she does not know what to get—either syrup of squill or ipecac. Mrs. Dunk doesn't care either. They yell up and down trying to decide. Harold on the second-floor landing rises and sits on his glider while the yelling continues. He is pained and annoyed. Before the two women resolve which medicine to get they jump onto another dilemma—to which drugstore should the daughter go. I don't know, the mother says, either one will be fine. The daughter hollers back. She wants Mother to tell her. But Mother purrs she wants daughter to decide. Finally, solicitously, young Dunk sings to her mother, "You tell me where to go."

"I'd like to tell you both where to go," Harold mumbles ever so softly.

Mrs. Dunk abruptly ends her conversation with her daughter: "It's no use. I can't hear a word you're saying. Somebody's shouting on the floor below."

The girl leaves, Mrs. Dunk retreats to her apartment and Harold lies down. Slowly, methodically the door to the Bissonette apartment opens. Amelia with knowing deliberateness asks her husband, "Who were those women you were talking to?"

"Mrs. Dunk upstairs."

"It seems you're getting pretty familiar with Mrs. Dunk. . . . *Upstairs.*" Slowly, methodically she walks back inside. Harold mumbles, "They were talking to me."

All quiets down and Harold returns to his slumber. This time a squeaky pulley on a neighbor's clothesline wakes him. He thinks it is a mouse and goes inside to get a mousetrap. He puts it by a small hole and says, "Eat that, you rat." He returns to bed.

The last interruption appears in the form of a huckster. The vegetable salesman is downstairs yelling out the menu on his cart. That is the last straw. Bissonette rushes into the house and returns with a shotgun. He stands next to the railing. The huckster has gone into the apartment below. Harold calls in his most unctuous tone, "Oh, vegetable man . . . vegetable gentleman." The rifle is cocked but the vendor does not appear. Harold gives up the hunt and returns to the couch holding the rifle in his hand. Dozing off, he drops the rifle and the thing fires, bringing the entire hanging couch and beam down with a bang. Bissonette slowly sits up, pulls out a fly swatter and kills a fly. End of scene.

The next day the car is packed and the Bissonettes head out to California. The Bissonettes and their belongings are stuffed into a convertible four-door Ford. They try conserving their meager money supply by picnicking. On this day they espy a beautifully manicured picnic area. Unfortunately, they do not espy the PRIVATE PROPERTY sign. They drive their rattletrap of a car loaded with gypsy

The picnic scene.

Filming the picnic scene in It's a Gift. Director Norman McLeod is seated in the chair at left. Note W. C.'s stand-in standing by (he is the man wearing the skimmer).

Arriving at their
dream ranch house.
Pictured are
Kathleen Howard,
Tommy Bupp,
Fields, Jean
Rouverol and Buster
the dog.

indifference across the luxuriously attended estate. Harold, while taking in the surrounding beauty, runs into a life-size statue of Venus de Milo, breaking her in two: "She ran right in front of the car." They park the car and settle down. Amelia unwraps the food, tossing the layers of papers to the wind. Norman throws empty cans at the cracked statue and Harold, trying to find some comfort, grabs a pillow to sit on. The dog rushes up and bites onto the other end. Harold fights back, pulling on the pillow until finally the canine's teeth tear a hole in it, sending feathers flying. Mrs. Bissonette, terribly distraught: "Those were my mother's feathers."

"I never knew your mother had feathers."

Eventually the caretaker and owner arrive to clear the tramps out. Amelia fights back, arguing with the caretaker, but Harold cowers, back to the car; "Don't argue with them, dear, they're beneath our dignity." Finally they drive away, and when Amelia asks Harold why he did not help her he responds, "I was just waiting for one of them to say something to me."

In California the Bissonettes ride past acres and acres of beautiful orange groves in the vicinity of their new place. Mrs. Bissonette apologizes to her husband, admitting that maybe she had been wrong about the entire affair after all. They pull over to a neighbor's magnificent orange ranch and ask a Mr. Abernathy directions to their place. The rancher says it is just down the road. The Bissonettes arrive. The house is a falling-down old shack and the land is fallow. Disgusted, Amelia speaks up first: "We traveled 3,452 miles for this!" Trying to save some face, Harold gets out of the car and fondles an overgrown weed: "Evidently, a young orange tree." He surveys the house, and everything he touches breaks: "I can spend a lot of my spare time fixing it up!"

The ax falls. Amelia grabs the children and deserts her "old fool" of a husband. Harold calls after them, "Come on back, I'll drive you." He leans against his car and it falls apart. Harold, totally defeated, walks over to the porch of his new home. Only the Bissonettes' dog stays with Harold. He pets the mutt kindly and hears a train whistle in the background. With his family running out on him, his car destroyed and his dream shattered, he mumbles forlornly to the dog, "That's what we'll have to take back—the old choo-choo."

Suddenly, off the road and into the dust Harold's new neighbor drives. Mr. Abernathy is in a hurry. He rushes out of his car and up to Harold. Abernathy explains that a racetrack is going to be built nearby and the operators miscalculated. Because of the afternoon sun, they will need the Bissonette spread for a grandstand. He tells Harold, "Don't let them kid you. . . . Hold out for any price." Harold needs fortification. He takes out his flask and starts to gulp.

Soon another car drives up Harold's dusty driveway. An entrepreneurial type, fancily dressed, steps out with an equally well tailored entourage following. The fast-talking businessman tells Harold he wants to put a gas station on the site and will pay him $5,000 for the property. Amelia and the family return to find out what all the excitement is about. Harold takes a swig and says no deal. Amelia yells for Harold to accept. He ignores her. The man says $10,000. A firm negative and another swig. Amelia calls him a fool. He steps past the man, grabs his wife firmly and tells her to keep out of it. "This is a private argument." He returns to the negotiations. The track owner offers $15,000, "and that's as high as I go." Harold pulls from the flask and says, "No!" The man is exasperated. "You're drunk!" This riles the old drunk:

"Yeah, and you're crazy. I'll be sober tomorrow, and you'll be crazy for the rest of your life."

The man asks Bissonette's price. Harold unfolds a pamphlet and points to a picture of the typical California orange grove. "This orange grove and $40,000—no, $44,000. Mr. Abernathy needs his commission." The man calls it a holdup, but turns to huddle with his partners. In no time he turns again and accepts the offer. Amelia faints. Harold gives Mildred his flask and tells her to give mother "some of this reviver." Amelia comes to and tells Harold, "You're an idiot, but I can't help but love you."

The last scene pictures the Bissonette family leaving in their enormous limousine. John Durston, Mildred's lover, is with them, but Harold stays home. He sits on his magnificent porch and pours himself a triple-strength gin, then grabs an orange from the nearby overhanging tree and squeezes a couple of drops into his glass. The last shot pans to a crate of oranges. The side of the box reads, "Bissonette (pronounced Bis-o-nay) Oranges."

(This last scene was shot at Fields' own home. He had recently moved from Toluca Lake and rented seven acres of land and a huge house in Encino, California.)

A personal note: In researching this book I went to the Lakeside Country Club, a Fields hangout, to ascertain if W. C. used their links in any of his golf routines. Everyone with whom I talked was quite helpful and very nice, and I found out he did use their course in a couple of his films. As a memento they gave me a copy of their heritage book, which recounts some of the club's history and lists their members, past and present. In the index I found the name of a Harold Bissonette. I immediately called the manager of the club and asked if Mr. Bissonette was a member, past or present. He told me that he was still on the active list, a member in good standing, and then divulged Mr. Bissonette's home number. I called

W. C. primping between scenes. Tammany Young waits on Fields off camera and plays Everett, his assistant, on camera.

Mr. Bissonette negotiating for a new orange ranch. He may be drunk, but "you're crazy. And I'll be sober tomorrow and you'll be crazy for the rest of your life." From left, Bud Fine, unidentified, Guy Usher, Del Henderson, Fields and of course Buster.

him. Probably in my excitement to talk with the real Harold Bissonette, I mispronounced his name. I asked for "Mr. Bis-o-nay." It was Harold on the phone. He corrected me: "It's Bis-o-net!"

He told me Fields got a kick out of the name and had asked if he could use it in his next film.

It's a Gift premiered November 30, 1934, to familiar reviews. The critics heralded Fields' comedy. Many claimed W. C. surpassed Chaplin as the greatest clown. All admitted that this movie would enhance Fields' following, and no one slandered W. C.'s ability to induce the greatest belly laughs from an audience. But nearly every critic knocked the quality of the film and the lack of a plot. One reviewer said the thing looked like it took two days to film and a couple hundred dollars to make. Another said it looked like Paramount had spent no money on any of Fields' productions.

True, they do look that way, but it never bothered W. C. He would not have been any more funny standing in the middle of a multimillion-dollar set. And Fields knew it. Indeed, for roles such as this one, a beleaguered husband scraping to make a living, the tawdry appearance of the film actually contributes to the comedy instead of diluting it. Fields probably knew that too.

As for the lack of a good story, that was not a new criticism. The critics wailed that Paramount never gave Fields a good story, even though his movies made their sides split with laughter. They all agreed that only W. C. Fields could play in a film for an hour and a quarter with no plot and still keep the audiences howling from beginning to end. But they still thought there should be a plot. Why? Fields could care less whether one scene logically dovetailed into another. He simply wanted to play his

special bits; it made no difference how loosely they were strung together. He never needed a story to present the laughs. Moreover, the critics had no right accusing Paramount of failing to give Fields a proper script. At this point in their relationship the studio gave W. C. a wide berth to create as he saw fit. This film was all Fields, nearly plotless and very funny.

For *It's a Gift* Fields once again raided his past successes to make a hit. As mentioned, this time he brought to sound film three of his stage routines from *The Comic Supplement:* the drugstore sketch, the back-porch routine and the picnic skit. These three bits constitute the majority of the film. They are self-contained. Each could play as a one-reeler and stand alone with no need of a story line to make it work. With a different "plot," Fields first packed these pieces into his silent film *It's the Old Army Game,* his first movie with Paramount. But in that 1926 film, Paramount kept sturdy shackles on the comedian. Because of that Fields thought poorly of the outcome. Now in 1934 W. C. had tried it again his way, unfettered, and with sound.

In a letter to a friend he compared the two back-porch scenes. About *It's the Old Army Game* he wrote: "That was really awful, but I sincerely believe that I had nothing to do with it being photographed the way it was." On *It's a Gift:* "Norman McLeod was kind enough to let me do my own version of the scene up at the Lasky Ranch for Paramount and that was really a very fine scene."

The studio even gave Fields the freedom to pick most of his own actors. Tammany Young was of course a Fields' favorite and he had a role in this film. And at the age of two and a half Baby LeRoy had fallen out of favor with the Paramount bigwigs because he was too old, but W. C. insisted on using him. They let him. However, he did not have absolute say. For instance, Paramount had held a "Search for Beauty Contest," with the winner promised a role in a feature-length film. Jean Rouverol won and she played W. C.'s daughter, Mildred, in *It's a Gift*. It was her first time in front of the camera. By the way, it was also Julian Madison's first time on screen. He played John Durston. Another actor, in this case a veteran, Charles Sellon, Mr. Muckle, seemed to have found his niche in the acting community playing invalids. Just a month before playing the blind and deaf hotel dick in this film, he acted as a valetudinarian stuck in a wheelchair in the film *Bright Eyes*.

This can be told now. There is a popular story about W. C. spiking Baby LeRoy's milk. My research and interviews all indicate it did happen, and it was during the filming of *It's a Gift*. Apparently LeRoy was in a cantankerous mood, crying and wailing and holding up production. The nurse had to feed him his bottle to keep the kid quiet. Solicitously, Fields came over to help. He asked the nurse if he could feed the little nipper. The nurse let him. After a few minutes W. C. asked the nurse if she would run across the street and pick up a racing form. The nurse agreed. While she was gone Fields dropped a couple of noggins of gin in the bottle and gave it to the baby. LeRoy sucked it up, then passed out. No one could revive the youngster and the day's shooting had to be cancelled. As Fields walked off the set he yelled to the director, "I told you the kid was no trouper."

As was mentioned, no matter what the critics said about the plotless, low-budget quality of *It's a Gift*, they universally praised W. C., and none too soon, because Fields and Paramount were headed for the negotiating table to hammer out a new contract. W. C. held the cards. Not only had he met with greater and greater artistic and box-office success, but now another studio begged for W. C.'s services MGM needed him for their production of *David Copperfield* Fields' prestige grew. He was on top now.

IT'S A GIFT

73 minutes
Sound, black and white
Released November 30, 1934, by Paramount
Produced by William Le Baron for Paramount
Presented by Adolph Zukor
Directed by Norman McLeod
Screenplay by Jack Cunningham from *The Comic Supplement* by J.P. McEvoy (and, uncredited, W. C. Fields)
Based on a story by Charles Bogle (W. C. Fields)
Photographed by Henry Sharp
Art direction by Hans Dreier and John B. Goodman
Sound recording by Earl S. Hayman
Song: "On the Banks of the Wabash"

CAST:
W. C. Fields   Harold Bissonette, proprietor
Baby LeRoy (Overacker)   Baby Ellwood Dunk
Kathleen Howard   Amelia Bissonette
Jean Rouverol   Mildred Bissonette, lovesick daughter
Julian Madison   John Durston, salesman
Tommy Bupp   Norman Bissonette, skate-wearing son
Tammany Young   Everett Ricks, clerk
Morgan Wallace   Jasper Fitchmueller, cumquats customer
Charles Sellon   Mr. Muckle, blind man, house detective
Josephine Whittell   Mrs. Dunk
Diana Lewis   Miss Dunk

T. Roy Barnes   Insurance salesman
Spencer Charters   Gate guard
Guy Usher   Harry Payne Bosterly, promoter
Jerry Mandy   Vegetable man
Patsy O'Byrne   Mrs. Frobisher, doing her wash
Del Henderson   Clarence Abernathy, farmer
Edith Kingdom   Old woman in limousine
James Burke   Iceman
William Tooker   Old man in limousine
Billy Engle   Bit
Jack Mulhall   Butler
Bud Fine   Driver
Eddie Baker   Yard attendant
Chill Wills and the Avalon
    Boys   Campfire rustics, singers
Jane Withers   Hopscotch girl
Buster   Dog

Filmed at Paramount in Hollywood.

The porch scene was shot at the Lasky Ranch. (The silent version was made in Florida.) The porch set stood until 1978, when it was destroyed.

Working title: *Back Porch*. Partial reworking of *It's the Old Army Game* (1926).

A one-reel non-theatrical excerpt from this film is entitled *The Big Thumb*, and a second excerpt is called *California Bound*.

David Copperfield

—1935—

Dale Carnegie once wrote, "When you talk to W. C. Fields, you feel as though he truly stepped out of a Dickens novel." If that be true, the novel would be *David Copperfield,* the character Wilkins Micawber. Charles Dickens' *Copperfield,* one of the greatest English-language novels, was fiction tightly intertwined with auto-biography. His characters were artistically drawn from his memories, from the people of his past. There is little debate in literary quarters, for instance, that Wilkins Micawber was Dickens' sketch of his own father.

It was fitting that W. C. Fields played Micawber in *David Copperfield.* Ever since 1915, the year Fields first used his voice on stage, reviewers often suggested that the comedian must have been molded by Dickens, that his delivery, his voice and his mannerisms begged for a union with Micawber. W. C.'s résumé certainly fit the role. His genealogy was pure English. His father, born and raised in Sheffield, England, never lost his thick accent. And his mother's lineage could be traced directly to the English countryside. W. C.'s life during his first few penurious years in vaudeville certainly seemed to imitate any number of Dickens' hardship tales. But perhaps the eeriest connection between W. C. and Wilkins occurred in 1880, the year of W. C.'s birth. That year an English artist painted all of the *Copperfield* characters, relying solely on Dickens' descriptions. His painting of Micawber could easily be mistaken for a drawing of W. C. Fields—vintage 1935. Micawber and Fields were kindred.

David O. Selznick spent a year preparing to put *David Copperfield* on film. First he went to England to look up the internationally famous Dickens authority Walter Dexter. Then he and Dexter visited the spots made famous in "Boz's" story. While in England he secured the talents of the fine novelist Sir Hugh Walpole to write the script, insisting that the author stay as steadfast as possible to the original story. (Walpole also had a small part in the final production, playing the Vicar of Blunder-stow.) Selznick had all the costumes made from scratch, keeping the styles authentic; then, the trade papers wrote, he had them washed eight times and soaked in coffee to give the appearance of age. The trades were filled with stories of Selznick's meticulous preparations. They claimed he even had doorknobs specially made to stay true to the story and the period, and that he went so far as to ship weeds and sand from the English shore to replicate the description of Peggotty's home. Seventy-two sets were built. The average movie may use twenty. In choosing the young Copperfield, it was rumored that Selznick and his casting crew interviewed over 10,000 children before choosing a young lad from Wiltshire, England, named Freddie Bartholomew. Selznick spared no expense to make this movie accurately, and the cost easily climbed over the million mark.

Selznick picked his cast carefully, but also with an eye on the box office. To play the impecunious Wilkins Micawber he insisted on casting Charles Laughton, although from the outset W. C. was under consideration. On May 17, 1934, Selznick cabled Louis B. Mayer from London: "If Laughton unavailable for Micawber, might like W. C. Fields. Can we get him? To avoid necessity of trying Paramount, think we should get word to Fields direct, who would probably give eye tooth to play

Micawber." Actually Selznick believed all along Fields was better suited for the part, but he wanted a "more important name," which at the time Laughton had. At least that is what the MGM sales department said, which assessed Laughton as more valuable commercially everywhere in the world except the United States, and Selznick saw *David Copperfield* as a potential international hit. Laughton read the script and refused the part. He told Selznick he could not play the role credibly, but Selznick pushed hard and finally Laughton reluctantly agreed.

After five weeks of continuous rehearsals and the shooting of several thousand feet of film everyone working on the picture agreed it was not reaching its potential. Something was missing. It was time to shoot Micawber's scenes. Everyone hoped that that would add the delightful right touch. It did not. After two days of filming it was clear that Laughton's Micawber was too dull, too lifeless and too unsympathetic. Indeed, his portrayal simply exacerbated the drudgery of the picture. Laughton knew it himself. He felt it from the beginning, and now after only two days of filming he was convinced. He refused to return to the set. He simply was not Micawber.

Selznick and George Cukor, the director, had to agree. Cukor recalled: "He didn't have the geniality or the innocence for the part." Again the producer and director searched for an international name to take the role. They turned to England and W. H. Berry. Although Berry was no great draw in the U.S., he definitely met the international-fame criterion. He wanted the part badly, but his wife was deathly ill. He would not leave her side. With Berry's rejection, Cukor lamented out loud, "We must have a good utility man to build up the picture by playing a good Micawber." Within earshot a Cukor assistant, remembering that Fields' name was bandied about before, spouted out, "Now how about W. C. Fields!"

"Get him. Fields is the man." And that is how W. C. became Wilkins Micawber. There is a great coincidence here. Almost ten years earlier to the day, *Poppy,* in which Fields first became a stage star, was headed for its English debut. Some of the original Broadway cast joined the English troupe, but Fields stayed in New York. The man who replaced W. C. as Eustace P. McGargle in London was none other than W. H. Berry. He bore a striking resemblance to Fields in both appearance and manner. Now Fields in a sense was replacing him as Micawber.

Fields was at Paramount beginning work on *Mississippi* and negotiating for a new contract when Cukor contacted the studio and the star. Both Cukor and Selznick told Paramount that no expense would be spared to secure Fields' talents. Quickly all agreed. Fields would cost $50,000—$25,000 to Paramount, $25,000 to the actor. That day W. C. drove over to MGM and began work. Micawber's scenes took a mere ten days to film. So for less than two weeks' work Fields got $25,000; but more, his work was so good and his characterization so exceptional that he was the hit of the show. Cukor and Selznick realized that and as a reward presented the comedian with top billing. George Cukor, always a brilliant director of literate, tasteful films, who was still directing major releases in his eighties, said in his later years that W. C. "was born to play Micawber—that rare combination of

Portrait study of Freddie Bartholomew and W. C. Fields as they appear in David O. Selznick's David Copperfield.

Twins!!! The near destitute Micawber clan, with a very worried daddy and a helpful David. "Nil desperandum," Mr. Micawber.

Ross-board art created for the original 1935 release depicting the entire cast. From left to right, Herbert Mundin, Basil Rathbone, and Edna May Oliver.

A scene from the film with Wilkins (W. C.) and David (Freddie Bartholomew).

the personality and the part. He was charming to work with."

The role was difficult for the creative Fields to play. Used to ad-libbing freely, now he was tied to Selznick's demand for a true re-creation of Dickens, and therefore had to memorize his lines—Fields' greatest failing. He talked about this: "The studio demanded so much authenticity that my speeches are practically cut out of the book. Every gesture of Micawber's is so faithfully described in the book that it gives an actor no chance to create. Usually, I add a good deal of ad-libbing to my roles, so this is difficult." In fact it seems W. C. never got his lines memorized. Madge Evans, who played Agnes Wickfield, remembered: "He didn't learn his lines. They all had to be written out for him on a great gazebo so that he could glance at them."

Keeping faithful to the story did not stop Fields from suggesting added bits. He spent quite some time trying to convince Cukor that Dickens "would have written in a juggling scene, but not having a showbiz background he didn't think of it." He argued that right after the death of David's mother "a little juggling was needed." Cukor did not see eye to eye with W. C. on that one. It was not a total creative prison for Fields, however. Cukor would film some of the comedian's antics, then later see if they would fit in the movie. For instance, whenever Dickens' Micawber faced black moments in his life he would ask

Maureen O'Sullivan, Lewis Stone, Freddie Bartholomew, W. C. Fields, Frank Lawton, Roland Young, Madge Evans, Lionel Barrymore,

for the shaving materials, suggesting he was ready to do himself in. When Fields as Micawber asked for his razor, he kept the company in stitches with his zealous but misdirected passes at his jugular vein. Unfortunately those bits were lost in the editing room. Although Cukor had to cut out many of W. C.'s impromptu gags, he recalled that "his suggestions and ad-libs were always in character," and not all of them were lost to the editor's scissors.

Cukor: "There was a scene in which he had to sit at a desk writing, and he asked me if he could have a cup of tea on the desk. When he got agitated he dipped his pen into the teacup instead of the inkwell."

Fields had another major concern about the role: "I'm worried too about Micawber's character. My other roles have been twentieth-century Micawbers, but where they always dropped their bluff and became human when they got around the corner the real Micawber never does this. I only hope that audiences will get the human side of him from my portrayal as you get it in the book."

The official title of the book and movie is *The Personal History, Adventures, Experience, and Observations of David Copperfield, the Younger.* And that is what it is. The movie begins with David's birth, six months after his

With Roland Young as Uriah Heep in a posed still from MGM's David Copperfield.

Wilkins Micawber with the grown-up David Copperfield (Frank Lawton).

father's death. Not wanting to raise the boy fatherless, Clara Copperfield marries Mr. Murdstone, a very mean man. Murdstone treats David quite badly, eventually sending him to a boarding school. Soon Clara dies and David returns to work in his stepfather's warehouse, where he meets Mr. Micawber. He moves in with the very poor Micawbers, but shortly thereafter Mr. Micawber is sent to debtor's prison. And soon after that David runs away to Dover to his Aunt Betsey, Mr. Dick and Nurse Peggotty's home.

Murdstone finds the boy and tries to get him back, but the three will not let the cruel stepfather have the child

Wilkins and the Mrs. (Jean Cadell) greeting David the man (Frank Lawton).

again. David returns to school, then meets Agnes Wickfield, who involves him in her father's business. Agnes falls in love with David, but young Copperfield considers her nothing more than a good friend. Another employee of Mr. Wickfield is Uriah Heep, who poses as a sycophant, but who in fact has been stealing from Wickfield for years. David and the now freed Micawber help expose Heep's nefarious business practices. Meanwhile, David has fallen in love with the exceptionally childish Dora Spenlow and, to Agnes' great grief, marries her. However, soon afterward Dora dies, breaking David's heart, but this in turn brings Agnes back and the two live happily onward.

The film opened on January 13, 1935, "with all the pomp and ceremony of old Hollywood's grand premieres," at Grauman's Chinese Theatre in Hollywood. "The audience contained more celebrities than any theatre in quite a while, and they followed the old premiere custom of applauding every name on the screen except for Charles Dickens, who never worked in Hollywood."

The reviewers praised the film, and Fields, with zeal. A few critics, however, who failed to understand that Cukor was not interested in "correcting" Dickens, complained that the film ran too long, at two hours and thirteen minutes, and at times became tedious. But those complaints were completely overshadowed by the vast majority of scribes who ranked the film top-notch. It was a great movie.

Some of the finest praise for Fields' work came from fellow actors. Will Rogers sent a telegram to W. C. on January 7, 1935, immediately after seeing a preview of *Copperfield:* "I don't believe there has been a picture made where one characterization stood out like Micawber's. That's to say nothing of the fine comedy of it, I mean the real clear cut character. It was great."

Probably the most fascinating letter Fields received came from the pen of Roland Young, Uriah Heep. He wrote Fields on January 19, 1935, the day after the New York City premiere of the motion picture, and included his own mini-review:

> I saw *Copperfield* last night. . . . I thought the picture held up amazingly well for such a long one. . . . In spite of vigorous cutting, I thought you surely walked away with the picture. The little Freddie—I thought—gave the best performance by a child I have ever seen. I liked Frank Lawton and attributed the too great sweetness to the writings of the late Charles Dickens, who in endeavoring to draw a picture of himself succeeded too well, and proved to the world that he must have been a pretty insufferable young man. The only person I really took exception to was Maureen O'Sullivan, and that I thought was by bad casting. Heather Angel would have been vastly better. George Cukor, I feel, did a grand job and a damned difficult one, and while I regret some of the lost scenes—such as your departure with your family for Australia—still, on the whole, I thought he had cut it rather brilliantly.

The papers here are very enthusiastic about the picture and the cast, tho' a couple of them seemed to think I was pretty badly miscast.

(Those couple of critics were wrong. Young was a brilliant Uriah Heep.)

Not only were the "papers" enthusiastic about *Copperfield,* but "Boz" himself was becoming quite a hit in Hollywood. Charles Dickens meant a hot box office for the studios in those Depression days. Universal's *Great Expectations* had just barely beaten *David Copperfield* into general release; MGM had just signed Ronald Colman to star in *A Tale of Two Cities,* set for production any day; and following that, it was announced, they would shoot *Pickwick Papers,* starring W. C. Fields. Fields loved Dickens. As a young vaudevillian he bought a complete set of his works, and admitted he saw himself in some of "Boz's" tales. Sadly, and for reasons unknown, he never got the chance to play Dickens again, but he never lost the desire. As late as 1943, and with W. C.'s blessing, Orson Welles tried to persuade any studio to make *Pickwick Papers* with Fields starring, but by then the motion picture executives felt the comedian was too ill to carry such an expensive undertaking.

Anyway, with the overwhelming success of *David Copperfield,* and some grand plaudits for Fields' work, W. C. was ready to renegotiate with Paramount from a position of strength. As Micawber would say, "In short, I have arrived."

A final note: Madge Evans shared scenes with both W. C. Fields and Lionel Barrymore on this picture. Married to playwright Sidney Kingsley, she was as bright as she was beautiful, as witness her insightful observations:

Lionel Barrymore was not a charm boy like his brother John. Lionel was more acerbic. Lionel was a frustrated artist. Lionel had not wanted to be an actor. He and John both spent their lives doing something they didn't want to do. In *David Copperfield* he came to the set reluctantly. He did his part, and he left as quickly as he could. He disliked acting, definitely, openly.

W. C. Fields was also a man who didn't like acting. He thought pictures were a ludicrous way of making a living. He was much more interested in drinking. But he was a funny man. Comedy is a very difficult art; it requires genius. Fields was not a Santa Claus type though. These men—Fields, the Barrymores—they were very clever men, very sardonic, very cynical. They didn't have illusions about what they were doing. They didn't have illusions about themselves, about the world. So that while they were clever, amusing, interesting to watch, they were not lovable, old, funny dears. They were strong characters. They were extraordinary. They were men larger than life. And that's what you like when you see them as actors, because that quality comes through with them.

DAVID COPPERFIELD

133 minutes
Sound, black and white
Released January 13, 1935, by Metro-Goldwyn-Mayer
Produced by David O. Selznick for MGM
Directed by George Cukor
Based on the novel by Charles Dickens
Adaption by Hugh Walpole
Screenplay by Howard Estabrook
Special effects by Slavko Vorkapich

Art direction by Cedric Gibbons
Costumes by Dolly Tree
Musical numbers by Herbert Stothart
Assistant director: Joe Newman
Photographed by Oliver T. Marsh
Edited by Robert J. Kern
Sound by Douglas Shearer
Press agent: Howard Dietz

CAST:
W. C. Fields   Mr. Wilkins Micawber (originally intended for
    Charles Laughton, who completed two days' shooting in the role)
Lionel Barrymore   Dan Peggotty
Maureen O'Sullivan   Dora Spenlow
Madge Evans   Agnes Wickfield
Edna May Oliver   Aunt Betsey Trotwood
Freddie Bartholomew   David, the child (originally intended for
    Jackie Cooper, then David Jack Holt)
Frank Lawton   David, the man
Lewis Stone   Mr. Wickfield
Elizabeth Allan   Mrs. Clara Copperfield
Roland Young   Uriah Heep
Basil Rathbone   Mr. Murdstone, the stepfather
Elsa Lanchester   Clickett
Jessie Ralph   Nurse Peggotty
Jean Cadell   Mrs. Micawber

Lennox Pawle   Mr. Dick, Aunt Betsey's friend
Violet Kemble-Cooper   Jane Murdstone
Una O'Connor   Mrs. Gummidge
John Buckler   Ham, Peggotty's nephew
Hugh Williams   Steerforth
Ivan Simpson   Limmiter
Hugh Walpole   The Vicar of Blunderstow
Mabel Colcord   Mary Ann
Herbert Mundin   Barkis, the carrier
Fay Chaldecott   Little Em'ly, the child
Florine McKinney   Little Em'ly, the woman
Marilyn Knowlden   Agnes, the child
Harry Beresford   Dr. Chillip
Renée Gadd   Janet
Arthur Treacher   Dishonest coachman
Margaret Seddon   Bit

Filmed at MGM in Culver City, with one second-unit shot done in Canterbury, England.

Academy Award nominee for best picture. Won *Film Daily's* 1935 award for best picture. Was among top ten grossing films of the year.

Previous filmings of *David Copperfield* were produced by Thanhouser in 1911 and by Associated Exhibitors in 1923. A subsequent adaptation was made in England in 1969, featuring Laurence Olivier and with Ralph Richardson as Micawber.

Mississippi

—1935—

After some truculent negotiations, Paramount and Fields reached an accord on a new contract. It was for one year. Fields would appear or star in three movies for the studio and receive $300,000, to be paid in weekly installments of $6,000. That out of the way, W. C. immediately started work again on *Mississippi*.

The story was an overdone piece based on the 1923 Booth Tarkington play *The Magnolia*. It was filmed in 1924 and renamed *The Fighting Coward*. In 1929 Hollywood made a talking version starring Charles "Buddy" Rogers and called it *River of Romance*. Now in 1935 they used the same plot, added Bing Crosby and W. C. Fields, and tagged it *Mississippi*. Some of the trade papers reported, however, that with Fields on the set the movie changed dramatically from the original. The studio hired Francis Martin and Jack Cunningham to write the script, but the papers reported that it was Fields who dictated it, or at least created his own bits of business and dialogue. The story goes that during filming W. C. kept the crew howling with his antics, while Cunningham shadowed W. C., writing down all of his ad-libs and sight gags to include in the script.

Directing the film was W. C.'s longtime friend Eddie Sutherland. The two had a rocky initial meeting in *It's the Old Army Game,* but by this point they were getting along just fine, primarily because now Sutherland let Fields do whatever he wanted in front of the camera, giving him little or no direction.

It is the Old South. Fields, Commodore Orlando Jackson, runs a Mississippi riverboat which occasionally docks near the plantation home of the strictly Southern Rumford family. There is a big party at the Rumford place celebrating oldest daughter Elvira's engagement to the Philadelphian Tom Grayson, Bing Crosby. Suddenly Elvira's former lover, Major Patterson, appears at the festivities to challenge Grayson to a pistol duel; winner wins Elvira. Grayson refuses the challenge, calling this courtly manner of problem solving disgusting. Elvira, however, born and raised on the plantation code, finds her fiancé's refusal cowardly and insulting. She tells her father to banish the Northerner from their home, and then agrees to marry Major Patterson.

Grayson heads upstairs and packs to leave. Rumford's youngest daughter, Lucy, finds Tom's actions honorable and sneaks into his room to beg him to take her with him. She secretly loves him. Grayson feels warmly toward the adolescent, but tells her she is too young.

Tom is a good singer and needs some money to get back home, so he heads for Jackson's riverboat looking for a singing job. He gets it. Besides operating a floating

Getting ready for the card-game scene in Mississippi, with Fields and Paul Hurst clearly visible. Director Eddie Sutherland, standing but partially hidden by the movie camera, gives gentle direction to W. C.

A scene at the Rumford plantation, with Bing Crosby standing next to Joan Bennett, and W. C. with Queenie Smith.

A publicity shot of the crooner and the comedian.

nightclub, Jackson spends time sipping mint juleps, gambling and telling tall tales. One of his favorite stories depicts him fighting fierce Indians in the old days, shooting them with three pistols one in each hand and the third between his teeth. When a listener informs him that pistols had not yet been invented, the Commodore has the answer: "I know that, but the Indians didn't know it." Later he refines the talk: "Unsheathing my bowie knife, I carved a path through this wall of human flesh dragging my canoe behind me." Meanwhile, Grayson is rehearsing a new song, "Swanee River," which the knowledgeable Commodore claims "is no good. It'll be forgotten in two weeks. People can't remember the tune." He walks away humming it.

During a card game later in the day Jackson tries to get rid of the five aces he dealt himself, but each time he draws a new card it is an ace. The other players also hold aces. When the skulduggery is discovered knives fly and guns shoot. The Commodore is spared a razor cut when Grayson quickly sticks a folding chair between the Commodore's face and the flying knife.

That same evening is Grayson's debut. The house is packed. Then Captain Blackie, a bully to whom Jackson owes some money, saunters into the crowd, disrupting the show and demanding that Grayson stop singing. He will not, and Blackie begins to tear the place apart.

Grayson, angry over the disruption, jumps from the stage to get Blackie. They struggle. Blackie pulls out a gun. They fight over it. Suddenly the gun discharges, killing Captain Blackie. Grayson calmly returns to the stage to finish his song as they carry Blackie away. Seizing the incident for publicity, Jackson convinces Grayson to change his name and billing to "the notorious Col. Steele—the singing killer." Colonel Steele's reputation spreads far and wide, with Jackson adding another notch to Steele's gun at each stop.

Meantime, Lucy has been attending school and growing up. Her class is on an outing, coincidentally not far from the riverboat. All the girls' conversation centers on the notorious Colonel Steele. They want to meet him, except for Lucy, who finds his reputation repulsive. But one night she does meet Grayson, and the singer realizes Lucy is not too young anymore. They hug and kiss, but Grayson does not tell her he is Colonel Steele. She soon finds out and quickly rebuffs his romantic notions. But this time a Rumford girl will not have her way. A few days later he invades the Rumford home playing the role of the notorious Colonel Steele to its fullest. He belittles the Major, shoots fear into the Major's bully brother and breaks down Lucy's bedroom door to get the hiding girl. He forces her to go down to the riverboat and he and Commodore Orlando Jackson explain the hoax behind the Colonel's reputation. Convinced, Lucy accepts Tom and they stay on the riverboat, presumably to live happily ever after.

The premiere of *Mississippi* was met with generally favorable reviews. Most critics claimed Fields was tops but Crosby was weak. They did not like the songs he sang, some fine work by Rodgers and Hart, claiming they did not embellish the crooner's voice. The criticism fits. The songs were fine, but they were for Lanny Ross, not Bing Crosby. Ross was supposed to star in this film, but for some reason, that fell through and Crosby filled in.

Bing Crosby captured star billing, but that did not seem to cause friction between him and Fields. They were cordial on the set but by no means close. Perhaps W. C. knew that he was stealing the show and it was better to keep relations with the star calm while working, because Bing would certainly be mad when he saw the preview. He was. He went to the studio heads and ranted and raved. The film was a comedy hit for W. C. Fields but a poor showing for Crosby. The crooner demanded changes in editing, additional scenes and at least one more song. Paramount caved in. Between the time of the preview to the time of public premiere at least one third of the movie was changed. Bing had his additional song plus a couple more love scenes with Joan Bennett. One of the critics' complaints was that the film was disjointed, a common fault of Fields' films, but in this case undoubtedly exacerbated by Bing's demands.

Apparently W. C. ad-libbed freely throughout the film, and Sutherland never tried to slow him down. The papers say that during the card game scene, scheduled to

A glaring Fred Kohler holds his own with W. C. in this scene from Mississippi.

W. C. confers with Irwin S. Cobb, who was visiting the set. They share an interest in cigars for one thing.

be a very short piece, Fields kept throwing in business, making the sequence three times longer than scripted. And another time W. C. got behind an enormous calliope and started playing. The notes were sour and steam poured from a dozen leaks. Finally the entire thing collapsed. It was put on film and stuck into the movie, but after the preview, when Crosby hollered so and Paramount agreed to more footage of the crooner, some scenes had to be cut, so the calliope bit was extricated. Another ad-lib from this movie became a famous Fields line: "Women are like elephants to me. I like to look at 'em but I wouldn't want to own one."

Fields' excessive use of alcohol was beginning to show. He was normally an insomniac, and the booze aggravated the malady. He started sleeping in a barber chair and taking long walks at night, but nothing helped. So in the mornings on the set the makeup artist spent extra time covering up the huge circles under the comedian's eyes. However, his humor never left him. Soon Fields began work on another film which he wrote. He threatened he would sing in this next picture just to get back at Bing.

MISSISSIPPI

80 minutes
Sound, black and white
Released March 22, 1935, by Paramount
Produced by Arthur Hornblow Jr. for Paramount
Presented by Adolph Zukor
Directed by A. Edward Sutherland
Based on the 1923 Booth Tarkington play The Magnolia
Adapted by Herbert Fields and Claude Binyon
Screenplay by Francis Martin and Jack Cunningham
Music by Richard Rodgers and lyrics by Lorenz Hart
Songs: "Down by the River," "Soon," "Swanee River," "It's Easy to Remember, But So Hard to Forget," "Roll Mississippi."
Photographed by Charles Lang
Art direction by Hans Dreier and Bernard Herzbrun
Edited by Chandler House
Sound recording by Eugene Merritt
Second unit director: Marshall Neilan

CAST:
Bing Crosby   Tom Grayson/the notorious Col Steele (originally intended for Lanny Ross)
W. C. Fields   Commodore Orlando Jackson
Joan Bennett   Lucy Rumford (originally intended for Elizabeth Young)
Queenie Smith   Alabam'
Gail Patrick   Elvira Rumford
Claude Gillingwater Sr.   General Rumford
John Miljan   Major Patterson
Edward Pawley   Joe Patterson
Fred Kohler Sr.   Captain Blackie
John Larkin   Rumbo
Libby Taylor   Lavinia Washington
Harry Myers   Joe, stage manager
The Cabin Kids (Ruth, Helen, James, Winifred and Fred Hall)   Themselves
Paul Hurst   Hefty
Theresa Maxwell Conover   Miss Markham
King Baggott   First gambler
Mahlon Hamilton   Second gambler
Stanley Andrews   Gambler with eye patch
Al Richmond   Gambler
Francis McDonald   Gambler
Eddie Sturgis   Gambler
George Lloyd   Gambler
Bruce Covington   Colonel

Jules Cowles   Bartender
Molasses and January   Themselves
Robert McKenzie   Show patron
Oscar Smith   Valet
Harry Cody   Abner, bartender
Forrest Taylor   Man at bar who orders sarsaparilla
Warner Richmond   Man who pulls a gun
Matthew Betz   Man at bar
Jack Mulhall   Duelist
Jack Carlyle   Referee
Bill Howard   Man in auditorium
Victor Potel   Guest
Jan Duggan   Boat passenger
Richard Scott   The second
James Burke   Passenger in pilot house
Helene Chadwick   Extra at opening
Jerome Storm   Extra at opening
Dennis O'Keefe   Extra
Ann Sheridan   Extra at engagement party and girls' school
Charles King   Desk clerk
Jean Rouverol   Friend of Lucy
Mildred Stone   Party guest
Mary Ellen Brown   Party guest
J. P. McGowan   Dealer
Clarence Geldert   Hotel proprietor
Mabel Van Buren   Party guest
Bill Harwood   Party guest
Fred (Snowflake) Toones   Valet
Lew Kelly   Man at bar
Arthur Millett   Extra
Clarence L. Sherwood   Extra
Bert Lindley   Extra
Roy Bailey   Extra
Warren Rogers   Extra
Jean Clarendon   Extra
Dan Crimmins   Extra
William Howard Gould   Extra

Filmed at Paramount in Hollywood.
Working title: A Cruise to Nowhere, originally also scheduled with Burns and Allen.
Remake of The Fighting Coward (Paramount, 1924) with Cullen Landis, Ernest Torrence and Mary Astor in the leads, filmed also as River of Romance (Paramount, 1929) with Charles "Buddy" Rogers, Wallace Beery and Mary Brian in the leads.

Man On The Flying Trapeze

— 1935 —

Fields collaborated with his old vaudeville buddy Sam Hardy on this one, with the credits for the original story reading Charles Bogle and Sam Hardy. Hardy was ailing and on the skids in Hollywood. He needed financial and, most likely, psychological help, so W. C. became his benefactor. This was typically Fields. The view of W. C. in his personal life as a curmudgeon simply was not true. Among people he liked he was generous and warm and an easy mark. He covered that side of him with a thin veneer of irascibility, but that fooled very few people. Particularly when it came to Fields' old vaudeville pals, he would go out of his way to lend a helping hand, and that was what he did for Sam Hardy.

After they worked on the original story the studio turned it over to scriptwriters. That was when the war began. W. C. hated Hollywood's contribution to the "literary world" and he let it be known. But it really made no difference how much he wailed against them. He never

followed the script anyway; he would either ad-lib or change his lines the night before shooting, much to the scriptwriters' irritation. Fighting with the writers on this film was particularly acerbic.

There were other problems. Evidently Fields had little say on casting in this picture and production had to be started over a number of times because of W. C.'s difficulty in dealing with Paramount's selections. At one point the studio finally gave in to the comedian. He wanted his favorite from the silent days, Mary Brian, to play his daughter in this opus, indeed he demanded it. You see, *The Man on the Flying Trapeze* bore a great similarity to *Running Wild,* and the loving daughter in that film was played by Mary Brian. He was convinced that Mary was the only one who could re-create this role. Ms. Brian was in New York at the time, but the studio sent for her anyway and rushed her back to Hollywood so production could resume.

"It's a quartet." From left, Tammany Young, Walter Brennan, Lew Kelly and W. C. singing "On the Banks of the Wabash," if "singing" it can be called.

More problems. While searching for a suitable director, William Le Baron, W. C.'s friend and producer, temporarily took over the directing duties, but then he caught a severe cold and had to quit. Clyde Bruckman, who directed Fields in *The Fatal Glass of Beer,* replaced Le Baron, but he too caught a severe case of influenza and had to leave for a couple of weeks, so Sam Hardy and W. C. grabbed the helm and directed the picture until Bruckman returned.

And more. W. C. himself fell quite ill during production. He sprained his ankle for the second time while playing tennis and still suffered from insomnia and other booze-related illnesses. It was a wonder *The Man on the Flying Trapeze* was ever made, never mind that the result was a minor masterpiece for Fields.

As was mentioned, the film was akin to *Running Wild.* Again Fields suffers from an antagonizing mama's boy, sissy stepson and a tyrannical, overbearing second wife. And just as in *Running Wild* he has a daughter from his first marriage who loves him. And the themes were similar. Fields begins both films kowtowing and rudderless, and he ends with courage and determination. But for *The Man on the Flying Trapeze* Fields added one more assailant to his manhood—a live-in mother-in-law. So the themes were similar but the plots were slightly different.

The movie begins with a classic Fields bedroom scene. Ambrose Wolfinger, W. C. Fields, is in the bathroom running his toothbrush along the sink while drinking and gargling from a flask. His wife, Leona, lying in bed, demands to know what he is doing. Ambrose swallows quickly: "Just brushing my teeth, dear." Apparently for the fourth time that night. Ambrose returns to bed and falls asleep.

From the air vent Leona hears singing voices. Marauders in the basement! Leona wakes Ambrose: "Ambrose! Ambrose! There are burglars singing in the cellar!"

"What are they singing?"

"What difference does it make—"

"Yeah, yeah." Ambrose listens for a while: "What terrible voices." He wants to sleep for a little longer, then go down. Ridiculous! Leona is afraid the burglars will eventually come upstairs and harm her sissy adult son, Claude. Ambrose slowly prepares to meet his fate. He checks through the nightstand for his gun. He pulls out walnuts and gloves and eventually grabs his firearm. While checking it he passes the barrel in front of his wife. Scared, she demands he be more careful.

"Don't worry. It isn't loaded."

"No, but you are."

The gun fires. Leona faints. Ambrose stands over her and with little remorse asks, "Did I kill you?" She comes to and calls him a fool. Ambrose says with slight remorse, "Oh, good, I didn't kill you."

The shot has aroused Mrs. Neselrode, Leona's mother, and Leona's son, Claude. They rush into the room. Leona and Ambrose excitedly explain the situation: "burglars singing in the cellar." Ambrose figures Claude could go down with him to apprehend the criminals. Mrs. Neselrode places herself between Claude and Ambrose, The poor boy could get killed. Wolfinger's daughter, Hope, rushes into the room. She hears her cowardly stepbrother refuse to join Ambroise and volunteers herself. It might be dangerous. Ambrose will not let her go and he heads downstairs alone.

He opens the door which leads down to the basement and trips, falling all the way down the stairs, and landing at the bottom on his posterior. He startles the burglars but not too much. It seems they had broken into Ambrose's applejack and are a bit bibulous. Ambrose introduces himself and the burglars offer him a drink. He accepts. After a few noggins they now have a trio. All three start singing "On the Banks of the Wabash." A policeman arrives and arrests the two burglars (who incidentally were played by Tammany Young and Walter Brennan). Ambrose has been having a good time and wants the cop to let them go. The officer has his duty to perform and in fact needs Ambrose as a witness. The four leave for the courthouse.

Justice is short and sour. The judge lets the thieves go but arrests Ambrose for manufacturing applejack without a license and puts him in jail. He calls home but his wife refuses to bring bail. Indeed, she, Mrs. Neselrode and Claude have a big laugh over Ambrose's plight. That irks Hope, so she grabs her meager personal savings, goes to the courthouse and frees her father.

Back home at the breakfast table he passively accepts his family's rebukes and Claude's taunts of "jailbird!" On the table there is only one piece of cold toast for Ambrose. But worse than his empty stomach and the opprobrium is Claude's announcement that he found a fifteen-dollar front-row seat to the wrestling match of the century between Meshobbab and Tosoff, slated for that afternoon. Ambrose quickly checks his coat pocket—nothing. So that is where Claude "found" the ticket. But he cannot complain, because Leona would kill him if she found out that he planned to take part of the day off to see the fight. Ambrose sadly leaves for work but decides to take part of the day off anyway and try to find an extra ducat somewhere.

Wolfinger has worked for the same company for twenty-five years without a day off. He is a memory expert. He keeps piles upon piles of papers on his desk in seeming disarray, but whenever the company needs to find some lost, nearly forgotten document, Ambrose searches for the vital information and just by jostling a few papers pulls it out. His boss, Mr. Malloy, does not particularly like Wolfinger but finds his exceptional ability to remember minute details an invaluable help. However, the second in command, Mr. Peabody, would love to find any reason to fire Ambrose.

Ambrose's secretary has a ticket to the fight and asks him if she can have the day off. Of course he lets her go.

Mr. Malloy calls Ambrose to his office. The boss wants to know all about a big client who is coming in

Baby LeRoy visits W. C. on the set of Trapeze and receives sage counsel on his Paramount contract from the foremost contract fighter of them all. Note: The armrest nameplate reads "Joan Bennett."

today. Ambrose remembers the man clearly, J. Farnsworth Wallaby. Their last meeting was five years ago. Wallaby has two boys—one of them a champion tennis player and the other "a manly little fellow." (A possible jibe at "Big" Bill Tilden.) Wallaby and Malloy had dinner that night and wound up at a speakeasy where Malloy somehow found a lady's garter and . . . the boss has learned enough.

Ambrose returns to his desk and musters up enough courage to go back and ask Mr. Malloy for the day off. He will be honest. When the boss asks Wolfinger the reason for wanting the free time, somehow Ambrose gives the impression that his mother-in-law has just passed away. Commiserating over the loss of a loved one, Mr. Malloy says, "It must be hard to lose your mother-in-law."

"Yes it is, very hard. Almost impossible."

Mr. Malloy asks how she died. It seems Mrs. Neselrode had fainted and to revive her they gave her a dash of alcohol, but it was poison booze and she died instantly. Ambrose gets the day off, but rumors spread throughout the business that Mrs. Neselrode drank herself to death. Mrs. Neselrode is a proud teetotaler who has boasted to Ambrose, "When I was a young and petty girl, I promised my mother that lips that touch liquor shall never touch mine." To which Ambrose replied, "That's a lovely sentiment."

Ambrose heads for the fight. Trouble! First he gets about four parking tickets while stuck in the same no-parking zone. Then he gets a flat tire right at the top of a steep hill. While he is taking off the flat the spare gets loose and rolls down the hill, with Ambrose giving chase, dodging cars, trucks, trolleys and trains.

Back at the Wolfingers' home, Ambrose's business associates have sent funeral floral arrangements. Leona thinks that possibly Ambrose has met with a fatal accident. She is not too concerned but calls his office anyway. Mr. Peabody, the second in command, extends his condolences for the loss of her mother. Indignantly Leona assures him that Mrs. Neselrode is very much alive. Mr. Peabody, the one who hates Ambrose, relishes the fact that now he has cause to kick Ambrose out of the firm.

Finally, at the arena Ambrose joins the long queue to the box office. But when he reaches the window the cashier slams down the SOLD OUT sign right in front of Wolfinger's nose. Ambrose settles for a knothole. Peeping at the fearsome match, he sees Meshobbab lift Tosoff over his head and throw him out of the arena. Ambrose rushes to the door to see the flying wrestler. Smack! The floating Tossoff knocks Ambrose to the gutter. The arena crowd pours out and with them is Ambrose's secretary. She sees her boss in the gutter and rushes to help. Then Claude comes out, takes in the scene, gleefully concludes that Ambrose is drunk and having an affair with his secretary, and skips home to tell his mother and Mrs. Neselrode.

The two old bats are already in a frenzy over Ambrose's lie to Malloy, then his firing and now this. They are thoroughly disgusted with Ambrose, but not surprised. Hope hears Claude's story and defends her father, calling her brother a liar. Enter Ambrose with black eyes, a broken hat, torn clothes, but holding a bundle of flowers for Leona—"a little nosegay." She grabs the

flowers and throws them in his face, then all three gang up on him. He is in no mood and sternly shuts them up. He was wrong to use Mrs. Neselrode's dying as an excuse to get off work. He admits he went to the wrestling match, but denies he was drunk or having an affair with his secretary. Claude counters. He saw the debauchery with "my own eyes." Ambrose warns, "Shut up, Claude!" Claude continues the assault. He threatens to hit Hope. That does it! Ambrose rears back and with a powerful, although uncoordinated, haymaker knocks Claude to the ground. With mounting anger, he takes a swing at Mrs. Neselrode, but the old biddy runs away just in time. Ambrose and Hope leave the house and find an apartment.

Back at the office, Malloy needs Wolfinger. An important customer, Mr. Muckenback, is coming to town. Peabody unctuously declares he fired Ambrose for lying and for taking the day off to see the wrestling match. Malloy demands that Peabody get him back immediately. Malloy does not begrudge a man one mistake in twenty-five years. He tells Peabody to get Ambrose on the phone.

Peabody finds Ambrose at the apartment. Wolfinger and his daughter are searching through want-ads with little luck. Ambrose has resigned himself to return to work, apologize and accept a 50 percent cut in salary. The phone rings. Hope answers. Peabody offers the job back at the same salary, but Hope and Ambrose think quickly. She tells him that her father has another offer from "Moe Litvak at the Irish Woolen Mills," at twice the salary and with long vacations. Peabody consults with Malloy and the boss agrees to match the offer. Hope says fine, under the condition that Ambrose's vacation time starts today with full pay. Agreed!

Leona returns to Ambrose, but this time under Ambrose's terms. Everyone is happy now, so as a conciliatory gesture Ambrose takes the entire family out for a spin in his new roadster. Hope and Leona join Ambrose in the front seat, while Mrs. Neselrode and Claude take the rumble seat. A storm hits—torrential rain. Ambrose puts up his convertible top and passes around a thermos of coffee. In the rumble seat Mrs. Neselrode and Claude get a thorough drenching.

The film opened nationally in August. The reviewers lined up again to acclaim W. C., but also to berate the low-budget appearance of the work and the slipshod plot. Nothing new in these reviews. The critics also hailed Kathleen Howard as Fields' wife, and W. C. could not have been more pleased. He had often told reporters that Ms. Howard was the only woman in Hollywood he would consider for his "reel" wife. The newspaper reports claimed he flatly refused to have any other woman play his spouse. Kathleen Howard was formerly a Metropolitan Opera singer, but after twelve years of warbling she quit and turned to fashion writing. Soon she became an editor of a women's magazine. She was doing a piece on Mitchell Leisen's film *Death Takes a Holiday,* and while she was on the set someone asked her to play a part. She did, and did it well, and her career in film was launched.

Another member of the cast, although not mentioned in any reviews, was Carlotta Monti, who played the part of Ambrose's loyal secretary. She had made herself notorious by publicly claiming that she was once W. C.'s paramour. She had asserted that her twelve years with the comedian, 1934 through 1946, were a time when she loved and cared for W. C. In the book *Close-up: The Hollywood Directors,* Ms. Monti was mentioned in David Wilson's piece on the career of William Wellman. In one segment he talked about Wellman's filming of *Robin Hood of El Dorado.* According to Wilson, William Wellman brought Robert Carson, a young screenwriter, along "to do standby dialogue." David Wilson wrote: "W. C. Fields' girlfriend, Carlotta Monti, played one of the camp followers of Murietta. She had just been thrown out of Fields' mansion, and she amused the cast and crew with her stories about the comedian. The one thing, she said, that she could never forgive him for was when he hit her on the head with a rubber mallet after kicking her down the main staircase."

Then Wilson quoted Robert Carson's recollection of Ms. Monti. Carson: "At one point Monti approached me, and she said that if she could just have her part—if I could just fatten her part—she would be, you know, very nice to me." Carson continued that he was madly in love with another woman at the time and nothing came of Ms. Monti's overture. This occurred two years after W. C. and Carlotta began their "love" relationship.

From her testmony at the probating of W. C.'s will, and from court documents filed when she sued Fields for the rubber hammer episode, it can best be deduced that Ms. Monti had a very practical interest in W. C.

Mary Brian was Fields' neighbor when he lived in Toluca Lake. She recalls, "He would always yell across the lake, 'I've got a script and you've got to be my daughter.' Lots of times Paramount would send a car for us both because we were so close around the lake. Now if he'd had a fight with Carlotta he would say to me, 'If you ever, *do,* . . .' whatever it was that she had done, 'I'll take you over my lap and you will get the spanking of your life.' "

She also recalls that "he was undemonstrative in speech, but with little nudges and things I knew that he liked me and was fond of me." What she didn't know at the time was that he saw in her the real-life daughter he never had, but wanted.

The Man on the Flying Trapeze was the most self-reflective picture W. C. Fields ever made. It mirrored his own life—his likes, his displeasures, his hurts and his triumphs. It was a sort of a creative autobiography. The irony of Ambrose being accused of dalliance with his secretary, played appropriately by Carlotta Monti, was not lost on Fields' friends. Furthermore, one could not easily miss the self-parody of Fields, famous for his inability to remember lines, playing the part of a memory expert. And Ambrose Wolfinger's desk looked strikingly similar to W. C. Fields' desk.

Through allusion, Fields also parodies his history with Paramount. Wolfinger got canned, but in a short time the boss discovered Ambrose's invaluable contribu-

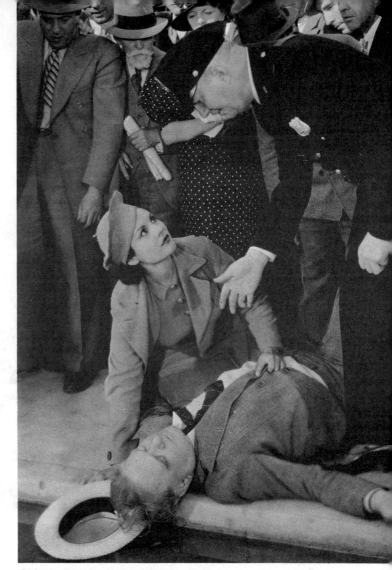

Carlotta Monti, playing Wolfinger's secretary, attends to her boss outside the wrestling arena in this scene from Trapeze.

tion to the firm and wanted him back at the same salary. Ambrose's agent, his daughter Hope, said the offer was unacceptable. With quick reconsidering the boss upped the ante to a satisfactory level and the memory expert had a job again. Paramount fired Fields in the silent days. A few years later the executives realized W. C.'s worth as a talking film actor and wanted him back at the same salary. With Fields' agent representing the comedian, he refused and Paramount upped the ante to a satisfactory level, and the memory inexpert had a job again.

But perhaps the most self-reflective aspect of the film concerns Wolfinger's family. In most of his movies Fields suffered from a bellowing, pugnacious, pretentious, nagging wife, a reflection of his own wife, Hattie. In this film, however, he added the extra ingredient of a sissy *adult* son named Claude. W. C. Fields had a son, W. C. Fields Jr. The younger Fields always used the name Claude, never Bill or William. At the time of this film Claude Jr. was thirty-one years old and a respected lawyer, but W. C. Sr. still considered the boy a sissy, babied by his domineering mother. Father and son fought quite a bit over the years, but by 1935 they started drawing slightly closer, but not close enough for the father to forget the

Stern looks from Oscar Apfel and Lucien Littlefield spell trouble for W. C. in Trapeze.

pain of years gone by. The son was a very religious man and condemned his father's rumored affair with Ms. Monti. So it was no small nettle that Wolfinger's son was the one who accused Ambrose of philandering with his secretary, played by the very same Ms. Monti. W. C. could never understand why his son turned from him. Oh, he knew Hattie had her hand in it, but figured the boy would grow away from her persuasion eventually. He never did completely. W. C. searched for a good reason why he was estranged from his son. Frustrated, he eventually blamed it on the boy's gender. He often said that if he had had a daughter she would have understood him, forgiven him, loved him and seen through Hattie's perfidy in a way a boy could not. Wolfinger had a loving, understanding daughter who sided with him against her mother. W. C. boiled with emotion—sadness and anger—over what he saw as his family's treachery and fought back on film, particularly in *The Man on the Flying Trapeze*. Deep down inside, W. C. always hoped that his wife and son would come back to him and accept him for what he was. They did not fully. But Wolfinger's family did.

Although Fields had trouble with his own son, he had no problems with his "reel" son in this picture. Fields took a strong liking to Grady Sutton, who played Claude in *The Man on the Flying Trapeze*. W. C. asked the studio to use him in his films whenever possible. Grady remembers what most of the actors who played opposite W. C.

remember, that Fields ad-libbed ad infinitum. "You never knew. In the dining-room scene he didn't say a thing while we rehearsed." But when the scene was being shot: "I was so fascinated by him that I was doing the business of eating but listening to him. He's going on like a wild man and a few minutes later I hear the director yell, 'Cut!' He said, 'Grady, why didn't you come in on your cue?' And Bill says, 'I didn't give the boy a cue. Leave him alone. I never give cues!' He got me over to one side and said, 'Now look, son, we'll work it this way. When you think I've said enough, well you just butt in.'"

Mary Brian, also, was struck by how "loose" the filming was. Fields scripts were generally one-tenth the size to which she was accustomed. W. C.'s scripts were nothing more than just an outline with practically no dialogue. Their sketchy nature allowed for the improvisation Fields liked. "He used to have the set completely lit," she remembers. "Every corner would be lit and ready for action because we never knew where we might end up once a scene began. He might say, 'Daughter! Find my bathrobe.' Well, we hadn't rehearsed it, but I'd have to go and look. Another time, my phone conversation about the Irish Woolen Mills at the end of the picture was not rehearsed. It was that loose."

So the set was completely lit. What about Fields? "He did drink," she says. "He always had a glass in his hand. He used it like a baton while working things out on the set. But he would just sip on it. I never saw it get in the way at any time. He'd just have a little glow on, but never drunken, never out of control.''

Ever wonder how the picture got its name? W. C. wanted to call it *Everything Happens at Once,* a fitting tag for the plot. At first, evidently, the studio liked the idea sufficiently well to commission some fine publicity artwork using that title. But then for reasons unknown they nixed it. *The Memory Expert* was a second choice, and in fact the European release bore that appellation, but Paramount did not like it either. Finally, the Paramount clique settled on *the Man on the Flying Trapeze.* Nowhere in the movie can the title be justified. Here is how a newspaperman explained Fields' reaction to the title changes: "*The Old Fashioned Way* was to be named *The Great McGonigle. It's a Gift* was formerly called *The Back Porch* and now he is writing a new story which the studio says will be called *The Man on the Flying Trapeze,* but which W. C. thinks should be called *Everything Happens at Once* and he confidently expects it will be released as *Lo, the Poor Indian.*''

To compound the confusion, Paramount had recently released a terrific Popeye cartoon also entitled *The Man on the Flying Trapeze.* Then there was William Saroyan's 1934 O. Henry Award-winning short story, "The Daring Young Man on the Flying Trapeze.''

But it turns out, as Mary Brian explains, that *The Man on the Flying Trapeze* was just a title that intrigued him: "He used it frequently as a working title and finally here they let him have his way.''

There were other name changes.

In the casting call sheet it was reported that Sutton's character name would be Claude Bensinger. But in Fields' original script the character had no last name Perhaps the studio arbitrarily surnamed him Bensinger, but by the time the film was released he had become Claude Neselrode. Here's why: W. C. and his sporting pals (to be used interchangeably with drinking cronies), who included the Barrymores, Gregory La Cava, Gene Fowler and John Decker among others, frequented Jim Jeffries' boxing barn in the San Fernando Valley. It was a place where local pugilists could test their wares while Hollywood's élite tested their prowess in show stealing by competing to see who had the best catcalls. One of Fields' favorite boxers was a fellow by the name of Claude Neselrode.

After completing filming in late May, W. C. became seriously ill. So ill in fact that many Hollywood newspapers claimed that *The Man on the Flying Trapeze* was most likely Fields' last film. The papers said that he was suffering from grippe, a bad back and severe pneumonia, but the truth was that alcohol was beating him. He had to go on the wagon. He hurried out of Hollywood and went to a small health spa at the base of the San Bernadino Mountains called Soboba Hot Springs, a favorite retreat of the Hollywood crowd. He spent about two weeks there drying out. That summer, Fields' friend Will Rogers died in a plane crash in Alaska, and W. C.'s co-writer on *The Man on the Flying Trapeze,* Sam Hardy, died in the early fall of 1935. After Hardy passed away, many thought W. C. Fields would be next to meet the "man in the bright nightgown.''

With Michael Visaroff.

W. C. officially becomes a Kentucky Colonel. True! Presenting the award is Mary Brian and friend and writer Sam Hardy. All this took place on the set of The Man on the Flying Trapeze.

But newspapers nevertheless kept Fields' name alive. Ed Sullivan, still a Fields fanatic, wondered in print how well Fields could fill a till at the box office: "I have taken girls to Fields' pictures and the lines that send me off into howls of laughter leave the girls quite cold. It has been proven that a star who doesn't appeal to women will not set up box office records." However, Louella Parsons argued the contrary: "W. C. Fields is comedy's king, taking the crown from Charlie Chaplin, and he is developing into a box office popularity." Indeed, a London paper claimed that W. C. was Paramount's biggest moneymaker. But the New York *Times* tempered that, saying that next to Bing Crosby, Fields brought the most bucks to the studio. Actually, both were wrong. It was Mae West whose pictures grossed the highest (and she was also the highest-paid woman in the United States in 1935). But W. C. Fields was right near the top.

Even though in general the Hollywood trades predicted doom for W. C., other newspapers kept rumors running that the "great one" was better and would be in front of the camera very soon. They were wrong. By October W. C. was still very sick and unable to fulfill his contract and make his third picture that year. Nevertheless, Paramount wanted him and hoped for his return by signing the comedian to another contract for the same $300,000 a year for three movies. As soon as the contract was signed the trades took the signal and stopped predicting W. C.'s demise and started stories about his next pictures. First announced was an adaptation of Julian Street's yarn "Need of Change." Then they said Fields would star in *Rip Van Winkle* with Lyda Roberti playing the sleeper's wife. Once again *Pickwick Papers* was the rumored movie, but none of these were made. Then *Don Quixote* was announced for Fields and shortly cancelled. And another proposed Fields vehicle—*Don't Look Now*—cancelled! Finally one more, *The Count of Luxembourg*, to star W. C. Fields and Irene Dunne. Cancelled!

By the beginning of 1936, W. C. swore he was in perfect health, but the studio demanded that he see one of their doctors. He did and the doctor certified that Fields had all systems go, but he had to stay on the wagon. He did not, but started work anyway on another remake of an old film.

THE MAN ON THE FLYING TRAPEZE

65 minutes
Sound, black and white
Released July 26, 1935, by Paramount
Presented by Adolph Zukor
Produced by William Le Baron for Paramount
Directed by Clyde Bruckman
Screenplay by Ray Harris and Sam Hary
Based on a story by Charles Bogle (W. C. Fields) and Sam Hady
Additional material written by Bobby Vernon and Jack Cunningham
Photographed by Alfred Gieks
Song: "On the Banks of the Wabash"

CAST:

W. C. Fields	Ambrose Wolfinger, memory expert
Mary Brian	Hope Wolfinger, his daughter
Kathleen Howard	Leona Wolfinger, his wife
Grady Sutton	Claude, his stepson
Vera Lewis	Mrs. Cordelia Neselrode, mother-in-law
Lucien Littlefield	Mr. Peabody
Oscar Apfel	President Malloy
Lew Kelly	Adolph Berg, the gildersleeve
Tammany Young	Willie the Weasel, burglar
Walter Brennan	Legs Garnett, burglar
Arthur Aylesworth	Night court judge
Harry Ekezian	Hookallockah Meshobbab, the Persian Giant
Tor Johnson	Tosoff, the Russian Behemoth
David Clyde	J. Farnsworth Wallaby, Australian sheep man
Ed Gargan	First patrolman
Eddie Chandler	Second patrolman, on motorcycle
James Burke	Third patrolman
James Flavin	Henry, the chauffeur
Sarah Edwards	Car owner
Carlotta Monti	Ambrose's secretary
Sam Lufkin	Ticket taker
Helen Dickson	Miss Dickson, president's secretary
Lorin Raker	Ring announcer
Heinie Conklin	Street cleaner
Michael S. Visaroff	Homicidal maniac
Harry C. Bradley	Peeved driver
Rosemary Theby	Helpful pedestrian
Jack Baxley	Night court officer
George French	Clerk
Billy Bletcher	Timekeeper
Robert Littlefield	Neighbor with correct time
Minerva Urecal	Italian woman in ambulance
Mickey Bennett	Office employee
Dorothy Thompson	Information girl
Albert Taylor	Clerk
Mickey McMasters	Referee
Charles Morris	Turnkey
Eddie Sturgis	Bystander at arena gate
Pat O'Malley	Officer
Keith Daniels	Ticket seller
Joseph Sawyer	Ambulance driver

Filmed at Paramount in Hollywood.

Working titles: *Everything Happens at Once,* then *The Memory Expert.*

Reworking of *Running Wild,* from eight years earlier, with Mary Brian repeating her role at Fields' daughter.

Part cut from the final release print: Charles French.

Poppy

—1936—

Rumors proliferated that W. C. was in pre-production on any number of movie projects or he was working diligently on his own script; but in fact for almost ten months Fields' ill-health kept him from the Paramount lot. Then in March 1936 Fields got a little better and started work again, but just barely. The rumored movie possibilities for W. C. were shoved aside to recapture a proven winner from long, long ago—*Poppy*.

Now push the clock back thirteen years. Fields was forty-three years of age and one of the top headliners on the New York stage, but not yet considered a star. Philip Goodman approached the juggling comedian to put him in a musical comedy. Scared, even recalcitrant at first, Fields finally accepted the offer and made a big hit on Broadway as Professor Eustace P. McGargle, F.A.S.N, in the Dorothy Donnelly play. He took a relatively weak script, ad-libbed freely, threw in his own skits and became a star. The play of course was *Poppy*. Two years later D. W. Griffith renamed the play *Sally of the Sawdust* and put it on film. Now, eleven years after *Sally* (née *Poppy*), Paramount wanted to again put Fields in the role of McGargle, freeing him from the household and placing him back in the midway. Paramount had no intention of changing the Fields formula for success: Put Fields' past works on sound film.

The stage play *Poppy* and the silent film *Sally* extensively displayed Fields' juggling prowess, but the fifty-

six-year-old W. C. squelched the idea of juggling for this 1936 film. He knew he had lost his great skill years before and did not want to present a second-rate imitation of his formerly magnificent talent, especially in view of his failing health.

All the trades thought W. C. was now in the pink, but he and Paramount knew otherwise. He had fallen off the wagon a few months earlier and was now drinking with more gusto than ever before. This in turn worsened his insomnia, which became nearly pernicious. And if that was not bad enough, during the filming of a scene for *Poppy,* in which Fields had to ride an 1890s type of bicycle, he fell off and broke a vertebra. (Sound familiar?) For most of the shooting of *Poppy* Fields wore a debilitating type of scaffolding device under his garments in order to keep his back straight. His ill-health, however, was only subtly discernible, and that was mostly through omission. Fields appeared on the screen much less in this picture than in his previous few movies, and long shots were used extensively so a double could be substituted for the comedian. (Not coincidentally that double was Johnny Sinclair, who had saved Fields' life nine years earlier on the set of *Two Flaming Youths* when W. C. fell off a bicycle and broke a vertebra the first time.) Even for some medium shots Sinclair donned a W. C. mask and played the role. On the other hand, when it came to Fields himself working in front of the camera, he gave

Gloria Swanson and Herbert Marshall visit W. C. on the Poppy set.

W. C. with Rochelle Hudson (Poppy). The cowboy on the right is of course Bing Crosby, who took a break from his shooting of Rhythm on the Range, *also produced by Paramount, to visit with W. C. on the Poppy soundstage.*

absolutely no indication of his ailments. Indeed, he played his bits and skits with verve—crisply, jauntily and youthfully.

Although this *Poppy* is by no means Fields' best film, W. C. did add some new and hilarious comic sequences.

The story is the same as the original *Poppy* with minor changes. McGargle runs the old army game, a shell game, and Poppy helps out. They enter Green Acres, a small town, to set up shop at a local fair. On the way he finds a dog, tells Poppy to wait for him and carries the canine to the local gin mill. He orders a drink and puts the dog down on the bar. The bartender recognizes the animal; it looks just like a neighbor's dog. McGargle assures him it is not: "The dog's a cross between a Manchurian yak and an Australian dingo." McGargle asks the dog what he will have. The dog answers, "Milk in a saucer." A trick of ventriloquism of course. The bartender is astounded. He wants to buy the dog. He will pay twenty

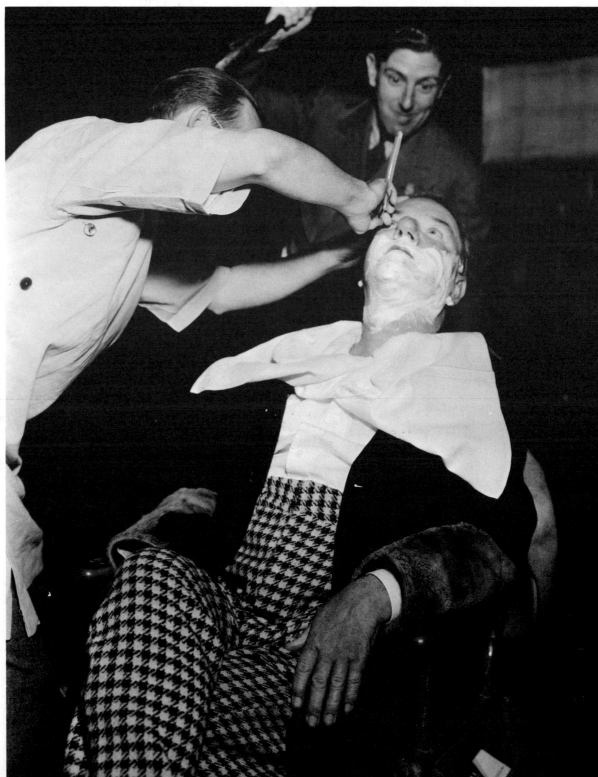

A variation on the burglar-catcher chair. Director Eddie Sutherland stands poised ready to strike his star in this gag photo from the set of Poppy.

dollars. McGargle grabs the money, finishes his drink and leaves. On McGargle's way out the dog speaks: "Just for selling me, I'll never talk again." Fields warns the bartender, "He probably means it. He's awfully stubborn." Exit.

Eustace and Poppy set up their booth at the Green Acres fair and begin to ply their trade. Someone says the Mayor is coming, and McGargle hides his shells and gives a lecture on the evils of gambling which impresses the Mayor. Poppy, on the other hand, impresses the Mayor's son. In no time the two fall in love. Eventually McGargle catches wind of an estate closing, the Putnam estate. The Putnams are forced to give their great inheritance to someone other than the legal heir because the legal heir, a girl of Poppy's age, has not been seen since she was a baby. Unless the girl shows up soon, the estate goes to someone else. McGargle hooks up with a crooked lawyer and they draw up a specious document proving Poppy is the lost Putnam girl.

Now Poppy and the Mayor's son are in love and they plan to marry. An engagement party is set. There McGargle gets tangled up in a hilarious croquet game and is slated to perform that evening on his beloved Kadula Kadula. But soon McGargle's scam is uncovered and he must take it on the lam. He grabs an old-type bike with the big wheel in front and the small wheel in back and outraces the police.

The marriage is cancelled and Poppy hides with a matronly woman who knows the Putnams and has taken a real liking to Poppy. Soon the woman finds Poppy's locket. She asks where she got it and Poppy says that her mother gave it to her a long long time ago. She does not remember her mother, because she died when Poppy was very young, but there is a picture of her inside the locket. The woman looks aghast! The photo is of the Putnam daughter. Poppy really is the Putnam girl. The marriage is set again and everyone lives happily ever after.

Released on June 19, 1936, *Poppy* received surprisingly good reviews, except that most critics bemoaned Fields' limited time on the screen. Nonetheless, they unanimously hailed W. C.'s return. That was premature. First it was time to break another vertebra. That is correct. This was the third time. He broke it soon after the filming of *Poppy*. Stories surrounding the incident vary, and the truth is hard to find, but two facts remain constant in all versions: One, Fields was out of bed for the first time since the break caused by the fall from the *Poppy* bike, and two, he was holding a good stiff martini. Evidently somehow or other the ground and his derriere collided and he broke his coccyx or tailbone. Here again the accounts diverge. Those who claim his glass broke assert that when Fields was told he broke his coccyx or tailbone he responded, "Worse than that. I've lost my drink." On the other hand, there are those who swear W. C. still had a full glass after the fall and yelled triumphantly, "I didn't spill a drop!" then passed out in pain.

Who says he never took direction! Well, at least for this photo Fields listens to instructions from Eddie Sutherland as Rochelle Hudson and others look on.

Here is how the studio captioned this one: "Brother visits comic. When W. C. Fields, Paramount comedian, became ill recently his brother Walter Fields of Philadelphia rushed west to be with him. Now that Fields is completely recovered and busy in Paramount's Poppy, his brother has decided not to return east after all. He is going into the real estate business in Los Angeles. He's a former fight promoter." The truth: Walter stayed in Hollywood with his brother because W. C. was still very sick. He never did pursue the real estate option, and did not return east until W. C. started to improve, months after this picture was taken. But, yes, Walter was a former boxing promoter and at one time, for a short time, shared the stage with W. C. in vaudeville. Members of the Dukenfield family were always surprised that the older brother became the famous comedian. They all claimed that Walter was twice as funny as W. C.

Candid shot with Catherine Doucet as they await preparations for the next camera setup in the croquet scene from Poppy. *Fields' ill-health is reflected in his pained expression in this still and his lifeless expressions in the rest. The studio took more still pictures of W. C. for this film than for any of his others, probably hoping to catch the comedian with some vitality. They never did.*

Whatever the true story, one thing was certain: Fields hurt terribly during the filming of *Poppy*, as evidenced by the shooting of the last scene in the motion picture. It was set up as a very tender moment between father and daughter. Poppy told McGargle that she will settle down in Green Acres. She will not continue traveling with her father. Fields gently held Poppy by her shoulders. "Let me give you one word of fatherly advice."

"Yes, Pop."

"Never give a sucker an even break." He patted her softly, turned, stole someone's hat, purloined a handful of cigars and walked outside in the elegant Fields manner. However, when he turned the corner, hidden from the camera's eye, W. C. fainted from the pain in his back.

A final note: This was the first time Fields worked with Bill Wolfe, a skinny, ugly tall character actor. From the beginning of Fields' career he took a particular interest in peculiar-looking people. He would use them over and over in his act. During the *Follies* it was Shorty, during his first years in Hollywood it was Tammany Young, whom he was still using, and now Bill Wolfe.

With *Poppy* finished, Fields' health deteriorated drastically. Not only was his back out of whack, but the booze-related maladies were proliferating. At times he claimed, "Gabriel is stalking me with his horn," or, "The man in the bright nightgown is coming to my door." Such fears, however, did not abate his intake of alcohol, but he did change its moniker from "tonsil varnish" or "demon rum" to "angel's milk." It would be a while before W. C. would work again.

POPPY

75 minutes
Sound, black and white
Released June 19, 1936, by Paramount
Produced by William Le Baron for Paramount
Associate producer: Paul Jones
Directed by A. Edward Sutherland
Assistant director: Richard Harlan
Based on the 1923 stage play *Poppy*, by Dorothy Donnelly
Screenplay by Waldemar Young and Virginia Van Upp
Music and lyrics by Ralph Rainger and Leo Robin, and Sam Coslow and Frederick Hollander
Song: "Poppy"
Costumes by Edith Head
Photographed by William C. Mellor
Art direction by Hans Dreier and Bernard Herzbrun
Edited by Stuart Heisler
Sound recording by Earl S. Hayman and John Cope
Musical direction by Boris Morros
Interior decorations by A. E. Freudeman

CAST:

W. C. Fields	Professor Eustace P. McGargle, F.A.S.N.
Rochelle Hudson	Title role
Richard Cromwell	Billy Farnsworth
Granville Bates	Mayor Farnsworth
Catherine Doucet	Countess Maggie Tubbs De Puizzi
Lynne Overman	Attorney E. G. Whiffen
Maude Eburne	Sarah Tucker
Bill Wolfe	Egmont
Adrian Morris	Constable Bowman
Rosalind Keith	Frances Parker
Ralph M. Remley	Carnival manager
Wade Boteler	Bartender
Tom Herbert	Astonished barfly
Dewey Robinson	Calliope driver
Tom Kennedy	Hot-dog vendor
Ada May Moore	Snake charmer
Charles McMurphy	Constable
Tammany Young	Joe
Cyril Ring	Yokel
Jack Baxley	Yokel
Frank Sully	Yokel
Harry Wagner	Yokel
Eddie Waller	Yokel
Del Henderson	Yokel
Doc Stone	Deputy sheriff
Malcolm Waite	Deputy sheriff
Dick Rush	Deputy sheriff
Jerry Bergen	Gardener
Grace Goodall	Second woman gossip
Gertrude Sutton	First woman gossip
Nora Cecil	Woman
Johnny Sinclair	Double for W. C. Fields

Filmed at Paramount in Hollywood.

Remake of *Sally of the Sawdust* from eleven years earlier. Adapted for radio broadcast on *The Lux Radio Theatre* in March of 1938.

The 1932 MGM picture *Polly of the Circus* echoes neither Fields picture, although Maude Eburne is featured in both talkies. The original Goldwyn version of *Polly of the Circus* (1917) featured the D. W. Griffith actress Mae Marsh as an orphan named Polly, who, like Poppy, is raised as a child of the circus.

An Interlude With Radio

"It is hard to tell where Hollywood ends and the d.t.'s begin"—W. C. Fields.

The trade papers said that immediately after filming *Poppy*, W. C. again went to Soboba Hot Springs to rest. While there, the papers said, he caught double pneumonia and was rushed to the hospital unconscious. The pneumonia persisted, rumor had it, and Fields lost over sixty pounds. His illness lasted more than a year, and he could not work. A Dr. Citrone took care of Fields for some of the time and charged the comedian $12,000 for about two weeks of treatment. W. C. felt the fee was outrageous and he refused to pay. The doctor sued. About a year later the case came to trial. In court it was revealed that Citrone had treated Fields not for pneumonia but for delirium tremens. The comedian lost sixty-plus pounds because he was forced to stop drinking for a while. Citrone claimed that W. C. drank two quarts of gin a day. Fields vehemently denied it. "It was only one quart."

Fields' face broke out in tiny exploding volcanos, and ruptured blood vessels turned his nose a brilliant red. But early on at Soboba, when he did not think he was so sick, he and Dr. Citrone would play golf. The physician was new at the game, so the comedian instructed him, emphasizing the need of the golfer to keep his eye on the ball. Fields would tell the doctor to concentrate and stare at the ball a long time before hitting it. While the doctor focused on the tee, Fields would sneak a miniature bottle of gin from his bag, gulp the contents, hide the empty, then tell the doctor, "Now hit the ball." This went on for all eighteen holes.

Because of the court battles with Citrone, word spread that Fields suffered from the d.t.'s, but W. C. made jokes about his illness: "It's a wonderful thing, the d.t.'s, you can travel the world in a couple of hours. You see some mighty funny and curious things that come in assorted colors." W. C. stayed off the hard stuff for nearly three months, but it is when he quit that the d.t.'s began.

It seemed the longer he kept off the booze the more bizarre the hallucinations became, so it was easy for W. C. to deduce that quitting alcohol was worse than drinking and that obviously the doctors did not know a damn thing. He soon returned to the bottle.

But, while in the hospital and suffering from the booze-induced apparitions, W. C. claimed he also contracted double vision. He could not read. To while away the hours someone gave the old gent a radio. Fields did not care much for radio and listened to it infrequently, but now he had to have something to crack the boredom. Much to his surprise, he liked it. ("I'll have the management send you up a radio" was the line W. C. scripted into *The Bank Dick* three years later, intending to comfort a bedridden bank examiner he had surreptitiously poisoned.) He would faithfully listen to Fred Allen, Joe Cook, Jack Benny and Burns and Allen.

In January 1937 Fields was still in a hospital bed while Paramount prepared for their silver jubilee program to be broadcast over the radio. It was to be held in honor of Adolph Zukor, and the Paramount brass wanted Fields to participate. He was too sick to go there, so they brought a microphone to him. Among the other Paramount stars heard over the airwaves that night of January 7, 1937, was a bedridden W. C. Fields. The comedian sent his greetings to Mr. Zukor from a hospital room. The audiences loved hearing Fields' voice, and they let the radio networks know. He was a hit.

Then, he said, the radio came to his aid again. He heard someone announce over it that he was at death's door. That got him mad. He jumped from the bed and started exercising a little, and in no time he was doing better. In April he was well enough to leave the hospital. He did admit, however, that indeed the "grim reaper took a swipe at me . . . but I had the presence of mind to duck just in time."

Once out, all the radio shows made Fields grand offers to guest-appear. He finally accepted Chase and

Here is the original caption: "He's a Jolly Good Fellow — Only W. C. Fields seems sad, very sad indeed, as the colleagues of Charlie McCarthy on the NBC Chase and Sanborn Hour *make merry at Charlie's redwood punch sociable. The cowboy in the center is Charlie. Standing, left to right, are Fields, Nelson Eddy, Edgar Bergen and Don Ameche. Seated, Robert Armbruster and Dorothy Lamour."*

Fields wanted out of radio and back into picturemaking. Here he sits with William Le Baron, the chief of production at Paramount, and Carlotta Monti, who gave her name as Carmencita LaVola, one of her many aliases.

Sanborn's lure and shared the mike with Edgar Bergen and Charlie McCarthy on May 9, 1937. Smashing! The trio of Bergen, McCarthy and Fields got such an incredibly great reception from critics and audiences alike that Chase and Sanborn immediately signed Fields to a sixteen-week contract at over $5,000 a week. He had fun, and at first he felt that radio work was easier than filmmaking. He could stay on the airways until his health completely returned.

This was not the first time W. C. courted offers to do radio. As early as 1935 Fields auditioned for NBC, and the company loved it and wanted to sign him; but: "I didn't think radio would go anywhere. I felt the same way about movies when I worked on stage. Now I'm ready to jump when television comes around."

Because of his ill-health, his Chase and Sanborn contract did not force him to attend rehearsals and also let him call in sick up until two hours before air time. His illness and the revelations from the Citrone-Fields court battle were a source of jokes between old "bugle beak" and "the woodpecker's flophouse." Charlie McCarthy said to W. C., "Mr. Fields, I read in the papers that you drank two quarts of whiskey a day. Ha-ha-ha. What would your father say if he heard that?"

"He'd say I was a sissy."

W. C.'s allegiance, however, was to Paramount. Once he was asked why he talked about his studio so often on the radio. "I owe the studio a debt. William Le Baron [then chief of production at Paramount, replacing Ernst Lubitsch] and others took a chance on me when others had no hope. *International House, Million Dollar Legs,* and *If I Had A Million,* these people put me in those pictures, and following their success Paramount gave me a contract. That's why my picturemaking will always come before my radio work. To me pictures mean Paramount. I'm going to make another picture for them soon and more pictures for as long as they want me. This radio business, by the way, is grand. I like it. I like to work on the air and I like to listen to other programs. No one except a person who was shut up as I was can understand what a great boon radio is. I like to think that maybe whatever I do on the air is helping to cheer up some poor guy who can't get out of bed or who is in a wheelchair. If the general public likes the show, and I think we have a great collection of great entertainers, then so much the better."

On September 18, 1937, Fields' contract with Chase and Sanborn ended. The company wanted to renew it, but the "original half man, half nose," as McCarthy called W. C., refused. Fields complained about the bad scripts the writers sent him and how he had to write the entire show himself once a week and how he could not take the grind. It sounds fishy. The *Chase and Sanborn Hour* was known for Fields' and Bergen's ad-libs. As always, the script meant nothing to W. C. He just wanted to get back into pictures, and after all, he still had contractual obligations to Paramount. He could not take the toll of working both radio and movies. So he quit the air and started writing his scenes for Paramount's next extravagant opus, *The Big Broadcast of 1938.*

Fields returns to Paramount, and by the warm welcome awaiting him in his dressing room it would seem the studio is happy to have him back. The message from Mitchell Leisen, which read "My doctor says don't work too hard," is prophetic. It is also funny because whoever made up the card misspelled Leisen's name. So much for Hollywood sincerity.

189

The Big Broadcast Of 1938

—1938—

The first one was in 1932, starring Bing Crosby, Burns and Allen, Kate Smith and the Mills Brothers. They called it simply *The Big Broadcast*. Then Paramount made a sequel, *The Big Broadcast of 1936*, with Jack Oakie, Burns and Allen, Charlie Ruggles, Mary Boland and a cameo by Bing. They did it all again the following year, with Mitchell Leisen directing, this time starring Jack Benny, Burns and Allen, Martha Raye and Shirley Ross. For *The Big Broadcast of 1938* Paramount wanted to use Benny once more. They had already signed Martha Raye and Shirley Ross, but for some reason Benny could not be cleared. In July of 1937 he was replaced by Fields. W. C. was still under contract with

Paramount, but he was also in the middle of his sixteen-week engagement on the *Chase and Sanborn Hour*. Dorothy Lamour frequently guest-starred on that radio program, and Paramount signed both of them to deliver the *Chase and Sanborn Hour* audience. All the *Big Broadcasts* followed the same format—a sort of filmed radio. The stars were well known for their on-the-air antics. However, the most striking similarity among the *Big Broadcasts* was the near absence of a plot. The movies were primarily loosely connected sketches and specialty numbers. Bob Hope used to crack that *Variety* had offered a $10,000 reward to anyone who could recite the plot after screening the picture. Well, here goes!

In *The Big Broadcast of 1938* W. C. plays the two Bellows brothers: S. B., a frivolous millionaire in love with booze, golf and billiards; and T. Frothingell, a relatively staid, self-possessed fellow who wears glasses and a mustache (a normal-looking mustache). The brothers own a luxury liner, the S.S. *Gigantic,* which is slated for a transatlantic race against the S.S. *Colossal.* The *Gigantic* contains a secret powerhouse in its belly which picks up electrical power from short wave radio broadcasts and transmits it to the propellers. T. F., aware of S. B.'s penchant for disaster, dispatches his brother to the *Colossal,* figuring S. B. will ruin the *Colossal*'s chances by his mere presence.

The race is today and S. B. must hurry, still he figures he can squeeze in eighteen holes before the gun. On the way to the links he stops to fill his limo with gas. Disaster! The attendants pander to S. B.'s every need while the millionaire gruffly orders them around. He needs air in his tires and gas for the car. While barking instructions his rear tire explodes and S. B. leaves in a huff, spilling gas all over. On the way out he yells, "Out of my way before I sue somebody." He tosses his lighted cigar out of the car and it ignites the station. Boom!

On the golf course, S. B. rushes from tee to green riding his golfcart/motorcycle/airplane with an army of caddies in hot pursuit. After a few good gags in a sand trap and other golfing parodies, S. B. is told the ships have already started the race. He drops the wings to his golfcart, steps on the gas and heads down the runway . . . ah . . . fairway, scattering his caddies: "Gangway, boys, gangway." He is airborne. He passes a few geese and somewhere over the Atlantic spots a ship and lands with a thud. He is on the wrong ship—his own, the *Gigantic.*

The *Gigantic* has a huge room in its hull which is fit for dancing, eating, drinking and entertainment. From the stage, radio broadcasts will be sent recording the ship's shows and periodically serving updates on the race. Buzz Fielding, Bob Hope, is scheduled to MC the broadcasts, which are supposed to begin soon, but Buzz cannot be found. He is still on the mainland. In jail! It seems Buzz has been married a few times, three to be exact, and has failed to pay the last installment on his alimony to the trio. You see, he bet his entire salary on the success of the *Gigantic.* With his failure to pay the three ex's, Joan, Cleo and Grace got a warrant for his arrest and put Fielding behind bars. Fortunately, Buzz's new love, Dorothy Wyndham, arrives and posts bail. The two rush to the dock, to board the *Gigantic.* Unfortunately, bail is not good enough for the three former spouses; they want their alimony and they do not need another ex-wife diluting their payments. So they dash to the *Gigantic.* All five arrive just in time! Mike, Ben Blue, has been handling the MC duties execrably. Buzz takes over, much to the relief of the crowd and, undoubtedly, the radio station.

After S. B. lands he takes a group of reporters on a tour of the ship. He brings them to the elaborate power plant, informing them confidentially, "This is our still." The Captain of the ship, knowing S. B.'s bent toward calamity, wanted the owner kept from the power plant,

A slimmed-down W. C. aboard his golfcart/motorcycle/airplane ready to take off in movies again with The Big Broadcast of 1938.

but too late now. Bob Hayes, the inventor of the new engine and chief engineer, hears of Bellows' tour and rushes to his plant just in time to see S. B. poke the tip of his umbrella into an electrical coil, shorting out the works. Frightened by the blaze of electrical arcs and feeling sabotaged by the elaborate contrivance, Bellows orders the door locked and demands that the engine never be used. Hayes is dumbfounded. Without his invention the *Gigantic* cannot win the race.

Down in the ship's ballroom, Buzz has just announced to the stunned crowd the *Colossal* has taken the lead. No one is more disappointed than Buzz. He tells his newest heartthrob, Dorothy, that if the *Gigantic* loses he cannot marry her. He will be broke. And then he has to remind Cleo, Grace and Joan that if the *Colossal* wins, no more alimony. That prospect unites all three ex's with Dorothy. They form a conspiracy. Grace will attract Bellows away from the power station while Dorothy will lead Bob Hayes down to the engine room to see what can be done to fix the device.

Getting gas! He will get a lot more gas later on from Paramount.

Stand clear and keep your eye on the club! (Caddy on far left is former Dead End Kid and now Dr. Bernard Punsley.)

Grace charms S. B. into giving her a grand tour, ending up on the bridge far away from the power house. To impress Grace, Fields suckers the bridge crew into a navigational closet and locks the door, then jauntily takes over the helm. Down in the engine room nothing seems to work—except for Bob and Dorothy.

Eventually the *Gigantic* crew escapes and the Captain retakes the helm. Soon there is an S.O.S. heard over the radio. S. B. recognizes the voice. It is his daughter Martha Bellows. He tells the Captain to let her sink. "Wherever she goes disaster follows. Seven years ago she crashed her plane into a mirror factory." The Captain overrides Bellows' orders and goes to the rescue. They find the small raft just in the nick of time. Martha was standing in the aft end of the rubber raft blowing gale-force winds into its makeshift sail while her partner, Scoop McPhail, egged her on. But she just stepped on the side of the rubber raft with her high heels, deflating the skiff. They fish Martha and Scoop out of the water. On deck, the first thing Martha sees is an enormous mirror. She takes one look and it shatters.

After creating a series of disasters, Martha ends up in a refuse duct. She crawls through and wends her way somehow to the power plant, where Bob has all but given up trying to fix the engine. Martha is immediately attracted to Bob and in her swoon falls against the dead power plant, giving a sharp jolt to one of the electrical coils. A metal piece falls out. S. B.'s umbrella tip! That was the problem all the time. Bob works quickly and gets the electrical engines humming, and now it will be a race to the finish.

Meanwhile, Buzz has been spending the afternoons with his first wife, Cleo. They have been drinking and talking and remembering old times in a song, "Thanks for the Memory." Slowly they realize they are still in love with each other. They want to try it again together. They are going to get remarried. That is all right with Buzz's fiancée, Dorothy. She has been spending her time with Bob Hayes, and they have fallen in love also, and they too decide to marry.

Up on the old brine, the *Gigantic* under full power now, has caught sight of the *Colossal,* the French coast and the finish line. It is going to be a squeaker. The *Gigantic* wins by a nose, and everybody is happy.

The Big Broadcast of 1938 broke into the public on February 18, 1938. The critics wrote particularly mediocre reviews—some bad, none good—but praised W. C.'s work, while taking time to complain that he was not on the screen enough. Fields had just finished a serious bout with delirium tremens and still suffered from a bad back and insomnia, but it seemed none of these maladies attenuated his talents or comic timing. Indeed, the only indication that W. C. might have been sick was his noticeable lack of girth, and that in fact made him look good.

Again the movie as not much more than filmed radio, and taken as such it was quite entertaining, although at first the discontinuity is jarring. Some of the radio pieces, self-contained, were good, others seemed to drag. Shep Fields and his Rippling Rhythm Orchestra used cartoons to enhance the audio, and that was pleasant, although it ran a little too long. On the other hand Kirsten Flagstad's number, "Brunnhilde's Battlecry," from the *Ring* cycle, although beautifully sung, was stunningly out of place. Fields knew that and tried to tie it into the rest of the film by ad-libbing a line right after the song, but Leisen nixed it, so Fields appealed to Le Baron: "I still say that my crack after the Flagstad number about the parrot on board would not offend anyone—including Miss Flagstad. It is entirely in character and should be tried in front of a regular audience. I have absolute confidence in it and further confidence it is not overstepping any bounds of propriety or good taste." Fields lost. On another complaint which failed with Leisen, W. C. again went to the Le Baron court of appeals. The comedian wanted the scene with Joan, Cleo, Grace and Fielding at the jailhouse axed. In his memo to his mentor W. C. wrote that he thought that scene was "irrelevant, immaterial and stinko!" Appeal denied.

Fields and the song "Thanks for the Memory" received the most praise from the critics. The song got an Academy Award, but Fields did not. The honor for the song brought Bob Hope and Shirley Ross another pairing later that year in the movie *Thanks for the Memory.* That film was not very good.

The Big Broadcast of 1938 was Bob Hope's first feature-length film; he had made only one short movie before this. Paramount did not envision much of a future for the ski-nosed comedian; in fact, they were planning on dumping him because they thought he was too much

Looking over the side (at absolutely nothing) are, from left, Dorothy Howe, Ben Blue, W. C. Fields, Grace Bradley (married to William Boyd of Hopalong Cassidy fame), Lynne Overman and Martha Raye. Richard Denning is in the back row between old pals Blue and Fields. (Fields, you will recall, once arranged to turn Ben Blue black and blue for stealing material.)

like Jack Benny. Under most circumstances, Hope should have been the star of the picture—he occupied more footage than any of the other actors—but his name came sixth on the credits. Martha Raye was listed above him because the studio really wanted to promote her, having decided that she had a great future in film, although soon they would change their minds. Bob Hope certainly had a warm spot for the movie, however. Even today his theme song is "Thanks for the Memory."

Hope was fascinated by Fields. Paul Jones (who became a longtime producer for Bob Hope) introduced the two and assured W. C. that Hope was just fine. In his book *The Road to Hollywood* Hope recalled: "Fields was naturally suspicious of strangers. But he accepted me into his confidence. I spent many hours in his dressing room, listening to his peculiar philosophy." As the two were swapping stories one day, a top Paramount executive knocked on the door looking for money for the studio Community Chest drive. It seemed everyone on the lot had by now donated except for Fields. Bob Hope remembered the exchange:

"Very nice of you to drop by, my good man," welcomed W. C. "I'd like very much to help you with your admirable drive. Unfortunately, there is a very compelling reason why I cannot." Fields grabbed the executive's curiosity. He was all ears. "You see," Fields happily continued, "I am a member of the F.E.B.F."

"The what?"

"F—— everybody but Fields."

Bob Hope admired W. C.'s habit of doctoring scripts. Not so much for what he did but how he did it. After analyzing a particular script, Hope learned, W. C. would then consult with the Paramount bosses and boast he could "fix the thing," for a price naturally—usually about $50,000.

One script Fields did not "fix" was a Paramount newsreel item called "W. C. Fields Acts Again." There was no script. The piece was shot on the set of *The Big Broadcast of 1938.* Paramount would often feature their contract players in their newsreels, generally for promotional purposes, but in this case Fields had been so ill that his return was indeed newsworthy.

He had appeared at least once before in a studio newsreel. In that one they filmed W. C. exercising in his backyard with two bathing beauties looking on. From a beam above his porch were hung two gymnastic rings. He grabbed the rings, pulled himself up, and then, out of the camera's view, someone obviously placed a stand underneath W. C.'s feet. With everything set his amazing feats of strength began. After completing an impossible half iron cross he hooked a ring under his nose and stretched out his arms, seemingly holding himself up only by his proboscis. When he lowered himself the two women felt his muscles and commented on his strength. He commented on their limbs and then went back into his house.

The newsreel item filmed on the set of *The Big Broadcast,* however, was considerably more intriguing.

Director Mitchell Leisen succumbs to the lure of liquor as a pleased W. C. looks on with a devilish air. Wonder what was in that drink? This was one of the very few tranquil moments between the director and the comedian.

W. C. photographed as he attends a preview of **The Big Broadcast** of 1938 *at the Paramount Theatre in Hollywood.*

The first part caught Fields, Le Baron and Mitchell Leisen between scenes. All seemed to be happy. Jokingly Leisen handed Fields a milk bottle. The comedian made an attempt to drink from it, but, alas, he could not muster up the courage.

From there the film cut to the links as it followed W. C. through a sequence from the golf scene in the motion picture. Not only do we see it as it actually appeared in *The Big Broadcast of 1938,* but we also see the scene being shot. We get a clear view of the old 35 mm cameras cranking away shooting the star as he plied his trade.

"W. C. Fields Acts Again" was a unique piece of footage. Of course watching Fields being filmed was fascinating, but it was equally fascinating to view the *apparent* comradeship between Leisen and his star at the beginning of this news item.

William Le Baron had recently ascended atop Paramount's regime as chief of production and of course indulged his friend W. C. in most respects, at some cost to Mitchell Leisen, the stylish director. Leisen was well aware of Le Baron and Fields' mutual admiration; and W. C., frankly, exploited the situation by taking license whenever possible. Fields' aggression against authority—any authority—was reason enough for trouble, but more, Fields was his own best director. And in Bob Hope's view that was why he resisted direction from a taskmaster like Leisen. Result—a problem. Evidently intent on causing the maximum amount of chaos in the least amount of time, W. C. purposely ruined scenes, used profanity and ad-libbed private jokes. Once he rattled off on a hilarious tangent and concluded by looking into the camera: "They're going to run out of film pretty soon."

Well, Leisen ran out of patience. He refused to direct W. C. any longer, and Eddie Cline was brought in to captain certain scenes with Fields. That was just fine with the comedian, because, of course, he directed Cline. Meanwhile, Leisen had a heart attack as shooting was concluding, and many people suggested that Fields brought it on. Said Mitchell Leisen of W. C. Fields: "He was the most obstinate, ornery son-of-a-bitch I ever tried to work with."

This was the beginning of the "absolute" Fields. He had just spent a year in the hospital bordering on death. He had plenty of time to think, to look at his past, to analyze the present and to form his future. For the past, he knew *he* was the best judge of his comedy. Although he did not know why people laughed, he knew how to make them laugh better than anyone else. The people he had listened to and followed over the years, against his better judgment, always proved wrong. For the present, he knew he would eventually recover from his illness, but it would not be long before "Gabriel blew his horn" for good. He did not think he had much time left.

For the future he would do it his way or not at all. He would, from now on, follow his own instincts, his own natural talent for comedy. With the people he liked he would treat them more generously than ever. For those he did not like, he would not hold his tongue. The future promised a lot more run-ins with Hollywood's big guns, with fights filled with vitriol and spite. Those in authority were always the villains in Fields' eyes. Future associations would reflect a nearly schizophrenic view of W. C. Fields. Half the people with whom he worked—most directors, producers, almost anyone in authority—will echo Leisen's assessment of him. The other half—most of his fellow actors and all of his friends—will call him the sweetest, dearest man who ever trampled a Hollywood studio. Both opinions were correct.

The box-office drought and the critics' not so colossal reception of *The Big Broadcast of 1938* helped Paramount decide to abandon their *Big Broadcast* format for good. Also abandoning ship would be some of Paramount's high-priced talent—most were pushed overboard.

With work finished on *The Big Broadcast of 1938,* Fields turned his attention to writing another script for Paramount: *Mr. Bumpus Goes to London.* And the result? . . . Mr. Fields goes to Universal.

THE BIG BROADCAST OF 1938 _____

97 minutes
Sound, black and white
Released February 18, 1938, by Paramount
Produced by Harlan Thompson for Paramount
Presented by Adolph Zukor
Directed by Mitchell Leisen
Story by Frederick Hazlitt Brennan
Adaptation by Howard Lindsay and Russel Crouse
Screenplay by Walter De Leon, Francis Martin and Ken Englund
Choreography by LeRoy Prinz
Music director: Boris Morros
Songs: "Thanks for the Memory," music by Ralph Rainger, lyrics by
  Leo Robin; "You Took the Words Right out of My Heart," by Jack
  Rock; "Zumi Zumi," music and lyrics by Tito Guizar; "Brunnhilde's
  Battlecry," from *The Ring of the Nibelungens* by Richard Wagner;

"The Waltz Lives On"; and "Mama, That Moon Is Here Again"
Photographed by Harry Fischbeck
Edited by Eda Warren and Chandler House
Assistant director: Edward Anderson
Musical adviser: Arthur Franklin
Art direction by Hans Dreier and Ernst Fegte
Sound recording by Gene Merritt, Don Johnson and Charles
  Althouse
Interior decorations by A. G. Freudeman
Costumes by Edith Head
Animated cartoon sequence by Leon Schlesinger
Special effects by Gordon Jennings
Additional scenes directed by Eddie Cline (uncredited)
Additional material written by Charles Bogle (credit delisted)

CAST:

W. C. Fields	T. Frothingell Bellows, millionaire playboy
W. C. Fields	S. B. Bellows, his brother (both parts originally intended for Jack Benny)
Martha Raye	Martha Bellows, his daughter
Dorothy Lamour	Dorothy Wyndham
Shirley Ross	Cleo Fielding, ex-wife number one
Lynne Overman	Scoop McPhail
Bob Hope	Buzz Fielding, radio MC (originally intended for Jack Benny)
Leif Erickson	Bob Hayes, seaman-inventor
Grace Bradley	Grace Fielding, ex-wife number three
Rufe Davis	Turnkey
Tito Guizar	Himself
Lionel Pape	Lord Droopy
Virginia Vale/Dorothy Howe	Joan Fielding, ex-wife number two
Russell Hicks	Captain Stafford
Leonid Kinskey	Ivan
Patricia Wilder	Honey Chile
Shep Fields and His Rippling Rhythm Orchestra	Themselves
Kirsten Flagstad	Herself
Wilfred Pelletier	Himself
Ben Blue	Mike
Archie Twitchel	Steward
James Craig	Steward
Richard Denning	Officer
Michael Brooke	Officer
Jack Hubbard	Officer
Bill Roberts	Officer
Clive Morgan	Officer
John Huettner	Officer
Bruce Wyndham	Officer
Kenneth Swartz	Officer
Lee Bennett	Officer
Rex Moore	Caddy
Bernard Punsley	Caddy
Don Marion	Caddy
Brooks Benedict	Pier extra
Irving Bacon	Prisoner, harmonica player
Wally Maher	Court clerk
Muriel Barr	Showgirl
Mary MacLaren	Woman
Florence Wix	Woman
Carol Holloway	Woman
Gertrude Astor	Woman
Nell Craig	Woman
Ethel Clayton	Woman

Gloria Willimams	Woman
Ray Hanford	Pilot
John Jennings	Adagio dancer
Harvey Karels	Adagio dancer
Harry Lauter	Seaman
James Burtis	Third reporter
Bud Geary	Helmsman
Jimmy Conlin	First reporter
Billy Daniels	Pageboy
Stanley King	Chauffeur
Rebecca Wassem	Extra
Sherry Hall	Second reporter
Jack Daugherty	Guard
Randolph Anders	Bartender
Paul "Tiny" Newland	Black gang sailor
Harry Wilson	Black gang sailor
Gus Glassmire	Bit
Lal Chand Mehra	Bit
Edgar Norton	Secretary to T. F. Bellows
Sheila Darcy	Haughty girl
Virginia Pound/Lorna Gray/Adrian Booth	Divorcee
Marion Weldon	Girl
Yvonne Duval	Girl
Dorothy Dayton	Girl
Gwen Kenyon	Girl
Nora Gale	Girl
Harriette Haddon	Girl
Joyce Matthews	Girl
Suzanne Ridgeway	Girl
Dorothy White	Girl
Helaine Moler	Girl
Paula De Cardo	Girl
Ray Hanford	Pilot
Don Brodie	Radio operator
Frank DuFrane	Radio operator
Mae Busch	Waltz costume extra
Jerry Fletcher	Second gas station attendant
Robert Allen	First gas station attendant
Auguste Tollaire	First official
Charles Millsfield Sr.	Second official
Charles Teske	Adagio dancer
Jack Dawson	Adagio dancer
Ted Meredith	Adagio dancer
Pete Rand	Adagio dancer
Edward Cutler	Adagio dancer
Ted O'Shea	Adagio dancer
Estele Eterre	Dress extra

Filmed at Paramount in Hollywood.
  Working title: *That Man's Here Again.*
  Previously, Paramount had produced and distributed *The Big*

Broadcast, made in 1932, and then *The Big Broadcast of 1936* and
The Big Broadcast of 1937. This fourth entry was the last of the
series.

The Paramount Parting

Writing the script went very slowly for Fields, but whenever he finished about ten pages he sent it to the studio. Adolph Zukor read over the work and found W. C.'s writing disappointing and his output unsatisfactory. Fields countered in a letter dated April 22, 1938, saying that even though he had submitted only ten pages they were "ten playable pages." Then W. C. complained about his impediments. He had written a story several times, but the studio writers "tore it down and added so much unplayable trite dialogue" that he had to rewrite everything. This opened the door to a full broadside aimed at Hollywood's comedy writers. He accused the lot of plagiarism, citing the example of a writer who gave Fields a complete scene. After reading the script W. C. told the man that he performed the same scene in his last picture. The writer laughed heartily. "Christ, I forgot where I stole that one from." Fields ended his letter to Zukor: "I am not writing this letter because I am piqued, but because I wish to assure you that I esteem your friendship and it would deeply grieve me if by hook or crook or misunderstanding you would lose the regard I know you have for me."

Five days later Fields turned in thirteen more pages, which made the script complete, and wrote Zukor telling him that the stuff in the envelope was fully playable pages, and although less than the studio writers' number of pages, that can be easily explained: "All descriptions of eyes, dresses, and fingernails have been omitted." Insufficient!

Paramount's frequent financial instability resulted in quite a large roster shake-up in the late thirties. Mae West, Marlene Dietrich, Gregory La Cava, Martha Raye and more were dumped by the studio and accepted with open arms by Universal. By May of 1938 W. C. Fields had joined the trek. Just one month after his last letter to Adolph Zukor, Paramount terminated its long relationship with their comic star. Producer Arthur Hornblow Jr., who headed the production of *Mississippi,* was happy with Fields' departure. He commented at the time that he would not work with W. C. again for "five million dollars." Fields wrote to his friend Jack Norworth about the divorce: "Paramount has given me my conge. I do believe that the motion picture business is on the down beat; however, it may be that I have outlived my usefulness. Either way, it's o.k. with me. However, when they told me to screw, I had the presence of mind to grab the salary check for the whole picture, and quite a goodly sum for some writing I did for them." (Note: Fields' one-year contract called for three movies for $300,000. The year was up and Fields had performed in only one picture. But he wrote a second and wanted to do it, yet Paramount said no. Fields felt he should be paid for the film anyway, plus some of the writing he did for *Big Broadcast of 1938.)* "And if that be larceny let them make the most of it.

"The director, the supervisor, the producer and the whole menage that was responsible for the fiasco of the 'BIG *Brody* of 1938' are all retained at the studio, which is another satisfaction and adds to my fiendish glee.''

He continued, writing that he has a radio date with Bergen and McCarthy for June 5, 1938, and hoped it would be good enough to give him monthly work. The letter sounded resigned but not depressed. His talent could not stay untapped too long. When word spread of the Paramount parting, offers came roaring in from radio and film. If W. C. had taken one job on the radio and one job in film, the trades said, he could have made $39,000 a week.

While W. C. perused the offers, rumors flew. In July some reporter caught Harold Lloyd in New York promoting his most recent film, *Professor Beware*. Lloyd told the newspapermen that he was also in the city scouting for some comedy material for the ex-Paramount star W. C. Fields. That became bold headlines: Lloyd and Fields to team—Lloyd producing, Fields starring. Fields loved the idea. For the first time in a long long time he would be working with a production executive who understood how comedy was made. Harold Lloyd certainly did. Both gentlemen responded favorably in the press to such a union, but for some reason a deal was never consummated.

W. C. did not jump at any of the offers; he merely looked at a few, but mostly he kept writing his own script. When finished in August he handed the idea to Universal Pictures. They liked it. Fields negotiated for $115,000 a picture and more freedom than Paramount gave him. Agreed! Fields now worked for Universal.

Also in August Mervyn Le Roy asked W. C. to take the title role in *The Wizard of Oz*, or play the cowardly lion, or grab whatever character he wanted, guaranteeing the comedian $5,000 a day and star billing. His agreement with Universal did not proscribe working with another studio; his contract was a one-picture affair. Negotiations with MGM continued. They came close to agreement. On September 9, 1938, the papers blared that Fields had signed to play the Wizard. That was not true of course. Fields turned down Mervyn Le Roy for two reasons, as the comedian explained. One, he was writing a totally Fields movie and desperately wanted to put in on the screen; and two, he did not think *The Wizard of Oz* was that hot a property. Fields now concentrated fully on his first Universal picture, *You Can't Cheat an Honest Man*.

Out of work and considering the prospects. The photo on the wall shows W. C. with Wiley Post and Will Rogers.

Still sick and ordered to stay on the wagon, W. C. Fields vows "No more booze!" He breaks that vow soon after the photographer leaves. Note: The publicity department would not release this still until the labels on the bottles were disguised.

You Can't Cheat An Honest Man

—1939—

For his first opus with Universal, Fields stuck to his winning formula of his recent Paramount years. He resurrected and reworked a piece from his past. The embryo of *You Can't Cheat an Honest Man* was a story called *Grease Paint,* a screenplay written for Fields in 1933 by H. M. Walker. It was a circus story, and for some reason it was rejected in the early thirties, and Fields' "original story" was made into *The Old Fashioned Way* instead. Now, starting fresh with Universal, and promised carte blanche, W. C. considered the old script anew. He decided to add plot elements from his silent movie *Two Flaming Youths,* and once again he became the circus faker, the lovable charlatan.

W. C. freely altered the two old scripts as the spirit moved him, adding brand-new scenes and comic bits. When he was finished he truly had an original screenplay, which he called *You Can't Cheat an Honest Man.* The title certainly befitted Fields' conception of himself. Throughout his career W. C. felt he was a man of integrity surrounded by cheats who tried to sell him short: vaudeville theatre managers who refused to pay him; Ziegfeld, who put Ed Wynn under Fields' pool table to steal laughs; Paramount, who promised him freedom then left him shackled on editing-room floors (Universal soon would follow suit); and a wife who stole his son. That was Fields' perception of the world around him. And yet, despite his ubiquitous perfidy, he was a success, a star with a bankroll to boot. Why? Because he was an honest man. He could not be cheated.

In 1936 Universal had changed its approach to filmmaking for the sake of economy. Carl Laemmle Jr. had just left, and with him went the prestige films he made which were bankrupting the studio. Universal returned instead exclusively to B moviemaking, with an eye on full-family entertainment. They were low-budget motion pictures with no major starring names, except for the rapidly emerging Deanna Durbin. Gradually over the years the studio developed its own modest stars for the program musicals, comedies, westerns and serials that had always done well. So by 1938 they could afford to take a chance on W. C. Fields, and they did.

Fields, as Larson E. Whipsnade, heads a severely indebted circus which must flee the law in every county in which it plays. The film opens with the circus wagons crossing the county line just out of reach of a sheriff's warrant. The law is Whipsnade's nemesis from the outside; from within the circus it is Edgar Bergen and Charlie McCarthy. Their contract, however, makes it impossible for Whipsnade to fire them. But, alas, he may not have to. Since Larson E. never pays his workers, McCarthy and Bergen have decided to quit the show. No sooner has the decision been made than Whipsnade's daughter enters the tent looking for her father. Victoria is a beautiful young woman. She asks Bergen her father's whereabouts. Bergen is smitten and he forces the conversation to last longer, finally asking Vicky for a date. She nervously agrees. Well, perhaps he will stay with the circus after all. Whipsnade really is not that bad. He quiets his dummy by telling him that Vicky has a younger sister.

Meanwhile, Larson E. works the ticket wagon. His employees run in and out of the wagon and Whipsnade always has something to say to them. With this constant chatter he still dispenses tickets to the eager customers but always is losing count of the change, in the customer's favor of course. He reminds every customer to "count your change before leaving the window. No refunds after leaving the window." What Larson E. does is double up the bills, making the customer think he is getting more change than is due, so they do not count the money at the window but run off to count the bonanza later. If they had counted at the window they would have gotten the right change, but in their hurry to cheat the cheater they lose. Thus, *You Can't Cheat An Honest Man.*

Eventually Vicky finds her father and during the conversation Larson is forced to escape a creditor. Vicky finds out about the circus's financial bind. Vicky has been courted by an extremely wealthy man, Roger Bel-Goodie, a pompous stuffed shirt of the lily-white-hands variety. Filled with compassion for her father's plight, she reluctantly decides to marry the rich guy. Her brother, Phineas, a son ashamed of his father and family heritage, is happy to hear the news, and so is the father. Phineas puts on the airs of the rich and has been arguing strongly

with Vicky to marry Roger. The union would advance Phineas' own career and station. But up until now Vicky has refused. Today, however, she will call Roger and tell the louse she will agree to the distasteful bonding. They set a marriage date. The wedding will be at the Bel-Goodie mansion.

While staying around the circus a few days, Vicky and Edgar have been getting along smashingly. They usually meet at the circus's hot-air balloon. This day Vicky has asked Edgar for a special meeting. She has to tell him of her engagement. Before their conversation, however, Vicky has to pack. While she is gathering her belongings, her father appears and talks soothingly to his daughter. She is late and tells Larson that she has to hurry, talk with Edgar and change, then race to the Bel-Goodie estate. With all magnanimity the father assures his daughter that he will tell the duo the distressing news and be as gentle as possible. Vicky thanks him and leaves.

Larson grabs a knife and a block of wood and heads for the balloon. He carries on a perfunctory conversation with the pair, but whenever the two are not looking Whipsnade takes a whack at the tether with his knife. Soon Edgar and Charlie are airborne, and unaware of the pending marriage. Larson runs back to his trailer, takes care of some business, then dresses for the evening's festivities. He puts his empty-headed sissy assistant, Grady Sutton, in charge, grabs the circus chariot, motored by two huge white horses, and heads for the Bel-Goodies'.

Up in the air Bergen and McCarthy assess the danger of their ride and decide it would be safer to parachute. They jump. Meanwhile, Vicky has her accelerator down to the floor in her convertible, trying to make the ceremony on time. An incredible coincidence! Edgar and Charlie land in the back seat of Vicky's car and the parachute comes to rest on top of the automobile. Unable to see, Vicky veers into a gas station, killing a gas pump and bouncing off a police car. The cops arrest the trio and lock them up. The guard on duty ignores Vicky's pleas to free her so she can get to her wedding. They simply have to wait for the judge. *Wedding!!!* Edgar hears the news for the first time. He is shocked and hurt; nonetheless he keeps a stiff upper lip and congratulates her. Finally the judge comes. He knows Bel-Goodie and lets Vicky go to the ceremony. Edgar and Charlie stay behind. For sure they will leave the circus this time. They are eventually freed and Edgar grabs a bike and rides down the road with Charlie on his back.

The Bel-Goodies anxiously await the Whipsnade girl. Phineas nervously mixes with the passel of "crème de la crème" assuring all that his sister will be arriving soon.

Finally Larson E. enters. The butler opens the door holding a card tray. Whipsnade mistakes it for a tip tray and throws out a few coins. He removes his cape and the butler takes it and folds it nicely on a chair. But Whipsnade opens it up, boldly revealing the inside, which with black lettering on white silk advertises the Whipsnade circus.

"A little free advertising."

Phineas walks up aghast and quickly folds the cape,

W. C. (Larson E. Whipsnade) is about to teach David Oliver why *You Can't Cheat an Honest Man*. *Grady Sutton looks on in the background.*

admonishing his father to be on good behavior. Larson looks around the joint and whispers to Phineas, "Looks like there's a lot of necks washed here tonight." Again Phineas reproves his father: "These people really matter."

"I know, son. They're the crème de la crème, the noblesse oblige . . . we have acrobats in our circus."

Roger's father, jowly and self-important, asks Larson the whereabouts of his daughter.

"She's gone to the barber shop for a facial. She may be some time. There are eight or nine men ahead of her."

Mr. Bel-Goodie decides to give Larson another chance. "I understand you're in big-game hunting." Phineas did not want the Bel-Goodies to know his father ran a circus, so he had told them he was a great white hunter instead. Whipsnade plays along. He tells them he was up at Lake Titicaca where he befriended a snake—a scream from another part of the room—Mrs. Bel-Goodie has fainted. She has an aversion to snakes and the mere mention of the word makes her pass out. The entire party rushes to her aid while Whipsnade, oblivious to the commotion, continues his story. He rambles on for a while about how this snake slept in the Whipsnade wickiup that night when a marauder entered. Mrs. Bel-Goodie slowly comes to. Larson is talking away about his *rattlesnake*—scream! She faints again. Whipsnade continues. Apparently his slimy little friend stuck his fangs in the ruffian's fetlock. Someone gets a taste of whiskey for Mrs. Bel-Goodie and Whipsnade wants one too. The whiskey has revived her. Larson continues, amid the pandemonium, that his snake—there she goes again—stuck its tail out the window and rattled for a constable. Someone asks Larson what all the fuss is about.

"Give, Queenie!" Shower time at the circus. If you don't have running water try an elephant's running nose.

With Eddie "Rochester" Anderson in Honest Man.

Whipsnade points to Mrs. Bel-Goodie: "Evidently she's had too much to drink."

Phineas finally pulls his father away and grouses about the disgusting story. Whipsnade admits it might have been too much and offers to make amends by telling the drummer story.

"No!"

"I could clean it up a bit."

Whipsnade finally saunters into the playroom. A Ping-Pong table sits in the middle of the room. A society matron leans casually against the wall. Larson goes over to speak to her. She is pulling on a cigarette, which is locked into a long cigarette holder. She drags, then exhales. "How's your Ping-Pong?" Smoke pours into Larson's face. Spitting out the fumes and not understanding the question, he takes offense: "Fine, how's yours?" Then he grasps the question and laughs lightly: "Ping-Pong, Ping-Pong . . . I was champion of the tri-state league and the Lesser Antilles many years ago."

A spiffy, proper sort of young man sets up at one end of the table, paddle in hand. A challenge. Whipsnade grabs the paddle at the other end.

"Serving!" the sport says.

"No thanks. I've had enough."

The man serves. The match is on. It is fiercely fought. All the Bel-Goodies' guests come to see. Back and forth the ball goes, and farther and farther from the net Whipsnade is forced. Finally he is in another room. He trips on the carpet, does a complete somersault and lands just below a ringing phone, which he answers. The game is over, and so is Mr. Bel-Goodie's patience. Mr. Bel-Goodie stands in front of Mr. Whipsnade and shouts a fusillade of fifty-dollar insults, concluding with "You egregious tartuffle."

"Is that in my favor?"

Phineas interrupts. "This is no time for levity, Dad."

"This isn't levity, son." To Bel-Goodie: "Declare yourself. Is that a male or female tartuffle?" Flustered, Mr. Bel-Goodie calls for his wife: "Mater!" Getting a kick out of the nomenclature, Larson E. responds, "He's calling for his mater." Then, mimicking the pretension, "Pater!"

Vicky shows up. Roger meets her at the door. She tries to explain her tardiness to her fiancé, telling him that a funny thing happened on the way over. Roger will not stand for it. He tongue-lashes Vicky for her inconsiderate behavior, then sends in a few stinging shots about her father, ending with "The only reason you're marrying me is for my money, my . . . my social prestige."

Vicky has had it too. "Why don't you get off the trapeze and get down to the sawdust where you belong." Phineas, Larson and the older Bel-Goodies join the fray with the rest of the party. Phineas hears insults about his father and has a change of heart. He starts to defend Dad. Larson hushes up the fight, and takes over himself. He delivers a few smooth cuts to the astonished crowd and concludes the tirade with "And if there is such a thing as a tartuffle, you're it." The sheriff enters. Larson sees him. "Great snakes!" Mrs. Bel-Goodie screams, faints! Larson E., Vicky and Phineas slip past the constable, jump on the chariot and off they go. On the way they pass Edgar pedalling in the opposite direction. Vicky yells to him that the marriage is off and tells him to hurry and come along. Edgar swings the bike around and pedals furiously to catch up, but Larson E. keeps riding hard and fast.

Released February 17, 1939, almost one year to the day of *The Big Broadcast of 1938*'s premiere, *You Can't Cheat an Honest Man* received the same old critical response: Fields is hilarious, but the story is disjointed, the

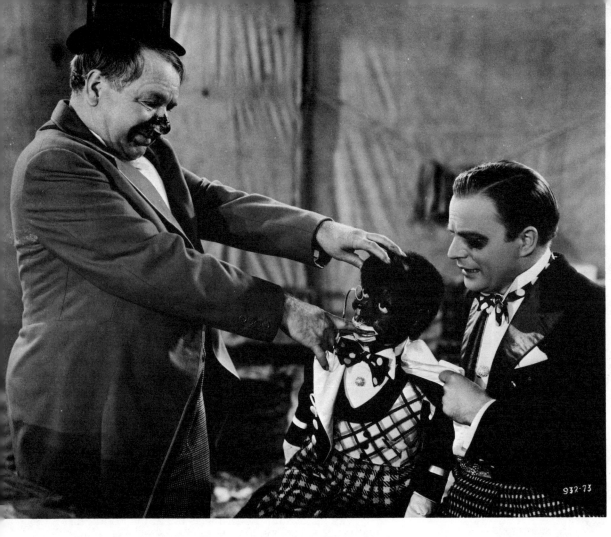

With Edgar Bergen and Charlie McCarthy, who is made up for a minstrel act on the fairgrounds.

plot is weak. But there was a new complaint. Some critics attacked W. C.'s characterization of Larson E. Whipsnade, saying he was a charlatan all the way through, not once given to pathos or sympathy, never once justifying the normal Fields description as the lovable larcenist. They said his irascibility never eased. True! W. C. complained about the same thing. Indeed, Fields was so angry about the butchering job in the editing room he refused to promote the picture when Universal asked him to: "Advertising the picture would add a few hundred thousand dollars to the gross and naturally swell my coffers. But, I am afraid that in this case it would only add to our embarrassment and humiliation. We certainly don't want to go on the air advertising we are releasing an obviously unfinished picture or that Universal is heedless to the entreaties of the artist, producer and the staff, who are offering their services without additional cost, so enthusiastic are they about the improvements that can be made with very little additional effort or expense."

Fields wanted tenderness in this film. From the very first scene he wanted to establish his character as a kind-hearted rogue. His initial scenario began with a piece he stole from *Sally of the Sawdust*. Gorgeous, Fields' wife, lies dying in bed after a fall from the trapeze. Before the "final curtain" she makes Fields promise to take care of the children and keep them away from the circus. Fields agrees, and as he wrote it in his scenario: "Then there is a tender scene between Gorgeous and myself." Surely such a sequence would have established

Whipsnade as a kindly character. Furthermore, Fields wanted the movie to conclude with a richly sentimental touch, but in both cases director George Marshall blue-penciled the idea. Fields went over his head.

In a letter to Cliff Work: "My only wish is to make this picture one that will stand, and without a story it is meaningless. My character is shot. The picture now is a jumble of vaudeville skits—Bergen and Fields in their vaudeville skits." (That should never have bothered old "plotless" Fields. The fact is W. C. here was mistaking character development for story line.) "The play which I had written has been written out. I suggest again that you shoot the opening scene of Gorgeous' death. This is a transition from low comedy to pathos, which has been employed by the finest writers since the days of Indian and Chinese drama and has not been altered. The scene outside of the Bel-Goodie home with me apologizing to the children, baring my heart to them, and the children deciding in my favor and giving their reason for coming back to the circus is most important. Then in the midst of the scene showing the children's love for their father and the father showing his real love for his children . . ." (Again, how much of this is pure art, and how much of it is W. C. creatively hoping that his son and his wife would come back to him? How much of this harks back to 1904, when Hattie, W. C.'s wife, refused to bring her newborn baby and rejoin her husband on his vaudeville tour? She never did join him. And this scene never made it to the screen.)

202

Fields' letter continues: "Cliff, it looks to me like sabotage. Someone with the reins in his hands is ruining this fine picture." (A lightly couched reference to George Marshall.) "It is overloaded with two-reel comedy and no story, no pathos, no believable characters, the humanness and the truth have been deleted."

George Marshall and W. C. Fields hated each other. "Bill Fields never made me laugh," said Marshall, who incidentally also directed W. C. in *Hip Action*. "He was one of the meanest men I ever knew." Yet this was the same movie in which Constance Moore and Edgar Bergen raved about that "wonderful gentleman W. C. Fields." This was the new post-illness absolute Fields. Marshall could not understand W. C.'s brand of humor. The director even wanted to cut the best and funniest piece in *You Can't Cheat an Honest Man*—the marriage reception at the Bel-Goodies' home. Fields won that point and we all should be grateful he did.

The battles on the set were hot. In a letter to Lester Cowan, W. C. complained that Marshall had yelled at him on the set "at the top of his lungs." He called Fields "an egotistical bastard." Explaining further, W. C. wrote, "It would be unfair if I didn't leave it to Mr. Marshall to tell you what I called him." Fields continued, saying that he had written the story and scenes, some that included Bergen, yet Mr. Marshall refused to let him see the rushes.

There were more battles to come, but before continuing the coverage it should be noted that W. C. was wrong. Pathos or not, *You Can't Cheat an Honest Man* was an hilarious motion picture. Now, back to the fights.

Eddie "Rochester" Anderson recalled one bout in particular. It was during the scene in which W. C. was selling tickets from a large ticket booth. At one point Rochester walked in and reminded Whipsnade that it was Wednesday and time for his bath. W. C. closed the ticket booth window and was supposed to leave out the back door with Rochester following. The two were to parade to the bathing area a few feet away, which consisted of four sheets tied together forming a box. Queenie, the circus elephant, would use her trunk as a nozzle and squirt water at the bathers.

For reasons of temperamental fate nothing went right in that scene. Marshall would yell, "Action!" W. C. would open the door with Rochester following and they would start their parade to the shower. The ticket booth was an old circus wagon, and the two actors had to walk down three steps to reach the ground. Every time W. C. got to the bottom of the steps Marshall would yell, "Cut. Take that again will you, Bill? The sound was off." Or: "Stop, Bill! I'm sorry the lights were just not right. Do it again." And so on and so on; and every time something went wrong Rochester and W. C. had to turn around and climb back into the wagon and wait for the director's yell, "O.K., Bill. You ready? Action!" The scene was taken over and over and finally on about the eighth try Marshall yelled into the wagon, "I know it will work this time, Bill. Are you ready? Action!" No door opened and no word was heard from inside the wagon.

"Bill! What's wrong in there?"

Inside, Fields locked the door and poured a drink and just sat there. Rochester was nervous: "I think we better get going." W. C. sat with his feet propped up on a crate and said, "If you walk out that door I'll see you don't do this picture." Marshall was banging on the door. W. C. hollered, "This time *we're* not ready." He stayed comfortably in that ticket office downing drinks which he made from his portable bar. Rochester simply shrugged and joined in. Outside, Marshall coaxed, then threatened, then pleaded, then ranted and raved, all to no avail. The comedian just kept pouring martinis, one after the other. Finally the yelling and pounding from outside stopped, and a little later there was no sound at all. Fields smelled a trap. After about ten minutes Rochester said, "I think they must have left the set. I'll bet you they all went home." No, it was still an ambush. "They're a tricky lot," Fields warned. "They're out there all right." Whatever doubts Rochester had, he kept them to himself. Time passed quietly, and after about an hour or so W. C. put down his drink and yelled, "Now, George, we're ready. If you do it right this time." No answer. W. C. opened the door. The stage was dark and empty. George Marsall had cancelled the day's shooting much earlier and had stormed off. With a satisfied look on his face Fields grabbed his drink and walked across that deserted set arm in arm with Rochester.

The fighting between Fields and Marshall became so acerbic that Universal finally brought in Eddie Cline again to direct W. C.'s scenes. But because of Fields' overall disgust and antagonism now, he baited Cline incessantly throughout the remaining production, with the essential distinction being he hated Marshall while deep down he loved Cline. According to legend it is our loss no one ever filmed the parody and byplay between Cline and Fields, their quarrelsome racket supposedly being funnier than any film they made together.

Fields had other run-ins on the set, including an initial encounter with his pal Edgar Bergen. Jules Stein ran the Music Corporation of America (eventually MCA would buy Universal), and they represented Bergen at that time. Since Bergen was a big name on radio, MCA felt he should have the right to pick a director and be assured a certain amount of time on the screen. Fields heartily complained about Stein's provisions and threatened to work for MGM on *The Wizard of Oz* before starting *You Can't Cheat an Honest Man*. Universal was in a hurry and worried about losing the volatile comedian, so they quickly worked out a settlement between the two. On the set, however, Bergen and McCarthy and Fields got along famously, with only one exception. Evidently at the end of each day's shooting W. C. would return home, completely change the script slated for the next day, and then in the morning demand a cast meeting. He insisted that everyone pay attention and keep awake. A chair would be drawn up for McCarthy too. One day Bergen closed McCarthy's eyes and Fields kicked the dummy out of the meeting for falling asleep. McCarthy was never allowed to come back. Other than that the comedian and the ventriloquist actually were quite fond of each other and held each other in high regard. They bantered and ad-libbed wonderfully well, and W. C. admired anyone who could keep up with his extemporizations.

The fighting over *You Can't Cheat an Honest Man* did not end in 1939. In 1943, when Fields used the same snake story from this picture for a radio program, a fellow named Harry Yadkoe sued Fields for plagiarism. Yadkoe claimed he had written the story, sent it to W. C., never received a reply, then heard the piece on the radio. Fields countered that Yadkoe had taken the story from his film, revised it slightly, then tried to sell it to him. He went on to say he felt that Yadkoe was so "feeble-minded" to pull such a stunt, he never bothered writing back. Since W. C. failed to write Yadkoe, the verdict went to the plaintiff. Leaving the courtroom, W. C. commented to the newspaper folk that he had been seeing snakes all night, "and as a result I have a terrible hangover."

Although unhappy with his treatment so far at Universal, Fields nevertheless began writing another film, which Lester Cowan would produce. On April 3, 1939, W. C. asked in a letter to Cowan if Universal had decided on which picture they wanted: "the South American story or the story of the theatrical mother and the infant prodigy with the inebriate father who is aced out of the family. I refer to the story I told you over the phone several days ago."(The combination of these stories could easily have been an inchoate script for the upcoming film, *Never Give a Sucker an Even Break.*) He concluded his letter: "Tell them [Universal] not to phone me as I want to keep everything on record from now on. I refuse to be shuttled around on this one as I was in *You Can't Cheat an Honest Man.*" Neither proposed picture was made, but a strange and totally unexpected collaboration came to pass instead.

YOU CAN'T CHEAT AN HONEST MAN
76 minutes
Sound, black and white
Released February 17, 1939, by Universal
Produced by Lester Cowan for Universal
Directed by George Marshall
Assistant director: Vernon Keays
Screenplay by George Marion, Jr., Richard Mack and Everett Freeman
Based on an original story by Charles Bogle (W. C. Fields)
Musical direction by Charles Previn
Photographed by Milton Krasner
Art direction by Jack Otterson
Associate: Charles H. Clarke
Gowns by Vera West
Set decorations by R. A. Gausmam
Sound supervisor: Bernard B. Brown
Sound technician: Robert Pritchard
Assistant to the producer: Cliff Work (uncredited)
Additional scenes directed by Eddie Cline (uncredited)
Edited by Otto Ludwig (uncredited)
Songs: "Hi, Charlie McCarthy" and "Camptown Races"

CAST:
W. C. Fields   Larson E. Whipsnade
Edgar Bergen   Himself
Charlie McCarthy   Himself
Mortimer Snerd   Himself
Constance Moore   Vicky Whipsnade
Mary Forbes   Mrs. Bel-Goodie
Thurston Hall   Archibald Bel-Goodie
Princess Baba/Valerie Brooke/Valerie
   Gregory   Herself, daughter of the Rajah of Sarawak
John Arledge   Phineas Whipsnade
Charles Colman   Butler
Edward Brophy   Corbett
Arthur Hohl   Burr, bill collector
(Pietro) Blacaman   Himself, Hindu animal hypnotist
Eddie "Rochester" Anderson   Cheerful
Grady Sutton   Chester Dalrymple
Ferris Taylor   Deputy sheriff
James Bush   Roger Bel-Goodie III
Ivan Lebedeff   Ronnie, Ping-Pong player
Irving Bacon   Jailer
Eddie Dunn   Cop
Jan Duggan   Mrs. Sludge, Ping-Pong spectator
James C. Morton   Judge
Walter Tetley   Boy with candy cane
Evelyn Del Rio   Little girl who cries
Delmar Watson   Boy in bleachers with slingshot
Lloyd Ingraham   Mayor
David Oliver   Man cheated at window
Ed Thomas   Butler

Lewis Morphy   Circus attendant
Edward Woolf   Thin man
Lee Phelps   Sheriff
Ethelreda Leopold   Blond girl at party
Frank Jenks   Jerry, assistant
Don Terry   Ping-Pong player
Ed Thomas   Butler with phone
Charles Murphy   Lon, roustabout
Ted Hardy   Russian circus performer
Bobby Hare   Circus attendant
Leyland Hodgson   Butler
Dorothy Arnold   Debutante
Si Jenks   Hillbilly
Joe King   Police officer
Frank Melton   First yokel
Ralph Sanford   Truck driver, customer for ring the gong
Eddie Chandler   Highway patrol officer
Dora Clemant   Bit woman
Leyla Tyler   Society woman
Jack Clifford   Riding master
Otto Hoffman   Mayor
Ray Moyer   Fire eater
George Offerman Jr.   Western Union messenger
Grace Goodall   Spinster
Minerva Urecal   Spinster
Dick Dickinson   Contortionist
Frank O'Connor   Cop
Bill Wolfe   Elwood, hillbilly twin, world's smallest giant
Bill Worth   Hillbilly twin, world's tallest midget
Drew Demorest   Barker
Kay Marlowe   Second deb
Jennifer Gray   Third deb
George Ovey   Circus attendant
Billy Engle   Circus attendant
Beryl Wallace   Girl
Jack Gardner   Ticket seller
Duke York   Bit man
Art Yeoman   Barker
Ernie Adams   Barker
James Lucas   Barker
Jack Kenny   Barker
Byron Munson   Ping-Pong player
Major Sam Harris   Wedding guest
Russell Wade   Wedding guest
Ralph Brooks   Wedding guest
Dale Van Sickel   Wedding guest

Filmed at Universal in Universal City.
   The one-reel non-theatrical excerpt from this film is entitled *Circus Slicker.*
   Reworking of *Two Flaming Youths* from a dozen years earlier.

PRINCESS BABA

W. C. filling in for Edgar with Bergen's other dummy, Oliver.

W. C., with a defiant countenance, and George Marshall evidently discussing a scene. Art Smith and Bill Wolfe look on.

My Little Chickadee

— 1940 —

A couple of months after the premiere of *You Can't Cheat an Honest Man* Fields submitted two new script ideas to Universal. The studio, however, had their own W. C. project in mind. Their comedian's scenarios were shunted aside for the nonce to make way for the resurrection of a mid-thirties rumor—team W. C. Fields with Mae West.

That was a Universal trend then. It started with the smashing success of *Destry Rides Again,* which paired Jimmy Stewart and Marlene Dietrich and convinced Universal that teaming two stars in the same picture made the box offices hum. The great response to *Destry,* a spoof of western films, directed by George Marshall, further convinced the studio to put the luminaries in the Old West. If it worked well once, the studio figured, repeat it until it dies—Stewart and Deitrich in cowboy garb, West and Fields in an oater. Soon after that, Universal added Tex Ritter to Johnny Mack Brown's western series to form yet another team.

Ms. West's career was just edging into eclipse after such a meteoric rise in the early thirties. On the other hand, Fields was still riding a popular tide. Surprisingly, and for some unknown reason, Fields agreed easily to sharing the screen with West and he began work immediately on a scenario for the picture, or what he liked to call an "epitome." Universal again tagged Lester Cowan to produce and Eddie Cline to direct. Fields felt less sanguine with those two. Even though he picked Cline personally to direct him in *Honest Man,* he still harbored bad feelings over the result of that picture and blamed anyone in authority for, in his own words, "its miserable outcome," and of course that included his friend Eddie Cline. Nevertheless he agreed to work with them and then geared up to cover his flank this time around.

W. C. finished his first "epitome" in one month and gave it to the studio at the end of March. With the scenario he added a list of prospective titles: *"December* and Mae, Honky-Tonk, The Little Lady, The Sheriff and the Little Lady, Pueblo, Pueblo and Denver, First Lady of Lompoc, and Husband in Name Only." Furthermore, he suggested Gene Fowler would be the perfect screen writer, but added, "Miss West and myself will both do a great deal of the writing on our own behalf." Fields' skits in the first draft were nearly all incorporated in the final release; however, the plot changed drastically.

In this his original "epitome" Fields went overboard with pathos and tender sentiment. Evidently he wanted to make up for his losses in Honest Man where compassion was edited out. Again W. C. wrote in his favorite scene: Madame Gorgeous, Fields' wife, falls from a trapeze and is dying. Fields rushes to her bedside. Ms. West, Gorgeous' friend, is also on hand and promises Gorgeous that she will take care of Fields. The scenario, and the violins, continue. After Gorgeous dies, W. C. and Mae head west, leaving the circus behind. Mae opens a honky-tonk in one of those ephemeral gold-mining towns, and for a while Fields works for her. Eventually Fields marries West, a marriage of convenience, simply to give her respectability in the town. After a shoot-out in which Mae gets wounded and W. C. kills the desperados, the town doctor attends to Mae. But Fields is brought to trial and accused of killing two men. He is acquitted of the murders but declared guilty of "being the best shot in town." Meanwhile, his wife and the doctor fall in love, but Mae does not want to hurt the good man to whom she is married and refuses to ask for a divorce. Sadly Fields overhears the conversation and, though broken-hearted, gamely devises a plan. He tells the doctor that he has met another girl and wants out of his current setup. Since he does not want to hurt Mae, he inveigles the doctor to take Mae off his hands. The doctor obliges. Fields, who by now has been appointed Justice of the Peace and Mayor, presides over the divorce and the marriage with a stiff upper lip. In the last scene he watches the two ride off into the sunset, then resignedly he gathers his belongings and his dog, climbs atop a bike with the huge front wheel and small back one, and rolls off into the sunset himself. Suddenly, the dog runs in front of the bike and Fields does a colossal flip. The end.

It was odd that Fields should incorporate that last scene. After all, he had already broken his neck twice, in two different motion pictures, falling off that same type of bicycle. Perhaps he was just trying to prove he could ride. Nevertheless, here again Fields took a traumatic experience from his past and tried putting it on film.

Universal did not use his plot, but parts of the scenario did survive story rewrites and film editing, including Fields tending bar with Squawk Mulligan; a card game; a lynching scene; and the device of marriage in name only. For some of these scenes Fields took lines and bits from earlier films. The card game included tricks from Mississippi, and his stories about fighting Indians were also taken from that movie. The line "Go out and milk your elk" he snatched from The Fatal Glass of Beer, and he included a checkers game skit first filmed in The Pharmacist. But the majority of Fields' skits were new, and to get them in the final release took a grand and bitter battle.

But first, before the main event, I should get a few of the minor wars out of the way here. At one point the script called for Fields to refer to Mae West as Chiquita. A South American ambassador caught wind of it and created quite a stink, claiming W. C.'s comic portrayal of the Spanish-speaking peoples of the world was disparaging to his culture. It was almost cut, but W. C. fought hard to keep it in and he won.

In another scene Mae West slipped out of bed and tried to buffalo Fields by putting a goat in her stead. When W. C. entered the bed to join his wife, he sniffed, then asked, "Have you changed your cologne, dear?" Rumor reported that Mae West made him cut it. On still another occasion W. C. improvised an affectionate appellation, calling Ms. West "my little brood mare." She kicked that one out also. Finally, although it is not a fight, there is a point worth mentioning here before we go on to the knock-down-drag-out. W. C.'s scene tending bar with Squawk Mulligan took longer to shoot than it should have. Evidently when Fields prepared for the take he got behind the bar and just stared at all the bottles. Eventually director Cline walked over and asked him what was wrong. Why was he holding up production? W. C. turned slowly and, with almost a sad look in his eye, answered, "After thirty years of drinking I've finally discovered that all that time I've been on the wrong side of the bar."

Now on to the main event.

About May 5, 1939, Mae West and Lester Cowan received Fields' "epitome." Cowan accepted it and assigned Grover Jones to write the script. Jones finished his draft near the end of July. The result turned W. C. all shades of red, and in a hastily drafted telegram to Mae West, Fields disclaimed any connection with Jones' product, arguing that the scriptwriter did not follow the original story line, concluding, "We'll probably have to get together in the end and write the tome ourselves." Then he tickled her feathers with flattery: "I also want you to know I have a great admiration for you as a writer, an actress, and for you yourself."

Evidently Cowan told Jones to rewrite the script. Near the end of August came rewrite number two. Jones claimed he incorporated more of Fields' work this time. Fields disagreed and angrily dashed off a letter to Cliff Work, a supervising producer at Universal:

"There are no interesting scenes or smart dialogue and it doesn't move. Mr. Jones has omitted my scenes. He has written a light comedy part. . . . He has me a sad-looking creature. . . . I go crazy and leap over rocks. I shout, 'She loves me, she loves me!' Now I ask you, Cliff, has he written this for Fields or Shirley Temple?"

The rage continued. Fields followed his letter to Cliff Work with an in-depth page-by-page critique of Jones' script. With sarcasm he cut the script to shreds and entitled his little review "Corn with the Wind."

This, Jones' second rewrite of W. C.'s "epitome" has Mae West kidnapped by a mob of redskins, but she saves herself by charming the savages with their favorite Indian songs, sung in Indian, and as Fields claimed in "Corn with the Wind," sounding awfully similar to "Frankie and Johnnie." She also cows the cowboys by singing the same songs to them, and thus abating their natural tendency to massacre Indians. Fields is characterized as a down-and-out prospector suffering from melancholia and a propensity for melodrama. He has been spit on by fate. Not only is his gold digging a bust, but he has lost the one thing he truly loves, Mae West.

It did sound like pure schmaltz. After Fields concluded his ridicule of Jones' second script, he wrote that Cowan and Cline thought they had a great story, and that Cline "had insulted me to my face by innocently asking me if Jones' original script wasn't my original story." Apparently Fields' tirades over the script were going on for quite some time, to the point that Universal threatened to sue Fields for $115,000, his salary for acting, if he did not get to work on the picture. So Fields added to his critique: "I repeat again, I will do any picture you suggest, even against my better judgment, for Lester [Cowan] has me scared about that one-hundred-thousand-dollar suit you are going to instigate against me."

Fields stayed clear of Cowan, hoping to get a better response from Cliff Work. Soon after that last letter and critique, Fields wrote Work again, on August 30, 1939, summing up the problem and giving a solution:

"The work I'm doing on the screen differs from that of anyone else. My comedy is of a peculiar nature. Naturally, no writers have been developed along the lines of my type of comedy and this is why I sometimes have differences with writers, supervisors and directors alike. I am misunderstood mostly by these departments, but the customers and the critics seem to get my point o.k." The solution: "Give me the final say on the cutting, the supervising and the direction and I will write the story gratis-free. Eliminate factional disturbances such as making it a director's picture or a supervisor's picture or a writer's picture. Make it a Mae West—W. C. Fields picture. . . all

this talk about my being ill and not strong and the kindly suggestion that I work about six hours a day is not necessary. I have never felt better physically or mentally in my life." It appears that Cowan had explained Fields' harangues as a symptom of his illness.

Then Fields threw his lance at his chosen director, Eddie Cline, in a September 1 letter to Cliff Work: "I picked Mr. Cline as a director because I thought him efficient, inexpensive and someone I could talk to and get a direct reply from, but recently when he laughed so heartily at nothing when Mr. Jones read his first script to us and in the presence of Mr. Jones thought it a great story, then later agreed the story was impossible . . . I felt he was not sincere." Also in this letter Fields reneged on his offer to write the script for free, telling Work that now he would have to pay: "Maybe it will give it more importance."

In mid-September W. C. finished rewriting his story and sent a copy to Mae West. In the cover letter he recounted some of the hot-tempered exchanges he had had with the trio—Cowan, Cline and Jones—and revealed his new tactic: "I'm giving them the silent treatment." He further told her his scrivenings were copyrighted and said he forbade Jones to use any of them, which essentially damned any Jones script. Probably the most interesting facet of these vituperative *Chickadee* exchanges was Fields' excessively cordial communications with MaeWest. W.C.seemed to have taken a "you-and-I-against-them position. Although no letters from her to Fields could be found, the graciousness of Fields' letters never changes, indicating that, at least before shooting, she responded in kind.

By the middle of October, nearly seven months since the bickering began, it seemed W. C. and Mae had finally gotten rid of Jones. Fields wrote to Cliff Work again: "I

Two mighty profiles meet head on in this scene from Chickadee. They belong to Margaret Hamilton (remembered forever as the Wicked Witch of the West) and W. C. (who was supposed to have played the Wizard of Oz).

"You're a plumber's idea of Cleopatra." Perhaps these were the soft words of love whispered to Mae West in this scene from Chickadee?

have read Mae West's script and I must admit that it is a far better script than mine." He then added that Ms. West had graciously agreed to a collaboration with him. He continued: "During my entire experience in the entertainment field, I have never had anyone catch my character as Miss West has." Finally he stated that he would demand a bundle from Universal for writing his dialogue for the picture.

So, who wrote *My Little Chickadee?* West or Fields? From Fields' original "epitome" a logical conclusion can be drawn. Mae wrote her material, W. C. wrote his, and then they collaborated (meaning ad-libbed) in the scenes in which they both appeared. The plot, however, was most likely Mae's idea. Ms. West on the other hand gave her account of the authorship. It was inaccurate, but she maintained that she wrote all but a few of the final script's 135 pages. She claimed Matty Fox told her that W. C. "fought them and held them up" until they agreed to

accord him co-author credit on the screen. Mae claimed she first saw the picture a month after release and learned only then about the screenplay billing.

In any event, the stars' script "alliance" worked well. Moreover, the two seemed to have conspired against Lester Cowan. Fields liked writing West about Cowan's silliness. At one point W. C. wrote that Cowan wanted to use the prizefighter Tony Galento in the film, then scoffed at the thought. By the end of October it appeared that Fields-West got Cowan relieved of his duties, even though he does receive screen credit as executive producer. Fields wrote Mae West on October 20, 1939: "Frank Pope of the Hollywood Reporter . . . called me at Chasen's [a restaurant in Hollywood and a favorite Fields hangout] and wanted me to confirm the rumor that Lester had been taken off the picture, which I refused to do. I told him Lester had a sore tooth and as far as I knew he was taking a forced vacation on account of this. I think this about closes everything without any mud slinging." Jack Gross took over from Cowan and W. C.'s relationship with him was friendly. For now, whew!

With that battle truncated, casting began. Rumors flew that Cary Grant had been brought in to play the part of a masked bandit. Never confirmed. On the other hand, Humphrey Bogart *was* given the script, but when he read it he refused the part: "I would read my lines at the end of which a note read, 'The following ten pages to be supplied by W. C. Fields.' Then I would read more of the lines followed with another note, 'The following ten pages to be supplied by Mae West.' "

Apparently these interruptions in the script continued all the way through. Finally Joseph Calleia was offered the role and he grabbed it.

Then Fields had some of his own casting suggestions. He wanted to use Grady Sutton, Bill Wolfe and Jan Duggan—members of W. C.'s self-advertised "Fields Comedy Company." He got Wolfe and Duggan but for some reason lost Sutton. Then Fields wanted George Moran, of Moran and Mack, the Two Black Crows. W. C. fought very hard to get the job for his old vaudeville friend. You see, a few years earlier Fields hired both of them for one of his films. The two were on the East Coast at the time and so headed across country in a car. On the way they got into a terrible accident and Mack was killed. That all but ended his partner's career. Fields later found out that George Moran was working a seedy theatre in San Francisco. W. C., feeling partially responsible, had to help his old friend and invited him to perform in *My Little*

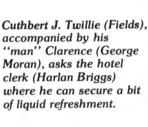

Cuthbert J. Twillie (Fields), accompanied by his "man" Clarence (George Moran), asks the hotel clerk (Harlan Briggs) where he can secure a bit of liquid refreshment.

Twillie trying to pass off his personal I.O.U. as bond for his card game with Morgan Wallace. "It's worth its weight in gold."

Guilty "of splitting a bottle with an Indian." W. C. and George Moran.

Chickadee. The studio agreed, and the remaining Black Crow played Fields' Indian friend Clarence.

The script written, the characters set, only one more hurdle was left—put it all on film. With the stars' egos finally in front of the camera, the seemingly cordial relationship between West and Fields dissipated. They battled long and hard to top one another on screen. When director Cline was asked what it was like directing the duo and their volcanic temperaments, he said, "I'm not directing them, I'm refereeing." During respites between scenes Fields antagonized Ms. West by yelling loud enough for her to hear things such as "Ah yes, she's fine figure eight of a woman, isn't she? A handsome lass if there ever was one . . . and exceptionally well preserved too." Or calling her "a plumber's idea of Cleopatra."

On her part, West fought back where Fields lived. The teetotaling Ms. West demanded that her contract contain a clause giving her the right to close the set if she ever caught Fields drunk. She had claimed that sure enough one day she found W. C. inebriated and, as promised, shut the set. Dick Foran was asked his version of the story. "The fellow drank all the time, but I never saw him drunk." He continued, saying he never remembered West closing the set, but perhaps he did not work the day she did it. Anyway, Dick Foran felt that possibly she caught Fields downing a noggin of gin, and since she believed if you took one drink you had to be drunk, she demanded an end to the day's work.

Both stars ad-libbed freely throughout the epic, which kept the crew in stitches. Some scenes had to be delicately cut to delete Cline's laughter at a surprise addition to the script.

In all fairness to both stars, their occasional bouts on the set were nothing compared to the expected battles.

The full blowouts, the major contention over screen time, or the titanic tantrums by one or the other over scene stealing never materialized, a definite relief to all involved. But do not get the impression they enjoyed themselves during the production or continued their pre-shooting cordiality. They did not.

Mae plays Flower Belle Lee, the unreluctant kidnap victim of the dreaded masked bandit. Her townspeople, convinced she and the desperado are lovers, kick her out of town, sending her to Greasewood City. She can return home only after gaining respectability. Miss Gideon, the town's head censor, chaperones Flower Belle. On the ride to Greasewood City the train is stopped on its tracks by a stonefaced Indian on horseback. A rack is hitched to the back of the horse on which lies a slumbering Cuthbert J. Twillie, W. C. The train's whistle awakens Twillie and he gathers his portmanteau to inquire of the engineer, "Do you have a private car with a room, a bath and an exclusive bar?" No! But Twillie gets on anyway. He tells his Indian friend Clarence to meet him in Greasewood City.

The train starts moving again, but soon Indians attack the iron horse on the lonely prairie. Flower Belle, the best shot on the train, is given two six-shooters to repulse the savages. Twillie on the other hand relies on a stinging "I hate you!" He gets caught between two cars when an arrow flies past. He catches it and throws it back at the attackers. Finally making it to the next car, he grabs a little boy's slingshot and starts to fire. The child protests. Twillie turns and commands the boy, "Go in there and fight

211

With George Moran (formerly of Moran and Mack) as they step outside the soundstage at Universal to rehearse a scene. Fields' physical appearance had begun to deteriorate, as shown in this unretouched photo.

like a man," pointing to the next car. Flower Belle's flashy shooting saves the day. The Indian attack is repulsed. Cuthbert walks back into her car as all around congratulate Flower Bells for her bravery.

Catching her name and smitten by her beauty, he sits next to Miss Gideon (a name from the Bible toters, no doubt) to gain more information about that "vision of loveliness." He says, "Tell me about that lady with the hothouse cognomen." Miss Gideon fills Twillie in on Miss Lee's repulsive past. The type of woman Cuthbert likes. He excuses himself and walks toward Flower Belle's seat. He pretends to be jolted by the train and falls on the seat opposite her. He introduces himself and asks her name.

"Flower Belle Lee."

"What a euphonious appellation—nice on the ears and a delight for the eyes." She asks his business and he opens his carpet bag to pull out a card, in the process revealing what looks like a lot of money. Money attracts. Twillie might be a practical catch. Cuthbert wants to kiss her "symmetrical digits"—her hand. She agrees. He likes it. "May I avail myself of a second helping?" He gets the nod. But he cheats, taking a few extra smooches. Now he hints of a union: "It is not good for a man to be alone."

"It's no fun for a woman either."

"Could we be lonesome together?"

She consents. The elated Twillie announces their plans of matrimony to the other passengers. Flower Belle spies Amos Budge, a gambling friend who travels in a minister's garb, and gets him to perform the ceremony.

Right after the wedding the train arrives in Greasewood City, where Mr. and Mrs. Twillie head for the hotel. Flower Belle takes the lead at the registration desk, asking for two rooms, much to her husband's chagrin. She grabs the honeymoon suite and gives Cuthbert the other room. Still hoping to consummate their marriage, Twillie follows his new bride to her boudoir, but she slams the door in his face. He bends down to the keyhole and tries to persuade her to open the door. "I have some very definite pear-shaped ideas to discuss with you." (A line that slipped past the censors.) Flower Belle lets it be known that nothing will happen between them this night, and Twillie retreats to his room sadly. He sets up home and heads for the bar. Outside, he runs into Clarence.

"New squaw?"

"New is right. She hasn't even been unwrapped."

With Cuthbert gone, Flower Belle slips into his room and rifles his bag. There she discovers that what she thought was money was merely coupons that Twillie hands out in his traveling salesman business. She goes back to her room and readies herself for the appointed evening tryst with her masked lover. Tonight he has promised to reveal himself by taking off the mask.

Back to Twillie, who has meandered to the bar. He needs money to join a poker game. He picks out a sucker at the bar and asks if he would like to cut cards, one hundred dollars a cut. The man puts down his money. Broke, Twillie pulls out a piece of paper: "I'm traveling light. The country is fraught with marauders. I'll give you my personal I.O.U. A thing I seldom give to strangers." The fellow balks, but Cuthbert interrupts. He signs the paper and shoves it next to the one hundred. "It's worth its weight in gold." The man reluctantly goes along and the challenge is on. Fields lets the sucker go first. He picks. "King." He shows Twillie the card, but Cuthbert turns his head: "Don't show me the cards. A gentleman's game." Cuthbert's turn. He picks the card, looks at it, then quickly returns it to the deck. "Ace!" He reaches for the money.

"I didn't see it!"

Twillie is affronted, then resigns himself. "Very well, very well, you nosy parker." He shuffles through the deck, finds the card, pulls it out and shows it to the man. "I hope that satisfies your morbid curiosity." He grabs the money. The other fellow steams. Twillie smiles congenially and asks the sucker if he would like another go of it. Seeing the anger rising in the fellow, Cuthbert bids farewell. "Possibly at some future date."

He takes his winnings to the poker table and with bravado throws the cash down. "Deal me in." Expecting a fistload of chips, he gets just one piece and he embarrassedly sits down. It is his deal. While he shuffles, he spins a yarn about how he single-handedly subdued the Indian attack earlier that day, ending with "It reminds me of the time I was in the wilds of Afghanistan. I lost my corkscrew and was compelled to live on nothing but food and water for several days." The players angrily prod him to deal. Twillie wins big, but eventually the cardplayers discover his skulduggery and manhandle the cheat.

While he was playing cards, Flower Belle had entered the bar killing time before her night rendezvous. Jeff Badger, the saloon owner, has been flirting with her. When the fighting at the card table breaks out, Flower Belle prevails on Badger to intercede for her husband. He does, then offers Cuthbert free drinks at the bar. There, Twillie entertains any who will listen, repeating the story of how he single-handedly fought off the fearful Indian attack. Three six-shooters, one in each hand and a third between his teeth. The enthralled crowd reaches to shake his hand, but he pulls back: "Watch that trigger finger." Badger suggests that the heroic Twillie should be Greasewood City's sheriff, a job that guarantees the office-holder only a few short months of life. Badger announces a banquet for the new sheriff, at which Mrs. Twillie will grace the throng with a song.

Soon Cuthbert sets up shop in the Sheriff's office, where he passes the time playing cards with Clarence. A game is on. Clarence holds "three squaws"; Twillie, "three chiefs." The Sheriff reaches for the assorted baubles and beads at the center of the table. Clarence, a bit disgruntled, bends over and picks up his bow and arrow. Cuthbert sees the sinister action and grabs his whiskey bottle by the neck. "What are you up to, you red rascal?" He breaks the bottle over the Indian's head, knocking him out. "The only thing they can arrest me for is splitting a bottle with an Indian."

Flower Belle's hayseed cousin enters the Sheriff's office to congratulate his "cousin-in-law." By now Clarence has recovered and Cuthbert kicks him out of the office: "Go back to the reservation and milk your elk." Cousin Zeb asks Twillie if Clarence is a full-blooded Indian.

"Quite the antithesis. He's very anemic."

Twillie asks Zeb to play cards. Zeb is quite eager. "Is this a game of chance?"

"Not the way I play it, no."

Meanwhile, Flower Belle has found another suitor, Wayne Carter, the upright Greasewood City newspaper editor. He wants a real schoolhouse with a teacher; he wants the streets cleaned so decent people can feel safe to walk them at night; and most of all he wants to run Badger and his ilk out of town. Carter brings her to the run-down old one-room schoolhouse where the pupils' ages range from preadolescent to grandfather. To one of the students she asks, "Is that a pistol in your pocket or are you just happy to see me?" (That too got by the censors.)

That night is the banquet for Sheriff Twillie. He sits at the end of the table in a cloakroom, while Badger and Mrs. Twillie sit next to each other in the middle of the room. The saloon owner extols Sheriff Twillie's virtues and ends by telling the crowd the lovely Sheriff's wife will sing for them. She keeps her promise and walks on stage to give a pleasing rendition of "Willie of the Valley," a sultry saloon song.

Later that night Flower Belle lets Cuthbert into her room—at last Twillie's first piece of nuptial bliss. He wants to take a bath first. While he cleanses himself Mrs. Twillie puts on a wrap to go into the night and meet her masked bandit, but before leaving she places a goat under the bed covers. Twillie primps in the bathroom, dries himself, puts on one of Flower Belle's lacy robes, smells her cologne, "Eau de Rocky Mountain Goat," sprinkles some on and heads for the bed. He sees the lump under the covers and concludes it is Flower Belle. He reaches under the covers to caress her tenderly: "You better take your coat off, 'dear. You won't feel the good of it when you go out." He pulls the covers back to reveal more of his love and finds the goat. Disappointed, he sleeps alone that night.

Very early the next morning a frenzied crowd bangs on Twillie's door. The stagecoach has been robbed by the masked bandit again. Twillie's half-awake response is not so convincing: "How unfortunate." The townfolk tell Twillie he needs a posse. He could not be more pleased. He tells them to do that and he will catch up with them later. The mob rushes to the streets and Twillie returns to bed mumbling, "Sleep! The most beautiful experience in life . . . 'cept drink."

The Sheriff wakes up early in the afternoon and heads for the saloon, eventually ending up tending bar with his old bartending friend from days of yore, Squawk Mulligan, a short, tough old man.

Soon a very small mean drunk woman stumbles to the bar, a legal no-no. Cuthbert tries directing her to a table, but she will not go. Instead she spits out the story of her and her husband's latest row. She ends the tiff by calling her husband a list of disparaging names, concluding the story with "He couldn't say anything to that."

Twillie: "Obviously you're too quick-witted for him . . . too quick at repartee. . . . Now will you sit over there."

She leaves and another customer enters. He heard Cuthbert had lost his wife. "I understand you buried your wife recently."

"I had to. She died."

Another customer at the bar comments on the toughness of the small woman who was so "quick at

213

Mae West and W. C. Fields review their script with director (or referee) Eddie Cline.

repartee." She did not scare the Sheriff. It reminds him of the time "I was tending bar on the Lower East Side. A tough paloma by the name of Chicago Molly comes in. We had lunch on the bar that day consisting of succotash, asparagus with mayonnaise and Philadelphia cream cheese. She dips her mitt in this melange. I was yawning at the time, and she hits me right in the mouth with it." Squawk walks out from behind the bar and busies himself. Twillie continues: "Well, I jumps over the bar and knocks her down." To Squawk: "Remember the time I jumped over the bar and knocked Chicago Molly down?"

Squawk grumbles, "*You* knocked her down? I was the one who knocked her down." Squawk continues working.

Twillie: "Yeah, yeah, you knocked her down—but I was the one who started kicking her." To the customer: "Have you ever kicked a woman in the midriff who had a pair of corsets on?"

The customer ponders a bit. "No . . . no. I just can't recall any such incident at this time."

"Well, I nearly broke my great toe. I never had such a painful experience."

"Well, did you ever see her again?"

Squawk cuts in: "I'll say. She came back the next night and beat the both of us up."

Defensively Twillie adds, "Yeah, but she had another woman with her."

After bartending, Twillie heads back to his office and catches a checker game in progress. With the same twist as in *The Pharmacist* he says to one player, "I wonder what would happen if you moved that piece"—indicating. The player moves per direction. Immediately his challenger jumps the table clear, and W. C. walks away.

That night Cuthbert decides he will steal some time with his spouse. He knows the apartment at which she is to meet the masked bandit, so he dresses in the masked man's disguise and sneaks off to the rendezvous spot. He puts a ladder to Flower Belle's second-story window and climbs inside. The place is dark. He calls, "Chiquita!" Flower Belle rouses from her bed. They kiss. Immediately she knows this is not her lover. Then she notes the enormous facial protrusion and quickly recognizes Twillie. Although not at all surprised, she does call her husband "a cheat." To which the ersatz masked bandit defends himself: "Anything worth having is worth cheating for." She kicks him out of her bedroom. As Cuthbert descends the ladder, Miss Gideon, who coincidentally occupies the lower apartment, catches him by the leg, hangs on for dear life, and screams for help. A mob shows up and takes over. They strip the black mask from the bandit's face. Twillie! Their own Sheriff is the masked bandit. A rope appears and the crowd escorts the Sheriff to the hanging barn. All the while Cuthbert pleads his innocence: "I was at a masquerade party impersonating a Ubangi." It does not work. At the gallows they place a noose around his neck. Someone asks if he has anything to say.

"Yes! This will be a great lesson to me."

Another person asks Cuthbert what is his last request.

"I'd like to see Paris before I die." They sneer.

"Philadelphia will do!"

Meanwhile, Flower Belle has been entertaining the real masked bandit. She begs him to help Twillie, revealing their marriage is one of convenience performed by a gambler not a minister. The masked bandit will help. Right before they spring the trap on Twillie, the masked bandit rides up on his horse, and to prove he is the real robber throws down a bagful of spoils from his latest stagecoach holdup. Then, just as quickly, he rides off. The crowd frees Twillie.

Flower Belle has revealed her fake marriage to Carter and to Badger. Flower Belle is also quite certain, and correctly so, that Badger is the masked bandit. The two, suitors now, argue for Flower Belle's hand, but she puts both off. She has not made up her mind. Twillie, meanwhile, has packed his belongings and is ready to leave Greasewood City for good. Flower Belle and Cuthbert meet in the lobby of the hotel. Miss Lee wants to know where her fake husband plans to go.

"I'm headed back east. I am going to sell stock in hair-oil wells." They exchange parting lines.

Twillie: "If you're ever out my way, come up and see me some time."

Flower Belle: "I'll do that, my little chickadee."

The movie ends with a shot of Mae's swinging derriere headed upstairs.

My Little Chickadee was released on February 9, 1940, nearly a full year after the premiere of *You Can't Cheat an Honest Man*. Most of the reviewers treated W. C. well, telling their readers that his recent illnesses had not denigrated his comic worth. The vast majority of the critics asserted Fields made the show, and indeed he did. The movie in general received terrible notices. Universally, the critics lambasted the weak plot and the incredible discontinuity, an old harangue, to be sure, but absolutely justified here. The film was even too disjointed for a Fields comedy. Although history has proven that *My Little Chickadee* outgrossed any other Fields-Universal film, it was certainly not his best picture for the studio. The motion picture never lived up to its pre-shooting expectations. On paper the comedy team of West and Fields seemed like a perfect marriage, but on film it was a disaster. Their widely divergent styles actually diluted their individual comic bits. He was making his movie and she was making hers, and that obvious distance between them was palpable; there was no magic in their interplay. They were not funny as a team. Mae West and W. C. Fields never really made a movie together.

Many of the critics took Mae West to task in this film. That was sad. Mae had hoped to regain her title as queen of the box office. She had dieted off twenty pounds and weighed in at a curvaceous 120, but the trades ridiculed her for trying too hard on screen and taking herself too seriously. Furthermore, Ms. West simply was not the enormous draw she had been. Pasted to a page in one of W. C. Fields' scrapbooks was a clipping from an unidentified trade paper. The tabloid rated the films Hollywood produced so that exhibitors could pick the big draws. This is how they rated *Chickadee*: "Box office draw—very good. (The name draw is responsible for good business. Mae West apparently is no help.)" Evidently when crowds lined up to see *My Little Chickadee* they went to laugh at W. C., not to snicker with Mae West.

The filming was finished, but rumors spread that the fighting continued. The story goes that Fields and West fought over star billing, and that the studio finally offered a compromise. The names would be written in the same script, the same size, and side by side. Knowing the left side would be the preferred spot, both the stars fought to put their names there. According to the gossip, Universal again calmed the storm, explaining to Fields that women go first. That quieted the comedian for a short while. Then, the story goes, one morning at 2 A.M. W. C. called Cliff Work: "When a husband and wife are introduced it's always 'Mr. and Mrs.' I should go first." And the acrimony started all over again. The story reeks of publicity hype. You see, Fields wrote a letter to Jack Gross, the unheralded producer of the picture, three weeks before the release of *My Little Chickadee*: "I would like to have the credits read:

Mae West	W. C. Fields
as	as
Flower Belle Lee	Cuthbert J. Twillie

Otherwise this definitely gives Mae West first billing. These trivial matters may seem picayunish, but precedents are precedents and they sometimes become aggravated and grow into mighty oaks." And the cast of characters was written that way. So, it seems, no real battle over billing came to pass.

But there still were real wars to be fought. The former Hays office, the movie-censoring clan, then headed by Joseph Breen, wanted to cut a favorite old Fields line. W. C. had tried to sneak it past the censors in other films and got the same response. The line: "I know what I will do. I'll go to India and become a missionary. I hear there's good money in that too." Breen cut it, while Fields fought for it. In the end the scissors boys won and Fields was surprisingly gracious. His last letter to Breen on the issue: "I am indebted to you for your kind explanatory letter. I know you are right [that the missionary line must go] and I shall henceforth hold my peace." The copy of Breen's letter cannot be found, but it sure would be interesting to find the logic of the cut.

When the movie came out and Mae West read the reviews praising Fields and knocking her, she was furious. At Paramount she had always been a bigger star than W. C., and now it looked as though he had upstaged her (a first in her career). Embittered, she refused to work with the comedian again. Indeed, she refused to ever talk to him again, or allow anyone to talk about him in her presence until the day she died. She hated W. C. Fields. In a discussion of the picture in her autobiography she tendered a particularly caustic observation of W. C. "I think that under the grotesque ruin of a clown Bill Fields was tragically aware of the wreck he had made of himself."

In 1973, when my first tome, *W. C. Fields by Himself*, was published, I made the typical TV and radio talk-show rounds. My first booking was a Los Angeles station. When they secured a date for my appearance, the producer of the show asked me if I would share the microphone with Mae West. I enthusiastically said yes. I really wanted to meet the living legend. When I arrived at the station for the interview there was no Mae West. I thought that maybe she planned a grand entrance later in the program, so I asked the producer when he expected her. He said she was not coming. "Why?" The producer walked me to the studio and explained, "I'll be honest with you, Mr. Fields. When we asked her if she would be on the show with you, she told us, 'I don't want to meet another Fields as long as I live!'"

A few months later my brother, Everett, ran into her in a Los Angeles restaurant. He introduced himself and asked about the old gent. All Mae said was "He was a great talent—a great talent." And then quickly walked away.

The time-consuming battles of *My Little Chickadee* were fought at possibly a great expense to Fields. Just as his first picture for Universal had prevented W. C. from doing *The Wizard of Oz*, the long gestation period of this second opus prevented him from returning to Broadway. There was no guarantee the comedian would have left Hollywood, but the extended shooting schedule of *Chickadee* obviated any choice. The Broadway show was a musical by George S. Kaufman, Moss Hart and Cole Porter. The trades announced that his co-star would have been Joan Crawford.

With *Chickadee* a box-office success, although a critical failure, Universal decided to let Fields do things his own way again. They gave him more freedom, or at least promised it, cut his supervision and let him work on his own script. He started right away.

MY LITTLE CHICKADEE

83 minutes (7,498 feet)
Sound, black and white
Released February 9, 1940, by Universal
Produced by Jack Gross (uncredited) for Universal
Executive producer: Lester Cowan
Directed by Edward Cline
Assistant director: Joe McDonough
Original screenplay by Mae West and W. C. Fields
Photographed by Joseph Valentine
Music score by Frank Skinner
Musical director: Charles Previn
Art direction by Jack Otterson
Gowns by Vera West
Edited by Ed Curtiss
Sound engineer: Bernard B. Brown
Song: "Willie of the Valley" lyrics by Milton Drake
   and music by Ben Oakland

CAST:
Mae West   Flower Belle Lee
W. C. Fields   Cuthbert J. Twillie, snake-oil salesman
Joseph Calleia   Jeff Badger (originally intended for Humphrey Bogart)
Joseph Calleia   Masked bandit (originally intended for Humphrey Bogart)
Dick Foran   Wayne Carter, newspaper editor
Margaret Hamilton   Miss Gideon (originally intended for Jan Duggan)
George Moran   Clarence/Milton, the "Red Rascal"
Si Jenks   Deputy
James Conlin   Bartender Squawk Mulligan
Bud Harris   Porter
Russell Hall   Candy
Otto Heimel   Coco
Eddie Butler   Henchman
Bing Conley   Henchman
Fuzzy Knight   Cousin Zeb (originally intended for Grady Sutton)
Anne Nagel   Ermingarde Foster, teacher
Ruth Donnelly   Aunt Lou
Willard Robertson   Uncle John
Donald Meek   Amos Budget, cardsharp
William B. Davidson   Sheriff
Addison Richards   Judge
Mark Anthony   Townsman
Fay Adler   Mrs. "Pygmy" Allen
Jan Duggan   Woman
Bob Burns   Barfly
Gene Austin   Saloon musician
Al Ferguson   Train passenger

Bob Reeves   Barfly
Dorothy Vernon   Diner
Morgan Wallace   Gambler
Wade Boteler   Leading citizen
Harlan Briggs   Hotel clerk
Clyde Dembeck   Boy on train
Jackie Searle   Boy
Billy Benedict   Lem
Delmar Watson   Boy
George Billings   Boy
Ben Hall   Boy
Buster Slaven   Boy
Danny Jackson   Boy
Charles Hart   Boy
Robert Beamish   Boy
Chester Gan   Chinaman
George Melford   Sheriff
James C. Morton   Townsman
Slim Gaut   Bowlegged man
Frank Ellis   Townsman
Bill Wolfe   Barfly
Otto F. Hoffmann   Pete, printer
Betty Roche   Charity seeker
Bob McKenzie   Townsman
Joe Whitehead   Townsman
John "Blackie" Whiteford   Townsman
Jeff Conlon   Townsman
Leo Sulkey   Townsman
Walter McGrail   Townsman
Hank Bell   Townsman
Charles McMurphy   Townsman
Alan Bridge   Townsman
Lloyd Ingraham   Townsman
John Kelly   Henchman
Jack Roper   Henchman
Eddie Hearn   Barfly
Vester Pegg   Gambler
Alan Bridge   Barfly

Filmed at Universal in Universal City.
   Parts cut from the final release print: Lane Chandler, Lita Chevret.
   Universal's original screenplay was entitled *The Jaywalkers*, written by Grover Jones with the intention of capitalizing on the studio's recent success with *Destry Rides Again*. Mae West's subsequent original screenplay was entitled *December and Mae*, with other suggested titles including *Herman*, *Honky-Tonk*, *The Little Lady*, *The Sheriff and the Little Lady*, *Pueblo*, *Pueblo and Denver*, *First Lady of Lompoc*, and *Husband in Name Only*.

The Bank Dick

—1940—

On January 29, 1940, W. C. Fields turned sixty years old. He had been in entertainment for forty-three years, in movies for twenty-five and in Hollywood for more than a decade. By now many critics had been touting Fields as the comic king, and there was no reason to believe his reign would end soon.

Upon completing *My Little Chickadee,* W. C. signed another contract with Universal, a contract that guaranteed him freedom to create his own brand of laughs. He would write the script, choose his director and have final say in the editing room. Matty Fox, Universal's vice-president, then growing impatient waiting for a Fields script,

suggested the comedian play in Nat Perrin's *Alias the Deacon.* W. C. would take the lead of a swindling card-player from the Old West. Wrong! Fields complained that it was too close to his card games in *Chickadee* and *Mississippi,* and besides he was writing his own script. He wanted to join the twentieth century again and throw a few jabs at domestic life. In rejecting Fox's idea, W. C. assured him that his own script would be ready in two weeks, that it would fit his own peculiar type of humor and, most importantly, it would be inexpensive. Fox really liked the inexpensive part, so he agreed to wait some more. Fields asked the V. P. for a modest writing

salary: "Just a little martini and sherry money . . . and I
assure you I am not drinking to excess these days." But
he was.

Complete freedom at a Hollywood studio at last, a
cherished birthday gift, nothing could stop him now.
Even when calls from the East begged him to return to his
beloved New York to star in another Broadway show that
would be created just for him, Fields said no.

By mid-January Fields submitted his scenario to
Universal, along with casting suggestions. He wanted
Gloria Jean to play a Little Lulu type and asked Matty

Fox to get Ann Sothern. For some reason Fox could
provide neither. W. C. also wanted the Universal executive to talk with MGM and secure the services of Mickey
Rooney. Fox tried, but Louis B. Mayer said no. That
annoyed W. C. The comedian wrote Fox: "I am sorry Mr.
Mayer pooh-poohed the idea of loaning Mickey Rooney.
Someday he may want the great actor Fields and we shall
say to him, 'nay.' " Finally, for the part of Og Oggilby
W. C. wanted Grady Sutton, with whom Fields had
worked in the Sennett short *The Pharmacist* and the feature-length films *The Man on the Flying Trapeze* and *You*

Can't Cheat an Honest Man. Grady was of course a member in good standing of the "Fields Comedy Company." The studio, on the other hand, wanted one of their own contract players for the part. "No!" Fields demanded. "I want Grady. I like to work with him. I like the way he reacts to me." The studio fought. Fields was adamant. "All right, then get yourself another Fields." W. C. got his way. His script called for two bank robbers, Loudmouth McNasty and Repulsive Rogan, and again here the comedian hand-picked the actors. For Loudmouth he hired George Moran, of Moran and Mack, the Two Black Crows. He had used Moran twice before—in *The Fatal Glass of Beer* and *My Little Chickadee.* Fields then employed Al Hill to play Repulsive Rogan. George O'Brien used to tell the story that Hill was once a real crook. The mob had stationed him on a film set in the early thirties. They needed some money laundered, so they got into the picturemaking business and Hill was told to make sure there were no cost overruns. He was tough and mean and carried a bulge under his coat. But while on the set he got interested in acting and wanted a part. They could not refuse him, so they put him into the film. He did well, and the acting bug never left him. So if O'Brien's tale is true, Al Hill went straight playing crooks in motion pictures.

By July Fields turned in the last few pages of his script. In total it was a very short piece, but in his cover letter to Matty Fox he defended its brevity: "As you probably know, I write my scripts short and they develop on the set, which I have found a far better premise both economically and practically."

W. C. had been sending the script bit by bit to Universal over the six-month span from January to July, and they in turn had been sending it to the Breen office for approval. The censors held their tongues until the last pages were submitted, and then just a week after receiving the final draft they sent their list of objectionable material to the studio and the star, a list nearly as long as the script. Fields fought them. Many of Breen's proscriptions were petty. For instance, at one point Fields scripted dialogue between a doctor and his patient. The doctor tells his charge to take two pills "in a glass of castor oil for two nights running." Breen objected to "castor oil" used so closely with the word "running," because of the cathartic purpose of the oil. Fields graciously suggested he would change it to cod-liver oil. (Some help.) Breen backed off and W. C. kept "castor oil."

The biggest confrontation between Fields and Breen centered on the name Fields gave to a bar in Lompoc, the town in which his film was set. He called the saloon the Black Pussy Cafe and Snack Bar. Breen said, "Objectionable!" Fields for the defense. He told him that his friend Leon Errol owned a bar and grill on Santa Monica Boulevard called the Black Pussy Cafe, and if it was good enough for Santa Monica it certainly was good enough for Hollywood. Compromise: Fields would have to name the joint the Black Pussy Cat Cafe. Loophole: That was the name printed on the door of the saloon, but throughout the movie W. C. always referred to the place as the Black Pussy Cafe. The arguing over the rest of the material went on for months, never acrimonious, always polite, but nevertheless a struggle.

More trouble. After guaranteeing W. C. a totally free hand on the film, the powers-that-were started to recant. They assigned a writer to rewrite the script, saying the original piece was unsatisfactory. The writer changed the script and Universal gave it back to Fields, saying, "See, this is better." Here we go again. After reading the script, Fields immediately put pen to paper and wrote to Eddie Cline, the director, and Jack Gross, the production supervisor:

"Dear Eddie and Jack: First Mr. Fox assured me I would be left to my own devices, and Mr. Work told Mr. Beyer [W. C.'s agent] I would be left alone. The script was to remain in toto." Then W. C. attacked the scriptwriters' changes: They wanted the picture to start with Fields selling snake oil. W. C. objected. He won. At some point in the picture they wanted him to receive a grand homecoming from his family. W. C. objected. He won. They wanted to change two of the characters. W. C. objected. He won. And so on. For every objection to the redraft, Fields got his way, proven by the final product. Fields concluded his letter: "I have devoted my life to story and comedy construction. Has the critic ever written for a low comedian? [Keep in mind that throughout the missive Fields cynically refers to Universal's writer as the critic, never the writer.] Where is the critic's name in the credits? . . . When the star finally appears upon the screen and if it is a dud the critic's name will not be mentioned or condemned. I am the one who will take it on the chin. I disagree with all the critic's suggestions, but thank him for his sincere and honest interest. . . If you let me alone as you promised I will work like a canine (or beaver, optional)."

The studio came back saying something had to be done if for no other reason than the script was too short.

W. C.: "Anent the length of the script. This has been written succinctly to avoid overhead and to allow for byplay, interpolations, and for extemporaneous dialogue."

Well, Universal tried again. They hired a Mr. Grayson to give shape to Fields' story but not to tamper with W. C.'s dialogue or characterizations. Universal told Fields that all Grayson was to do was beef up the script. W. C. went along with it, but when he received Grayson's fifty-nine-page revised script, he discovered that the studio's boy had in fact changed the basic story. W. C. shot back. He tore the new piece apart and accused Cline, Gross and Grayson of lying.

Try it again. By the end of August a new revised script was handed to the comedian. That was it. This time Fields took his case to the top banana, Nate Blumberg, president of Universal Pictures:

"August 22, 1940—Dear Friend Nate: I have received the latest script as changed to suit the council [studio heads] by a neophyte whose bump of Fields humor is a dent. . . . I don't know to whom to appeal. The director, Eddie Cline, knows little about what goes on. The same can be said of Jack Gross, the supervisor. . . . Matty Fox assured me this one would be done my way. I am sorry he is not here now to champion the cause of both the studio and myself. . . . I assure you if I am forced to do this picture as is now written it will not only

Edgert Sousè ("accent grave over the 'e' ") at the door of his favorite haunt, the Black Pussy Cat Cafe, which Fields constantly refers to as the Black Pussy Cafe, much to the distress of the censors.

other daughter for this film Elsie Mae Adele Brunch Sousè. In real life W. C. had two younger sisters. The older one was called Elsie May, the other, Adel.) Ms. Merkel recalled that the director had told the entire cast and crew to be on the set at nine A.M. sharp. By 9:05 everyone was there except for W. C. Nine-thirty came and went. Ten slipped by, ten-thirty passed, and then somewhere around eleven Fields strolled onto the set. His secretary, Magda Michael, followed close behind carrying a flask in a leather pouch.

Fields casually prepared himself for the day's filming as the cast and crew scurried to their respective working locations—two hours late. No one complained. Una Merkel said that W. C. did not act arrogantly or conceitedly; he acted as if he had shown up perfectly on time. He did not apologize, neither did he seem embarrassed for making everyone wait. And strangely no one on that set acted slighted. They too seemed to think W. C. had come to work right on time. Director Eddie Cline never spoke a word of reproach. Ms. Merkel said that it all seemed quite natural.

The scene to be shot was set in a large opulent dining room in the wealthy Sousè's home. (A moving picture quirk. When a studio films a movie they rarely start at the beginning and run to the end. Generally, they shoot scenes in what seems like random order and sometimes, as in this case, the first scene put on film is the last scene in the script.) Egbert, W. C., is positioned at the head of the table. He gets up to go to work. Myrtle runs to him and plants a kiss on his forehead and says, "Have a good day, Pater."

Well, the very first thing W. C. said to Una Merkel on their very first meeting at the very first rehearsal was "I'm sorry about my foul-smelling breath." Ms. Merkel did notice a slight scent of alcohol. It was eleven A.M., W. C. was two hours late and the only word of contrition came as the result of the smell of booze on his breath. It did not bother Una. She told him, "Why Mr. Fields, on you it smells like Chanel Number Five."

"Honey, you're in."

From that point to the end of her filming stint with the "great one," she said, "He was absolutely wonderful to me. . . . W. C. Fields was one of the nicest men I ever worked for."

Egbert Sousè ("accent grave over the 'e' ") is an unemployed dipsomaniacal bumbler, disrespected by his two daughters and harassed by his wife and mother-in-law. Agatha, Mrs. Sousè, spends her days complaining about her husband's smoking, drinking and unemployment. Mrs. Hermisillo Brunch, Agatha's mother and a harridan, rocks on her rocker keeping her eye out for any sign of Egbert's faults so she can squeal to Agatha. The oldest daughter, Myrtle, a not altogether intolerable simpleton, treats her father more with indifference than vituperation. But the youngest girl, Elsie Mae Adele Brunch Sousè, is a thoroughly insolent child with a disconcerting violent streak.

be detrimental to me, but to Universal Studios."

The very next day Blumberg wrote Fields. The Universal president had interceded and sent word to all those involved in the production that Fields was guaranteed a free hand and a free hand he would be given. W. C. wrote back thanking Blumberg.

In September 1940 Fields began production on probably the only feature he made that was completely, unequivocally his own creation. Una Merkel, who played W. C.'s addlebrained daughter, Myrtle, remembers that first day on the set. (Incidentally, Fields christened his

It is morning and Egbert is headed downstairs. His wife, daughter Elsie Mae and Mrs. Brunch await him in the living room. Egbert is puffing on a cigarette and almost in sight of his family when he hears Mrs. Brunch suggest that the reason he is late is because he is in his room smoking. He stops and curls the lighted cigarette into his mouth.

Every day, with today being no exception, he excuses himself from the house on the pretense of looking for a job. He smiles oddly at the bunch, then heads for the door. Elsie Mae aims a catsup bottle at his head, then shoots. Bull's-eye! He walks out the door, picks up an enormous porcelain vase from the front porch, turns and takes aim at his daughter. Just then Myrtle bounces up the stairs onto the porch. She has brought her boyfriend. She interrupts Dad to introduce her fiancé, a dim-witted sissy. "Father, this is Og Oggilby."

"Og Oggilby! Hmmmm, sounds like a bubble in a bathtub." Egbert hands Og the vase and heads out.

Meanwhile on the streets of Lompoc a movie company is working on location. Their day's shooting is being held up because the director, A. Pismo Clam, is drunk. The production manager, Mackley Q. Greene, knows nothing about shooting a film and now he is in charge. He needs a solution so he heads for the Black Pussy Cat Cafe. Coincidence! That is precisely where Egbert Sousè spends his days job hunting.

Sousè already occupies a place at the bar. After Egbert orders his drink he asks his friend Joe Guelpe the bartender, "Was I in here last night and did I spend a twenty-dollar bill?"

"Yep!"

"Oh boy! What a load that is off my mind. I thought I'd lost it."

Mackley Q. Greene orders a stiff one himself and tells the bartender his woes with the nearly comatose A. Pismo Clam. Sousè listens for a while then interrupts. He tells Greene about his long association with "Fatty Arbuckle, Charlie Chaplin, Buster Keaton and the rest of 'em." The production manager is impressed, or at least desperate, and turns the shooting over to Mr. Sousè.

Four stagehands carry Egbert on a palanquin from which the new director barks orders to the actors through a megaphone. Suddenly Sousè falls over backwards. Plop! right in the middle of Lompoc's main street. That is all right. He has to talk to the actors anyway. He has found the underlying problem with the film. He approaches the two actors. One is a very tall man, the other a short, very short, woman. The male lead, Francoise, is dressed in top hat and tails, the woman, Miss Plupp, wears a dress. With his keen artistic eye Sousè decides some judicious cutting is in order, plus a slight story change. He arbitrarily rips a number of pages from the script and decides to make the plot a football and circus story. The tall man will be the hero on the field, the woman a fan. Egbert's family walks up and Elsie Mae shouts that she wants to be in the picture, but Sousè pushes her away. Elsie Mae continues to wail while Agatha demands that her husband put the little girl in the film. Confusion abounds with the Sousè family yelling and the actors complaining that the new plot will not fit their present attire. Egbert finally sees Joe Guelpe heading for the bar; he tells the actors to practice their lines and makes a hasty retreat to the Black Pussy Cafe.

Too late to catch up with the bartender. Joe has left. Egbert reads the sign hanging on the door, OUT TO TEA— JOE. Sousè is patient. He walks over to the Lompoc Municipal Bus Line's bench and sits down to wait for the cafe's reopening.

In another part of Lompoc, the villainous duo of Loudmouth McNasty and Repulsive Rogan are robbing the Lompoc State Bank. Og works at the Lompoc State Bank and coincidentally Rogan and McNasty go to his window to steal the money. After they seize the bundle,

A time for high spirits at the Black Pussy Cafe. From left, Shemp Howard (of Three Stooges fame), Dick Purcell, W. C. and Bill Wolfe.

Sousè replaces the drunken director A. Pismo Clam. (Approximately 150 miles north of Los Angeles, not far from the real town of Lompoc, is a small community named Pismo Beach, which is well known in California for its delicious clams, thus A. Pismo Clam.)

Og faints and hits his head against the alarm button. The crooks rush out and the chase is on. They hide in an alley right behind Sousè's bench. One of them wants to split the money right there. The other argues they should still be on the lam. A fight ensues. McNasty is knocked unconscious. Repulsive Rogan runs. As he takes off he flings McNasty's gun away. It hits Sousè, knocking him over the bench backwards and landing him atop Loudmouth. By the time the cops and the crowd show up Egbert is standing over the crook. Obviously all conclude that Sousè single-handedly apprehended the ne'er-do-well. He receives oblations from the gathered throng, including Og, who tells his future father-in-law to go to the bank on the morrow, where undoubtedly he will receive a grand reward from Mr. Skinner, the president.

After all the excitement, Egbert needs some reviver. He heads for the Black Pussy Cafe and between swigs tells Guelpe how the bandit pulled a knife on him this long—no, this long . . . this long. Actually it was an assegai. He picks up the day's paper, the Lompoc *Picayune-Intelligencer,* which pictures Sousè, and with

banner headlines tells the story of his heroic capture. Proudly he carries the paper home to impress his family. He shows the paper to his wife, who is busy playing Chinese checkers with Mrs. Brunch. As he shows her the article he tells her the harrowing tale but she is too busy to care, and Mrs. Brunch grabs the paper and throws it into the fireplace. Resignedly he returns to his room.

The next morning he heads for the bank. Mr. Skinner is a self-important phony. However, he accepts Egbert graciously. Sousè goes through his monologue on the dangerous capture, which Skinner takes with doubt. Finally, putting an end to the yarn, the president stands up to give Egbert his string of awards: First, a hearty handclasp. (The camera freezes on the two hands meeting. Skinner's fingertips lightly touch Sousè's palm.) Second, the bank's calendar, which pictures a painting of a reclining nude captioned "Spring in Lompoc." Third, a job, as bank detective, "or to revert to the argot of the underworld—a bank dick." Skinner explains why Sousè does not receive a desk job. By starting on the bottom, he elucidates, Egbert can learn the banking trade in all its aspects. Who knows? One day he may even take over the job of vice-president. Then he tells Sousè, "The bank opens promptly at ten."

"Oh well, that's all right. If I'm not here on time you just go right ahead without me. I'll catch up with ya."

Egbert leaves the office and talks to Og. "I'll come in here with one of those disguises on. If you recognize me go like this." He brings his hand under his chin and waves it laterally. "Now if you don't recognize me go . . ." He tries to think of another sign, then it dawns on him. "Well, if you don't recognize me you won't know what to do."

It is time for lunch. Sousè heads for the Black Pussy Cafe. After Egbert has hefted a few drinks a slick, dapper con man wearing a floppy Panama hat and fancy clothes enters the taproom. J. Frothingham Waterbury searches the tavern for a likely sucker. Egbert Sousè! He interrupts the bank dick to explain his dire position. For some reason or other he has to sell his entire holdings in the Beefsteak Mine very cheaply. The lucky buyer will make millions, eventually earning "a big home in the city, balconies upstairs and down. Home in the country. Big trees. Private golf course. A stream running through the rear of the estate. Warm Sunday afternoons fishing under the cool trees, sipping ice-cold beer. And then this guy comes up the shady drive in an armored car from the bank and dumps a whole basket of coupons worth hundreds of

thousands of dollars, and he says, 'Sign here please on the dotted line.' "

"I'll have a fountain pen by that time."

"I'd rather part with my dear old grandmother's paisley shawl than to part with these bonds."

"Yes, it must be tough to lose a paisley shawl." Sousè agrees to take the bonds off the man's hands. He tells Waterbury to wait for him; he will get the money. Egbert heads for the bank. He pulls Og aside and asks him to borrow money from the bank surreptitiously. Og refuses, telling him it would be stealing. Sousè argues it is not stealing, merely a loan that Og can pay back in a few days when he gets his bonus. Nobody will miss it. Besides, think what it will mean if Og gets the money; he can marry Myrtle and buy a house. He reiterates Waterbury's story in the inimitable Sousè way: "You'll get a beautiful home in the country, upstairs and down. Beer flowing through the estate over your grandmother's paisley shawl."

"Beer?"

"Beer! A man comes up from the bar. Dumps $3,500 in your lap for every nickel invested. Says to you, 'Sign here on the dotted line.' " Og is reluctant to take a chance.

"Take a chance. Take it while you're young. My uncle, a balloon ascensionist, Effingham Huffnagel, took

Sousè in charge changes the script arbitrarily (not unlike what Fields did in real life during this production) by ripping out a few pages. Here, he directs François and Miss Plupp (Reed Hadley and Hyather Wilde) in an entirely new story of his own. Elsie Mae Adele Brunch Sousè (Evelyn Del Rio) demands a part in the picture while Mrs. Agatha Sousè (Cora Witherspoon) and Egbert's mother-in-law, Mrs. Hermosillo Brunch (Jessie Ralph), make sure she gets it. (Incidentally, in real life W. C. had two sisters. The older one was named Elsie Mae, the other Adel.)

a chance. He was three and a half miles up in the air. He jumped out of the basket of the balloon and took a chance of alighting on a load of hay.''

"Did he make it?"

"Ah . . . no . . . no he didn't. Had he been a younger man he probably would have made it. That's the point—don't wait too long in life.''

Og is weakening. Sousè continues: "Don't be a fuddy duddy! Don't be a moon calf! Don't be a jabbernowl! You're not those, are you?'' That caps it. Og sneaks the money from the vault and gives it to Sousè. Sousè runs back to the saloon and hands the dough to Water-

bury for the bonds. Og and Egbert are now the proud owners of the Beefsteak Mine. All nice and simple. Remember by the end of the week Og can replace the five hundred dollars.

The next day at the bank Sousè is happily going about his chores when he spots some trouble. A small boy dressed in a cowboy outfit is brandishing a toy pistol. Egbert thinks it is real. He does not want to rush. He acts casually as he slowly larrups up behind the kid. Then he pounces on him, grabbing the boy by his throat. The boy's mother breaks the hold and sneers at the bank dick. The little boy makes fun of Egbert's nose. The joke is too

"I'd rather part with my dear old grandmother's paisley shawl than to part with these bonds,'' says J. Frothingham Waterbury, trying to sell what he thinks are bogus bonds to the bank dick.

. . . and Sousè trying to sell Og Oggilby (Grady Sutton) on the bond scheme. "Beer flowing through the estate over your grandmother's paisley shawl." "Beer?????"

insolent for the mother to take without reproach. She tells her son not to make fun of other people's infirmities, ending with "You'd like to have a nose like that full of nickels, wouldn't you?"

Then real trouble walks in—J. Pinkerton Snoopington, the fastidious bank examiner. He will be checking the Lompoc State Bank's books. Snoopington wants to see the president, but Sousè intercepts him. He tells the bank examiner that Skinner is out playing golf and is not expected back until midnight. While waiting for the president to return, Sousè will be more than pleased to give Snoopington a tour of Lompoc. J. Pinkerton begrudgingly agrees. They walk the streets while Sousè points out the sights, telling Snoopy that the town has three drugstores. "One actually sells medicine." Fortunately the tour ends in front of the Black Pussy Cafe. Egbert suggests they go in for a snort. Although prissy and straight, Snoopington says yes, so long as they can pick a booth in some out-of-the-way corner and close the blinds. No problem.

Sousè takes Snoopington's order, then goes to the bar. He asks Joe, "Has Michael Finn been in here today?"

"No, but he will be." Guelpe mixes the drinks and drops the drug into Pinkerton's glass and serves.

After two spiked drinks Snoopington becomes deathly ill. He asks Sousè to help him to his hotel, the New Old Lompoc House. Before entering the hotel Sousè warns Snoopington to pull himself together, because the hotel is a respectable joint. Sousè gets the key from the registration clerk and helps the bank examiner upstairs. Suddenly Egbert comes flying down the stairs, through the lobby and out the door. He returns with Snoopington, who is now rumpled and dirty, and carries him through the lobby and to the stairs. He comments to the hotel manager, "This is the same man. Just fell out the window. Friend of mine. Caught him on the first bounce."

Sousè puts Snoopington into bed and calls the eminent Dr. Stall. The doc rushes over. Sousè asks, "How's business, Doc?"

"Fair, fair. I don't suppose we'll ever get another whooping cough epidemic again." He checks Snoopington and quickly diagnoses the illness and prescribes the cure. "What you need most of all is rest—no exercise." He pulls from his bag a bottle of huge white horse pills. "Take two of these in a glass of castor oil for two nights running, then you skip one night."

Snoopington: "I thought you said I wasn't to take any exercise."

"You take me too literally." The doc then explains the dosage procedure more succinctly. Stall tells J. Pinkerton to stay in bed for three nights, but Sousè needs the fourth day so Og can return the money. He knocks the cane on the floor four times, then pretends to play golf, yelling, "Fore!" and Stall finally gets the picture and prescribes that a fourth day in bed will be necessary if complications develop. Stall leaves and as Egbert prepares to depart he wants to test the effectiveness of the Mickey Finn one more time. He turns to the bank examiner. "Gonna have the missus bake you a nice coconut custard

No tour of Lompoc would be complete without a visit to the Black Pussy Cafe. Sousè with J. Pinkerton Snoopington (Franklin Pangborn).

pie with saddaloid pudding." Snoopington jumps out of bed and makes a mad dash for the bathroom. Sousè leaves satisfied.

The next morning, just when Egbert is trying to assuage Og's battered nerves by telling him Snoopington will not be around for a few days, Og faints. Sousè turns around to see why. Snoopington, looking pallid and weak, has walked into the bank. Sousè suggests that J. Pinkerton should still be in bed. Not this bank examiner. "Mr. Sousè, if duty called I would go into the tsetse fly country of Africa and brave sleeping sickness if there were books to be examined." Sousè tries other dilatory measures on the bank examiner. First he smashes Snoopy's hand in a letter press. "That'll interfere with your writing, won't it?"

"Fortunately I'm left-handed." Second, Snoopington drops his glasses on the floor and Egbert steps on them. He lifts the shattered glasses and returns them to Snoopington, "Oh! Sorry! And I try to be so helpful. I hope that won't interfere with your auditing the books." J. Pinkerton Snoopington has an entire case filled with glasses. Pinkerton becomes suspicious, not only of Sousè's apparent unwillingness for him to examine the books, but also because every time Og looks at Snoopy the teller faints dead away.

Suddenly Waterbury enters the bank. Waterbury goes to the back office to get his bonds back from Og while Sousè opens the day's paper. In the headlines it reads that the Beefsteak Mine has struck it rich. "A bonanza." Egbert rushes into Og's office and without comment swings a haymaker which knocks the swindler right through the window. Og is shocked: "What are you doing? Just as I was getting some of my money back." Sousè throws the newspaper down on Og's desk; the bank teller reads. He's rich. This calls for a celebration. Og has to work but Sousè figures the bank can get along without him, so he heads for the Black Pussy.

"A friend of mine. Caught him on the first bounce." The penance for a visit to the Black Pussy Cafe.

As Egbert reaches the bank door he recognizes someone. The man pulls a gun and marches the bank dick back into the bank. It is Repulsive Rogan, in for his second try at heisting the Lompoc Bank. He pushes Sousè to Og's window. Repulsive demands the money. Egbert calmly urges, "Do what the gentleman tells you to, Og." Og turns over the money, and then ducks and pushes the alarm. Clang! Clang! Repulsive and Egbert run out of the bank. There is a convertible car parked in front, keys inside. Rogan demands that Sousè drive. The chase!

Sousè rips away from the curb. Og, the bank president and a few other people jump on the running boards of another car and pursue. The car is owned by Mackley Q. Greene, the production manager. He has come to the bank looking for Sousè. The chase leads to country roads, and in order to ease the tense robber Egbert points out the interesting sights, naming the trees and so on, but Rogan puts a halt to the tour telling Sousè just to drive.

The cops are catching up. Rogan tells Sousè to step on it. He does. The floor falls out. Then Repulsive tells Egbert to clean his filthy windshield. Sousè is too busy. He lifts the windshield from its joints and hands it back to Rogan. "You wipe it off—I'm driving." The bank dick surveys the car—not a pleasant-looking auto at all. "The resale value of this car is going to be nil after you get over this trip."

Sousè's reckless driving scares Rogan and the crook wants to take over the steering. "Give me that wheel." Sousè detaches the wheel from the driving column and starts to hand it back. "Here it is, but it won't do you any good in that back seat." Rogan leans over and pushes it back on the column. Same thing happens when Rogan demands that Sousè use the emergency brake. Egbert hands it back and tells the criminal to use it. Suddenly Sousè notices the rear wheel is falling off the car right at the time he is bordering a steep cliff. Egbert looks at the cliff and then the tire. "Going to be very dangerous."

Near the end of the ride Repulsive stands up in the back seat to jump out, but a low-slung tree branch knocks him in the head and he slumps over. Sousè does not know that and keeps driving furiously. Finally, without a back wheel and kissing the shore of a large lake, Sousè stops, slowly gets out of the car and comments to the unconscious Rogan, "You'll have to take the boat from here on anyway."

By now, Skinner, Og, the cops and Mackley Q. Greene have arrived. Sousè is a hero again, but also rich. The capture of Repulsive Rogan reaps a huge reward, another hearty handclasp from Mr. Skinner, but best of all, the story Egbert told on the film set while substituting for A. Pismo Clam was jotted down by the production manager and given to the head of his studio. The man loved it and the assistant has a royalty check for Sousè. With the Beefsteak Mine, the bounty for the capture of Repulsive Rogan and the film contract the Sousè family is fabulously wealthy.

The final scene is shot in the huge Sousè mansion. His insulting and mean family is tamed and loving to their breadwinner hero. Sousè, dressed in tux and tails, leaves the breakfast table while all the family line up for a good-bye kiss. The butler is waiting at the door with a silk top hat ready for his boss. Sousè grabs a safari hat instead and places it on his head. He asks the butler his sartorial opinion. The butler suggests the top hat is more appropriate. Egbert leaves the house properly attired but slightly disconsolate, feeling out of place surrounded with all his wealth. He lazily kicks a can along the ground until he hears the familiar whistling of Joe Guelpe heading for the Black Pussy Cafe. He looks up and with great glee sees his fast-walking bartender headed for work. Sousè runs after him trying to catch up to Joe and join him in a morning libation at his favorite bar. Nothing will ever change the Sousè of old.

The Bank Dick had Fields' stamp from beginning to end. The shooting was over in mid-October and it was now time to write the credits. Fields had his hand in that too. He wrote the fellow in charge, "Please do not forget, in making the credits on the screen both the story and the screenplay are to be credited to Mahatma Kane Jeeves. . . . There is not one line to my knowledge of Grayson's used in the script." Incidentally, speculations or explanations for Fields' use of the pseudonym Mahatma Kane Jeeves have ranged from the laughable to the bizarre. Here is the last word on that: Fields got a kick out of the old English drawing-room dramas, the ones in which the butler was usually named Jeeves. It seemed that any time the typically stuffy English aristocrat in these old melodramas would leave his mansion invariably he would call to the butler, "My hat, my cane, Jeeves." Well, at the end of The Bank Dick when Sousè was leaving his mansion Fields had written, although he never did say the line, "My hat, my cane, Jeeves." Or said quickly, "Mahatma Kane Jeeves." True.

Fields previewed the film around the first of November then went back to work and suggested a whole slew of changes. The studio went along with them all. If you watch the film carefully you can see that some of the best verbal jokes were post-dubbed by W. C., probably exactly as they occurred to him while watching the previews. Clearly no attempt was made at a precise lip sync, which is no less funny.

The almost completely W. C. Fields production, The Bank Dick, was released November 29, 1940, to the comedian's best film reviews ever. The "great man" finally proved his point. He knew what was best for him. On seeing the film, Mack Sennett called to tell W. C. that he should receive an Academy Award for his work. Fields, who had recently presented Sennett with his Oscar, knew better. "They don't give those to comedians." In a newspaper article William Saroyan said, "Mahatma Kane Jeeves should receive the writer of the year award."

With W. C. in full control, this was probably the most tranquil set on which he worked. But although serene for Fields, it must have been terribly disquieting for director Cline, because, the story goes, W. C. did not give one line

as written. For example, at one point when Fields was in the Black Pussy Cafe he was slated to hold a conversation with Bill Wolfe. Wolfe just stood there as Fields talked and when he was finished W. C. walked away ending the scene. Wolfe never had a chance to say his lines. It worked perfectly and it was kept in the picture just that way.

And another scene at the Black Pussy Cafe born on the spur of the moment was bartender Shemp Howard pouring Sousè's "usual," a shot of whiskey with a water back. Howard could not find a correct glass in which to put the water, so he grabbed an old fashioned glass and used that. Unperturbed at the size of the glass, and while the camera was still running, Fields got the idea to use the water back as a finger bowl instead. He washed his digits and dried them on a paper towel, them crumpled the paper towel and flipped it over his shoulder and then kicked it back up with his foot. The trajectory was so straight that it looked as if someone hiding behind the bar threw the paper towel back up.

Another completely extemporaneous addition was during the directorial sequence. This was the scene in which Sousè took over from the drunken director A. Pismo Clam and helmed a motion picture shot on location in downtown Lompoc, Sousè's hometown. One day as a joke Eddie Cline appeared on the set sitting on a palanquin. When Fields saw it he kicked the director off the chair and went through a series of gags on the portable throne which brought the crew to their knees. So Fields and Cline decided to put some of that stuff into the movie. What difference does a plot make?

Probably the most telling ad-libbing, and the most ironic, occurred during the shooting of this same scene. Reed Hadley played François, the actor Sousè directed. In 1972 Richard Bann interviewed Hadley; here is what the actor had to say:

Repulsive Rogan (Al Hill) makes his getaway with Sousè behind the wheel.

The greatest comedian I ever worked with was W. C. Fields. I made *The Bank Dick* with him at Universal. I had a scene where I played a ham actor who, at a height of six feet three inches, towered over my leading lady, who was about five feet tall. In addition they gave me a silk top hat to wear. The fascinating thing about working with Bill was that each take was different. Here I was, having studied the script, expecting a specific cue from Mr. Fields. But he would usually say something quite different, and the first few times actors would be a little startled. But whatever he said, Bill would usually express the general idea of what was actually written in the script. It certainly kept me on my toes trying to figure out when Bill was through talking so that I could say my lines.

The irony here was thick. While Sousè changed the script as shooting was under way so too in life Fields was changing his lines during shooting. This clearly was another perfect example of Fields' art imitating his life, and so immediate, too.

Also it was in this scene that W. C. took a swipe at Hollywood, or himself, or both. François was dressed in top hat and tails only to learn Sousè had done a hasty rewrite. Now he was to be a football star. François was incredulous: "In these clothes?"

"You can change your hat." Then Sousè told him of more changes. François found it impossible to follow the twisted tale, but Sousè reassured him: "Don't give it a second thought, I've changed everything."

Mackley Q. Greene, a representative of the producers, overheard Sousè's story line and wrote a synopsis for his boss. By the end of the movie we found out that the studio loved Sousè's stupid story, gave him ten grand for the rights and wanted him to direct it. In short the studio executives were so dumb they bought the plotless story of a complete bumbler. At the same time, Universal was buying the works of W. C. Fields, which were devised in the same fashion.

Whether or not Fields was ridiculing the studio or himself made little difference in their relationship. At this point almost everyone was happy: Fields loved his freedom; the studio loved the financial success of *The Bank Dick;* and the critics loved Fields. The only people not happy were the citizens of Lompoc, a real-life small community very close to Vandenberg Air Force Base in California. W. C. constantly mispronounced the town's name, and the citizenry was furious at him for depicting their village as dull and backward.

Except in Lompoc Fields was right on top still, and for the first time in a long time completely happy with his studio. In January 1941 W. C. gaily began work on another script for Universal, but the good feeling would not last long.

Egbert Sousè, now respectable, really has not changed much, not unlike W. C. Fields. Pictured clockwise from left, W. C.,
butler Ed Thomas, Evelyn Del Rio, Una Merkel, butler Joe North, Cora Witherspoon, Jesse Ralph and Grady Sutton.

THE BANK DICK

74 minutes
Sound, black and white
Released November 29, 1940, by Universal
Produced by Universal
Directed by Edward Cline
Supervisor: Jack Gross
Original story and screenplay by Mahatma Kane Jeeves (W. C. Fields)
Musical direction by Charles Previn
Photographed by Milton Krasner
Art direction by Jack Otterson
Associate: Richard Riedel
Edited by Arthur Hilton
Collaborating director: Ralph Ceder
Sound supervisor: Bernard B. Brown
Technician: William Hedgcock
Gowns by Vera West
Set decorations by R. A. Gausman
Additional material written by Dick Carroll

CAST:
W. C. Fields   Egbert Sousè
Cora Witherspoon   Agatha Sousè
Una Merkel   Myrtle Sousè
Evelyn Del Rio   Elsie Mae Adele Brunch Sousè
Jessie Ralph   Mrs. Hermisillo Brunch
Franklin Pangborn   J. Pinkerton Snoopington, bank examiner
Shemp Howard   Joe Guelpe, bartender
Richard Purcell   Mackley Q. Greene, of Tel-Avis
Grady Sutton   Og Oggilby, bank teller
Russell Hicks   J. Frothingham Waterbury, con man
Pierre Watkin   Mr. Skinner, bank president
Al Hill   Repulsive Rogan (screen credits erroneously list Filthy McNasty)
George Moran   Loudmouth McNasty, alias the Wildcat (screen credits erroneously list Cozy Cochran)
Jack Norton   A. Pismo Clam, director
Pat West   Assistant director
Reed Hadley   François, leading man
Heather Wilde   Miss Plupp
Harlan Briggs   The eminent Dr. Stall
Bill Alston   Mr. Cheek, teller
Eddie Dunn   James, the chauffeur
Jan Duggan   Mrs. Muckle
Bobby Larson   Clifford Muckle, her son
Bill Wolfe   Otis

Patsy Moran   Lady with fruit hat
Charlie Sullivan   Driver
Becky Bohanon   Girl
Larry Harris   Boy
Frank Lester Ward   Boy
Tommy Braunger   Boy
Emmett Vogan   Hotel desk clerk
Max Wagner   Shirtless ditch digger
William J. O'Brien   Extra during filming
Emma Tansey   Old woman on bench
Jack Roper   Extra during filming
Charles Hart   Extra during filming
David Thursby   Extra during filming
Dorothy Haas   Herself, the script girl
Fay Adler   Stenographer
Russell Cole   Bank employee
Pat O'Malley   Officer
Billy Mitchell   Moses, black man withdrawing money
Fay Holderness   Lady passerby
Nora Cecil   Lompoc ladies auxiliary
David Oliver   Teller with airy straw hat
Jack Clifford   Officer
Margaret Seddon   Old lady in car
Eddie Acuff   Reporter
Mary Field   Woman
Eddie Coke   Young man
Gene Collins   Boy
John Rawlings   Bit man
Sam Rice   Bit man
Lowden Adams   Valet to François
Vangie Beilby   Old lady with dog
Dorothy Vernon   Bit, old lady
Bonnie Washington   Miss Plupp's maid
Joe North   Butler
Ed Thomas   Butler
Melinda Boss   Secretary
Monte Ford   Director's assistant
Frankie Van   Director's assistant

Filmed at Universal in Universal City.
   Parts cut from the final release print: Eddie Hearn, Kay Sutton, Ethelreda Leopold, Harriette De Bussman, Clyde Dembeck, Virginia Dare, Patsy O'Byrne.
   Working title: *The Great Man.* Originally released in Britain as *The Bank Detective.*
   The one-reel non-theatrical excerpt from this film is entitled *The Great Chase.*

Never Give A Sucker An Even Break
—1941—

It has been repeated often, but it is true. It is the essence of W. C. Fields' art. It cannot be overstated. The pain in his life was the fuel for much of his comedy. Again, his movie wives were shrewish, pretentious and overbearing—Fields' perception of his own wife, Hattie. His film sons were disrespectful sissies and mama's boys — W. C.'s view of his own son, W. C. Jr. His daughters were inevitably sympathetic to the father, opposed to the mother—the comedian's projection of what his personal life would have been like had he had a daughter, not a son. In his movie depictions of middle-class life these three characterizations rarely vary, and he wrote it and played it that same way over and over and again and again.

Originally, the pain in W. C.'s domestic life came out in angry letters to Hattie, but eventually it surfaced in the form of laughs, not the least being that it was a woman who "drove me to drink. It is the one thing I'm indebted to her for." And yet, surprisingly, the family kept in touch through the years. Once a week W. C. wrote a letter to Hattie along with a check, and by the mid-thirties Fields and Fields Junior reconciled, never to the point of a true father-and-son relationship; it was too late for that, but there was love and they were cordial. His familial portrayals could have been devastating to his wife and son, but fortunately it seemed they never caught on.

By means of his films Fields helped settle old scores, real and imagined. The irony was that W. C. was being paid vast sums of money to "get even" in this way. Few if any have been so well paid, or even paid at all, to settle personal grievances or express hostility.

This life-art connection was part of his circus films as

well. He took the low-life vaudeville theater managers who swindled him in his penniless days of one-night stands and portrayed them on the screen. Fields played their roles with one important difference, however. In his artful depiction he added a touch of sympathy.

And more. In many of his movies the Fields character ends up rich and happy, usually by some incredible stroke of serendipity. Again, an artistic representation of his own life. W. C. could never explain his own success. On one hand he was extremely lucky. He worked hard of course, but he was bursting with talent which he did not fully understand. He was once considered the greatest juggler in the world, but when asked how he did it, he often responded, "I simply had a fatal facility to juggle." The coordination to toss balls came very easily. Sure, he put in long hours refining the art, but the basic talent was inexplicably there. So he put his juggling talent on stage with no intention of becoming a comic juggler, but as one reviewer noted, "There was something about him, the way he walked, the way he carried himself, something in the face that naturally made people laugh." Moreover, Fields' display of anger when he missed a trick, or dropped a hat or cane or ball brought, much to his surprise, howls of laughter. So, by accident he added comedy to an already brilliant juggling routine. Indeed, Fields admitted he never knew why people laughed, he just knew how to make them laugh.

On the set or stage he never stayed up late at night writing lengthy scripts or memorizing lines or trying to figure out the proper staging for the best laughs. He merely followed his own instincts at the time of performance, and this natural style made us all laugh. It almost all came too easily for him, and he could never grasp how he became so successful. His movies depicted that. He was an unregenerate, unrepentant and unreformable bungler as Sousè, Bissonette or McGargle who stumbled or fell into great wealth or success, but the man remained unchanged. Fields the star in Hollywood was the same as Dukenfield the poor boy in Philadelphia. Success did not change him.

With that in mind, it was inevitable that his very real fights with Hollywood's producers, directors and writers would sooner or later become the subject of ridicule in one of his motion pictures. And so it came to be in 1941, when W. C. Fields wrote a script entitled *The Great Man*. This was the second time Fields wanted one of his movies called *The Great Man*. He tried to slip the title past the Universal executives for his last picture, but they rejected it and called it *The Bank Dick* instead. Now he tried it again, but again lost. Universal changed the title to *Never Give a Sucker an Even Break*. Fields took it philosophically. "It doesn't matter anyway. Their title won't fit on a marquee, so they'll cut it down to 'W. C. Fields . . . Sucker.' "

It took four months to write the script and on April 15, 1941, Fields submitted the finished copy to the Breen office. The censors made a frontal attack. Two days later Joseph Breen himself wrote a six-page list of objections and sent it to W. C. Breen broke the suggestions into two categories, "Vulgar and Suggestive Scenes and Dialogue" and "Jocular References to Drinking and Liquor."

Fields again fought, and he won some points and lost others. In one scene Fields had his niece throw a brick at two bratty kids; Breen felt that would be offensive to parents. Fields won that one. In regard to the references to drinking, Fields had to cut some of them, not all.

But in one scene Fields got back at the censors. It was a scene in which he entered a soda fountain. He ordered an ice cream float. Then, completely breaking from character, he looked straight into the camera: "This scene was supposed to be in a saloon but the censor cut it out. It'll play just as well."

In newspaper interviews W. C. complained about the censor's red pen penchant: "Why, those guys won't let me do anything. They find double meaning in commas and semicolons in my scripts. As an example, they made me cut a line out about a drunk. The line reads, 'He's tighter than a dick's hat band.' Now what's wrong with that? They also won't let me look at a girl's legs. I'm just looking not saying anything and they censor me."

And of course there were other troubles. Even after the great success of *The Bank Dick* the studio for some reason started putting strictures on W. C. again. First they

Here is a compliment to the "great man" so easily identifiable even with his back to the camera. That is Gloria Jean running toward him. Of course there is no Esoteric Pictures—this is the gate to Universal — but for Sucker *they renamed the studio Esoteric. The original caption to this still reads: "Coming to work at the studio, W. C. Fields as 'Himself' meets Gloria Jean as 'Herself,' in Universal's* The Great Man." *That was the title Fields wanted for this film, and it seems for a time at least the studio bigwigs agreed; but alas, they changed their minds.*

complained about the script. When Fields turned in his first script it was a total of twelve pages. The studio demanded more, so he turned the twelve into ninety-six. The producer complained, "You haven't lived up to your contract. It's still too short, plus you were supposed to hire writers and you haven't yet." So W. C. got a couple of writers and instructed them to leave everything the same but add descriptive material such as "Beautiful girl adorned in blue fox and in a gown styled by the Rue de la Paix" and so on. With the added material the script stood at 156 pages. Fields handed it to the producer, but there were still some problems. "This is a very workmanlike job, too long however. We'll get our writers to cut it down." And W. C. accused Universal of putting fifty writers on it. Fields explained the rest: "They produced the worst script I ever read. I was going to throw it in their faces when the director [again, Eddie Cline] told me not to. He said, 'We'll shoot your own script. They won't know the difference.' We did—and they didn't."

Production was ready except for one thing. W. C. had to sign a very unique contract first. Universal would not use a real person's name in a movie unless they could get a release from that person. The release agreement provided protection against a lawsuit. In *Sucker* Fields played himself for the first time in his career and therefore Universal made him sign an agreement that read like this: "W. C. Fields will not sue the studio over W. C. Fields' portrayal of W. C. Fields in *Never Give a Sucker an Even Break.*"

W. C. Fields is headed for the Esoteric Studios for a script conference with a producer. On the way he stops to admire an enormous poster advertising his last movie, *The Bank Dick*. Standing nearby are two wastrels named Butch and Buddy who asperse the motion picture. Fields

While looking at the ad for The Bank Dick *those two little brats Butch and Buddy called the picture a "buptkie," causing the star, W. C. Fields to retaliate in this scene from* Sucker.

glares. The kids recognize him and scram. W. C. returns to admiring the poster when a shapely young woman walks past. Fields tips his hat: "Hiya, tootie pie, everything under control?" She ignores him, but her escort, whom Fields did not see, coldcocks the comedian, sending him flying over a hedge.

He brushes himself off and heads for the studio. Zombie-like Bill Wolfe intercepts him, asking for a part in the new picture. Fields puts him off, tells him to come by the house sometime. But what time?

"Oh, a couple o'clock."

W. C. decides to grab a bite to eat before his meeting. A fat, surly waitress takes his order. Fields asks if there is any goulash on the menu. The waitress wipes off a spot from the corner of the sheet. "That's roast beef gravy." W. C. tries to be very pleasant: "Is that steak New York cut?" Without a word the waitress takes her pencil and scratches out "steak" from the menu. Still cordial, W. C. asks, "Do you think it's too hot for pork chops?" She crosses out pork chops.

"Ah, that practically eliminates everything but ham and eggs." She crosses out something on the menu.

"No ham either. Eggs are entree! Give me two fomented eggs with butter in a glass."

"Cup!"

"Cup. . . . Yes . . . cup, and some whole wheat—"

"White!"

"That's fine—some white bread. Yes, and a cup of mocha java with cream."

"Milk!"

"Milk." After the meal W. C. says something about the food, to which the waitress takes umbrage. W. C. defends himself: "I didn't squawk about the steak, dear. I merely said I didn't see that old horse that used to be tethered outside here."

The waitress complains about him being too free with his hands.

"Listen, honey, I was only trying to guess your weight."

Fields heads for the producer's office. In the outer office a secretary works the switchboard. W. C. introduces himself but unbeknownst to him she is talking to someone on the line. "You big hoddy-doddy. You smoke cigars all day and drink whiskey half the night." W. C. grabs a handful of cigars from his pocket and throws them into a waste can. The secretary continues: "Someday you'll drown in a vat of whiskey." W. C. mumbles, "Oh, death where is thy sting?" Finally the shapely secretary says good-bye and disconnects the line. Fields gets up and starts to leave. Then the secretary, played by Carlotta Monti, says to him, "I beg your pardon, what did you say?" W. C. comes back. He gives her his name, and she says that Mr. Pangborn has been expecting him. W. C. goes into the inner office.

Fields begins to read his script when the intended leading lady walks in. Fields tells her the picture begins in a poolroom and she will be wearing a beard. She is in a twit but W. C. happily reassures her that she can play the rest of the picture "with an absolutely clean-shaven face." She leaves in a huff. Franklin Pangborn, the producer, then decides to read the script himself. In the

Gloria Jean displays her great form by tossing a well-deserved brick at Butch and Buddy as Fields looks on approvingly. The two wastrels were added to the film gratuitously. They serve no purpose to what little plot the film had.

movie and in the script Gloria Jean plays Fields' niece. Pangborn reads, and the script comes to life.

Evidently, in Fields' script he also is an actor. However, he has just decided to quit the movie racket and to fly somewhere that looks a lot like a gypsy village. Although his niece, also an actor, is in the middle of production, she nevertheless quits her career to join her uncle.

The two ex-actors take an unconventional plane which has quite unconventional trappings, including sleeping berths like Pullman sleepers and an open-air observation deck. At night in the sleeper and the next morning in the bathroom Fields creates quite a bit of havoc and later tries to relax on the open observation deck. Gloria, who hates to see her uncle drinking, is still asleep, so W.C. steals sips from his flask. He furtively keeps looking for Gloria to come bouncing onto the observation deck. Each time he looks over his shoulder he holds his flask near the ledge of the open window. Gloria finally shows up and Fields hides his bottle. In order to buy time to complete his liquid breakfast, Uncle W. C. gets Gloria to hunt down the flight attendant and find out the estimated time of arrival. She leaves. Fields reaches for his flask, which he has balanced precariously on the window ledge. He knocks it over. He jumps after it!! He catches up to the bottle in midair, screws the top back on and now all he has to worry about is the landing.

Luck would have it that he alights on an enormous

bed which is atop a huge butte. Bounce! Bounce! Bounce! He finally comes to a soft rest. The bed is in a courtyard abutting an enormous mansion. Fields straightens himself out and suddenly sees this vision of loveliness standing right in front of him. He introduces himself. The woman seems confused. She does not know what he is. He is a man. Ouliotta has never seen or heard of a man before. Since birth she has lived on the butte with only her mother and their huge dog. W. C. sees opportunity and introduces the young woman to the game of "squidgilum." He instructs her to put her hands atop her head and close her eyes. She does. Then W. C. kisses her. Ouliotta loves the game and goes a couple more rounds, until Fields hears a threatening growl from behind. He looks to see a large, long-fanged dog held on a leash by an even larger long-fanged woman, Ouliotta's mother, Mrs. Hemoglobin.

Ouliotta explains the exciting game to her mother and now Mrs. Hemoglobin wants a go at it. When she closes her eyes W. C. makes a mad dash for a basket which is used to get up and down the butte. The basket hurtles the two thousand feet to the bottom and dumps its occupant unceremoniously. Here the movie within the movie stops.

Back at the studio, Pangborn throws the script on his desk; Fields urges him to continue. The producer picks up the script and starts reading some more.

Back to the movie within a movie. Coincidentally W. C. has fallen just on the outskirts of this gypsy-like village. He changes into the accepted garb of the natives and heads for the nearest bar. At the saloon Fields tells his story of landing at the Hemoglobin estate and his quick retreat. He is informed that the old lady is fabulously wealthy. W. C. quickly changes his view of Mrs. Hemoglobin and decides she was not that bad after all. Another barfly overhears the conversation and sidles up to Fields. They split a couple of noggins of hundred-proof goat's milk. The man also wants to woo Hemoglobin and be-

comes Fields' rival for the old bat. (The credits describe his character simply as the "Rival." He is played by Fields' old friend from the Broadway days, Leon Errol.)

About the same time, Fields hears the sweet sound of his niece's singing. After she had landed she had to hitch a ride to the gypsy colony on an ox-drawn cart. Uncle and niece have a happy reunion and Fields invites her to the bar. Concerned about his drinking, she asks what is in his glass.

"Goat's milk, dear."

"What kind of goat's milk?"

"Nanny goat's milk."

Fields tells his niece about his plan to marry Mrs. Hemoglobin and her riches. Gloria does not like the idea of her uncle marrying for money, but he cannot be dissuaded. Meanwhile, Leon Errol has started his climb up the butte. Fields has dressed in a battered top hat and tails and ascends the mountain in the basket. Gloria accompanies him. He beats Errol to the summit, and when his rival finally appears W. C. throws him back down the cliff. The wedding is set. The marching music commences, and all the while Gloria tries talking her uncle out of the match. As he walks down the aisle he takes one good look at Mrs. Hemoglobin, decides Gloria is right and the two rush for the basket. They jump in and begin their lightning descent. Gloria is worried. Fields assuages her: "It's all right, dear. Don't start worrying until we get down to 1,999. It's the last foot that's dangerous." Thud!

The scene switches back to Pangborn's office. The producer is apoplectic. He tells W. C. the story stinks and kicks the comedian out of his office.

That is it. Fields has been kicked out of Hollywood. He will leave Gloria behind so she can finish school. He picks up his niece and tells her his plans. She wants to go with him. He warns her, "You want to grow up and be dumb like Zasu Pitts?" She does not mind and Fields agrees to take her. But first Gloria has to get some clothes. He parks in front of a department store and

Mrs. Hemoglobin (Margaret Dumont) surprises W. C. Fields (Himself) kissing Ouliotta Delight (Susan Miller).

In story conference with Mrs. Pastrome (Minerva Urecal), Mrs. Heather Pangborn (Mona Barrie), with her hand resting on her clean-shaven chin, and Franklin Pangborn (Himself), the justifiably worried producer at Esoteric Pictures.

hands his niece a dollar and a quarter: "Go in there and buy yourself several outfits." She leaves; Fields waits in his car. He notices a police car parked in front of him and so, with nothing else to do, he walks up to exchange small talk. When he gets to the window he hears on the police radio "Two crooks have just held up the bank for $150,000 . . . that is all."

"That is all! $150,000 ain't hay, is it?"

The police are annoyed with the interruption. The radio comes back with a description of the crook: "He has apple-red cheeks, cauliflower ears and mutton chop whiskers."

"Sounds like a full-course dinner to me. What, no apple pie?"

The cops tell him to be quiet and then they take off. W. C. returns to his car.

Inside the store a fat middle-aged woman is looking for baby clothes for her expected grandchild. She is in a hurry. She has to drop the clothes off at the maternity hospital, then rush to catch a plane. She gets the clothes, runs outside and demands the doorman get her a cab immediately. Fields sees her concern and asks if he may help her. Yes! The woman slips into the back seat. "I've got to get to the maternity hospital right away." Seeing the woman's girth and her anxiety, he concludes she might give birth in his back seat. He steps on it. He speeds through the streets of Los Angeles creating havoc. He gets stuck behind a hook and ladder and quite accidentally the ladder sinks its claws into the roof of Fields' car. The back driver of the fire engine lifts the car in the air to get it out of harm's way. Finally the car comes loose and spins onto the front lawn of the maternity hospital. Attendants rush out, retrieve the fat lady, and take her to the maternity room. Fields' car is a wreck and so is he. He steps out of the demolished auto just as Gloria Jean drives up in a taxi. His niece looks at Fields with affection: "My Uncle Bill . . . but I still love him."

"Fields . . . *Sucker*" made it to the silver screen on October 10, 1941, to surprisingly good reviews. Surpris-

ing because this was probably the most plotless movie of Fields' career. It seems the majority of the critics finally gave up grousing about the lack of a story in his movies. Most of them praised W. C. to the hilt, wrote glowingly of his comic talent and finally admitted that this great comic actor had proved beyond a doubt that he needed no story to incite belly laughs.

Of course, as was usually the case, not all the critics applauded the film. And since in this Universal three-some—*Chickadee, Bank Dick* and *Sucker*—Fields had nearly complete control of at least his own scenes from writing to directing to starring, any negative comments brought vituperative letters from the comedian. When Walter Winchell panned *Chickadee,* claiming that W. C. and Mae hammed so much fighting for the limelight that they ruined the picture, Fields wrote him calling him "slimy" and "cowardly." When Jimmy Fiddler wrote in the *Hollywood Reporter* that *Sucker* stunk, Fields fired back, writing the publisher about that "stinko" reporter. But he left his sharpest rebuke for the *Christian Science Monitor,* which wrote about *Sucker:* "W. C. Fields acting out a story with results that are by turns ludicrous, tedious and distasteful. There is the usual atmosphere of befuddled alcoholism." Watch out; here comes the "great man." He wrote the editor:

The Christian Science Monitor day in and day out the same old bromides. They no longer look for love and beauty but see so many sordid things that Mary Baker Eddy did not see in this beautiful world she discovered after trying her hand at mesmerism, hypnotism and spiritualism before landing on the lucrative Christian Science racket. When I play in a picture in which I take a few nips to get a laugh (I have never played a drunk in my life) I hope that it might bring to mind the anecdote of Jesus turning water into wine. And wouldn't it be terrible if I quoted some reliable statistics which prove that more people are driven insane through religious hysteria than by drinking alcohol.

About drinking. During *Sucker* Fields changed his alcohol habits. He quit his favorite concoction of pineapple juice and rum and switched to gin, claiming the former was fattening. But no matter the poison, it was killing him. The booze swelled his feet painfully and between scenes he would return to his dressing room and prop his feet up on pillows to ease the throbbing.

Other than Mae West's prohibition, this was probably the first time Fields had been warned to curtail his drinking on the set. With the youngsters around, Gloria Jean and Butch and Buddy, the studio marms, knowing Fields' bent for the hard stuff, threatened to close the set if the polyp-nosed comedian drank in front of the young innocents. To insure peace Universal put up a partition between the youngsters and Fields, so that in between scenes W. C. could take a drink in hiding. One day Fields walked out from behind the barrier bringing a bottle of amber fluid to his lips. Gloria's teacher screamed her condemnation and threatened to shut the place down. Fields slowly removed his hand from the label and showed it to the teacher: "Listerine, my dear, just Listerine." He returned to his dressing room to get the real stuff.

Gloria Jean's mother, Mrs. Schoonover, often visited the set. She remembered Fields as a lonely man. She said he would often invite her to his dressing room between scenes because he wanted to hear simple things: Where was she from? Where did she live? Or swap stories about the good old days, just plain talk. Gloria (who is still a

beautiful woman with loads of talent) remembers Fields kindly, too. She said he was such a *gentle* man, very considerate, and he seemed to take a real liking to her. (Maybe he saw in her that daughter who understands him and sides with him?) W. C. once joked, "Too bad Gloria isn't a little younger or I'd marry her myself." Gloria was a demure young woman being groomed as an adolescent star to succeed Deanna Durbin, who had matured. (Incidentally, Durbin lived across the street from W. C., and her incessant singing practice, of quick runs up and down the scales, drove her neighbor to distraction. W. C. publicly bragged that his shotgun was loaded and "aimed to kill.")

Fields liked Gloria Jean probably as much as he hated Butch and Buddy. These kids were wisecracking brats. One day the two were playing around with a bow and some arrows when Fields complained to the director, "I do not wish to be shot in the ass by one of those arrows." The boys were in earshot of W. C.'s remark and so was their studio cicerone. The teacher complained to the line producer Jack Gross. Gross wrote to Fields about it and Fields wrote back, "With reference to that garrulous female who sits on the set and gossips audibly all day through both rehearsals and takes . . . who snitched on me for saying, 'I do not wish to be shot in the ass by one

Fields gallantly kissing Mrs. Gregory La Cava's hand while W. C.'s friend and former director Gregory La Cava looks on. Fields' other friend and present director Eddie Cline boldly holds the Hollywood Reporter, *which proclaims in large headlines, "Studio Ban on All Visitors." The La Cavas seem unconcerned.*

Director of Sucker *Eddie Cline in a heated script conference with Otis Cribblecobbis while the real author relishes Otis' taciturnity.*

of those arrows,' within hearing distance of those two grand little troupers Buddy and Butch [they were commonly known as Butch and Buddy but Fields never gave them that satisfaction], I have no wish to demoralize those little chaps and I shall be more cautious in the future. It is my fervent wish that the holy Bible or an edition of Shakespeare never falls into their hands until they are old enough to stand up.''

Never Give a Sucker an Even Break was Fields' last feature-length starring film. Like Esoteric Pictures firing Fields in the movie, Universal Pictures did the same, only in real life. The studio did not renew the independent-minded comedian's contract. Universal wanted to try a fresh approach to comedy. Abbott and Costello had just burst forth on the scene with *Buck Privates*. Eventually, the duo would swell the studio's box-office coffers and stay great moneymakers for years to come. Old names like W. C. Fields were expendable. Of course it never helped that W. C. had alienated so many big shots. His last great success, *Sucker,* had been at the expense of his "sponsors," and now, so soon after that last picture, they cut him loose. They probably figured that they had the last laugh at *his* expense this time. With *Sucker* such a swipe at Hollywood picturemaking and W. C.'s incessant clamoring for artistic freedom, he certainly did not endear himself to the Universal brass. Indeed, one studio executive remembered Arthur Hornblow Jr.'s remark when Paramount axed Fields and quipped that Paramount's

price was too cheap. Universal would not work with Fields again for "*ten* million dollars.'' Fields was out, but he was in good company. Lots of esteemed comics were then floundering. Laurel and Hardy, Harold Lloyd, Harry Langdon, Buster Keaton, the Marx Brothers, all were forced into lousy pictures, when there was any work at all. But perhaps another reason for Universal jettisoning Fields was the comedian's love for the bottle. The alcohol was exacting its fare. W. C. had been in bad health for years now. There were big sums of money involved in picturemaking, and the studio may have been reluctant to take a chance on a star who might not be able to complete production.

Nevertheless, Fields still worked on new scripts and was always anxious to start another movie. He even elicited the help of Orson Welles to push some studio into making *Pickwick Papers* with the old Micawber in the starring role. But most of the studio heads felt W. C. was too sick to carry the burden of another feature film. The idea died. Broadway again called for him, but Fields did not want to go back there: "New York is a great old burg, but I love the open spaces and the sunshine and the money in movies.''

But no movies were planned for him.

W. C. wanted back into filmmaking, so he announced publicly that he was on the wagon for life now. On November 10, 1941, he said in an interview, "Don't tell the studio heads I'm on the wagon, because now when I call them a name over there they'll know I mean it. I'm not going to drink water though. My friend died of drinking too much water; his was a case of internal drowning." The truth is he did not stop drinking at all. A month after his announcement he and John Barrymore were sitting around the house on a pleasant Sunday. It was noon, December 7, 1941. They were sipping and listening to the radio. Then a bulletin interrupted the program. The Japanese had just bombed Pearl Harbor. It was war! Fields bolted from his chair and got to the phone. Barrymore did not listen in, he figured W. C. was calling a friend or a relative relaying the dreadful news. Fields came back and they started drinking again, talking about the prospects of fighting the Japanese and the Germans. About half an hour later a delivery truck pulled up Fields' driveway. Barrymore looked out the window and saw the driver unloading case after case of gin. He counted forty. Barrymore now knew the reason for Fields' earlier call. He turned to his friend mockingly: "Uncle Claude, why only forty cases?"

"Because I think it's going to be a short war."

Although Fields would appear in three more movies, only in cameo, and work in a twenty-minute routine on another one, in which his scene was cut before release, *Never Give a Sucker an Even Break* was really his last hurrah in Hollywood. The last time he would star. The last time he would make a film all his own. It was a fitting ending to his madcap movie career, to make a motion picture that stung the Hollywood establishment with its surreal satire of how *"they"* made movies. The studio may have fired him, but he had the *real* last laugh because *Sucker* still plays to the delight of audiences more than forty years after its stinging indictment of *"they"* was first issued.

NEVER GIVE A SUCKER AN EVEN BREAK

70 minutes
Sound, black and white
Released October 10, 1941, by Universal
Produced by Universal
Directed by Edward Cline
Screenplay by John T. Neville and Prescott Chaplin
Original story by Otis Criblecoblis (W. C. Fields)
Photographed by Charles Van Enger
Cameraman: Jerome Ash
Art direction by Jack Otterson and Richard H. Riedel
Edited by Arthur Hilton

Musical direction by Charles Previn
Musical score by Frank Skinner
Sound supervisor: Bernard B. Brown
Costumes by Vera West
Set decorations by R. A. Gausman
Associate director: Ralph Ceder
First assistant director: Howard Christie
Assistant second unit director: Melville Shyer
Songs: "Estrellita," "Comin' through the Rye," "Otchi Tchorniya," "Here Comes the Bride"

CAST:

W. C. Fields	The Great Man (as himself, Bill Fields)
Gloria Jean	His niece
Leon Errol	His rival
Billy Lenhart	Butch
Kenneth Brown	Buddy
Margaret Dumont	Mrs. Hemoglobin
Susan Miller	Ouliotta Delight Hemoglobin
Franklin Pangborn	The producer at Esoteric Studios
Mona Barrie	Mrs. Heather Pangborn, his wife
Charles Lang	Pete Carson, a young engineer
Anne Nagel	Mlle. Gorgeous
Nell O'Day	Salesgirl
Irving Bacon	Tom, soda jerk
Jody Gilbert	Tiny, the waitress
Minerva Urecal	Mrs. Pastrome, cleaning lady
Emmett Vogan	Steve Roberts, engineer
Carlotta Monti	Producer's receptionist
Leon Belasco	Pianist
Dave Willock	Johnson, the assistant director
Billy Wayne	Foreman on Stage 6
James "Brick" Sullivan	Fire truck driver
Harriet Haddon	Redhead

Marcia Ralston	Stewardess
Duke York	Tough guy who assaults Fields
Emma Tansey	Old lady with newspaper
Claud Allister	Englishman bitten by a dog
Jack "Tiny" Lipson	Huge Turk, the cigarette salesman
William Gould	Doorman
Michael Visaroff	Coachman in Russian village
Eddie Bruce	Cameraman
Jack Roper	Joe, drinking Jarno
Charles McMurphy	Officer
Frances Morris	Nurse
Frank Austin	Diner with high blood pressure
Irene Colman	Stewardess
Kathryn Sheldon	Air passenger, spinster
Kay Deslys	Mrs. Wilson
Emil Van Horn	Gargo, the gorilla
Bill Wolfe	Himself
Jean Porter	Passerby
Vic Potel	Mr. Clines, Russian magistrate
Dave Sharpe	Ubiquitous stunt double
Prince	Himself, the Great Dane

Filmed at Universal in Universal City.

Parts cut from the final release print: Al Hill, Cora Witherspoon, Lloyd Ingraham, James C. Morton, Dick Alexander, Armand "Curley" Wright, Jack Chefe, William Alston, Hank Mann, Patsy O'Byrne, Walter Lawrence.

Working title: *The Great Man,* the title preferred by Fields. Originally released in Britain as *What a Man!* In 1933 MGM had made a feature called *Never Give a Sucker a Break,* directed by Jack Conway. Fields himself had used the phrase twice in text titles for *It's*

the *Old Army Game* (1926). H. Allen Smith credits Wilson Mizner as the original source of this motto, but in fact Fields himself first ad-libbed this line in the 1924 stage play *Poppy.*

In an economic expedient, Universal reused intact the climactic chase footage as the finale for Abbott and Costello's 1944 film *In Society.*

The one-reel non-theatrical excerpt from this film is entitled *Hurry, Hurry.*

The Laziest Golfer

The film begins with W. C. standing at a tee at the bottom of a little hill. He chips the golf ball up the hill. It bounces near the top then rolls back down and lands on the tee again. He never has to move except to swing. After a couple of these lazy shots Fields sits down on a director's chair right next to a portable yet fully stocked bar. He addresses the camera saying that earlier he sliced a ball over his fence and toward Deanna Durbin's house. The errant golf ball sailed through a window. "She was hitting a high C at the time." The ball flew into her mouth and, "black and blued one of her tonsils." Fields "invited her over for a little gargle." But the talented singer refused his peacemaking overture. And that is where the film ends.

Copies of the movie indicate it was never released, it certainly was never edited. Perhaps it was supposed to be part of an intended USO series, something like the *Hollywood on Parade* group, but there is no mention of the piece ever being shown; there are no reviews, no advertisements, no contracts. Now it is just an odd bit of footage showing Fields relaxed at home, sipping a few and telling a tale. He used little makeup, so the movie revealed a face pocked and battered by booze; nevertheless he seemed comfortable.

He once talked about the short, saying he really was not the Laziest Golfer, but that his friend Gregory La Cava was. According to W. C., La Cava, who lived in Malibu, would rise early and tee up at low tide, then smash his golf ball into the sea. Then he would return home, relax, drink some and wait for the high tide to return his ball.

Dressed, sober (there is no doubt) and ready for conscription. W. C. Fields and John Barrymore are profiles in courage.

W. C. ran a spoof campaign for the presidency in 1942. He put his platform into a book which he titled *Fields for President*. Of course his campaign slogan was "Never give a sucker an even break." In his Dodd, Mead publication W. C. humorously attacked big government and the money burners at the IRS, but despite his losing campaign Fields was still very patriotic. During the war he and John Barrymore actually tried to enlist, creating some grand chaos at the induction center. When asked why they went to join, W. C. responded, "I heard our country needed a few more tanks." He was seriously concerned about the war, and when the USO approached him to make a short film for the troops Fields graciously agreed.

The movie was shot in W. C.'s own backyard. He was renting a beautiful Spanish-style mansion then which was tucked in the Hollywood Hills' Los Feliz district. His two undulating acres of property contained a tennis court and an Olympic-size swimming pool.

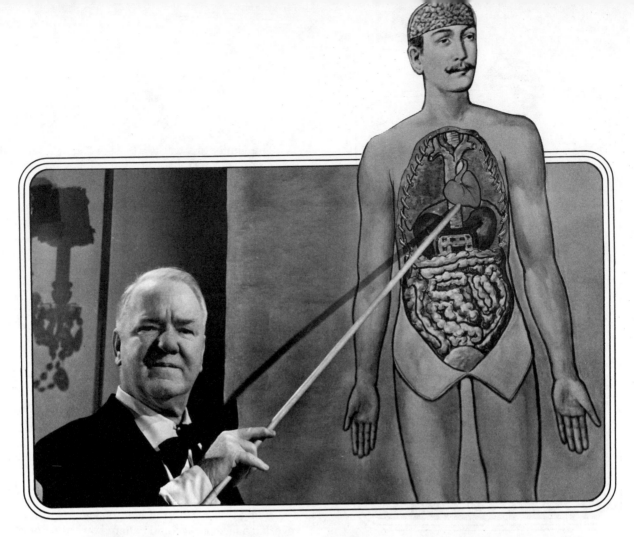

Tales Of Manhattan
—1942—

Twentieth Century-Fox courted Fields even before he began shooting *Sucker*. They wanted him to do a bit for their upcoming extravaganza entitled *Tales of Manhattan*. W. C. had never planned to do it. He had expected to be cranking out films for a long time at Universal, but they had abruptly squelched that idea. So he called Fox and told them he would be thrilled to work on the movie, and twelve days after the preview of *Sucker* Twentieth Century signed Fields for *Tales*. By November 14th the studio had the entire cast under contract. In early January they started production, and on the thirteenth of that month Fields worked for Fox for the first time. He put in five days, received $50,000, and then went home.

Tales of Manhattan follows the life of a tail coat as it passes from owner to owner. It begins with the wealthy and ends with the poor.

We first find the coat in an opulent love triangle among Charles Boyer, Rita Hayworth, and Thomas Mitchell.

Then the threads step down from that luxurious New York penthouse to a scene with Henry Fonda, who is married to Ginger Rogers in an intended satire of wedlock.

Next the coat adorns Edward G. Robinson who wears it to his upper-crust law school class reunion. The used coat hides the fact that Robinson is a hopeless alcoholic whose addiction has brought him financial ruin.

Fields, as Mr. Postlewhistle, dons the cutaway next. He bought the frock at a second hand clothiers operated by Phil Silvers. Postlewhistle is a montebank without a midway. He will wear the ill-fitting garment to Mrs. Clybourne Langahankie's mansion this evening where he is posted to lecture on the salubrity of cocoanut milk and the maleficence of liquor. His speech will be just one more of an endless series of "intellectually stimulating" talks that Mrs. Langahankie hosts in her sumptuous home for the enlightenment of her clucking group of friends (and to the near terminal nausea of Mr. Langahankie). Revenge for Mr. Langahankie! He and the butler dump liberal doses of alcohol into the large bowl of cocoanut milk. That should liven up his wife's little affair.

The time has come. The guests are ready. Postlewhistle approaches the lectern while telling his assistant,

Shicklegrubber, to dispense with the cocoanut milk. That accomplished, Postlewhistle begins his speech with his own glass in hand. He sips. He discovers that his cocoanut concoction never tasted so good. He continues the lecture as planned, downing "angel's milk" and castigating "demon rum." He lowers a diagram of a man's internal parts to illustrate alcohol's path of destruction. He points to a particular part of the anatomy, "The liver!" He mumbles, "It is very good with bacon." He continues aloud, "This majestic organ falls easy prey to the elixir of Saturnalia." By now the audience is in an alcoholic swoon and when one of the stuffiest matrons asks her husband to open a window, why the old chap throws a vase through it.

Postlewhistle wraps up his speech while Shicklegrubber passes the hat. When his assistant returns, Postlewhistle grabs the liquored generosity of his audience and stuffs the bills into his pockets. As he leaves the room he accidentally trips a lever and a wall spins 180 degrees revealing Mr. Langahankie, stewed to the gills, standing behind his erstwhile secret bar. Postlewhistle bellies up and orders a one finger shot glass of booze. Mr. Langahankie graciously obliges, but when he hunkers down to pour the smidgen of liquor, Postlewhistle stops him. Evidently his request had been misunderstood. Illustrating with his own finger, Postlewhistle instructs, "Not horizontally! Vertically!" Mr. Langahankie fills the glass to the rim.

After W. C.'s turn, Paul Robeson, Ethel Waters, and Eddie Anderson find the coat in an empty lot in their neighborhood. They check the pockets, find a wad of dough and divy up the money among themselves and their neighbors. Although playing the unflattering roles of Stepin Fetchit sorts, they use oddly communistic slogans in their dialogue.

Tales of Manhattan ends with the formerly fancy coat adorning a worthless scarecrow.

Possibly the Robeson, Waters, and Anderson scene was written by Paul Robeson, a fine actor, a great singer, a professional football player and a member of the New York Bar, who was a communist and who suffered greatly for his political beliefs.

Twentieth Century-Fox gave a private critics preview of *Tales of Manhattan* in May of 1942. The reviewers gave the film halfhearted notices, but once again praised Fields' turn as the showstopper and revealed that he got most of the applause. The bit was far from Fields' funniest or best work. Certainly it was humorous, but it was not the rollicking scene written about then, or for that matter, rumored to be over all these years. It had some disquieting touches that diminished the comedic effect. Although, it was W. C.'s wont to point a mocking finger at his own adversities (to put parts of his life on film), in this instance it was a little too unsettling to be knee-slapping. Postlewhistle's discussion of the pernicious effects of alcohol on "that majestic organ," the liver, bespeaks of W. C. Fields' own liver and the beating he has been giving it for the past decade or so. This clip clearly reveals Fields' alcohol-related physical decline. He did not appear well at all. Now we know that it would be only four short years before his "majestic organ" would succumb to the pummeling, and thus the liver line tends to make one wince.

Furthermore, it was quite obvious that W. C. ad-libbed freely throughout, as he did in all of his films, but this time those asides did not seem to flow naturally. He seemed to be struggling to birth his extemporaneous remarks. Of course they were funny, but the feeling he was working so hard took the edge off the laughs.

Finally, as of this writing, there is no known filmed transitional tag to this piece that would explain how the coat got from the Langahankie's soiree to the black neighborhood. The script had called for a robbery at the Langahankie's gathering, and the thieves were to use the coat to pile their booty, unaware that the tattered frock contained Postlewhistle's honorarium. It was scripted that the crooks would flee, take a plane, and in midair divide the loot. Then, to destroy the evidence, they would toss the coat overboard, still oblivious to the cash inside. So it seems the people of the press never really saw a completed version of *Tales.*

But even with these drawbacks, it is fairly simple to understand why the critics lauded W. C.'s bit. In the context of the film, which was very stylistic and occasionally dour, Fields was a breath of fresh air, and coming near the end of the film, that was exactly what the audience wanted. Besides, Fields' routine was completely out of sync with the spirit of the picture and that certainly made it the most memorable scene. By the time the reviewers penciled their critiques this so-so piece became hilarious. They simply remembered that W. C. purloined the picture once again. As one critic wrote: "The response to Fields was far greater than the response to Boyer, Fonda, Laughton, Rogers, and Hayworth. Furthermore, W. C. got the highest salary," [at least twice the salary, in fact, of any other actor in the movie] "and stole the show and Twentieth Century-Fox will give him top billing while the other actors scream."

Tales of Manhattan was released nationally on October 30, 1942 without W. C., despite the critics accolades for his scene. They could not understand why, and began to speculate in print. Some of the gossip writers claimed that the other artists created such a stir over the billing that in order to maintain peace, and protect themselves from possible lawsuits, the studio *had* to remove Fields from the film. But in fact this comedic segment did not fit in, and thus hurt the overall picture. Plus, *Tales* ran too long and Postlewhistle's part was the easiest to excise without damage to the plot. Sometimes it is necessary to remove what is best to make the whole run smoother. Nonetheless, without Fields, and still with tepid notices, the motion picture was successful enough at the box office to warrant a sequel.

After they had cut Fields' part Jimmy Fiddler wrote that W. C. planned to sue Fox over it. That made big news, but Fields vehemently combated the rumor, threatened to sue Fiddler and wrote a denial of it in the *Hollywood Reporter* in which he threw a few handfuls of mud at the critic. It was an excessive response by Fields just over a little tongue wagging, but most likely the "old gent" was hoping for a long-term contract with Fox and he felt Fiddler's gossip could ruin that prospect.

But it was probably Fields himself who wrecked any chance of an extended association with Fox. He was still nearly impossible to direct; and Fields and Julien Duvivier, the French director of *Tales,* clashed often. The Frenchman could not understand W. C.'s manner of acting or his ad-libs. At one point Fields as Postlewhistle extemporized to his assistant, Shicklegrubber, "Come here, my anemic blood bank." Duvivier demanded, "Cut! Cut! . . . Blood bank? Blood bank? What is this blood bank?" Of course Duvivier wanted Fields to read the idiot cards verbatim, and of course Fields would not. The fight was on. Buster Keaton and the stylish director Mal St. Clair (who, incidentally, directed Keaton in two shorts) had been loaned to Fox to mediate between W. C. and Duvivier, according to the trades, but they offered little in this case. When the fight between actor and director started, Keaton and St. Clair were laughing too hard to arbitrate. (Imagine Keaton laughing?) Fortunately Fields won that round without arbitration.

Then a little later Duvivier, pleased that for once W. C. followed the script, felt a little tiny direction here would make the scene work perfectly. "Now, I want you to laugh at the end of the line." Too much direction. Fields countered, "I never laugh in my pictures. I'll give

you a cynical smile, but a laugh . . . Never!" A few days after that encounter Duvivier again gave W. C. some directorial notes and Fields lashed back: "Sir, I am not an actor. I am a clown. If you want an actor you had better get someone else." And he stormed off the set. W. C. may have felt he had gone too far on that one, because the following day he returned to the set with a seven-foot olive tree instead of the customary branch.

Again Fields wanted to stay with Fox, but they did not want him. He wanted to hook up with any studio to make his own feature-length comedies even if it meant a cut in salary, but no one wrote or called. To keep busy he did a few radio appearances, but they were just guest shots. He wanted work, but no one seemed to want him. It was the tailspin of his career, abrupt and inexorable.

TALES OF MANHATTAN

118 minutes (10,663 feet)
Sound, black and white
Released Ocbober 30, 1942, by Twentieth Century-Fox
Produced by Boris Morros and S. P. Eagle (Sam Speigel) for
  Twentieth Century-Fox
Directed by Julien Duvivier
Assistant directors: Robert Stillman and Charles Hall
Screenplay and original stories by Ben Hecht, Ferenc Molnar,
  Donald Ogden Stewart, Samuel Hoffenstein, Alan Campbell,
  Ladislas Fedor, Lazlo Vadnai, Lazlo Georog, Lamar Trotti, Henry
  Blankford; and Buster Keaton, Ed Beloin and Bill Morrow (uncredited)
Photographed by Joseph Walker
Musical score by Sol Kaplan
Musical direction by Edward Paul
Orchestrations by Clarence Wheeler, Charles Bradshaw and Hugo
  Friedhofer.

Vocal arrangements by Hall Johnson
Songs: "Glory Day," by Leo Robin and Ralph Rainger; "Fare Thee
  Well to El Dorado," "A Journey to Your Lips" and "A Tale of
  Manhattan" by Paul Francis Webster and Saul Chaplin; "All God's
  Children Got Shoes"; "Great Getting Up in the Morning."
Art direction by Richard Day and Boris Leven
Set decorations by Thomas Little
Costumes by Irene, Dolly Tree, Bernard Newman, Gwen Wakeling
  and Oleg Cassini
Makeup by Guy Pearce
Unit manager: J. H. Nadel
Edited by Robert Bischoff
Sound recording by W. D. Flick and Roger Heman

CAST:

Charles Boyer	Paul Orman	Christian Rub	Wilson	Esther Howard	Bit woman
Rita Hayworth	Ethel Halloway	Adeline de Walt Reynolds	Grandmother	Ted Stanhope	Chauffeur
Thoma Mitchell	John Halloway	Sig Arno	Piccolo player	Paul Robeson	Luke
Eugene Pallette	Luther	Forbes Murray	Dignified man	Ethel Waters	Esther
Helene Reynolds	Actress	Buster Brodie	Call boy	Eddie "Rochester" Anderson	Reverend Lazarus
Robert Grieg	Lazar	Frank Jaquet	Musician	J. Carroll Naish	Costello
Jack Chefe	Tailor	William Wright	Skeptic	Clarence Muse	Grandpa
William Halligan	Oliver Webb	Frank Dae	Elderly man	George Reed	Christopher
Charles Williams	Paul's agent	Renèe Austin	Susan	Cordell Hickman	Nicodemus
Eric Wilton	Halloway's butler	Frank Darien	Grandpa	John Kelly	Monk
Ginger Rogers	Diane	Dewey Robinson	Proprietor	Lonnie Nichols	Brad
Henry Fonda	George	Tom O'Grady	Latecomer	Charles Gray	Rod
Cesar Romero	Harry Wilson	Edward G. Robinson	(Larry) Avery L. Browne	Phillip Hurlic	Jeff
Gail Patrick	Ellen	George Sanders	Williams	Charles Tannen	Pilot
Roland Young	Edgar, the butler	James Gleason	Father Joe	Archie Savage	Bit
Marion Martin	Squirrel	Harry Davenport	Professor Lyons	Rita Christiani	Bit
Frank Orth	Secondhand dealer	James Rennie	Hank Bronson	Laura Vaughn	Bit
Julia Griffith	Crowd extra	Harry Hayden	Soupy Davis	Ella Mae Lashley	Bit
Curly Twyford	Bird man	Morris Ankrum	Judge Barnes	Olive Ball	Bit
Joseph Bernard	Postman	Don Douglas	Henderson	Alberta Gary	Bit
Connie Leon	Mary	Mae Marsh	Molly	Johnny Lee	Bit
Charles Laughton	Charles Smith	Barbara Lynn	Mary	Blue Washington	Bit
Elsa Lanchester	Elsa Smith	Paul Renay	Spud Johnson	Maggie Dorsey	Bit
Victor Francen	Arturo Bandini	Alex Pollard	Waiter	Gino Corrado	Spectator
		Don Beddoe	Whistler	Hall Johnson Choir	Themselves

Parts cut from the final release print: W. C. Fields, Margaret Dumont, Ellinor Van Der Veer, Phil Silvers, Gibson Gowland, Jerry Bergen, Dot Farley, Marcel Dalio, Chester Clute, Julia Griffith.

Working title: *Stars over Manhattan.*
Concert scene shot at the Los Angeles Philharmonic Auditorium.

Follow The Boys

—1944—

After *Tales of Manhattan* and for the rest of 1942 and most of 1943 there was no paying work for W. C. Fields. He spent most of his time in and out of hospitals suffering from "pneumonia" again Then in the early spring D. W. Griffith heard rumors that a major studio was interested in producing *Pickwick Papers* and asked Fields if he would be available to star. W. C. was excited and wrote back that after recovering from his most recent ailment he would definitely pursue the matter energetically from his end. Nothing came of it.

By September W. C. was in pretty good health and made a guest appearance on radio with Bergen and McCarthy. It went pretty well, but he was not asked back. Later that month Universal Pictures asked him to help out on a syrupy patriotic movie they planned to call *Three*

Cheers for the Boys, but which was released as *Follow the Boys*. Eddie Sutherland coaxed Universal into using the comedian again, but it was surprising that Fields took the role, particularly after his unceremonious heave-ho from the studio just a few years earlier. He was a prideful man who remembered wrongs for a long time. Perhaps his recently enforced absence from the picture business made him swallow his pride and accept any job from anyone. He most definitely was not wanting for cash, but he loved the limelight. On the other hand, W. C. was strongly patriotic and he could have easily buried the hatchet if it would help "the boys."

The movie followed a vaudeville format in which many of the big stars performed their specialties. Universal asked Fields to reproduce his old pool routine. He

Fields proving to his director Eddie Sutherland that he had not lost a thing in the juggling department.

"The woodpeckers' flophouse" ain't going to steal the show tonight from "old bugle beak." W. C. Fields, Edgar Bergen and that dummy Charlie McCarthy as they appeared on the air in September 1943.

scarred and puffy and W. C. looked "worn and torn," as James Agee, the *Time* magazine critic, put it, "but as noble as Stone Mountain."

After seeing the rushes Fields was pleased. He wrote to Eddie Sutherland about how happy he was that the scene worked so well and praised his old friend for his stupendous direction. Evidently on the set the actor and director talked about working some more together, because Fields continued in his letter: "I am still mulling over your suggestion of the West-Fields combination. Do you think something along classical lines like Cleopatra and Antony or some other great lovers in history might attract the customers to the box office if done by Maizie-Waizie and myself or do you think just a knock down drag out comedy would fit the bill?" He concluded this missive with a line that hints at desperation: "I am leaving it to you, for you have reinstated me in the flicker racket. An old-fashioned hug and deepest appreciation." Certainly W. C. could not have been very comfortable at this time in his life.

There was more talk of work. Fields wrote to Fred Allen about a rendition of the dentist sketch to be put into a movie. Fields knew the movie moguls looked upon him with a jaundiced eye so he added magnanimously, ". . . but if the Chinese people [Fields' euphemism for studio heads] decided against having me in the picture you are welcome to any parts, or the scene in toto, free, gratis, and with my compliments." Nothing came of it.

However, in December of 1943 W. C. was approached to do cameo appearances in two more movies.

The movie begins on the last night of vaudeville in New York City. This last bill stars the Three Wests. Tony West (played by George Raft) is breaking up the trio to try his luck in Hollywood. In Tinsel Town he joins the chorus of a motion picture but during rehearsals he candidly and boldly criticizes the lead dancer, Gloria Vance. Instead of feeling insulted Gloria admires Tony's chutzpa and decides to make him her dancing partner and husband. Then comes December 7, 1941. The Japanese have just bombed Pearl Harbor and Tony intends to end his stage career and enlist, but he is rejected. Undaunted, he spearheads the Hollywood Victory Committee, a group of stars that will travel to the front line and entertain the troops. His hard work disrupts his marriage to Gloria, eventually forcing her to leave her husband. Tony cannot stop doing his good work for the war and takes his traveling group of stars across the sea. The ship is torpedoed. Back home, Gloria now finally realizes Tony's devotion and she takes over where he left off.

Sound familiar? The plot bears a likeness to a silent picture Fields made in 1928, *Tillie's Punctured Romance*, a real bomb. In that film it was a traveling circus that headed for the trenches to entertain the troops. Not

W. C. with Paulette Goddard rehearsing the Chase and Sanborn Hour *radio program in September 1943. The kiss may be an approving gesture for Paulette's divorce from rival Charlie Chaplin.*

We will let the studio's old caption stand: "Dictating letters to his secretary off stage on the set of Three Cheers for the Boys *[retitled* Follow the Boys] *at Universal's studios, W. C. Fields found himself surrounded by an autograph-hunting group of servicemen visiting the studio on a U.S.O. tour. Bill, one of the all-stars appearing in Charles K. Feldman's production, which tells the story of the entertainment world's war effort, obliged with pleasure. Lost in the crowd above is Magda Michael, whom he calls 'Mickey Mouse.'"*

During a break in Follow the Boys *Lou Costello stopped by the set to meet W. C. Fields. Abbott and Costello's* In Society *(1944) uses virtually all of the last reel from W. C.'s* Never Give a Sucker an Even Break, *the chase scene.*

surprisingly, Eddie Sutherland directed that too. Maybe that was how he got the idea to use Fields again.

W. C.'s routine lasted about fifteen minutes. He walked into an army mess hall and was asked to perform on the pool table. Besides re-creating his great billiard act he added a bit of juggling as well. Although the juggling was sharp, the scene had very few of Fields' ad-libs. The juggling must have been difficult to do after so many years dormant, so perhaps he cut his throw-aways to concentrate on the legerdemain.

Released for general consumption on May 5, 1944, *Follow the Boys* got surprisingly good reviews for such a terrible film. Quite possibly the critics felt hesitant to lambast a patriotic movie while a war was being fought. Under different circumstances the film probably would never have been released, never mind given such high

marks by the reviewers. With hardly an exception, the critics talked mostly of Fields' short piece as being the stealer. They claimed he dominated the movie with just fifteen minutes on screen. His pool routine seemed more refined and slicker in this picture than in his earlier efforts, but his physical condition made one wince. The face was started his moving picture career with it, and fittingly he would perform it in one of his last films.

They filmed his scene in December. It took a mere day and a half to shoot, for which Fields received twenty-five grand. It must have seemed like old home week for the comedian—dragging out his now antique vaudeville pool table, working again under Eddie Sutherland's direction and sharing the scene with one of his favorite straight men and a card-carrying member of the Fields comedy company, Bill Wolfe.

FOLLOW THE BOYS

118 minutes
Sound, black and white
Released May 5, 1944, by Universal
Produced by Albert L. Rockett for Charles K. Feldman Group Productions
Directed by Eddie Sutherland
First assistant director: Howard Christie
Original screenplay by Lou Breslow and Gertrude Purcell
Musical direction by Leigh Harline
Musical production numbers devised and staged by George Hall and Joe Schoenfeld
Photographed by Dave Abel
Art direction by John B. Goodman and Harold H. MacArthur
Edited by Fred R. Feitshans Jr.
Sound recording by Bernard B. Brown
Set decoration by Russell A. Gausman and Ira S. Webb
Costumes by Vera West and Howard Greer
Special effects by John P. Fulton
Songs by Sammy Cahn and Jule Styne; Kermit Goell and Walter Donaldson; Billy Austin and Louis Jordan; Dorothy Fields and Jimmy McHugh; Sheldon Brooks, Inez James and Buddy Pepper; Phil Moore, Leo Robin, W. Frank Harling and Richard Whiting; Roy Turk and Frank Ahlert; and Dick Charles and Larry Markes
Songs: "The Bigger the Army and Navy," "I'll Get By," "Mad About Him Blues," "I'll Walk Alone," "I'll See You in My Dreams," "Beyond the Blue Horizon," "Good Night," "Furlough Fling," "Shoo Shoo Baby," "Swing Low, Sweet Chariot," "Merriment," "Besame Mucho," "Sweet Georgia Brown," "Is You Is, Or Is You Ain't My Baby?" "Tonight," "I Feel a Song Coming On," "The House I Live In," "A Better Day Is Comin'," "Andrews Sisters Medley," "Kittens with Their Mittens Laced," "Some of These Days"

CAST:

George Raft	Tony West, hoofer
Vera Zorina	Gloria Vance (Bertha Lindquist), dancer
Charles Grapewin	Nick West
Grace MacDonald	Kitty West
Charles Butterworth	Louise Fairweather
George Macready	Walter Bruce
Elizabeth Patterson	Annie
Theodore Von Eltz	William Barrett
Regis Toomey	Dr. Jim Henderson
Ramsey Ames	Laura
Spooks	Junior
Lane Chandler	Ship's officer
Cyril Ring	Laughton, *Life* photographer
Emmett Vogan	Harkness, *Life* reporter
Frank Jenks	Chick Doyle
John Cason	Soldier at radio
Clyde Cook	Stooge
Tom Hanlon	Announcer
Charles King	Soldier
Bill Wolfe	Zoot suit man (Fields' routine)
Mack Gray	Lieutenant Reynolds
Molly Lamont	Miss Hartford, secretary
John Meredith	Blind soldier (MacDonald number)
John Estes	Patient
Ralph Gardner	Patient in leg cast (MacDonald number)
Daisy	Fifi
Doris Lloyd	Nurse
Charles D. Brown	Colonel Starrett
Nelson Leigh	Bull Fiddler
Addison Richards	MacDermott, *Life* editor
Frank La Rue	Mailman
Tony Marsh	First officer
Stanley Andrews	Australian officer
Leslie Denison	Reporter
Leyland Hodgson	Australian reporter
Bill Healy	Ship's officer
Ralph Dunn	Loomis
Billy Benedict	Joe, soldier
Grandon Rhodes	George Grayson, guild member
Howard Hickman	Dr. Wood
Bobby Barker	Soldier, Fields' stooge in audience
Dick Nelson	Sergeant
Don McGill	Man in office
Franklin Parker	Man in office
Don Kramer	Soldier
Edwin Stanley	Taylor, film director
Roy Darmour	Eddie, assistant director
Carl Vernell	Terry Dennis, dance director
Tony Hughes	Bit man
Wallis Clark	HVC committee man
Richard Crane	Marine officer
Frank Wilcox	Cpt. Williams, Army doctor
Jimmy Carpenter	Soldier
Bernard B. Thomas	Soldier
Eddie Kover	Dancer
Clair Freeman	Dancer
Bill Meader	Dancer
Ed Browne	Dancer
John Duane	Dancer
Nicholai	Dancer
Luis Torres	Dancer
Allan Cooke	Dancer
George Riley	Jimmy
Steve Brodie	Australian pilot
Carey Harrison	Colonel
Jack Wegman	Mayor
Billy Wayne	Columnist
Jack Whitney	Soldier
Walter Tetley	Soldier
Anthony Warde	Captain
William Forrest	Colonel
Odessa Lauren	Telephone operator
Dennis Moore	HVC officer
Nancy Brinkman	Telephone operator
Bill Dyer	Messenger boy
Thurston Hall	Bit
Janet Shaw	Telephone operator
Jan Wiley	Telephone operator
Martin Ashe	Man in office
Duke York	Military policeman
Joel Allen	Soldier
Carlyle Blackwell	Soldier
Lennie Smith	Jitterbug
Michael Kirk	Soldier
Mel Schubert	Soldier
Stephen Wayne	Soldier
Bob Ashley	Jitterbug
Jackie Lou Harding	Girl in montage
Genevieve Bell	Mother in montage
Lee Bennett	Acrobat
George Eldridge	Submarine officer
(Baby) Marie Osborne	Nurse
Nicodemus Stewart	Lt. Reynolds, U.S.A.F.
George Shorty Chirello	Welles' assistant
Janice Gay	Magic maid
Jane Smith	Magic maid
Marjorie Fectan	Magic maid
Doris Brenn	Magic maid
Rosemary Battle	Magic maid
Lolita Leighter	Magic maid
Mary Rowland	Magic maid
Eleanor Counts	Magic maid
Linda Brent	Magic maid

GUEST STARS:
Jeanette MacDonald, Orson Welles' Mercury Wonder Show, Marlene Dietrich, Dinah Shore, Donald O'Connor, Peggy Ryan, W. C. Fields, the Andrews Sisters, Arthur Rubinstein, Carmen Amaya and Her Company, Sophie Tucker, Delta Rhythm Boys, Leonard Gautier's "Bricklayers," Augustin Castellon Sabrias, Ted Lewis and His Band, Freddie Slack and His Orchestra, Charlie Spivak and His Orchestra, Louis Jordan and His Orchestra, Louise Beavers, Clarence Muse, Maxie Rosenbloom, Maria Montez, Susanna Foster, Louise Allbritton, Robert Paige, Alan Curtis, Lon Chaney Jr., Gloria Jean, Andy Devine, Turhan Bey, Evelyn Ankers, Noah Beery Jr., Gale Sondergaard, Peter Coe, Nigel Bruce, Thomas Gomez, Lois Collier, Samuel S. Hinds, Randolph Scott, Martha O'Driscoll, Elyse Knox, Philo McCullough.

Filmed at Universal in Universal City.
  Working title: *Three Cheers for the Boys*.
  "I'll Walk Alone" by Sammy Cahn and Jule Styne was nominated for an Academy Award.

Song Of The Open Road

—1944—

It seemed cameos were the order for Fields these days. He had a smart turn in *Follow the Boys,* critically praised anyway, so there was still a role in Hollywood for the aging and sick comedian. These were not good movies; time has proven that. Fields hated them, but there was nothing else for him, and besides they paid well.

Song of the Open Road received mammoth publicity because United Artists wanted to push their new singing star, Jane Powell. The movie was her showcase.

Jane Powell plays herself. In the film she is a successful child movie star but not happy in the Hollywood scene. After making a movie about the Civilian Conserva-

tion Corps she decides that working for the CCC will give her a purpose in life. She happily rejects her next big role, packs her bags, dyes her hair and dons a new hairdo to disguise her fame, and bicycles off to help pick a tomato crop that is near destruction because of a lack of back benders. With naive idealism as her guide, she joins the pickers' camp and succeeds in alienating the gang. She thinks of herself as a fine mechanic, and to prove it she nearly ruins a half dozen bikes. Then she considers herself an adviser to the lovelorn, but just about destroys two perfectly good romances. When it comes time to pick tomatoes the work crew has totally excluded her from the force. Dejected, she returns to Hollywood. Out in the fields, however, they still do not have enough pickers; and worse, a succession of other disasters follow, portending the total destruction of the crop. But who comes back from filmland to save the day? None other than the previously ostracized Jane Powell, who brings back a truckload of Hollywood stars to help in the picking. The luminaries perform out on the open road, bringing in large audiences who in turn assist in bringing in the tomatoes.

Fields' sequence with McCarthy and Bergen, plus the added bonus of Charlie McCarthy Jr., was funny but not up to the sparkle of their radio feuds or their work in *You Can't Cheat an Honest Man.*

Even after United Artists' pre-release hoopla the film got below-average reviews and low attendance. Jane Powell received good notices only as a singer and a star for the future, not as someone to see in this film. Fields perked up the reviewers' interest, and they mostly credited Bergen, McCarthy and Fields for bringing the show up from a completely unacceptable picture to an almost mediocre piece. Fortunately, the movie rarely plays now, so history most likely will not judge Fields unkindly for his work in it.

The last cameo was on its way, and although Fields' work in these final three pictures was considerably less than gratyfing at least it was work, and he loved that.

SONG OF THE OPEN ROAD
93 minutes
Sound, black and white
Released June 21, 1944, by United Artists
Produced by Charles R. Rogers
Assistant to the producer: William J. Fender
Directed by S. Sylvan Simon
Assistant directors: Maurie Suess and Phil Carlstein
Screenplay by Albert Mannheimer
Based on an unpublished story by Irving Phillips and Edward Verdier
Musical direction by Charles Previn
Music by Walter Kent and lyrics by Kim Gannon
Musical presentations by George Dobbs
Photographed by John W. Boyle
Art direction by Bernard Herzbrun
Edited by Truman K. Wood
Production manager: Val Paul

CAST:
Charlie McCarthy   Himself
Edgar Bergen   Himself
Jane Powell   Herself, child star
W. C. Fields   Himself
Bonita Granville   Bonnie
Peggy O'Neill   Peggy
Jackie Moran   Jack
Bill Christy   Bill
Reginald Denny   Director Curtis
Regis Toomey   Connors
Rose Hobart   Mrs. Powell
Sig Arno   Spolo
Irene Tedro   Miss Casper
Pat Starling   Herself
Sammy Kaye and His Orchestra   Themselves
Condon Brothers   Themselves
Hollywood Canteen Kids   Themselves
Lipham Four   Themselves
Chuck Faulkner Band   Themselves
Catron and Pop   Themselves
Charlotte Treadway   Bit

Unretouched photo from **Song of the Open Road.**

Sensations Of 1945
— 1944 —

Sensations of 1945 was W. C. Fields' last film—an un-flattering ending. Andrew Stone wanted W. C. to write his own bit, then star in it. The film would follow the vaudeville-type format of *Follow the Boys* and *Song of the Open Road*. So Fields once again went back to his stage days and produced a piece he first performed for Earl Carroll in 1928, "The Caledonian Express." In the *Vanities* version W. C. played five characters. It received raves, but in the screen version he played just one character and much of the fast-paced comedy in the original was lost.

For the third straight time there is not much to say about the plot except it was a string of sketches tied by a flimsy story.

A father and son own a publicity agency specializing in the sensational, but there is trouble at the helm. The father is a freewheeling sort with creative, although crazy, ideas, while the son is sane, conservative, businesslike. In order to shake up the company the father decides the front office needs new blood, so he puts one of his clients in charge, a dancer (played by Eleanor Powell). Her wacky schemes shock the stolid son. There is animosity and distrust. At one point W. C. Fields is brought in to perform one of his old routines, which he does. In the scene he and Louise Currie walk up to a British railway carriage which has a sign in the window reading RESERVED FOR LORD ROBERT ROBERTS. Fields dismisses the sign and boldly sits down with his beautiful companion. Currie worries they might be thrown out of the car, but W. C. assures her no one would dare. They do dare, but Fields refuses to budge. At one point a stumbling drunk vies for the compartment, but Fields hits and batters him around, finally knocking him down.

The movie ends when Eleanor Powell sprains her ankle and the son comes to the rescue. They not only become friends but the boy finally realizes her flashy ways are good for business.

Louise Currie has said that W. C.'s eyesight was so bad he could not read the cue cards, so the director had to use a huge blackboard on which to write the lines. She added that her scene with him had to be taken over and over, his ad-libs were poor and W. C. could not read his lines and play the scene simultaneously. Currie said that eventually Fields would get his part right, but by then she had forgotten her lines.

W. C. was funny but not the master of a movie as he was before. Perhaps he just gave up trying to steal a film. Besides, he hated these types of motion pictures, but it was all he could get at the twilight of his career. He complained about Hollywood in a letter to his sister Adel on July 10, 1944, just two weeks after the release of *Sensations of 1945:* "Whilst the critics have panned the hell out of the last two pictures I have been in, they have been pretty kind to me. The producers have cut me down in these pictures to practically nil. They're new types of pictures, taking some little starlet and surrounding her with names and in their effort to make the little girl a star they ruin the picture, as the little girls haven't the experience to carry the load. But when they are willing to pay me twenty-five grand for a day and a half or at the most five days I go after it like a trout for a worm, and then in turn our dear Uncle in Washington takes about ninety percent of it. It is a peculiar situation all around. These movies are just high class vaudeville put on the screen and since vaudeville has died in the flesh how in hell are they going to draw people in to see a picture of the real McCoy?

Sensations of 1945 was W. C.'s last motion picture. A year later he was dead. Friends bought a memorial ad in the *Hollywood Reporter* which hailed W. C. as "the most authentic humorist since Mark Twain."

Fields' re-creation of his Earl Carroll Vanities *sketch "The Caledonian Express" for his last film,* Sensations of 1945. *Pictured here with Bill Wolfe and Louise Currie.*

W. C. Fields created a singular characterization so indelibly etched that even today the weakest comic impersonation of him can still bring a smile to the sourest of faces. Luckily we need not settle for that. Many of the silent films are lost (a tragedy), and wonderful pictures such as *It's the Old Army Game* are scarcely shown outside of museums and archives, but the talkies, W. C.'s finest work, are still accessible. Television, video tapes, film societies—it is there we can still enjoy W. C. Fields undated, as fresh as ever, proving his line in *The Bank Dick* was true, "We're making motion picture history here."

SENSATIONS OF 1945

87 minutes
Sound, black and white
Released June 30, 1944, by United Artists
Produced and directed by Andrew L. Stone
Assistant to Mr. Stone: Carley Harriman
Assistant producer: James Nasser
First assistant director: Henry Kesler
Screenplay by Dorothy Bennett
Based on an original story by Frederick Jackson and Andrew Stone

Musical direction by Mahlon Merrick
Photographed by Peverell Marley and John Mescall
Art direction by Charles Odds
Edited by James E. Smith
Dance director: David Lichine
Music by Al Sherman and lyrics by Harry Tobias
Interior decorations by Maurice Yates
Acrobatics director: Charles O'Curran

CAST:

Eleanor Powell	Ginny Walker	Woody Herman and His Band	Themselves	Constance Purdy	Bit woman
Dennis O'Keefe	Junior Crane	David Lichine	Himself	Betty Wells	Bit woman
C. Aubrey Smith	Dan Lindsey	Richard Hageman	Pendergast	Ruth Lee	Bit woman
Eugene Pallette	Gus Crane	Marie Blake	Miss Grear	George Humbert	Bit man
Mimi Forsythe	Julia Westcott	Stanley Andrews	Mr. Collins	Earl Hodgins	Bit man
Lyle Talbot	Randall	"Uncle Willie"	Himself	Bert Roach	Bit man
Hubert Castle	The Great Gustafson	Gene Rodgers	Himself	Grandon Rhodes	Bit man
W. C. Fields	Himself	Mel Hall	Himself	Joe Devlin	Bit man
Sophie Tucker	Herself	Johnson Brothers	Themselves	Anthony Warde	Bit man
Dorothy Donegan	Herself	Flying Copelands	Themselves	Willie Pratt	Bit man
The Christianis	Themselves	Les Paul Trio	Themselves	Bill Wolfe	Bit man
Pallenberg Bears	Themselves	Wendell Niles	Announcer		
Cab Calloway and His Band	Themselves	Louise Currie	Bit woman	Working title: *Sensations of 1944.*	

EPILOGUE

I still stay up late at night to watch my grandfather's movies, and I still laugh uproariously. But now I see so much more beyond just the laughs. I see an artist at work, and in nearly every one of his films I see the self-portrait of that artist.

There was little difference between Sousè, Bissonette, Bisbee, McGargle, McGonigle, Whipsnade and the rest of them, and W. C. Fields. What made this comic mirror of himself more than a banal self-indulgence, however, was the honesty and clarity of his vision. He dug deeply into himself and brought to light something we all recognized, and that made it art. In using his life, his likes, his hates, and his dreams as the blood and guts of his art, he drew a portrait we all understood—a portrait of twentieth-century man, of alienation and redemption. I doubt if Fields actually intended to depict the historical angst of modern man, but he did.

In these modern times man feels bewildered, pressured to conform and a lack of control over his own destiny. The individual has gotten lost in the vastness of society.

Fields was lost too, alienated from his family and society; and when he displayed this personal alienation on screen he addressed most of us. W. C. said it did not make a damn bit of difference whether or not we controlled our destinies. The only thing important to him artistically was the dignity and integrity of the individual.

That, I believe, is the core of Fields' popularity. Certainly we laugh at his marvelous humor, his lines and his antics, but we also applaud and smile and feel proud that his characters survive with dignity no matter the insults surrounding them. We rally behind these characterizations today, and most likely so will the generations to come, because they represent the glory of the individual.

Our only redemption, says Fields, is knowing oneself, and being that. So, whether Sousè, Bissonette or Bisbee ends up with serendipitous wealth, or it is McGargle, McGonigle or Whipsnade flim-flamming a meager existence, the character never changes. In no purely Fields film do we feel sorry for his character, never mind the chaos swirling around him, because human dignity and self survive, the individual remains unstained. That is the greatest glory. That is what makes us smile, makes us feel good. So even when he looked his worst, "worn and torn," he nonetheless was "as noble as Stone Mountain."

At the end of his career, when Hollywood would not trust him with any worthwhile film work, Fields probably was not too hurt. He probably knew he would have the last word. He probably knew that no matter what the studio tried to do to take away his dignity—whether it was assigning him insulting roles in terrible films or, many years after his death, trying to sully his shade with an insulting movie about his life—his art would survive. W. C. Fields won.

And so his career came to a close among the echoes of a nascent time when William Claude Dukenfield tossed balls on a beer-hall stage in Atlantic City. At the end he played bit parts in three insignificant motion pictures, which were really nothing more than ". . . vaudeville put on the screen." It was a cruel epitaph for such a great artist. Frustrated and very sick, W. C. Fields left the movie business for good.

Not long after that, W. C. lay in a hospital bed, his condition serious. It was the Christmas season 1946; and Gene Fowler, the writer; John Decker, the painter; and Dave Chasen, the restaurateur, paid a visit to their ailing friend. The trio walked quietly down the hall, each hiding a bottle of Christmas cheer under his coat. When they entered Fields' room they found him reading . . . the Bible! One of them asked, "Uncle Claude, why are *you* reading the Bible?"

It is written that he looked up from the book and with all the self-confidence of a tenured lawyer rasped, "Just looking for loopholes."

He probably was.

A few weeks later he fell into a coma. Then on Christmas day he awoke. He looked at the only two people holding vigil, his secretary, Magda Michael, and a nurse. He brought his forefinger to his lips to signify quiet, winked, then closed his eyes; and "the man in the bright nightgown" took him away.

I always wondered what that wink meant. Perhaps he knew he had cheated the grandest cheater of them all, mortality. Through his art W. C. Fields lives today. He was an honest man, and "you can't cheat an honest man."

ACKNOWLEDGMENTS

First of all, and with deep love and respect, I must thank my grandfather, W. C. Fields, and my father.

I also want to thank my brothers, Bill (and his wife, Linda), Everett, and Allen, and a special hug for my sister, Harriet, for their love and encouragement.

Also I wish to give a humble bow and honorable mention to my mentor and friend Tam Mossman.

Furthermore, I must give my heartfelt thanks to those who put me up (and put up with me) during my travels while researching and writing this book: my mother-in-law, Mrs. Thomas Aragona, and her sons and daughter, John, Richard, Robert and Regina; Alexander and Mary Ellen Gordon, and Richard Feiner (who also had the original idea for this project and convinced me to write it).

This work took five years to bring to print and the vast majority of that time was spent in research. A great deal of data was stored in our family archives, but by no means all of it. I had to fill in the gaps. I needed more facts on Fields' life; I had to find missing stills; I needed to view films; and it was necessary to ferret out supplementary information on the movie industry in general. I found no lack of willing and caring help from institutions and individuals dedicated to the history of motion pictures. We all owe them our thanks because they are the true guardians of this unique art form. In alphabetical order: The American Film Institute; The British Film Institute; The British Museum; John Cocchi; Bob Deflores; William K. Everson; Herb Graff; Leslie Halliwell; Claude Heisch (WCCO-TV); Harry Jones (WCCO-TV); Milt Kennin; Paul Killiam Shows; Vick Knight; Pat Montgomery (Archive Film Productions, Inc.); David Parker (Library of Congress); Helen Reitheimer; Samuel M. Sherman; Anthony Slide (Academy of Motion Picture Arts and Sciences); Paul Spehr (Library of Congress); The Society for the Preservation of Variety Arts; Carl Flemming and Milt Larson; Universal Studios; the University of California at Los Angeles; The Victoria and Albert Museum; and Alain Weill.

A special hearty handclasp and thanks goes to Richard W. Bann, my friend, research associate and filmographer, for his care and dedication to this book. His diligent and meticulous work has been an inspiration to me. Moreover, Richard conducted key interviews for this book and provided nearly half the photographs. (Incidentally, the balance of the photos came from the collection W. C. Fields maintained himself, presently owned by W. C. Fields Productions, Inc.)

With deep gratitude I must acknowledge those wonderful people who shared in my grandfather's life, who knew him, worked with him and understood him. Thank you for your insight into W. C. Fields, and for giving so unselfishly of your time: Eddie "Rochester" Anderson; Richard Arlen; Edgar Bergen; Harold Bissonette; Grace Bradley Boyd; Billy Bletcher; Mary Brian; Louise Brooks; George Burns; George Chandler; Louise Currie; Richard Currier; Jan Duggan; Adel Dukenfield; LeRoy Dukenfield; Madge Evans; Dick Foran; Will Fowler; Dorothy Granger; Reed Hadley; Margaret Hamilton; Ruth Hall; Bob Hope; Gloria Jean (and her mother, Mrs. Schoonover); Una Merkel; Magda Michael; Constance Moore; Jack Mulhall; Jack Oakie; Nell O'Day; David Sharpe; Grady Sutton; Regis Toomey; Harry Watson; and Jane Withers.

I would also like to thank those who were directly involved in the presentation of this book and who went beyond their prescribed duties to bring it to fruition: Andrew Charron (editorial assistant); Carol E. W. Edwards (managing editor); Toni Lopopolo (editor); and Alex Soma (who is responsible for the beautiful design of this book).

Finally, a warm thanks to the memory of Al Kilgore.

Ronald J. Fields
New York

INDEX

Aasen, John, 63
Abbott, Bud, 237
Alden, Mary, 50, 51
Alderson, Erville, 28
Alice in Wonderland, 125–126
Allen, Gracie, 110, 111, 115, 127, 129, 130
Allen, Judith, 141, 143, 145
Alter, Lou, 77
Ameche, Don, 188
America, 21
American Venus, The, 29
Ames, Adrienne, 132, 133, 137
Anderson, Eddie "Rochester," 201, 203, 241
Apfel, Oscar, 178
Armbruster, Robert, 188
Astoria Studios, 58, 59

Baby LeRoy, 120, 123, 143, 146, 147, 152, 155, 160–161, 175
Ballyhoo, 77–78, 99, 106
Balmer, Edwin, 31
Bank Dick, The, 51, 62, 72, 187, 217–229, 231
Barber Shop, The, 101–106, 122
Barrie, Mona, 235
Barrymore, John, 167, 238, 239
Barrymore, Lionel, 165, 167
Bartholomew, Freddie, 162, 163, 164, 165
Beery, Wallace, 62, 64
Bennett, Joan, 170, 171
Bennett, Mickey, 38, 39
Bennett, Richard, 88
Benny, Jack, 190
Bergen, Edgar, 188, 189, 197, 199, 202, 203, 243, 244, 249
Berkeley, Busby, 72
Berle, Milton, 65
Berry, W. H., 163
Big Broadcast of 1938, The, 15, 190–195
Big Tree, Chief, 64
Birth of a Nation, The, 15
Blanche, William "Shorty," 14, 29–30, 32–33, 46, 59, 73–74, 77, 130–131
Blane, Sally, 69
Bletcher, Billy, 94
Blue, Ben, 72, 191, 193
Blumberg, Nate, 219–220
Bogart, Humphrey, 210
Boland, Mary, 127, 129, 130
Boyer, Charles, 240
Bradbury, Ray, 137

Bradley, Grace, 193
Breen, Joseph, 215, 219, 231
Breese, Edmund, 111
Brennan, Walter, 174, 175
Brian, Mary, 56–58, 60, 64, 173, 177–179
Brice, Monte, 65, 66, 73
Briggs, Harlan, 210
Brill, Leighton, 77
Broadway After Dark, 19
Broadway Headliners, 72
Brock, Louis, 72, 73
Brooks, Louise, 29, 36, 37, 39–40, 66, 71
Brown, Kenneth, 232
Bruckman, Clyde, 174
Bupp, Tommy, 158
Burke, James, 129
Burns, George, 110, 111, 115, 127, 128, 130
Burns Brothers, 10

Cadell, Jean, 166
Calleia, Joseph, 210
Carroll, Earl, 69, 71–72, 74
Carter, Louise, 134, 137
Cavanna, Elise, 90, 92, 94, 99
Chandler, George, 95, 97–98
Chaplin, Charlie, 13, 41, 47, 65, 69, 160
Chase and Sanborn Hour, The, 188–189, 190
Chasen, Dave, 253
Christie, Al, 65, 68
Christie, Charlie, 65, 68
Citizen Kane, 47
Clair, John T., 103
Clansman, The, 15
Clark, Bobby, 64
Cline, Eddie, 84, 194, 203, 206, 207–208, 211, 214, 219, 227, 232, 236, 237
Cobb, Irwin S., 171
Comic Supplement, The, 23, 25, 26, 30, 39, 48, 77, 152, 160
Conklin, Chester, 60, 62, 64, 65–67, 68–70, 81, 89
Conway, Jack, 63
Cooper, Gary, 87
Corbett, Gentleman Jim, 28, 29
Costello, Lou, 237, 246
Cowan, Lester, 204, 206, 207–210
Crosby, Bing, 168, 170, 171, 182
Cukor, George, 163–165, 166
Cunningham, Cecil, 87
Cunningham, Jack, 148, 168
Currie, Louise, 250–251

David Copperfield, 23, 161, 162–167
Davidson, William B., 108
Davies, Marion, 20–22
Decker, John, 253
Del Rio, Evelyn, 223, 228
Dempster, Carol, 27–30, 31–32
Denning, Richard, 193
Dentist, The, 15, 90–94, 122
Destry Rides Again, 206
Dieterle, William, 81
Dietrich, Marlene, 206
Donnelly, Dorothy, 18
Dooley, Ray, 25, 72
Doucet, Catherine, 186
Dressler, Marie, 124
Duck Soup, 84
Duggan, Jan, 144, 210
Dukenfield, Adel, 10, 11, 223
Dukenfield, Elsie Mae, 10, 223
Dukenfield, James, 10
Dukenfield, Kate, 10, 23, 76, 105–106
Dukenfield, LeRoy, 10
Dukenfield, Walter, 10, 11, 185
Dumont, Margaret, 234
Durbin, Deanna, 236, 239
Duvivier, Julien, 241–242

Eddy, Nelson, 188
Egan, Jack, 50
Errol, Leon, 81, 89, 100, 219, 234
Erwin, Stu, 110, 111, 114
Evans, Frank, 56
Evans, Madge, 165, 167

Famous Players-Lasky Corporation, 29, 34
Farley, Zedna, 90, 92, 93, 94
Fatal Glass of Beer, The, 62, 72, 76, 95–98, 207
Fazenda, Louise, 65–67
Fercke, 124
Fields, Lew, 64
Fields, Shep, 192
Fields, Mrs. W. C. (Hattie Hughes), 7, 8, 10–11, 25
Fields, W. C., Jr., 7, 8, 10–11, 25
Fine, Bud, 160
Fitzgerald, Cissy, 59
Flagstad, Kirsten, 192
Fleming, Susan, 84
Follow the Boys, 243–247
Fonda, Henry, 240

Fools for Luck, 68–70
Ford, Harrison, 20, 32
Ford, Paul Leicester, 20
Fowler, Gene, 207, 253
Fox, Matty, 217–219
Foy, Mary, 38
Frisco, Joe, 72

Gallagher, Skeets, 51
Gaumont Company, 12, 14, 15
Gaxton, William, 40
George White Scandals, 18, 19
Geraghty, Tom, 40
Gish, Lillian, 46
Goddard, Paulette, 245
Golf Specialist, The, 15, 73–76
Goodman, Phillip, 18–19, 23, 25, 30, 34
Grady, Billy, 82
Grange, Red "The Galloping Ghost," 77
Granger, Dorothy, 93
Grant, Cary, 210
Griffith, D. W., 15, 21, 25, 27, 29, 31–33, 34, 243
Gross, Jack, 219, 236

Haddock, William "Silent Bill," 15
Hadley, Reed, 223, 227
Hamilton, Margaret, 208
Hammerstein, Arthur, 77, 78
Hammerstein, Oscar, Jr., 77
Hammerstein, Reginald, 77, 78
Hardy, Sam, 23, 173–174, 179
Hare, Lumsden, 110, 111
Harris, Marcia, 45
Hatton, Raymond, 62, 64
Hayworth, Rita, 240
Hearst, William Randolph, 19, 20, 21
Henderson, Del, 137, 160
Herbert, Hugh, 82
Her Majesty Love, 79–81, 82
Hicks, Russell, 224
Hill, Al, 219, 227
Hill, Doris, 66
Hip Action, 107–108
His Lordship's Dilemma, 14–17, 73
Hollywood on Parade (B-10), 139–140
Hope, Bob, 191, 192–193
Hornblow, Arthur, Jr., 196
Howard, Kathleen, 134, 137, 158, 176
Howard, Shemp, 221, 227
Howe, Dorothy, 193
Hudson, Rochelle, 181, 182, 184
Hughes, Hattie, *see* Fields, Mrs. W. C.
Hurst, Paul, 169

If I Had a Million, 86–89, 119
International House, 109–115, 122
Irving, George, 137
Irwin Burlesquers, 10
It's a Gift, 23, 26, 35, 49, 51, 148, 152–161
It's the Old Army Game, 23, 26, 34–41, 45, 47, 66, 152, 160

Jamison, Bud, 91, 94
Janice Meredith, 20–22, 33
Jean, Gloria, 231, 233–235, 236
Jones, Bobby, 107–108
Jones, Clifford, 121, 122
Jones, Grover, 207–208
Jones, Paul, 40, 66, 193
Joyce, Peggy Hopkins, 109–114

Keaton, Buster, 69, 242
Keith, B. F., 10
Keith Orpheum Circuit, 10
Kelly, Lew, 174
Kennedy, Madge, 18, 23, 24
Kennedy, Tom, 66
Kenton, Erle C., 133, 137, 138
Kenton, James B. "Pop," 135, 138
Kern, Jerome, 25, 30, 76
Kohler, Fred, 171

La Cava, Gregory, 45, 46, 53, 57, 58, 236, 239
La Cava, Mrs. Gregory, 236
Laemmle, Carl, Jr., 199
Lamour, Dorothy, 188, 190
Lasky, Jesse, 31, 35
Laughton, Charles, 87, 162–163
Lawton, Frank, 165, 166
Laziest Golfer, The, 239
Le Baron, William, 21, 32–33, 36, 40, 47, 72, 79, 85, 109, 146–147, 150, 174, 188, 192, 194
Leisen, Mitchell, 189, 193, 194
Lenhart, Billy, 232
Le Roy, Mervyn, 19, 197
Lewyn, Lewis, 116
Lillie, Beatrice, 72
Littlefield, Lucien, 178
Lloyd, Harold, 47, 197
Lord, Pauline, 148, 151
Lugosi, Bela, 110
Lulu in Hollywood (Brooks), 29, 39, 66
Lunt, Alfred, 28
Lyon, Ben, 79–81

McCarey, Leo, 129, 131
McCarthy, Charlie, 15
McCullough, Paul, 64
McEvoy, J. P., 23, 25, 48, 130, 132, 152
Mack, Charles, 62, 64, 72
McKenzie, Robert, 135
MacLane, Barton, 121
McLeod, Norman, 126, 148, 150, 157, 160
Madison, Julian, 161
Mad Wolf, Chief, 64
Mankiewicz, Hermann, 46–47, 63–64, 82–84, 88–89
Mankiewicz, Joseph, 82–84, 88–89
Man on the Flying Trapeze, The, 23, 57, 58, 173–180
Maritza, Sari, 110
Marshall, George, 107–108, 202–203, 205
Marshall, Herbert, 182
Martin, Francis, 121, 122–123, 168
Marx, Chico, 139
Marx Brothers, 59
Mayer, Louis B., 162, 218
Maynard, Ken, 22
Meek, Donald, 48, 50
Menjou, Adolphe, 19
Merkel, Una, 220, 228
Michael, Magda, 245, 253
Miller, Marilyn, 79, 81
Miller, Susan, 234
Million Dollar Legs, 63, 82–85
Mississippi, 77, 168–172, 207
Mitchell, Thomas, 240
Monti, Carlotta, 173, 177, 188
Moran, George, 62, 64, 72, 96, 210–211, 212, 219
Morgan, Frank, 47
Morrison, Joe, 144–145, 146

Motion Picture News, 46–47
"Mr. Bisbee's Princess" (Street), 42
Mrs. Wiggs of the Cabbage Patch, 148–151
Mundin, Herbert, 164
My Little Chickadee, 62, 72, 206–216

Never Give a Sucker an Even Break, 72, 230–238
North, Joe, 228

Oakie, Jack, 83, 85
Oland, Warner, 108
Old Fashioned Way, The, 23, 72, 141–147, 198
Oliver, David, 200
Oliver, Edna May, 164
O'Sullivan, Maureen, 165
"Other Face of W. C. Fields, The" (Brooks), 39
Overman, Lynne, 193

Pallette, Eugene, 70
Pangborn, Franklin, 110, 111, 225, 226, 235
Percival, Walter C., 120
Peter Pan, 58
Pharmacist, The, 99–100, 118, 207, 214
Pitts, Zasu, 148, 149, 151
Platt, William, 63
Poole, Bessie, 40, 59, 66–67
Pool Sharks, 11, 12–13, 15, 130
Poppy (film), 23, 30, 181–186
Poppy (play), 18–19, 20, 21, 23, 24, 25, 27, 30, 35, 39, 48; *see also Sally of the Sawdust*
Post, Wiley, 197
Potters, The (film), 48–52, 68
Potters, The (play), 48
Powell, Eleanor, 250
Powell, Jane, 248–249
Punsley, Bernard, 192
Purcell, Dick, 221
Pyle, C. C., 77

Raft, George, 87
Ralph, Jessie, 223, 228
Ralph, Julia, 43
Rapf, Harry, 19
Raskin, Barnett, 57
Rathbone, Basil, 164
Raye, Martha, 193
Raymond, Gene, 87, 88
Reisner, Charles, 68–69
Ripley, Arthur, 103, 105, 106
Roach, Hal, 47, 65
Robeson, Paul, 241
Robinson, Edward G., 240
Robson, May, 88
Rogers, Ginger, 240
Rogers, Will, 18, 23, 25, 63, 179, 197
Rooney, Mickey, 218
Roseman, Edward, 55
Ross, Bud, 12, 13, 14–17
Ross, Lannie, 171
Ross, Shirley, 192
Rouverol, Jean, 158, 161
Ruben, J. Walter, 69
Ruggles, Charlie, 86, 127, 130
Running Wild, 53–58, 59, 173–174
Rush, Dick, 129
Ruskin, Harry, 77

St. Clair, Mal, 242
Sally of the Sawdust, 23, 27–30, 31, 34, 59, 76, 130, 181, 202
Sellon, Charles, 154, 161
Selznick, David O., 162–164
Sennett, Mack, 15, 65, 72, 76, 84, 85, 90–91, 94, 95, 97–98, 99–100, 106
Sensations of 1945, 250–251
Shotwell, Marie, 54, 56
Show Boat, 25, 30, 76–77
Side Show, The, 63, 64
Silvers, Phil, 240
Sinclair, Jerry, 43
Sinclair, Johnny, 63, 181
Six of a Kind, 127–131
Skipworth, Alison, 87, 88, 89, 119–124, 127, 129, 130
Smith, Art, 205
Smith, Paul Gerard, 72
Smith, Queenie, 168, 170
Song for the Open Road, 248–249
So's Your Old Man, 42–47, 50, 51, 73, 132
Steamboat Bill Jr., 69
Stein, Jules, 203
Stewart, Jimmy, 206
Stone, Andrew, 250
Stone, Lewis, 165
Stotesbury, Edward, 39–40
Stotesbury, Mrs. Edward, 39–40
Street, Julian, 42
Sutherland, Eddie, 39–41, 65–67, 109, 110, 115, 168, 169, 171, 183, 184, 243–246

Sutton Grady, 100, 178, 200, 210, 218–219, 224, 228
Swain, Mack, 65
Swanson, Gloria, 182

Tales of Manhattan, 240–242
Taurog, Norman, 148, 151
That Royle Girl, 31–33, 34
Thomas, Ed, 228
Tillie and Gus, 119–124, 248
Tillie's Punctured Romance (1928), 23, 65–67, 68, 73
Two Flaming Youths, 23, 59–64, 141–142, 198

Urban, Joseph, 20
Urecal, Minerva, 235
Usher, Guy, 160

Vanities, 69, 71–72, 73, 74, 76, 91, 93, 95, 250
Visaroff, Michael, 179

Walker, H. M., 198
Wallace, Morgan, 210
Walpole, Sir Hugh, 162
Walton, Charles, 34
Waters, Ethel, 241
Waters, John, 61
Watson, Harry, 106
Weber, Joe, 64

Welles, Orson, 167, 237
Wells, Jacqueline, 121, 122
West, Mae, 180, 206–216
White, George, 18
White, Victoria, 23
Wilde, Hyather, 223
Wild Man of Borneo, The, 46–47
Wilson, Clarence, 121, 123
Winchell, Walter, 25
Winninger, Charles, 76
Witherspoon, Cora, 223, 228
Wizard of Oz, The, 47, 197
Wolfe, Bill, 186, 205, 210, 221, 233, 246, 251
Work, Cliff, 207–208
Wynn, Ed, 11, 14

You Can't Cheat an Honest Man, 23, 197, 198–204, 205, 206, 249
Young, Roland, 166–167
Young, Tammany, 118, 130–131, 134, 136, 137, 147, 149, 151, 152, 153, 155, 159, 160, 174, 175
You're Telling Me, 15, 132–138

Ziegfeld, Florenz, 11, 14, 18, 23, 25, 29, 30, 34–35, 48, 75, 76–77, 100
Ziegfeld Follies, 75
Ziegfeld Follies of 1915, 11, 12, 14, 18, 73, 130
Ziegfeld Follies of 1925, 25, 30, 39, 40, 48, 79, 99, 100
Zukor, Adolph, 196